Murder, Inc.

Burton B. Turkus was assistant District Attorney of Kings County (Brooklyn) during the Murder, Inc. investigations. Sid Feder worked as an Associated Press staff writer for seventeen years, and contributed to the Saturday Evening Post, True, *and* Collier's, *among others.*

Murder, Inc.

The Story of "the Syndicate"

BY BURTON B. TURKUS
AND SID FEDER

DA CAPO PRESS
A Member of the Perseus Books Group

This Da Capo Press paperback edition of *Murder, Inc.* is an
unabridged republication of the edition published in New York in
1951. It is reprinted by arrangement with Ann Turkus and Berte
Feder.

Cataloging-in-Publication data for this book is available from the
Library of Congress.

First Da Capo Press edition 1992
Second Da Capo Press edition 2003

ISBN 0–306–81288–6

Published by Da Capo Press
A Member of the Perseus Books Group
http://www.dacapopress.com

Da Capo Press books are available at special discounts for bulk
purchases in the U.S. by corporations, institutions, and other organizations. For more information, please contact the Special Markets Department at the Perseus Books Group, 11 Cambridge
Center, Cambridge, MA 02142, or call (800) 255–1514 or (617)
252–5298, or e-mail j.mccrary@perseusbooks.com.

2 3 4 5 6 7 8 9 — 06 05 04 03

To Harry Feeney,
a great reporter

Contents

Introduction

In the spring of 1950, Burton Turkus, a former assistant District Attorney, asked me to write a book with him on the fantastic ring of killers and extortionists that *is* organized crime in the United States. It was an assignment at which any newspaperman would leap. This was the first authentic story, proved by data and record, of how this ring controls and operates, as big business, every racket, extortion and illegitimacy across the nation. By technique and personnel, it was responsible for the unbelievable total of approximately a thousand murders in the decade up to 1940. The killing, though, was not then and is not now done for fun, for passion or for robbery; it is solely for the preservation and improvement of the vast business interests: the rackets. The ring came to be known, a decade ago, as Murder, Inc. Today it is the Syndicate.

Burt Turkus is easily the best-informed man in the United States on this incredible country-wide network of organized crime. The reason is simple: the mobsters themselves told him. In 1940, while he was an assistant District Attorney in Brooklyn, a number of the ranking killers turned stoolpigeon. From them—from the "inside," in other words—Mr. Turkus learned of the organization and its innermost workings. Their disclosures were so thorough that he was able to prosecute seven of the ring's members—and put all seven in the electric chair, including Lepke, whose power and rule as czar of labor-industry extortion has never been equaled. To this day, Lepke remains the lone ganglord ever to be sent to the chair by the Law.

Long before the trials were over, the gangsters took to calling Turkus "Mr. Arsenic."

He does not conform to the general pattern of the prosecutor. He dotes on the theatrics of the courtroom and the criminal trial. But he is neither politician nor publicity hound. He looks like the movie version of a D. A.—suave, dynamic in conversation, sharp. Meeting him, one can readily believe that, as prosecutor, he did put seven men accused of murder in the first degree into the chair.

Before that, in private practice, on the other hand, he defended seventeen men accused of murder in the first degree—and not one of them got the chair. However, he has never defended a criminal in organized crime, unless assigned by the court as pauper's counsel.

He was and is a political independent. The District Attorney during the Murder, Inc., probe was William O'Dwyer, a line Democrat. As a result of the successes against the Syndicate killers, O'Dwyer became Mayor of New York and, more recently, United States Ambassador to Mexico. Turkus ran for county judge (on a Republican ticket)—and was defeated. He hasn't run for anything since, except, perhaps, for the bus to take him to the subway station.

Here, then, is the story of Murder, Inc., in Turkus' words. He himself maintains that his own part in the investigation was entirely as a lawyer, and was made possible by Louis Josephs and Sol Klein, the other assistant District Attorneys who worked with him, and by Detective Frank Gray, his aide, who still is a "top cop" on the force. The end result is all that impresses Turkus, even now.

"All it takes," he says, "is a break from within. No matter what anyone claims about being clever or brilliant, there is only one way organized crime can be cracked. Unless someone on the inside talks, you can investigate forever and get nowhere."

It takes, too, he adds, an end to the corrupt politician, for it is his contention that if the betrothals of gangster and politician were broken, organized crime could not last forty-eight hours.

News columns were overcrowded with the approach of World War II in 1940, and, as a result, only a small part of this "inside" story reached the outside. The facts of how extortion, murder and politics were put together by a group of specialists and formed into a nation-wide "business" are still there for anyone to see— if he can get on the inside.

I suppose the origins and growth of the Syndicate were not unlike that of any huge business amalgamation. The criminal gang first sprang up in this country in the battles between labor and industry just before and after World War I, with such figures as Li'l Augie Orgen, Kid Dropper, and Lupo the Wolf Saietta, an early ruler of Mafia. With the coming of Prohibition, although maintaining their positions as enforcement squads for both management and labor in industry, the mobs waxed fat on alcohol profits. Then came the heyday of Owney Madden, Al Capone, Dutch Schultz, Big Bill Dwyer and their ilk. The organization known as Unione Siciliano began to grow up, too, until in 1930 and 1931 it blossomed into its own. Perhaps the most striking developments of gang growth under Prohibition were the comparative ease with which the underworld could put a corrupt finger on law enforcement and the casual attitude with which the public viewed the dumping of bullet-ridden bodies in doorways and gutters. At about the same time, Café Society was coming into its own and, perversely, it was considered rather smart to know a gangster personally.

With Prohibition about to be repealed, the two problems that faced the ganglords were first, naturally, to develop new ways of profitable illegitimacy, and, second, to put a stop to indiscriminate killing. The murder of one beer baron by another had come to be accepted as the elimination of unneeded surplus, but it was obvious to the gangsters that the public would hardly stand for such promiscuous slaughter once Prohibition was gone.

To solve these problems, the Syndicate was born. The chief reason for its quick universal acceptance was that the end of Prohibition's crazy era brought an end to the insane egoistic ganglord of the Dutch Schultz breed, who settled everything with a bullet. Lucky Luciano, Costello, Lepke, Zwillman, the Fischettis—they were and are the modern type who believe in arbitration.

The government of the Syndicate is actually set up under a board of directors who dictate all policy. There was not then and there never has been any one mob magnate with more power than any other in national crime. The very fact that one "expert" tries to pin such authority on Costello, another on Lucky Luciano, and so on, seems to us conclusive evidence that individual control does not exist. Along with the board of directors, the moblords provided for a kangaroo court, made up of the bosses themselves, which serves as the judicial branch of the government, with irrevocable power of life and death.

Since the origin of the Syndicate, there has been no killing of a gang boss that was not "okayed"—from Dutch Schultz in 1935 to Charley Binaggio in 1950.

To insure their organization, one and all concentrated on developing connections, on municipal, state and national levels. The cartel is so finely organized that it can swing elections in many places—and can do it, too, regardless of which political party holds the reins.

The Kefauver Senate Committee did an admirable job of making the public sharply conscious of much of this danger that, although once exposed, had been forgotten through the years. For that, it must receive the thanks of all honest citizens. However, as we will point out, the Committee, as an investigative group, omitted much that, with only very little more prying, would have and should have been uncovered, in order to paint the exact picture of this menace. More important, in several instances, the Committee drew an unfortunate misconception of the organization, most notably in the importance it attaches to the cohesive control of Mafia, which, actually, was purged twenty years ago, and in pointing up a scattered few ganglords above others, in an amalgamation where every territorial mob boss has as much to say as any other.

But, make no mistake about it: Murder, Inc., was and is the national Syndicate. The head men were so well protected that Lepke remains the only one to enter a death chamber since the underworld organized its government. The Syndicate is with us today, not only in Brooklyn, but wherever there is crime, as it took a United States Senate Committee a full year to find out and report in 1951.

Sid Feder

September 1951.

Murder, Inc.

1.

Don't blame it all on Brooklyn

Murder, Inc.: National Syndicate—one thousand killings, coast-to-coast—Pittsburgh Phil, traveling salesman in homicide—the Mazza Mob goes to Minneapolis—the blueprint is the same today.

EARLY in 1940, while digging into the source of local felony, the District Attorney's office in Brooklyn ran head on into an unbelievable industry. This organization was doing business in assassination and general crime across the entire nation, along the same corporate lines as a chain of grocery stores.

The ensuing investigation exposed a vast network dealing in every known form of rackets and extortion, with murder as a by-product to that "business"—an incident to the maintenance of trade. The disclosures, in fact, uncovered a national Syndicate with coast-to-coast ramifications. It is, moreover, the same national Syndicate decried today by all law, up to and including the United States Senate, but far more closely knit than is generally and popularly believed.

As a member of the District Attorney's staff, I prosecuted the board of directors of the death department of this cartel, and sent seven men to the electric chair. (One other is serving eighty years.) Five of these seven were members of the self-styled Brooklyn combination, the branch office which served as the firing squad for all of the organization. The other two were ranking magnates in the national underworld. One was Lepke, most powerful of all labor and industrial rackets czars; the other, his operations manager, Mendy Weiss, a hulking mobster who coolly ordered murder on a country-wide basis. Their only connection with Brooklyn was as contract employers of the combination. They operated strictly on a trans-America scale.

3

In all the history of crime, there has never been an example of organized lawlessness equal to the Syndicate. Details are not for the squeamish—this is a warning here and now. In a ten-year period, upward of one thousand murders were committed from New England to California, Minnesota to New Orleans and Miami, by the combination, either directly or through the technique it developed. They were done for the Syndicate. The technique became, and, in fact, remains to this day, the blueprint for organized gang throat-cutting. However, murder, I must emphasize, was not the *big* business. The rackets were. The assassinations were ordered, contracted and performed solely to sustain those rackets.

Fantastic? It can't happen in your town? It did!

The facts were corroborated in testimony that satisfied juries and the highest courts in the land; they were documented in affidavited truths; they were unfolded, in fact, by the killers themselves. In our investigation, for the first and only time, the Syndicate was "broken from within," which is the only way organized crime can be attacked. Abe (Kid Twist) Reles, an arrogant self-glorifying gang leader who murdered more than a dozen men, turned State's evidence, along with a number of his less illustrious cohorts, and the pattern of national organized gangland was exposed. This was an association in which every mob of any importance in the United States had membership. It was a national ring put together on the lines of a cartel.

The blueprint has never worn out. A Charley Binaggio is killed in an open political clubhouse in Kansas City; a Detective Lieutenant, Bill Drury, is "rubbed out" in Chicago on a September day in 1950 for becoming too "nosy"; a Buggsy Siegel is eliminated as he sits reading a newspaper in the living room of a California mansion; Philly Mangano, an original Murder, Inc., staff gunman, is dropped into a Brooklyn swamp in 1951 with three bullets in his head. All make it brutally evident that the pattern is still in use.

There was no method of murder their fiendish ingenuity overlooked. They used the gun, the strangling rope, the ice pick—commonplace tools for homicide. There was the unimaginative mob-style ride, the shotgun blast on the lonely street. And there were the bizarre touches, too. Dozens were dropped into quicklime pits. Others were buried alive, cremated, roped up in such a way that

they strangled themselves by their own struggles for life. The killers thought they had come up with an especially appropriate effect
the night they tied a slot machine to the body of a pinball operator
who was "cheating," and dropped him into a resort lake.

The Syndicate's tentacles reached everywhere and anywhere. It
brought organized crime to California to stay; Cleveland's infamous Mayfield Road Gang and Chicago's Capone crew, which
continued operations after Scarface Al's finish, staffed that Far
Western office with able hands. A Seattle hoodlum, still in the
picture today, represented the Northwest.

Frank Costello's New Orleans slot machines were linked up,
and the Fischettis of Chicago and Tony Gizzo and his heirs in
Kansas City. The Purple Gang of Detroit held a franchise. The
racing wire service had many connections with it in ensuing years.
The Miami gambling ring (also known as the Northern Mob)
belonged, and the St. Paul combination. The New Jersey outfit,
Lepke and Charley (Lucky) Luciano in Manhattan . . . Cleveland, Boston, Chicago, Seattle, Philadelphia, New Orleans, Mil-
waukee, Dallas—whatever the locale, the underworld of every
community of any size in the nation was "in."

A string of hideouts from coast to coast and into Canada was
cunningly fitted into the outline. In the late thirties and early
forties, as the heat of the Dewey rackets investigations in Manhattan and our murder probe in Brooklyn intensified, potential
witnesses were sent out of town in all directions. One would go to
Salt Lake City, where the relative of a minor mob affiliate had a
prominent business. Several more would hurry off upstate, to the
Saratoga area where the Spa offered accommodations large enough
for groups. We learned of at least one who went to New Orleans
and was told there would be a job waiting with Frank Costello on
the slot machines. Sun Valley, Idaho, was a refuge for California
boys. A former New York hoodlum operated a popular hostelry
there. Kansas City was one of the most cordial hideout locales.
Mendy holed up between Kansas City and Denver for almost two
years, while New Jersey and New York sought him for murders
and the federal government hunted him for narcotics enterprises in
New York and Texas. The mobsters who turned State's evidence
told us that, in Detroit, concealment was ready at all times for

killers who were too "hot" at home. Wherever they went, Syndicate hoodlums on the lam were warmly received.

Little about the organization has been changed up to now. Each mob operated its own racket or rackets independently, collected its own take, was forced to cut no one in. Besides its own operations, each co-operated with every other mob. On some of the larger takes, the various gangs shared the profits, as they continue to do today, in matters like gambling and narcotics. The ties that bound them, and bind them yet, lay in a formal code of ethics, a set of bylaws ruling all, a board of governors for policy-making, a kangaroo court for justice, with complete and final say on life and death. All these were legislated when a group of the very top ganglords agreed to amalgamation in 1934. All are very real and concrete today.

The national ring deals in rackets big and small. No avenue of easy money is neglected. That is its reason for being: quick, easy illegal money. There are gambling and vice on a national scale, the profits running into appalling figures; dope-peddling, national and international. A far-flung loan-shark extortion operated from a Detroit-Brooklyn axis. More damaging to the general welfare, the mobsters tear at the very heart of honest business with their industrial rackets and labor extortions. They have controlled whole industries. They have raised the price of food and household commodities, boosted clothing costs and affected the pocketbook of virtually every average citizen in America.

Hard-working laborers have been forced to pay tribute in kickbacks from their day's wages. That has applied to any number of unions in which the thugs "muscled" power. The parasitic pirates hire out to foment or break strikes for fancy fees. On occasion, they have even hired out to both sides in the same dispute. They are that versatile. They infiltrated many unions and, once in, have any number of ways to make them pay off. Take one popular example:

The mob's fronts inside the union would incite a faction of the membership into pushing through a vote for a wage increase. The fronts generally were union delegates (through phony elections). Thus, they would carry the wage demands to the employer. The employer knew that refusal meant acid on valuable merchandise, bombings, wrecked trucks, smashed windows—and beatings. The employer gave in. Now the fronts switched the attack.

"This is going to cost you $50,000 a year in wages," they would say. "If you give us $25,000 cash, you won't have to give the raise. We'll straighten it out."

The deal would be made. The $25,000 would go into the mob treasury. The fronts would sorrowfully report that the raise had fallen through—maybe next time it would win. Any union men who objected were killed or savagely beaten.

The Syndicate was, in short, a powerful drain on the very economy of the country, more common than peculiar to every section. It still is.

Now, in the operation of an industry of such magnitude and character, murder was necessary, at times, to prevent interference with business. That is where the Brooklyn branch came in. With its special talents for killing, this was the Extermination Department for Murder, Inc. These killers were not for hire. Their services were limited exclusively to the Syndicate, for use when business required. It was not at so much per throat-cutting or ice-picking or bag job, but rather murder on a year-round flat fee from those gangs in the organization which used the service. It was murder by contract; murder by retainer.

Not that these mobs did not have their own staff killers. But, as often as not, it was desirable to import out-of-towners for such matters. Thus, one of the combination's slaughterers could be— and frequently was—brought into Cleveland or Boston or Hollywood to do a job, and then depart. No one would even know he had been around. Except, perhaps, the victim—and he would be very dead. The boys in the town where it happened, benefiting from advance information, would have iron-bound alibis set up.

Yet, during the entire investigation and prosecutions of 1940 and 1941, through all the drawn-out legal tricks by which the seven convicted killers tried every court and appeal to avoid walking that last mile—and through the ten years since—Murder, Inc., has been irritatingly labeled a Brooklyn production exclusively, like the baseball Dodgers or the sardine-packed beach at Coney Island. Even now, people say that Murder, Inc., was Brownsville and East New York and Ocean Hill, those neighborhoods in northeast Brooklyn which spawned these experts at death. Actually, on the national scene, Murder, Inc., was about as peculiar to Brooklyn as the hot dog.

If a traveling salesman lives in New York and has a sales territory in Iowa, Kansas and Nebraska, his business would hardly be classed as a New York operation. In just the same way, the Brooklyn triggermen were the traveling salesmen of the national crime cartel.

Harry Strauss was one of them. They called him Big Harry and Pep and, mostly, they called him Pittsburgh Phil, because he was the dandy of the outfit. Pittsburgh Phil would fairly purr when you referred to him as the Beau Brummell of the Brooklyn underworld. To the others, homicide was purely business; to Pep, it was practically ecstasy. He reveled in manslaughter; delighted in death.

"Like a ballplayer, that's me," he explained his enthusiasm once to an associate. "I figure I get seasoning doing these jobs here. Somebody from one of the big mobs spots me. Then, up to the big leagues."

He was vicious as a Gestapo agent, as casually cold-blooded as a meat-grinding machine in a butcher shop. He had such a lust for bloodletting that he would volunteer to handle "contracts" even when it was not his turn to work. He was such an eager and capable killer that when out-of-town mobs had special traveling salesman "commissions," he was the first choice, in most instances, to be sent out.

In the course of our investigation, various of the mob informers "sang" of the exploits of Pittsburgh Phil. It was quite an aria, for Phil killed more than thirty men in more than a dozen cities. He took on assignments in Boston and Chicago, Philadelphia and Miami and Detroit. The Connecticut State Police, for instance, were baffled for seven years by one particularly messy murder. When they heard of our discoveries of Big Harry's handiwork at homicide, they decided their unsolved murder bore the earmarks of his technique.

It seems that as the chill fall dawn came up on November 20, 1933, the first rays of the sun etched out all that was left of Al

Silverman, ex-convict and bootlegger, dangling from a barbed-wire fence in Somers, Conn. Al had been stabbed. His face had been battered so it could not have been recognized even by his pals, Lepke and Longy Zwillman, who does business in Newark and to this day is referred to as "the King of Jersey." Motive? Take your pick. Murder, Inc., was not advertising its contracts in the papers, those days.

The police of Detroit, too, had a murder that fitted the artistry of Pittsburgh Phil, with the possible collaboration of Happy Maione, who was head of the Ocean Hill hooligans, one of the two squads in the Brooklyn troop. He was called Happy because he wore such a perpetually surly look that when he walked along the street, the neighbors would actually pull down the shades.

Harry Millman, a Detroit gangster, was marked for murder in the summer of 1937. The local boys ingeniously placed a bomb under the hood of his car, set to go off as soon as he stepped on the starter. Only, that was the day Millman sent Willie Holmes to pick up his car for him. It was Willie who was blown into little pieces. Millman was wary now. The job needed an outsider he would not recognize. So the Detroit mob called for help. Three months after the bomb backfired, Millman was in a crowded restaurant one evening, at dinner hour. Two men walked in, poured twelve slugs into him, wounded five other diners, and walked out. No one ever saw the two gunmen again—no one, that is, who could identify them. However, no one would have been surprised if Pittsburgh Phil and Happy Maione were aboard an eastbound plane that evening.

Naturally, Pittsburgh Phil filed no records for posterity. Many of his deeds were so unusually "good," though, that even he, close-lipped as he was, had to tell his pals when he returned from a selling trip. Thus, they became gossip in the underworld, legends of bloodletting. And when some of his very close friends started to talk during the murder investigations, they told us. That is how we found out about the time the mob boss in Jacksonville, Fla., sent word that he had a contract.

Clearly, the man who had incurred the displeasure of the Jacksonville boss was allied with the underworld, although a man's station in life had nothing to do with the mob's decision to kill him. The local leader did not want to employ his own torpedoes. It was the sort of extermination that would bring the police around the next day, checking up on alibis.

Pittsburgh Phil, always eager to oblige, was assigned. A day or two later, he and his little black bag landed at Jacksonville airport. The contents of Pep's bag were varied. There usually was a gun. Since he was versatile, there might be a rope or an ice pick. Of course, there was also fastidious Phil's clean shirt.

Waiting at the airport was one of the junior officers of the Jacksonville chapter who was to "finger" the victim to be. He drove Phil past the man's home. "That one on the right there—on the corner," he indicated. "The one with the stone stoop. The guy comes out at the same time every morning. You're lucky. It's an easy pop."

This was definitely the wrong approach to the inflated ego of the visiting killer. "You fingered the bum—you did your job," he snapped. "Never mind how easy it is; I'm doing this."

Overnight, Phil pondered the setup. He had had only one quick glance at the spot, and that, in the dark. Something about it, however, did not look right to the expert technician. Next day, he set out to look over the layout by himself. Precisely at eleven, just as his local informant had said, the prospective victim walked out of his cottage. For a moment, he paused on the stone steps, taking in the warm Florida sunshine.

As the man stood there, Pittsburgh Phil's hunch was confirmed: this was no place for a murder. Here was a house on a corner. That meant two-way traffic. The hour was approaching noon. Housewives, motorists, delivery people, bill collectors—all with eyes and memories—were stirring. Besides, no preparations had been made for a getaway car, with an expert wheelman. There was no "crash car," to block pursuit. No getaway route had been mapped. None of the careful preparedness by which the Brooklyn troop made itself the top in its field. Evidently, the local hoods were simply fingering the victim and leaving the job completely to the visitor.

"These guys are farmers," Phil shrugged, annoyed that they should be so ignorant of finesse in the fine art of assassination, Brooklyn style. It was all right with Phil, though, that they were leaving him alone. "At least, these farmers won't get in the way," he thought. Nevertheless, he was completely irked at the entire job. It was becoming complicated.

Next morning, as the victim left his home at eleven and started up the street, he did not notice the dapper, custom-tailored stranger who picked up his trail.

"Even if it takes all day, I'll tail him and find the right spot," Phil vowed.

Where his quarry went Phil followed. He sat at the next table in the restaurant when the man stopped for dinner. He noted every movement. Finally the victim walked up to the ticket window of a movie theater. Never realizing he was marked for murder—and that it was right behind him—the man disappeared inside. Phil did the same. He was pleased to note that the crowd had gathered early, and that his target took a seat in the very last row.

The gangster leaned against the wall in the dark and contemplated the silhouette of his man. As he leaned there, Phil's hand, quite by chance, came in contact with a glass panel set in the wall. He looked down. The panel fronted an oblong niche. Printed on it was the message:

TO BE USED IN CASE OF FIRE.

Inside, as in countless public buildings, was a sturdy ax for combating flaming walls. A bright light lit in his bloodthirsty skull. Here were the means, the weapon and the method for getaway all neatly delivered, as if he had placed an order for it. Now it was "an easy pop."

"I take the ax and sink it in the guy's head in the dark," the killer's mind worked rapidly. "It's the kind of a thing that will make a lot of holler. Dames and guys will make a run out of here. I just run with them—and the getaway is a cinch. This is a natural."

He slid the panel back. His fingers curled eagerly, almost longingly, around the ax handle. He felt it for heft. It would never strike Phil as odd that he was about to bury the blade of a fire ax into the head of a man whose name he would very likely never know.

He moved in, the ax hanging from one hand, concealed along

his leg. Another moment or two, and the job would be neatly done. But at that moment, the target did something that has annoyed anyone who has ever gone to a motion-picture theater. Another patron, well up in front, rose and walked out, leaving a vacant seat. Phil's intended victim leaped alertly to his feet and dashed for the "empty."

That did it. That was the last disappointing straw. Disgusted, he slammed the ax back into its wall box. He stormed out of the theater and back to his hotel. It was the final touch. Even Pittsburgh Phil's lust for murder couldn't keep his interest alive now. It was a jinx job, he was positive. Thoroughly fed up with the hoodoo contract, he headed for the airport and took the first plane back to Brooklyn.

The next day he reported to his boss. This was essential. He had left a contract unfilled. A complaint from the Jacksonville commander could convene the cartel's kangaroo court. Desertion from an assignment in the mob is every bit the serious life-and-death matter that it is in the Army in a combat zone in time of war.

"Those Florida jerks wanted me to do a cowboy job," he sneered. To both Pittsburgh Phil and his boss, sinking an ax into a man's head in a darkened theater was perfect technique. To shoot a man off his front doorstep, without the mapped-out getaway, the "hot" car, the other fine details carefully worked out, was truly a "cowboy job." The boss understood at once.

To the boys on the Corner—Kid Twist Reles and Blue Jaw Magoon—Phil dolefully told of his frustration.

"Just when I get him set up—the bum turns out to be a God-damned chair-hopper," he mournfully concluded.

By mergers, trade agreements and intensive salesmanship—backed by its artistry at carrying out contract murder—the Brooklyn combination was able to grow from a position as just another gang across the East River (and not the most powerful, at that) to one of pre-eminence in its field in the national crime industry.

With all its throat-cutting, though, the troop never overlooked the fact that, to the Syndicate, murder was secondary to the rackets which were the source of income. And the bandits of Brooklyn, Inc., were deep in those. Early in our investigation, any number of ties that bound them to cross-country crime came to light.

Louis Capone, for instance, had excellent connections with the Purple Mob in Detroit in the loan-shark operation, which covered a wide portion of the nation. Louis was no relation to Scarface Al, except that both were murderers and thugs. Suave and well groomed, with iron-gray air, Louis had the appearance of a diplomat. You could almost picture him in striped trousers and a tail coat.

Capone ran a pasticceria—the old-world trade name for a shop dealing in thick black coffee, rich pastry and assorted delicacies. The place was a success. It is feared, however, that the excellent spaghetti sauce and the creamy cakes so popular in the sidewalk cafés of Rome and Naples were only a front for Louis in Brooklyn.

One of the regular patrons was Albert Anastasia, overlord of the water front. Back in the early days before syndication, when the Brownsville thugs of Kid Twist Reles and the Ocean Hill hooligans of Happy Maione were just wild punks, Louis used to feed them. And, from filling their stomachs, it was no trick at all for him and Anastasia to advance to filling their heads with ideas on lawlessness, especially since they were already well along the road to self-education in this field.

Capone held considerable power in the Syndicate through his Detroit contacts. When Dukey Maffetore, just a punk in the Mob, turned informer in the spring of 1940, he mentioned the matter.

"The Purple Gang and the Brooklyn combination," Dukey explained, "controlled the loan-shark racket all over. They had a real close deal. Every week they exchanged money for the shylocking."

The partnership must have been obvious, indeed, if Dukey, who was only on the fringe, was cognizant of it.

Our informers said both Capone and Anastasia were allied with Joseph Doto, who is far better known by his underworld label of Joey Adonis—or Joey A., for short. In those days, Adonis lived in his bombproof home in Brooklyn, and for years had been especially close to Lucky Luciano and Frank Costello. Today he re-

sides in a mansion in Fort Lee, N. J., high on the Palisades towering above the Hudson, but close enough so that his influence can
still be felt in Brooklyn—politically, socially and industrially. And
one of his neighbors still is Albert Anastasia, who followed him
across the river and himself built a palatial home on the Palisades.

Until 1951, Adonis had been arrested time and again on charges
up to and including assault and grand larceny. He had good
friends, though, and his total penalty had been a fine of one hundred dollars. In May of 1951, he was hauled in on gambling charges
in Bergen County, N. J., and pleaded *non vult*—meaning no defense. It appeared that at last the Law had overhauled "Mr. A.,"
for he was eligible to a sentence of eighteen years. Instead, he
drew a term of two to three years from Judge J. Wallace Leyden,
and his attorney said he would be eligible for parole in ten months.
The *New York World-Telegram* referred to Mr. A., at his sentencing, as "the laughing boy of the underworld."

Adonis' connections with Costello, and certain Chicago, Detroit, Cleveland and Western mobsters, in gambling in Florida,
Saratoga and Nevada have been most remunerative. For years, he
also has enjoyed—until the summer of 1951, at least—an exclusive government-protected monopoly for hauling automobiles
from the Ford Motor Company's largest Eastern plant, at Edgewater, N. J.

That Joey A. outranked Anastasia in Murder, Inc., is a virtual
certainty. To this day, Adonis stands high on the national board
of governors of the Syndicate. No one, in fact, stands higher than
this hard-faced hoodlum who looks like a movie version of a
gangster. Reles placed him in the picture as the co-ordinator and
mediator of intergang disputes anywhere in the ring. Some idea
of Adonis' eminence can be gleaned from the marked tone of
profound reverence that comes into the voice of any hoodlum,
anywhere, whenever he mentions "Mr. A."

In Florida, besides gambling, the Brooklyn combination was
associated with other mobs in the jewelry robbery racket. When
Reles began his remarkable recounting of the varied virtues of the
Syndicate, the jewel "heists" were prominently referred to.

"A lot of people think this Brooklyn troop is just a small-time outfit," he said, putting the proper perspective on matters. "Well, we got good connections. You know how the New York gangs case dames with a lot of jewelry in night clubs, and then take them. We been working with the Chicago and New York guys in Florida for a couple years now, and it's even better."

The Florida race tracks, the gambling traps, the luxury hotels evidently were excellent bases for carrying on such midwinter work. The victims themselves co-operated to some extent, for it is no secret that most feminine visitors to the Miami area look on the trip as an excursion in exhibitionism.

There were any number of other connections the troop acquired. The bookmaking operations reached across New Jersey and into Pennsylvania. Through Lucky Luciano, there were narcotics over a wide area. Florida gambling was so closely linked that many underlings were given jobs as "spotters" or strong-arm men in the clubs there. Some of the same executives of ten years ago still run the Florida traps today.

However, neither the hideout system nor the jewel thefts nor the shylock and gambling and narcotics rackets brings out the completely national outline of Murder, Inc., as sharply as the death dealt out from the Atlantic to the Pacific and way stations. As a matter of fact, in addition to convicting seven of the slayers in Brooklyn, we furnished our witnesses—and in some cases, the killers as well—to outside prosecutors to clear up many contracts the troop handled for the Syndicate far from its home base —as far away as Hollywood, Calif.

As soon as word of our sensational findings became known, law-enforcement agencies in Pennsylvania and Minnesota, Massachusetts and California and various other points dusted off long untouched files on unsolved homicides and asked if our aviary of songbirds had mentioned them. The Pennsylvania State Police reopened the eight-year-old killings, in the Scranton area, of Lew Marcowitz (a ride job), Jack Steinberg (shotgun) and Sam Wichner (stuffed in an automobile luggage compartment). Massachusetts prosecutors were reminded of the much-headlined Dave Green killing, among the bodies that had been left around.

There was one intriguing skein of slayings that jumped from

New York to St. Paul, Minn., which we never did put entirely together into one piece. The production was, however, the unmistakable technique of Murder, Inc.

On the lower East Side of Manhattan, a violent and unrestrained environment that spawned many of the infamous, one who made a fortune in bootlegging was Abe Wagner. However, at the start of 1932 Wagner's position was threatened by a rising new gang. Eventually this Mazza Mob decided it was strong enough to eliminate competition—by the customary means.

On February 20, 1932, Wagner was riding down sprawling, scrambling Suffolk Street in his shiny sedan. On Suffolk Street, children dart in and out, and pushcart peddlers show an alarming unconcern for moving vehicles. A car must proceed slowly. As the glistening vehicle crawled past No. 66, what seemed to be all of the shooting members of the Mazza Mob suddenly opened up with their guns. They riddled the automobile until the door on the near side resembled the nozzle of a shower. But Wagner rolled out of the other door, and was out of sight, on foot, before the gunmen had a chance to take aim.

Now, Wagner was not one of the trigger-happy gangsters who would immediately start a gory underworld war because of such pointed animosity, especially when the other side evidently was at least as powerful as his own army. His maxim was that it is better to be a live coward than a dead gang boss. He became decidedly respectful, and cautious enough to sue for peace. He knew his enemies could always be contacted at the Hatfield Hotel, at the upper edge of the explosive East Side. The following day, he sent his partner, Harry Brown, and his brother, Allie, as emissaries. He provided them with a sizable bankroll.

"See can you pay them off," he instructed hopefully.

The rival mobsters accepted the tribute; at any rate, the funds were never returned. But guns flashed at the peace meeting, and when the shooting stopped, Allie Wagner was dead.

Mrs. Pauline Wagner, mother of eight, mourning her youngest son, was practical enough, nevertheless, to realize it was only a question of time until the guns would turn on her older boy once more.

"Take Goldie and go away somewhere for a while," she wept. "Go now, so I won't worry. Hurry."

The older son hardly needed the urging. He had already decided the same thing. He sold what few possessions he had, and he and his bride Goldie got out of town. The Mazzas were left in complete charge, especially since they had, by this time, aligned themselves with the local powers-that-be. They were well acquainted with Lucky Luciano, who had, shortly before, moved in as head man of Unione Siciliano, the modern Italian society of crime.

In March, 1932, only a month after Wagner departed, the Lindbergh baby was kidnaped at Hopewell, N. J. One of the first names mentioned in connection with the infamous abduction was that of the New York bootlegger who had disappeared from his old haunts.

"We have a tip that Wagner was seen in the vicinity of Hopewell about a month before the kidnaping," revealed Colonel H. Norman Schwarzkopf, head of New Jersey State Police.

The police were unsuccessful in their efforts to locate Wagner; the Mazzas, on the other hand, soon knew, through the underworld grapevine, exactly where he had settled. They decided that Wagner alive, even on the run, was not good for their business. They dispatched a triggerman to eliminate him.

Wagner, however, was no neophyte in gang warfare. He appreciated full well that torpedoes would be along, and he kept an ever watchful eye. As a result, he saw the triggerman first; just soon enough to get home the first shot. The hood who had come to kill him wound up dead himself.

Shortly afterward, for one reason or another, Wagner had to make a hurried trip to New York. As unobtrusively as possible, he slipped into his mother's three-room apartment. Nevertheless, he was spotted. He was home no more than an hour or two before someone whispered to his mother that his enemies knew he was back.

"Go quick," the frantic mother urged, pushing him toward the door. "Don't wait."

They would be after him in earnest now, Wagner realized. He returned to his hideaway only long enough to pick up Goldie.

They pushed farther west, and finally landed in St. Paul. There, Wagner changed his name to Loeb. He changed his calling, as well. At least, to all intents and purposes, he hawked oranges and bananas, instead of delivering hijacked Scotch and bathtub gin, from a truck his mother bought for him.

The Mazzas learned of all this very quickly. This time, the stubborn thugs were determined Wagner had to go. Two shooting aces were sent out to do the job. Our informers said the pair were from the Bug & Meyer Mob, run by the arrogant Buggsy Siegel and his businesslike partner, Meyer Lansky.

The two aces caught up with Wagner in a restaurant in the Midway, between St. Paul and Minneapolis. It was one of those spots with eating place downstairs and living quarters above. Deliberately, the gunmen pumped seven bullets into the incognito bootlegger. And as he lay there, they clobbered his head with their pistol butts. They were unhurried. They had orders to get the job done; get it done, they did.

So intent were they, though, that they were caught at their work. They said their names were Joseph Schaefer and George Young, which, of course, were aliases. Both had been sought for two and a half years for a job that rankles federal manhunters to this day —the murder of federal agent John J. Finiello in a raid on the Rising Sun Brewery in Elizabeth, N. J., in 1930.

Meantime, the dead man's sudden widow identified him only as Loeb, a fruit peddler. For that reason hardly a word of the murder reached the press of the Atlantic Seaboard. The killers, unidentified themselves for several days, refused even to talk about it. On Thursday of that week, however, Mama Wagner called a "press conference" back on teeming Rutgers Street in downtown Manhattan.

"My boy was murdered out in St. Paul last Monday," the grief-stricken mother sobbed. "The same murderers killed him as killed my Allie here. I knew they would. But why? Why? My boy was always so good to me."

The New York newspapermen rushed to police for verification of Wagner's violent end. Amazingly, authorities said it was all brand new to them. Nor had Colonel Schwarzkopf in New Jersey heard of it. He revealed, however, that, as far as the Lindbergh kidnaping was concerned, he was no longer anxious to get Wagner.

"We did want him," admitted the state police head surprisingly. "But his fingerprints don't check any we have."

The newspapers turned to St. Paul authorities for light, but there, they knew the man only as Loeb, a fruit peddler. In fact, another man had come forward, identified himself as "J. Loeb, uncle of the dead man," and derided any identification of the corpse as Wagner. To this day, no one has the vaguest idea who the "uncle" was.

St. Paul police brushed off Mama Wagner's insistence. How, they shrugged, could an old woman in New York know her gangster son was a murdered fruit huckster a thousand miles away? The newsmen returned to the little apartment on the East Side. But Mrs. Wagner was adamant. Of course, the widow in St. Paul would supply no information to police and newsmen. That was the code of the trade, wasn't it?

"Look." Triumphantly, through her tears, Mama Wagner waved a yellow slip of paper. "Here is a wire from my daughter-in-law —from Mrs. Goldie Wagner. She says my boy was killed Monday, and she wants money to send his body here. I sent her twenty-five dollars; that is all I had. If it wasn't my son, how would I have the telegram?"

That proved it. The newsmen appealed to New York authorities to ask for fingerprints of the victim. Eventually, more than a week after the murder, the mystery was cleared up.

The captured killers were valuable workmen. Buggsy Siegel did not want to lose so handy a pair. The immediate concern was to keep them from the electric chair; the question of their freedom could be worked out later. A fortune was spent—and the pair did escape the chair, by drawing life sentences. Ever since, for more than fifteen years, all methods and means have been tried to obtain their freedom.

Pardons were denied time and again, but the killers were not forgotten. By 1940, Buggsy Siegel had become Syndicate boss in California. He came east on a business trip along about then— eight years after Wagner was mowed down. He stopped off at Stillwater to visit his unfortunate friends. The Bug was determined to redouble efforts in behalf of the imprisoned pair. Arriving in

New York, he called a meeting of the Syndicate's directors and demanded as much. As a result, the combination's songbirds told us, all sorts of efforts were made.

Once, the worst killer in the Brooklyn troop—with the un-killerlike tag of Dandy Jack—was paid $35,000 to go to Minnesota and "set those two guys out on the street." His objective was to blast a hole into the prison through which the murderers could walk out! The payment was made by a top New Jersey boss—close friend of Buggsy—in a cabaret in Little Ferry, in northern Jersey. Efficient as he is, Dandy Jack was hardly that capable. As of right now, the two killers are still in the Stillwater (Minn.) Penitentiary.

"You know, Tommy Gibbons was—and still is—sheriff of Ramsey County," points out George Barton, the veteran columnist of the *Minneapolis Star Tribune,* as if that may have had something to do with it. Perhaps it has. The sheriff is the same Tommy Gibbons who, back in 1923, gave the unforgettable Jack Dempsey probably the worst fifteen rounds he experienced as heavyweight champion of the world.

From these and other operations, it would appear that Murder, Inc., and its insidious manner of moving around the national scene must have been fully uncovered to public view a decade ago. It wasn't.

In fact, it has always been a major surprise to me how little of its gigantic cross-country outline was actually presented for public understanding, since it was all there to see—for those who looked. Not too many grasped the coast-to-coast architecture of assassination and rackets. One of those who did quickly spot something considerably larger than a purely old-home-week production was the late Harry Feeney of the *New York World-Telegram.*

Harry was a round little Irishman who could smell a story a mile off. On the very first day of the investigation, he pointed up the nation-wide connections. On the second day, he came up with the inspiration for the name that has stayed with the cartel to this day—Murder, Inc. I remember his animated conversation with his assistant City Editor (now City Editor) Bert MacDonald, as he and the other reporters phoned in their stories from the D. A.'s office.

"It's just like Bethlehem Steel," he emphasized excitedly. "It has a board of directors, a treasurer—that's the bagman—and runs like a big syndicate."

However, the full impact of a national government-within-government that made its own laws and carried on its own brand of justice never did strike the public with any considerable force at the time. And the chief cause lay in as unrelated a subject as the buildup to World War II, just then under way. Each time our probe came up with a development that might display the reach of this octopus of lawlessness, the war came up with a greater sensation.

Late in 1941, we finally tried Lepke. The testimony involved people in high places—even as high as the late Sidney Hillman, who was president of the giant Amalgamated Clothing Workers and, just then, Director of the Office of Production Management in the federal government and very close to the White House. The war, however, was getting closer daily. Less than one hundred hours after Lepke was sentenced to die, the Japanese touched off the powder magazine at Pearl Harbor.

It made no difference, therefore, whether Murder, Inc., was an office under someone's hat on a Brownsville street corner, or a giant cartel stretching from Boston to Hollywood, with connections in the highest political places. Sons and brothers and husbands were fighting for their lives by the millions in every corner of the world.

Beleaguered makeup men, laboring to fit all of the big story into just so many newsprint columns, had to cut down on everything else—and that included the first denouement of the unbelievable edifice of national crime. The stories that the stoolpigeons told—these stories that opened the eyes to the overall operations—had, largely, to be laid aside. Only the highlights of each day's developments could be "run," and the highlights rarely touched on the national structure of the Syndicate—the appalling import of Murder, Inc., on every man's security and pocketbook and daily life.

Had the full beam of publicity been turned on the ring as a

national entity when the lid was lifted ten years ago, today's drive on crime would have had a far more advanced start. Public clamor would have demanded widespread action far sooner.

For, make no mistake about this: the organization of Murder, Inc., the national Syndicate that was founded in 1934; the "bomb-proof" technique it developed and by which it protected itself from law enforcement—these are the same cut and pattern as the crime ring that has caused countrywide furore through 1950 and '51. The organization we broke open in 1940 is the same one that required a Kefauver investigation in 1950.

2.

A full mooner starts
a chain reaction

A new assistant D. A., and 200 murders—the political acumen of William O'Dwyer—Willie Sutton, the FBI's most wanted man, recruits some talent—Dukey and Pretty sing the opening chorus— gangster turns policeman: it could only happen in Hollywood.

TAKE a list of two hundred murders, all unsolved, and a map on the wall with a mark on it for each murder, and you have the District Attorney's perfect recipe for how not to be jubilant with his job.

I can vouch for it. The list was on the desk of the brand-new assistant District Attorney, in charge of the Felony and Homicide Section, early in 1940. That meant me. The map was on the wall behind the desk. In addition to a mark for each murder, there was also one for every other felony committed in New York's biggest borough . . . extortion, robbery, assault. Just name it, we had it.

Every section showed some scattered lawlessness. But in the northeast, to the naked eye, it was all marks and no map. There, in Brownsville, East New York and Ocean Hill, it was a blighted area—a pesthole. Through ten years, the murders had piled up in those sore spots. In one strip less than two miles long and three-quarters of a mile wide, two dozen or more men had been shot, stabbed, strangled, hacked to bits or cremated, and left in the gutter, on vacant lots or in stolen automobiles. A good many bodies had never been found at all.

The stack of violent deaths was enormous. We had the Medical Examiner's reports on them; we had the statements of witnesses, for what they were worth. But we did not have one item on which to peg a case; no case on which to get a conviction.

We knew there were mobs working. Any detective could tell

you that. We knew, for instance, that Kid Twist Reles, fat and vicious, had an outfit in Brownsville with his pal, Buggsy Goldstein, and that they would stop at nothing. We knew Happy Maione in Ocean Hill headed a gang of hoodlums, which included the moronic Dasher Abbandando, and we suspected they were no strangers to bookmaking, prostitution and loan-shark activities. We felt that Louis Capone, in spite of his dignified restaurateur's front, must be connected in some way, because he showed a re-markable interest in these thugs. We knew Pittsburgh Phil and Vito Gurino were tied up somehow in the goings on.

But neither we nor anyone else dreamed that these men were more than just local aggregations, limited to the areas in which they roamed. That had always been the scope of plug-uglies in Brooklyn. Even hoodlums like Johnny Torrio and Al Capone operated only locally until they left town and headed west. If anyone had suggested that a large part of the 200-or-so unsolved murders plaguing us was wrapped up in an appalling aggregation of about a thousand assassinations all over the country, and could be laid to the same crew of killers, we would have laughed at them.

We went to work on this localized premise—treating each group as a separate small fraternity of felony. But no matter what ap-proach you took, where was the evidence? Courtroom evidence, that convinces judge and jury.

How I arrived at that desk, with the map behind it, went back, you might say, to the biggest cash robbery in American criminal history. To be accurate, it is only the second biggest now, since a set of holdup men walked into the Brinks Express Company in Boston in the spring of 1950 and helped themselves to a million dollars and some change. Until the Brink job, however, Brooklyn held the record for sixteen years—ever since August 21, 1934, when ten skilled machine-gunners nailed an armored car near the Rubel Ice Plant, just off the water front, snatched up $427,950, ran the step or two to the docks and disappeared in two waiting speedboats.

For six years, the ten were wraiths. Then, Archie Stewart was bothered by his conscience—after he was sentenced to sixty years for a bank robbery in Pine Bush, N. Y. This chronic criminal had been a mastermind of what the State called "the crime of the century." He told the entire story. Three of the ten were available. Stewart Wallace, who had only one hand, and Joe Kress were in Sing Sing. The third was Tom Quinn, a rumrunner and one of the getaway boatmen.

Originally, Sam Leibowitz was counsel for Kress. He was then one of the nation's brilliant criminal lawyers. As the trial opened, however, Leibowitz bowed out and was replaced by Vincent Impellitteri. (In 1950, Impellitteri was to complete another notable replacement program—winning the mayoralty of New York when William O'Dwyer resigned to become ambassador to Mexico.) I was in private law practice then. One afternoon, then-County Judge William O'Dwyer stopped me as I was leaving the Criminal Courts Building. He turned on the irresistible charm which has been the man's most remarkable asset as a public figure.

"I wish you would take the defense of this man Wallace," he said. As the court, he had a perfect right to assign me. If assigned, a lawyer has an ethical obligation to accept the defense of any indigent prisoner, without compensation in any case short of murder. At that moment, though, my calendar happened to be particularly heavy, and this had all the earmarks of a long drawn-out trial. Besides, although no lawyer has the right to prejudge guilt, it is only human, at times, to sense no real defense. This case had exactly that flavor.

"Judge," I countered, "if you are giving me a choice in the matter, I would rather not undertake it. But—if you insist . . ."

"It is incumbent on me," he replied, "to put someone on for Wallace comparable to the attorneys for the other defendants." That was the O'Dwyer charm at work. Few have been able to resist it.

There wasn't much the defense could do in this case. The State had too many loaded guns. The trio was convicted.

One afternoon, a few days later, O'Dwyer sent word that he would like to see me. He mentioned the weather and the state of my health. "You did a good job on the Rubel trial," he went on. "You got everything out of it there was."

"Nice of you to say so, Judge," I acknowledged. And I thought, "He didn't send for me just for that." He hadn't.

"I am going to be the next District Attorney of Brooklyn—and I want you on my staff," he announced.

It wasn't one shocker; it was two. First, a man elected to the county bench wins a fourteen-year term at $25,000 annually; the District Attorney's term is for four years at $20,000. Second, I was a political independent with no backing; I didn't even belong to a political club. And organization leaders have more than enough party workers to supply a new D. A. with all the assistants he can use.

"That doesn't make any difference," O'Dwyer shrugged. "Let me worry about the politics."

"You're paying me quite an honor, Judge. But let's leave it this way for now—when you're elected, we'll talk it over."

It did not make sense that he should even want the job. The bench was a "soft touch" compared to the sniping any District Attorney must expect. And it can mean $25,000 a year until the age of seventy, for, once a judge is elected the first time, both parties usually endorse him in ensuing elections.

So, when O'Dwyer set out to become District Attorney at what appeared a sacrifice, I was firmly convinced that he was motivated by the public interest. Any number of others took a different view. Mayor Fiorello LaGuardia was one. Afterward, he raised the issue of O'Dwyer's political acumen as against any sacrifice.

"O'Dwyer had it all planned all along," stormed the Little Flower. "He knew where he was going. That's the reason he named Burt Turkus to his staff. He wanted someone he could point to and say, 'See, I run a nonpartisan office.' "

He went on to link O'Dwyer to the most notorious ganglords in the nation, as have many others since. In 1939, though, the evidence was all the other way.

O'Dwyer won the election. "Burt," he proposed one afternoon shortly afterward, "the job I want you to do is to handle the murder cases."

Now that would be a pleasure. The trial court always has gripped me. The proposal represented an opportunity to remain with the clash and action of the criminal case. So, as of January 1, 1940,

Burt Turkus, a political independent, became assistant District Attorney in charge of the Homicide Section, in the administration of William O'Dwyer, an organization Democrat.

Brooklyn is famed far and wide as the City of Churches. Here was an incongruity hard to match: the City of Churches with two hundred or so unsolved murders. And what murders on that list, early in 1940:

A body strangled, ice-picked, left in a stolen car on a lonely street; two men stripped, stood against the wall of a garage and shot full of holes; a cremated "package" on an empty lot; a hacked-up corpse in a trunk under a bridge; a "bag job" in a sewer.

There was no continuity, no set pattern. The list showed simply that all these violent deaths had never been accounted for to the Law. In many instances, of course, the police had pretty good suspicions about the who, and, in some cases, even the why. But suspicions are not legal evidence. Geographically, though, we knew where we stood.

A silhouette of Brooklyn, in outline, roughly resembles a headless woman wearing a bustle—the bustle being the Fort Hamilton Government Reservation, guarding the mouth of the busiest harbor in the world, at the western end of the borough. No reflection is intended, of course.

Now, where the neck of the lady would be, in the far northeast corner, there is a quiet, ever-green acreage in which are the burial grounds of many denominations—Cypress Hills, Cemetery of the Evergreens, Salem Field, Mt. Carmel, the Hungarian Cemetery, Mt. Lebanon, one ofter another. The dead have no prejudices concerning segregation. And on the lower edge of these peaceful green hills and gravestones is the section where murder happened so often. A likely spot to make homicide a habit!

It is not a very large area—not over two miles, north to south; three miles, east and west. In those half-dozen square miles, bordered on one edge by cemeteries, on the other by the lonely sand dunes of the Canarsie Flatlands—between Long Island's rural acreages and the placid Eastern Parkway residential regions—the three trouble spots form a rough triangle. East New York is at the easternmost point, with Brownsville alongside. This, incidentally, is no indictment of Brownsville. It has produced eminent citizens. Many men and women labor to cut away the anchor of environment dragging at its youth. However, for years, tough guys have come from the area. There were times, in fact, when it was advisable for the pedestrian, caught out in Brownsville after dark, to take the middle of the street; and carry as little cash as possible. At the northern apex of the triangle is Ocean Hill, centered at the intersection of tree-shrouded Eastern Parkway and wide, busy Atlantic Avenue, both through thoroughfares across Brooklyn.

The rise of killings and assorted felony in the City of Churches obviously was the work of hoodlum groups springing up here and there in that tricornered area and on its rim.

There was, we agreed, one way—one jumping-off spot—to begin the cleanup. Up to now, these thugs had things pretty much their own way. We could start pushing them around; make them uncomfortable—drive them off the street corners. There is where we started.

Police were assigned to every intersection. Wherever one of these bums was loafing, he was made to move. Toughs were yanked unceremoniously off the corners at every opportunity and charged with any "rap" on which we could bring them in. There might not be enough to convict all of them—these swaggering gangsters were slick. But they could no longer set and hatch. This played hob wth the street-corner crap games that were the neighborhood pastime; whether it would erase any of the marks from the map remained to be seen.

It was, however, excellent preventive medicine. Kids were growing up on those streets. A hood, loudly flaunting his affluence-without-work, would park his shiny new convertible in the neighborhood parking lot, swagger down the neighborhood main street with a lacquered doll on his arm, saunter into the neighborhood bar and begin tossing money around for drinks for the boys. This tends only to breed admiration in the local youth—admiration and envy. Easily influenced kids dream of the day they can achieve the same wonderful estate. Envy quickly advances to the imitative.

Our drive to push the plug-uglies around no longer left them a corner on which to light, or a bar or poolroom where they could congregate. When the kids saw their idols being thrown into police wagons—thrown, that is; not tenderly helped in by the arm—it tended to plant the idea that perhaps their heroes were not such heroes after all. In any language, this is good crime prevention.

As the new broom started to sweep in earnest, the underworld became a little edgy. "Maybe the smart thing would be to get outa town and lay low until it cools off," some of them reasoned. All they got was a sneer from the hotheads.

"Leave town—nuts," snarled the hottest hothead of all, Happy Maione. "Who does that bum in the D. A.'s office think he is? If they keep on pushing us around, we'll start leaving packages on every corner in Brooklyn. That'll keep them good and busy."

This delivery service, mob style, means but one thing: a "package" is a body. Maione made sure the grapevine carried his message back to the District Attorney's office. It was the mob's declaration of war.

One day in late January, twenty-two of the hoodlums were rounded up in one batch. All were convicted of vagrancy or consorting with known criminals. Ken McCabe, another of the assistant District Attorneys, worked overtime prosecuting the tough guys. Among them were such rich pickings as Maione and Abbandando and Blue Jaw Magoon, a most valuable—and very tough—mob henchman. All were treated to stays of sixty or ninety days at the State's expense. For that long, at any rate, they would stay off the corners—and their central corner, in particular.

The heart of the Brownsville-East New York area is Pitkin Avenue. The neighbors firmly believe Pitkin Avenue compares with Fifth Avenue or State Street or Market Street or Lincoln Drive or any other promenade famed for its shops and shopping. But it was not in the glare of Pitkin Avenue's lights that the mob had its headquarters. Four blocks south is a busy intersection under the El tracks. This is the crossing of Saratoga and Livonia Avenues. One square away is a playground where children romp until they are old enough to decide whether it will be the road to honest citizenship or punkdom, hoodlumism and, if they do not stop a bullet first, mob big shot. That intersection was referred to by the mobsters as the Corner—in capital letters. The important point was a candy store. It was open twenty-four hours a day, which is why its owner was known as Midnight Rose. This shop and its corner, we were to learn, was the assembly room and dispatch bureau of killers—the office of the mob. It was a handy, central location. Less than two miles to the west is Ebbets Field, where the Dodgers play.

There was an easy connection between the Corner and the Ocean Hill base. Reles or Pittsburgh Phil or brazen Buggsy had only to drive up Saratoga Avenue to Eastern Parkway, turn right for six blocks to the heavily trafficked corner of Atlantic Avenue. That was operational headquarters of Happy Maione and his strong right arm, Dasher Abbandando.

Now that we had started our cleanup from the corners, we were in a more ticklish spot than ever. Soon, the vagrancy terms would expire; the hoods would be back on the streets again—no doubt ready for business as usual. The Felony and Homicide Section pondered where to turn next, at just what spot to take a hold. The more we pondered, the less light came through. And just about then, the postman dropped a letter in the District Attorney's office. It was on the not-so-elegant stationery of the City Workhouse on Rikers Island. Its message, as well as I can remember now, was:

Dear Sir:

I am doing a bit here. I would like to talk to the District Attorney. I know something about a murder in East New York.

Harry Rudolph.

It seems everybody who had been anybody in law enforcement knew Harry Rudolph—and they all said the same thing about him.

"That Rudy," they said. "He's off his rocker. He's nuts."

Detectives called him a "full mooner," a term that dates back to the days of witchcraft, when the new moon was supposed to make people do strange things who were caught out in it. A full mooner's wheels do not go around in proper synchronization.

Rudolph was serving an indeterminate sentence for a bit of light-fingered illegality—a misdemeanor. Since his incarceration was limited, he, certainly was not animated by the prospect of a reduced sentence as reward for information. Nor would the desire for transfer to more comfortable quarters inspire him. Rikers Island is as good a jail to be in as any—if you have to be in jail. We decided to see what he had on his mind. It was a sort of "what can we lose?" approach. The first thing Rudy said was he hated the Brownsville mob very much.

"Those rats killed my friend Red Alpert," he yelped. "I saw them do it."

It was a startling statement, for, up to that moment, Red Alpert had been one of the bodies left in a gutter. The details on our list ran true to form:

Alpert, Alex, alias Red. 19 years old. Small-time hoodlum. Shot at the edge of a yard. Nov. 25, 1933. No witnesses.

In more than six years, no one had admitted knowing a thing about it.

"I'll tell you who did it, too," Rudy expounded. "Those Brownsville guys—Reles and Buggsy and Dukey Maffetore. They took Red when he came out of his house."

Then Rudy complained that no one ever listened to him. For one entire year, he had been rambling about a murder and about the Brownsville mob, and all he had managed to stir up was a queer look.

In his eagerness to be believed, Rudy yanked his shirt up and exposed a curving expanse of abdomen. Sliced into the flesh was an old but ugly scar. "That's what they did," he pointed to his memento. "They stood two feet away from me and shot me. And I picked the bullet right out with my fingers."

No wonder no one would believe him. How can you believe a man who says he was shot in the stomach at a range of two feet, and not only lived, but plucked the bullet out with his bare hands?

To us, however, the all-important fact was that here was a man who said, "I saw Kid Twist and Buggsy and Dukey kill my pal." Fact or fiction, for the first time, someone was naming names. It was enough to ask the grand jury for an indictment. And that would keep the Kid, the Bug and Dukey off the streets—until a trial, anyway. So, Harry Rudolph was taken before the grand jury and that same afternoon, an indictment charging murder in the first degree was voted. It was a beginning, even though the prospect of securing a conviction on the unsupported say-so of the victim's somewhat eccentric friend was not one to give any prosecutor a feeling of delight.

Billy Sullivan—Captain William A. Sullivan, chief of the Twelfth Detective District—took a couple of men that same night and started looking for Buggsy and Kid Twist through the area. There was, however, no sign of the top command of the Brownsville thugs.

Late in the evening, they headed for the restaurant adjoining the huge market on East New York Avenue, where some of the hoodlums used to stop for a late snack. The captain and his men waited through many cups of coffee. At 1 A.M., with no sign of Buggsy or Kid Twist, the police decided to call it a night. Captain Sullivan went over to the man at the sandwich counter.

"Tell Reles and Buggsy I want them at my office at eight o'clock tomorrow morning," he directed.

Now, in their gun-and-gang careers, the Kid and Buggsy had been arrested seventy-six times between them, for everything, including murder. And between them, they had served a grand total of about fifty months. As a result, they were not particularly impressed when they received Captain Sullivan's message in the early morning hours.

"The same old crap," they chorused blithely. At 8 A.M., they sauntered jauntily into Captain Sullivan's office and said, "Here we are," with an air of, "This is the old walk-in-and-walk-out." Neither of them was ever on the street again in his life. They actually walked in and gave themselves up voluntarily on the one murder rap that did not go "out the window!" The same afternoon, Dukey Maffetore was picked up near his home.

At our request, Reles was remanded to the Tombs in Manhattan; Buggsy went across the bay to the jail on Staten Island, and Maffetore drew the Bronx County jail, far up near the Yankee Stadium. That way, they could not meet on the walk or huddle in exercise periods and reassure each other with, "It won't be long; just sit tight."

Reles and Buggsy were the tough guys. We just let them sit. We had our eye on Dukey.

Dukey Maffetore was a sleek young man who read comic books while the rest plotted murder. They would give him his orders; he would fold up his literature with a sigh and carry out some job that could lead him to the electric chair. Having completed his chore, Dukey would place his shoulder against a building again with a satisfied smile, and get back to *Li'l Abner* or *Superman.*

When Dukey was arrested in the Red Alpert murder, he was twenty-five, and he had not done an honest day's work in over seven years. Yet, he had never been convicted of a crime. All the Brownsville boys seemed lucky that way in those days.

Many interesting characters frequented the crap games of East New York. They were a source of personnel for an independent "businessman" with a burglary, a heist or a hijacking on his mind. Dukey knew one of these free-enterprise executives as Sutton, and one night Sutton singled out Dukey at a dice game.

"Do you want to make some money?" he asked.

"Doing what?"

"Driving a car tonight for a while."

The proposition sounded like an easy dollar to Dukey. He agreed. That night, Maffetore drove, with Sutton beside him, giving directions, and two others in the rear. Sutton said "stop" at a corner where there was a bank. The three dismounted.

"Wait here," commanded Sutton, and Dukey figured, "They must be casing the bank."

He was just sitting there when two policemen turned the corner and headed straight for the car. "So, I jump out and get away from there," Dukey told the boys later. "I guess those guys are going to stick up the bank."

He never saw Sutton again. It is probably just as well he didn't. On the Federal Bureau of Investigation's annual list of "the most wanted men in America," the name of Willie Sutton, bank robber, has led all the rest since 1949.

Someone described Dukey once as a hard-boiled flyweight. That stood until he faced murder. Then Dukey was just a flyweight, and a shaky one, at that. He was the obvious prospect for us to work on. We realized he would not know too much—but he was the best we had. We were certain Reles and Buggsy could never be cracked.

Now, small-shots like Maffetore will, sometimes with greater regularity than the big shots, observe the underworld code about "ratting." The fact that it is punishable by death—their own or that of someone they love—weighs heavily on the punks. They learn early that no place is safe for a "canary." In jail, a man can be cut down with a shiv driven silently into his neck; in the outside world, he and his loved ones are inexorably sought out. However, the Law has certain forces with which to counteract this terror. Isolation is one. Dukey received this "cold-storage" treatment—and the loneliness that accompanies it. The comic books had not dulled Dukey's imagination. Frantic thoughts raced through his mind. And no one—absolutely no one—came to relieve them. Then, suddenly, Dukey had a visitor. Detective Lieutenant Jack Osnato strolled into his cell and said, "I thought you might be lonesome." He said it in a friendly tone, and he said it in Italian, the tongue Dukey knew better than English. Jack Osnato knew his way with hoodlums. He had come up through the ranks, beginning with pounding a beat.

"Those guys are making a sap out of you," he jeered at Maffetore. "You'll be a sucker sticking with them." He didn't press the matter too hard then. All he wanted to do, that first time, was to plant the seed. But he came back again, and chatted in Italian, and offered cigarettes—and gave Dukey pep talk No. 2 for convincing small-shots.

"Those guys eat steak and drink champagne, and go to Florida," he drew the picture. "You stay in Brooklyn and pick up a buck where you can."

But the mob instinct is strong. Dukey remembered pictures in the papers showing what happened to stoolpigeons.

Lieutenant Osnato continued slowly and carefully, and in a couple of days, Mike McDermott took a hand. Mike was a colorful, smart cop, who also had come up the hard way. He was Deputy Chief Inspector, commanding Detective Headquarters in both Brooklyn and Staten Island. Later, he was to become chief of security at the government's atomic energy plant at Oak Ridge,

Tenn., when it was supposed to be the most closely guarded secret in the world. A huge, ruddy-faced Irishman, Mike is as clever a detective as ever hit a police department. Osnato was a friend of O'Dwyer; Mike was not. But Mike was all policeman. In spite of personal feelings, he was a tremendous help to the prosecutor's office. Between them, McDermott and Osnato started a friendly race to crack Maffetore.

"You guys are trying to make me squeal," cried the distressed Dukey. It had taken him a while, but he finally recognized the tactics.

"Sure we are," admitted McDermott. "Why don't you think of your wife and kid? They'll be evicted soon, when they can't pay the rent. Reles' family isn't going to be thrown out, you can bet that."

"The hell with you guys," whined the terrorized tough guy.

That's the way it went for some little while. Then Dukey sobbed out, "Who'll believe me if I do talk?" The weakling was ripe. Mike and Jack suddenly switched to a tougher line.

"Look," Osnato snapped. "You got it pretty soft in this can— a radio, a chance to get fresh air. The grub is good. If you keep on like you are, I'll see that you go to Raymond Street [Brooklyn] where there's dirt and bedbugs and cockroaches."

The break came during the week of Lincoln's Birthday. Harry Rudolph sent word to the District Attorney again. "A guy in the can here," he said, exploding a new rocket, "told me it's worth five grand to me if I change my story and square Reles and Buggsy and put them on the street, and let Maffetore take the rap."

"Who is it?"

"It's a guy named Frosch."

Frosch was well known to us. He was one of a family of professional bondsmen who handled much of the bail business for the Brownsville hoodlums. At that time, Frosch was in jail in connection with the bail-bond racket, and had admitted he was a "fixer" of many things—including policemen.

Corroboration of Rudolph's story was available. Vince Ricardo said he was in the adjoining cell and heard the offer made. Ricardo's identity always has been kept secret, for the simple reason he was a professional stoolpigeon from Los Angeles. He had been planted in the jail to aid a special investigation which had nothing to do with Murder, Inc.

Naturally, we made certain that Dukey was fully informed on how the big shots were scheming to get themselves clear. And when Osnato next walked into his cell, Dukey broke. In a matter of minutes, he was on the way to the District Attorney's office. He talked for an hour and a half—and that was long enough for him to unburden himself of just about everything he could remember about the mob.

"When I was twenty," he said, starting with his background, "I got in with the mob. I went into the shylock business. Pittsburgh Phil gave me the territory. He made me borrow the money, to start out, from his brother, Alex. Sure, I had to pay it back at the regular shylock interest. Pretty Levine was my partner until 1938."

But murder—what about murder? He denied the Alpert job flatly.

"But in 1937," he went on, "one night in May, me and Pretty are standing on the Corner, and Pittsburgh Phil tells us to steal a car."

They did, and delivered it, as Pittsburgh Phil directed, to Happy Maione and Dasher Abbandando.

"A couple days later," he added, "I see in the papers a guy is found dead in that car."

Any more? Well, the previous Labor Day, at Buggsy's command, he had driven "a little guy" he didn't know over to Reles' house.

"They choke him there," he related. "Then Buggsy sets fire to him on a lot."

The Duke was not reticent, but his mind and his speech worked laboriously.

"Buggsy or Reles or Pittsburgh Phil or one of those guys tells me do something, I do it," he explained hesitantly. "If I don't, I'll get myself killed."

Now that Dukey had sung, we were very little better off, however. He admitted stealing a car and delivering it, and the car wound up as a hearse. That is a long way from making out a murder case. He said he chauffeured a victim to his murder, and to his cremation pyre. That made him an accomplice. As such, he would require corroboration, by law.

It was clear that Dukey knew but a limited "song," because, as we had feared, he was on the fringe of the gang; he did only what he was told. He never learned the whys and the wherefores. What was needed was someone with bigger things to talk about; someone a rung higher on the gang ladder.

"Oh, then you should go get Pretty," Dukey himself offered. "He is smart. He knows more than me."

So, we went and "got" Pretty Levine.

Pretty had big blue eyes and curly hair, and dimples that caused much palpitation and fluttering of the eyelids among the Brownsville girls. He married a belle who was one of the beauties of Brooklyn. Some of his friends were unkind enough to suggest she was wasted on a punk, even one as pretty as Pretty was.

Where Dukey had the I.Q. of a boy probably half his age, Pretty's mind was clear. At one time it was said around the Brownsville "office," that if Pretty kept his mind on his work, Kid Twist was even thinking of advancing him from punk to hoodlum. That, of course, was before Pretty tried to go straight. That was toward the end of 1937, and Pretty had just married Helen, who was slim and barely twenty. He decided he would give up the life that had involved him in half a dozen murders before he was twenty-three.

It is remarkable that the mob didn't kill him at once. What probably saved Pretty was that he let no one know what he had in mind. He moved out of Brownsville, and simply didn't hang around any more. He managed to obtain a truck, and he over-came his thorough repugnance for work, hauling garbage and sand and ashes. He and Helen were able to get along until about September of 1938, when Helen had to go to the hospital for the arrival of their daughter.

"The bill is $100, payable before the patient leaves," the hospital, coldly efficient, notified Pretty. Pretty did not have $100. In desperation, he sought out the loan-shark department of the Brownsville combination.

"I need a C-note," he announced to Pittsurgh Phil. "Can I get it on the six-for-five?"

"Sure you can, kid," the big shot said to the punk who used to drive his murder cars. "All you need is an okay."

That meant a pair of co-makers from among the mob's personnel. Pretty still had some friends, and two of them were willing to say "good" for him, which was the shylocks' endorsement. But Pittsburgh Phil said, "No good; those two don't have it themselves. You got to get two better."

Out went Pretty again, and rounded up another pair willing to co-sign his note. Finally, he was granted the paltry sum by the mobsters for whom, only a few months earlier, he had risked sitting in the electric chair. And he got the money on the same basis as any other sucker: $1 interest per week for every $5 borrowed—or else.

In the weeks that followed, there was never enough to repay the shylocks. Eventually, he had to default. With the shylocks, default comes under the heading of hazardous occupation—and co-makers are in the same boat. For the sake of his own health and the health of the friends who vouched for him, Pretty went back with the gang.

When Dukey suggested Pretty as a source of information in 1940, detectives just went to his home, and there he was. We didn't know it then, but we had won a race with murder—double murder. It is shuddering to contemplate how closely the investigation of Murder, Inc., came to foundering before it ever got under way. Actually, both punks already had been marked for execution—and for exactly the same reason they were so valuable to us alive: they were the potential weak spots. And they were still alive only because the mob worked with such precision in perfecting plot detail.

The order for their execution had been issued in mid-January— the same day twenty-two of the hoods were sentenced for vagrancy and consorting.

"We got to take care of anybody who might rat," Pittsburgh Phil had cautioned, spotting trouble ahead. The list was carefully scrutinized. Dukey and Pretty were placed at the top of those who had to go. Dukey was a recognized weakling, and Pretty had tried to quit the gang.

Had it been deemed imperative, there is no question that the mob would have erased them as quickly and completely as switching off a light. But these thugs still could not believe we meant business. They told each other that the wholesale vagrancy arrests, which they called "tickles," were "something for the D. A.'s office to look good in the papers with." These plug-uglies were usually accurate in anticipating the Law. But they never suspected that the prosecutor's staff was going to delve into old murders. How could they? We ourselves didn't know what we were going to explode.

Thus, the mobsters saw no particular urgency for the elimination. They could take time for all details, and carry it out when the occasion was propitious. February 9 was set for Dukey's assassination, and March 1 for Pretty's. The indictment for Red Alpert's murder saved Dukey's life. He was arrested just one week before he was to be killed. Dukey fingered his ex-partner on February 20, and Pretty was brought in just nine days before the gang had his farewell party scheduled. Because of the mob's adherence to plot and technique, the Law got its first peek at the unbelievable operations of the underworld's most competent killers.

The average citizen, the neophyte in criminology, no doubt imagines that all you have to do to get the little guy to talk is put the squeeze on and, like an orange in a press, everything gushes out.

Actually, the big shots will talk faster. It took a masterful job by McDermott and Osnato to get Dukey to open up. Even then, he sang only because of the conviction that he was being abandoned. When it came to being exasperating, though, Pretty was the star.

It was made quite clear that Dukey had involved him in various crimes which headed him straight down the road toward prison. But Pretty just clammed up. Through the dragging hours of two full days, no one could get even a grunt out of him.

It was imperative to us that he open up. The break from within had to be widened. It was whispered that Pretty had a lovely wife. Perhaps, if she were brought down . . .

The lovely Helen had no baby sitter. She had to bring the sixteen-month-old daughter with her. The child was as beautiful as the mother. Helen and Pretty embraced fervently. He was a mobster, but you could see this affection was genuine. They were all that mattered to each other. Little Barbara grabbed her daddy around the legs, and was lifted up to join in.

"You want your husband, don't you?" Helen was asked. "Then it's up to you to get him to talk."

She turned to him, hands clenched anxiously. "Please, please," she implored. "For our sake, tell the truth."

Tears streamed down her cheeks. The child began to cry. Soon Pretty was sniffling, too. If it had kept up much longer, I felt I would have had a hard time to keep from doing the same.

Pretty became almost hysterical. "I can't talk," he choked. "How can I talk?"

"You must," his wife sobbed. "For us, you must."

Pretty jammed his hands against his mouth, as if trying to hold the words in. "I can't talk," tumbled forth again. That ended the interview.

What kept this peanut of the mob from talking? Under the wing of the Law, what did he have to be afraid of? He knew—and we hadn't learned yet—that where Murder, Inc., was concerned, jails were not safe and even the walls of the D. A.'s office might have ears. The heart-stopping thought of what would happen to his wife and daughter kept his mouth shut.

In the end, only drastic means were left. I remember thinking of the old remark about father giving junior his first spanking, saying, "This hurts me worse than it does you." Once more, Helen was sent for. Her eyes were red-rimmed and worried. The curly-haired small-timer was tortured by her anguish. What was going through his mind was this:

Dukey had talked some. Suppose he (Pretty) revealed what he, personally, had done. Would the D. A. stand for it? More to the point, if he didn't implicate anyone else, would it keep the heat of the mob off? As Helen continued sobbing her pleas, he reached a decision.

"I'll talk about myself," he burst out. "Then leave me alone. I won't talk any more than that."

In the presence of his wife, Pretty blurted out his part in the one crime Dukey had confessed first—"Me and Dukey took the car, and a stiff was left in it a couple days later." And, wife or no wife, that morsel was all. He rigidly refused to admit even, as Dukey had, that the theft was on Pittsburgh Phil's orders, or that they had delivered the car to Happy and the Dasher.

"Don't ask me any more questions," he repeated dully, time after time.

This was simply unreal. Here was an errand boy of the gang willing to confess himself right into prison, and maybe close to the death chamber. But not a word about others. Yet, he knew that the very killers he shielded would have killed him as casually as lighting a cigarette.

"Go ahead and put me in jail," he said stubbornly.

It was time to get very tough. "You're going to jail, all right," I told him. "And so is your wife. She was here and heard your confession. That makes her a material witness."

Pretty went wild. "I told you about myself," he screamed. "What do you want from her? She didn't do anything."

We had a threefold motive, however. First, Pretty's continued silence made the severest methods necessary. Second, we were not at all sure just how much Helen did know. It would be a very strange wife, indeed, who was married to a hoodlum and didn't know it—and more besides. Finally, now that he had confessed even this tiny bit, she was eligible, under mob methods, to be snuffed out.

Helen was placed in the Women's House of Detention. Any time Pretty wanted to see her, she would be sent up, and he would be brought over from jail. Still he would not talk. He kept chanting one single refrain:

"Do what you want to with me, but leave my wife alone."

Each time, with his wife listening, he would get the same answer, "You have the key to her cell—and you can unlock it."

And still he would not talk.

"These men will protect you," Helen reassured him. "They won't let us get hurt. Those other men are no good. Tell the truth."

Pretty stood the strain for twenty-four days. On the twenty-fifth, he and Helen and their baby were alone in the room for perhaps half an hour. When I walked in, he had his arms around them.

"If I talk, will they be safe?" was the first thing he demanded.

"You have nothing to worry about," I insisted.

"Why should I keep my wife in jail for those rats?" Only he didn't use the word "rats." "I'll tell everything, and I'll take my chances." He cursed the mob. Pretty had finally broken. It was St. Patrick's Day, and one reporter covering the District Attorney's office noted, "The good St. Pat has come to Brooklyn to drive more snakes away."

The Red Alpert job had started the whole ball rolling—and Pretty's first words were, "Dukey didn't have a thing to do with Alpert." It was not an auspicious opening for his long-awaited song. Only much later, by putting a lot of bits of information together, did we learn that he was telling the gospel truth.

Red Alpert had been a very tough kid in a neighborhood where, it had been rumored, children teeth on .45-caliber pistols. By the time he was sixteen, he was making his living breaking the law. He had such a hatred for a police uniform that he would not even wear a blue serge suit. He was mostly a petty burglar, without mob affiliation. Even a small-time crook, though, occasionally stumbles into a haul. In the summer of 1933, Red came up with a bundle of gems from some transaction.

Red was not well enough established to have an outlet for valuable trinkets. He knew, however, that the Brownsville mob would have ways and means of disposing of such articles. He looked up Pittsburgh Phil.

"I got some nice stuff here," he displayed his loot. "Gimme three G's for it. It's worth a lot more."

"I'll give you seven hundred," was the counteroffer. Pittsburgh Phil's tone indicated he expected neither hemming nor hawing. However, no one—not even the swaggering Brownsville thugs—awed Alpert.

"You know what you can do for seven hundred," he snapped. "You can go to hell."

This was heresy in Brownsville. No one spoke to Pittsburgh Phil like that. The fashion-plate plug-ugly would kill a man with the same relish he acquired the very latest in haberdashery.

"Here's seven hundred . . . take it or leave it," he challenged.

Red told Pep once more, specifically, what to do with his seven hundred, and he walked disdainfully away.

Phil was incensed. But, outweighing his urge for redress for the disrespect was his greed for the jewelry at his proffered price. You might think a cut-throat like this would simply have pulled out a pistol then and there, shot the insolent burglar and taken his treasure. These killers, though, were specialists. Almost invariably, they murdered only after careful planning and discussion among all the partners.

Returning to the Corner, Phil gathered the clan. "Imagine that punk telling me what he'll take," he sneered, irate. That the jewels were worth every bit of the $3,000 Alpert asked was of no moment. Phil wanted Red brought in for proper punishment —which meant, of course, the complete erasure of the independent young thief, and the acquisition of his gems. To avoid arousing Alpert's suspicions, it was decided to have a stranger go after him —one whose association with the combination he would not suspect.

"He doesn't know Pretty—Pretty's the guy for it," suggested Reles. Pretty remembered the occasion well. His report to us on developments went this way:

"I'm standing on the Corner talking to my friend, Joey, when Buggsy comes along and says, 'Come on down in the candy store.' I go down, and Reles and Pep and Louis Capone are sitting at a table. They say, 'Bring Red Alpert down to us here.' Me and Joey go down to get Alpert. But Alpert won't come.

"Joey says, 'Let's go around the back and grab him from the back.' We go around, but Red must guess what we're doing. Before I know what's happening, Red is there and puts a gun on my head. I don't even see him. Joey gets excited and starts shooting, and Alpert runs. Nobody gets hurt. Joey and me come back to the candy store and tell them what happens. They say, 'Okay—let it go.'"

This did not mean, of course, that Pittsburgh Phil's rancor had cooled—or his desire for the jewels. "I can't go to see him, because he knows what I am after," he confided to Reles and Buggsy. "You two go down there."

Buggsy and Kid Twist made the trip. "Pep wants the ice for seven hundred," they offered. Alpert laughed in their faces.

"I told Pep the hell with him—and the hell with you guys, too."

Red shouldn't have done it a second time. He had now defied the three top torpedoes. The trio summoned Walter Sage, an associate.

"It's your 'hit,' " Pep ordered. "You're a good friend of Alpert. He won't get suspicious if you come around."

Pretty completed the story, although he knew none of these motivating details.

"I saw Walter Sage with Buggsy and Pep and Reles," he related. "Then Buggsy comes over to me and Dukey. He says, 'Youse two better go sleep together some place tonight. Something is gonna happen.' I had a room over on Williams Avenue then. Dukey and me stay there that night. The next day, I read in the paper where something happens. Red Alpert got hit."

Continuing his song, Pretty dipped next into the playland of upstate New York, the Catskills, and revealed half a dozen assassinations. All appeared then to involve Brooklyn gang stuff only, as if the mountains were something of an annex for the combination. Up to that point, whenever a body had bubbled up to the surface of a Catskill lake or was left on a dusty roadside, all that Sullivan County authorities had was a corpus delicti. No witnesses, no motive—no anything. Pretty's revelations shocked Sullivan County District Attorney Bill Deckelman.

"We," was his amazed gasp of realization, "have been a dumping grounds for the last ten years."

In the modus operandi of the national Syndicate, the matter of friend killing friend was—and is—not considered at all unusual. In fact, a contract to murder even a blood relative is no occasion for outrage. Either the man assigned does the job—or he "goes," himself.

Thus, Walter Sage did not let his friendship for Red Alpert stand in the way. Walter always did his best for the mob. He handled several more jobs through the years. His devoted service ultimately was rewarded with promotion to the post of district manager in charge of slot machines in Sullivan County. The machines provided excellent returns in the Catskill resort belt, as they always do among light-hearted, free-spending vacationers.

For a year or two, Walter's administration was eminently satisfactory. In midsummer of 1937, however, the directors of the combination detected something about Sage's accountancy by which all the proceeds were not reaching the mob treasury.

"What does that bum think—he's a trolley-car conductor?" demanded Kid Twist in the ensuing business meeting. "It looks like he figures all the nickels and quarters that stick to the ceiling belong to us, and he takes the rest."

The violation was most serious. It was decreed that Sage must be taught a lesson not to fool with the combination's collections. A permanent lesson. Pittsburgh Phil and Gangy Cohen would be the "professors." They were Walter's best friends. Sage lived with Pittsburgh Phil when he was in Brooklyn. Gangy, a 230-pound giant, was his roommate and first lieutenant in Sullivan County.

Pretty happened to be taking his vacation in the mountains just then. Two days after he arrived, Pep came to see him.

"What're you doing tonight?" he inquired. And before Pretty could answer, the eager executioner continued, "Whatever it is, drop it. Meet me in front of the Evans Hotel with your car."

Pretty was there promptly. "Sit tight and keep your lights out," Phil directed. After some minutes, a car sped by. Its headlights blinked once, bright and dim, in a quick flash.

"Tail them," ordered Pittsburgh Phil hurriedly.

For a mile or two, Pretty trailed the tiny red taillight. He was close enough to hear the scream that came from the other car eventually. The automobile drifted to the side of the road and came to a stop in a wooded area. Pretty braked just behind it.

What had happened in that car was this:

Gangy had suggested a ride through the hills to his buddy, Walter Sage. Walter might suspect something if anyone but his old pal, Gangy, made the date. Sage sat in front with the driver. Gangy and Jack Drucker, another transplanted Brooklyn badman, were in the rear. As they wheeled through the summer night, those in the rear leaned forward time and again to tell a joke, discuss the baseball pennant races—all the usual chit-chat.

They reached a lonely spot, where tall trees pressed in on the mountain road. The signal was given by the driver—some innocuous remark, previously agreed. One of the men in the back seat slid an ice pick out of his pocket. He leaned forward, as he had done any number of times during the trip. This time pleasant conversation was omitted.

His left arm snaked around Sage's neck and jerked back. The mob calls it "mugging." Holding the slot-machine manager in this strangling grip, the man plunged the pick into Walter's neck and upper chest thirty-two times as methodically as a pile driver. Sage struggled fiercely at first, then convulsively, and finally was still.

"He's done," one of the others said, and the pick-wielder released his grip. The car stopped. The tail car came up.

Pretty saw the doors open on each side of the murder car. From one, he saw Jack Drucker emerge slowly, an ice pick in his hand. From the other, Gangy burst out as if fired from a cannon. With a loud whoop, he disappeared into the woods.

"What the hell?" said the surprised Pittsburgh Phil. Then he and Drucker busied themselves pulling out the body of Walter Sage, who had just lost his job as general manager for slot machines in Sullivan County. The corpse was loaded into Pretty's automobile and driven to the shore of one of the popular lakes dotting the mountains.

There, a pinball machine was lashed securely to Sage's chest, and the entire package was dropped into the lake. The pinball machine was a symbol. Pittsburgh Phil preened himself over this touch. It was the object of Sage's larceny, and he would forever bear it in his last resting place. This was the lesson the mob felt Walter had to be taught. It also served a decidedly utilitarian function. With that anchor, the corpus delicti would stay put on the lake floor—at least until the water had decomposed it to make identification impossible.

Now, a body immersed in water will rise to the surface because of the buoyancy of gases which fill the intestinal tract. These killers kept themselves informed on such matters. Imagine their surprise, then, when the cadaver suddenly popped to the surface in just ten days, despite the perforations and the weight. They investigated, and, as a sequel to the lesson for Sage, they learned one themselves, in anatomy.

Perforations made by a tool such as an ice pick, while the victim is alive, are virtually sealed by blood pumping from his still-beating heart. Thus, the gases do not escape. Not enough holes were opened in Walter Sage after he was dead for the corpse to lose its buoyancy, and the body worked its way up. Still strapped to it was the object lesson—the pinball machine.

"Think of that," Pittsburgh Phil shook his head in wonder. "With this bum, you gotta be a doctor, or he floats."

On the night Walter Sage was done in, Gangy was moving very fast through the mountain woods when last seen. The gangsters couldn't figure out what got into him. Gangy, however, had his reasons. Having completed his assigned portion in the departure of his very good friend, the gangster giant was suddenly stricken with the inspiration that now he was just as marked as Sage had been, on the grounds that he knew too much. That is why he lit running, and did not stop until he had put a large patch of woodland between himself and recent companions.

One night, many months later, Pretty and Dukey were wasting an hour or two at a neighborhood movie in Brownsville. The film was *Golden Boy,* the story of a prize fighter. One scene depicted a fight arena, with a prolonged flash of ringside fans leaping and cheering for the celluloid gladiators.

Pretty blinked. "Hey," he nudged Dukey, "there's Gangy."

"Where?" Dukey twisted his head, looking. "Where?"

"Up there—in the picture. The guy waving."

Dukey finally located it. "Gee—that's him all right," he acknowledged.

"Wow," cried Pretty. "Wait till the troop hears this."

Bubbling over with their information, they did not even stay for the rest of the picture. This was a rare opportunity for the punks—to be able to astound all the big shots. They headed for the Corner.

"We just see a picture down at the movie," the loan-shark partners chorused as they joined their superiors, "and guess who's in it?" They gave no one a chance to answer. "Gangy's in it," they effervesced in self-importance.

"You're nuts," was the unanimous response. "How could that bum get in the movies?"

"We're telling you," insisted the strutting small-shots.

The executives still disbelieved, but Pretty and Dukey were

so positive that all of them went to the movies . . . Reles and Buggsy and Happy and Blue Jaw and Abbandando and Pittsburgh Phil and Louis Capone.

"There . . . that guy . . . by the ring," Pretty pointed, as the scene flashed across the screen. "That's Gangy."

Everyone took a good look. "Geez . . . that's the fat bum, all right," conceded Reles. All Pittsburgh Phil could say was, "Well, I'll be damned."

What had happened was that Gangy emerged from the Catskill woods some distance from where he entered on the night of Sage's murder, and he made for a railroad station. He boarded a train heading west—as far west as he could go.

The long ride gave Gangy a great deal of time for reflection. By the time he stepped into California's golden sunshine, he was laughing about the whole thing. He reasoned that the mob had given no sign of intending to harm a hair of his head. His fears, he became convinced, had been groundless. But, since he was in California, he decided to stay a while. Gangy had friends in Hollywood, among them a number of actors who are popular and respected by millions to this day. Through one friend or another, Gangy got himself onto the film lots. Tall and husky, he was kept busy with bit parts.

The mob kept the secret well after discovering Gangy's new career. Not until three years later—after our probe had begun, and just about the time Pretty decided to sing—was Jack Gordon of the films unmasked as Gangy of the combination. Then, one evening, a Sullivan County policeman was in a theater suffering the lower end of a Class B double feature, when a figure on the screen jerked him to attention. It was an apparition. Sullivan County law enforcement had been hunting that figure for three years, to answer questions about murder.

District Attorney William Deckelman and Sheriff Harry Borden and some state troopers were on the next plane out. They found Gangy well established as an actor. He and his family were ensconced in a cozy cottage just across the street from the studio. And all but a very few of gangster Gangy's film roles had been as —a policeman!

Pretty was not exactly a fount of information; he didn't know enough. But for a while, he was a steady useful trickle, supplying leads to launch our investigation. His picture of operations in Sullivan County, a hundred miles from the gang's lair, provided the very interesting disclosure that no matter where they were, when the Brownsville boys were around, murder always happened.

The blue-eyed punk was still on the fringe, though. He placed Maione and Abbandando, Louis Capone and Pittsburgh Phil, Buggsy and Reles squarely in an organization of killers. But he did not know where or how each fitted into the whole. Neither he nor Dukey knew even where the power lay. To both, Pittsburgh Phil was top man.

As far as those 200-odd unsolved murders in Brooklyn were concerned, we had a man on first base, but we were a long way from scoring. No convictions could be obtained against any of the bosses on what the two small-shots said. Their material was promising—nothing more. For example, when we whisked them to Sullivan County, indictments were voted there against Gangy, Pittsburgh Phil and three others in the assassination of Sage and Irv Ashkenaz, which Pretty also mentioned; but when Gangy was brought back from movieland and tried, he was acquitted in spite of their testimony.

A better break-from-within was life and death to the probe. And if it did not come, our office was going to be holding a very large bag, for the promise in the recitals of Pretty and Dukey had been screamed in headlines across the nation.

We had, however, produced one excellent effect. Brooklyn mob society was tense and stewing. Each hoodlum was wracking his brain trying to recall whether Pretty or Dukey had been close when he committed some crime. Friend became a bit suspicious of friend. Naturally, we did everything we could to further the uneasiness. There are handy ways of disseminating rumor to reach the underworld. We let little things drop here and there . . . "Pittsburgh Phil is talking," the whisper would go out, or "Buggsy offered to sing."

All of this, though, did not gainsay the bald realization that our investigation was going to collapse unless we got a top mobster who had all the answers—and would give them out loud. He had to know why the killings were done, as well as how, and his revelations had to be dovetailed and unquestioned.

We had to have a Buggsy or a Happy Maione who would put the finger on the rest and reveal the machinery. We needed, in brief, a canary that could sing good and loud—and on key. A Reles would do. Do? He would be the exact, perfect fit! Of one thing in this mess, though, both the Law and the mob were positive: Kid Twist would never break. It was legend in the police department how the Kid was arrested and worked over time and again—but never a word out of him.

And then, Mrs. Kid Twist Reles walked into the District Attorney's office.

"My husband," she announced, "wants an interview with the Law."

3.

Song of murder
on a holy day

The head hoodlum had fat fingers—the man who wouldn't squeal, does—the Syndicate gets its first exposure—ten-year mystery: why did Reles talk?—rackets are big business; murder, incidental.

IF A total stranger walked up to Kid Twist Reles and, without a word, bashed him in the face, I could understand it. That was the reaction you got from one look at him.

The Kid had eyes that were shiny agates, hard and piercing, and you didn't like them at all. He had a round face, thick lips, a flat nose and small ears, stuck close to his kinky hair. His arms had not waited for the rest of him. They dangled to his knees, completing a generally gorilla-like figure.

Kid Twist's most striking characteristic, though, was in his fingers. They were strong; they strangled men. Where ordinary fingers start to taper at the ends, the Kid's became spatulate. The tips were big and flat. They reminded you of a set of hammers, hung at the end of an arm. You could almost picture this low-browed bandit driving rows of nails into a board merely by snapping the fat heads of his fingers down, one by one.

And he was tough. Very, very tough. He did not have the loud nerviness of his buddy, Buggsy. Nor did he kill just for the pleasure of killing, like Pittsburgh Phil or surly Happy Maione. Reles was just tough all over. Tough enough to organize the overthrow of the racket regime that ruled Brownsville and East New York before him, even though he was shot twice doing it—once in the back, once in the stomach.

Even Reles' mind was tough—and cunning. Take the time he and another hoodlum had a vendetta going. The other was called Jake the Painter. They had threatened to kill each other on sight.

51

One evening, in September, 1932, they came face to face on a street. It just happened that Reles was not carrying "the piece." The piece, in mobdom, is also known as the rod, equalizer, cannon, blaster, that thing. In plain English: a gun. The other mobster hauled out his piece and was about to let go.

Reles fancied himself as a psychologist; prided himself on his self-possession under stress, and a sadistic sense of the dramatic. There was a lot of the ham actor in the Kid.

"What's the use killing me here?" he said softly to Jake the Painter, although looking squarely into the unfriendly end of a pistol. "The only thing that'll happen, is my mob will get you. That ain't smart."

"They gotta get me first," snarled the other.

"Don't worry—they'll get you."

The man with the gun hesitated, and Reles went on persuasively. "There's plenty of room for everybody," he urged. "You and me together, Jake—we could clean up, the way you know the painting business. You could come in with us." Reles pressed his advantage. "Let's talk it over like a couple of smart businessmen," he suggested. "Let's go have a drink."

Jake went along, not quite convinced. He should have remembered that the Kid, oddly enough, did not drink. And he should have remembered that the Kid was never known to buy a drink, either.

After several libations, Reles' reasoning made sound sense to Jake the Painter. When the sworn enemies walked out of the speakeasy, they were chums, to all intents and purposes. As they strolled along, the Kid turned to his would-be slayer of a few minutes before.

"Look, Jake," his tone was warm, inspiring confidence. "What do you want to be found with the piece on you? For what?"

"What do you mean?" Jake was puzzled. "What's the difference?"

"The difference is you got a record. Suppose the Law comes along now and frisks you." The Kid was solicitous. "Gimme the damn thing . . . lemme ditch it."

"Geez, I never thoughta that. You're always using your head, pal." And, with utmost faith, Jake placed the gun in his new friend's hand. Nonchalantly, Reles accepted the weapon. Just as nonchalantly, he turned it around—and fired a string of shots into the trusting mobster-painter.

As Jake toppled into the gutter, the conniving killer flipped the pistol into a sewer. He scampered around the corner and dashed two blocks at top speed. There, had witnesses been noticing, he suddenly switched from a man-in-a-hurry to an apparently reeling drunk. He staggered to a store window, raised his foot and deliberately drove it through the glass. He wobbled on very slowly, allowing the proprietor plenty of time to grab him.

Kid Twist was in the police station, giving an excellent performance of a man in a happy haze, when the alarm came in: A body had been found in a gutter with half a dozen slugs in it. Jovially, Reles nudged the detective.

"Well, chum," he hiccoughed confidently, "this is one they can't hang on me. I was right here all the time."

Kings County Judge George Martin called him "more vicious than Dillinger." Squat and beetle-browed, the Kid was Brooklyn's Public Enemy No. 1 from 1931, when he climbed to the top of the crew of killers, until he walked into the police station in 1940, sneering about a murder rap he regarded as a laugh. He was the most virulent and dynamic agent of the mob. He had a speech defect that was, incongruously, almost a lisp, and a peculiar kind of walk that always made him look as if he were trying to kick his shoes off.

They called him Kid Twist after a lower Manhattan hoodlum of an earlier day. The blustering badman of Brownsville would sooner have thrown a dollar bill away, though, than admit he was anything but entirely original. What he lacked in stature (he was five feet two) was doubly made up in inflated ego.

He sported an air of importance that changed, chameleon-like, when he was cornered, to a feigned bewildered, "I don't know," or an attitude of good fellowship. In his heart, he felt he was more than a match for any lawyer or detective.

He enjoyed a greater reputation for frugality than any Scotsman. Yet a favorite stunt of his was to carry a fat roll, with a one-thousand-dollar bill on the outside, just to flash around and impress people. He loved money only a bit less than his spatulate trigger finger, but he never trusted banks.

He was a moral imbecile—but a shrewd moral imbecile. At thirteen, he was sent up the first time—five months in the reformatory at Chauncey, Mass., for juvenile delinquency. At fifteen, he was an expert at extortion. At seventeen, when a girl he tried to pick up wouldn't respond, he slammed her against a wall with his motorcycle.

"But I made restitution," he explained, as if that took care of everything. It must have. He received a suspended sentence, although when the police grabbed him, his machine was still on the scene.

Kid Twist Reles was one paradox after another:

He didn't drink; but he was a bootlegger in the late twenties.

His wife said he was her loving mate; yet he had dozens of girls set up and doing business in prostitutes' nests.

Mrs. Rose Kirsch was corroboration of the Jekyll-Hyde in the squat murderer.

"Didn't you know he was a killer?" she was asked.

"A killer? No," was her unhesitant reply. "He was very good in the house."

She was his mother-in-law.

Reles proudly gave his occupation as "soda jerk" when he was arrested in his earlier days. That, however, did not befit his position as he progressed. So, he acquired an interest in a small eating place, and from then on would casually remark, "I am a luncheonette proprietor," whether he was asked or not.

Nothing abashed the Kid. In 1934, he was sentenced to three years for assault, for breaking a bottle of oil over the head of Charles Battle, a garage attendant, who hadn't moved fast enough for his fancy. The judge castigated him blisteringly.

"Reles is one of the most vicious characters we have had in years," asserted the jurist. "I am convinced he will eventually either be sentenced to prison for life, or be put out of the way by some good detective with a couple of bullets."

Reles leaned to his lawyer and whispered a sneering message, which the attorney reported.

"I will take on any cop in the city with pistols, fists or anything else," the Kid defied the court. "A cop counts to fifteen when he puts his finger on the trigger before he shoots."

In his career, Kid Twist was arrested in Brooklyn and in Chauncey, Mass., in North Scituate, R. I. (1930) and in Jersey City, N. J. (1931), in Florida (1936 and 1938), and in Sullivan County, in upstate New York (1939). He committed just about every act of violence against which there is a law (see Appendix 1).

There were any number of crimes, of course, which do not show on his BCI (Bureau of Criminal Identification) record. He committed eleven murders by his own peculiar reckoning. We knew of fourteen in which he was a definite principal. He pointed out that he hadn't pulled the trigger in one of the others, and in another had only held one end of the strangling rope, and had not yanked it. Hence, he simply could not understand how he could be called the murderer in those. There were countless complaints against him for extortion, "protection" tribute, and accompanying vandalism and violence. Shopkeepers were crippled, who refused his "protection." There were slot machines, bookmaking, shylocking, gambling, beer-running. Once, earlier, he and his mob beat a recalcitrant beer-garden proprietor over the head with a chair because he refused to use their brew. He whipped out a gun on a street one day and wounded three men while trying to hit one.

From June 11, 1930, when he was picked up for murder the first time, until February 2, 1940, when he was taken off the streets for good, he was arrested on some charge or other on an average of once every seventy-eight days—excluding the time he spent in prison. But he walked out, free and clear, time after time.

Often, the same magistrate cleared him for a series of serious crimes. One, who was later removed from office, granted him freedom on bail in a before-dawn proceeding on one occasion. The magistrate's explanation was that he "didn't know" Reles was a dangerous character. Yet, in the course of the five preceding years, Reles had appeared before this same magistrate—and been discharged—for homicide, for felonious assault and for consorting with known criminals.

Most hoodlums who live long enough to be bosses generally run into convictions and jail sentences while they are still punks. By the time they arrive they have learned the ropes. Kid Twist ran true to the pattern. Four of his six brief prison visits occurred before 1928. From 1930 to 1934, he was arrested twenty-three times and walked out on every occasion, except for a thirty-day stint pinned on him in Jersey City in 1931 as a disorderly person. After his visit to Elmira, for hitting Battle with a bottle, ended in 1936, he never again spent a day in prison until he walked in voluntarily in 1940. One of the more remarkable things about his record, too, was the fact that although he was charged with murder six times, he never faced a jury for any one of them. Magistrate's Court was content to discharge him for "lack of evidence."

It was most obvious that Reles bore a charmed life where the Law was concerned. He also boasted about the amount of "ice" he had to pay out to keep the charm working.

Kid Twist started racketeering in 1927, as a punk. He started murdering in 1930, when he was putting together his own mob to take over in Brownsville. He never stopped either activity.

There was no doubt that he was highly regarded by the killer crew. Throughout the entire thirty months he was in prison, beginning in 1934, he received a weekly sum from the combination. Mikey Syckoff, one of the loan-shark agents, brought it to him faithfully, along with gang gossip and general good tidings.

"Mikey would say he was my brother to get in to see me," he explained.

In Brooklyn, Mrs. Reles, too, was handed a weekly amount while her husband was "away." Mob policy was never to have a member worry unduly over his loved ones during an enforced vacation. When Reles was freed, $1,600 and a new car were waiting for him, so he could come home in style. These thugs had a social code. It was good business, too; it impressed the hero-worshipping kids, from whence came the hired hands for the gang. The stylish return of the prodigal proved no loss of face or position.

The chunky killer was born in East New York. When his

"career" ended, he was thirty-four; he had a six-year-old son, and his wife was expecting another child. He went to school through the eighth grade. As a boy he spent a few months in a printing plant. At sixteen he and a confederate slugged a warehouse watchman and stole a truckload of dolls. From that day on, if Reles ever again turned an honest dollar, it was sheer accident.

His criminal education was complete, but he took a continuous postgraduate course as he ran into the Law again and again. Once, he was questioned about whether or not he had committed bigamy, one of the few illegalities not charged to him at some time or other. He squirmed at the query.

"I just don't recall," he evaded.

A year later, the matter was brought up again at another interrogation. This time, the Kid was very positive he had never been a bigamous husband. He was asked if he had refreshed his memory about it in the interim.

"Not refreshed my memory," he was serious and candid. "The last time I didn't know what bigamy was. Now I looked it up."

From this, it may be gathered that there was a bit of the philosopher in the first vice-president of the assassination army. There was. Forced to question him about assassination for hours on end, I reached a point one afternoon where I wanted to hear anything but bloodletting. It was at the time when Hitler and Mussolini were on their mad way toward trying to take over the earth.

"What," I asked, "do you think of the international situation?"

The question might produce a laugh. This loathsome hoodlum, with his warped intellect—what could he know about international affairs?

He leered, and with his habitual superior scorn he spat out, "It's a cinch." That was Reles for you. The whole civilized world frightened over what the axis dictators were up to, and to this gorilla, "It's a cinch."

"What do you mean—a cinch?" I asked, annoyed.

He slammed his hand on the table. "They're just the same as the combination," he declared. "We are out to get America by the pocketbook . . . the whole Syndicate. When we have to, we kill people to do it. Hitler and Mussolini—they're trying to do the same thing. Only, they're trying to get the whole world by the pocketbook. So, they are killing people by the millions to get it."

I had expected logic as much as I would expect Happy Maione to donate his week's bookmaking take to a police benefit. But then, who could spot a gangster better than another gangster?

On January 15, 1940, during our drive to rid the streets of hoodlums, Kid Twist was picked up on a street corner. He was brought before a magistrate and charged with vagrancy. He sighed.

"It's getting so I got to carry a bondsman around with me," he lisped petulantly. Then he reached into his pocket, brought out a large thick roll—and counted out the $1,000 bail as if he were buying a pack of cigarettes.

Nine days later, Harry Rudolph told his version of Red Alpert's assassination. The following morning the Kid walked in and gave himself up, convinced it was "another one of those things." This time, no roll could free him. He was sent to the grim, towering Tombs.

Happy Maione, held on a vagrancy charge then, was sent to the Tombs, too. Reles got word to the sour-faced felon. "Don't worry, Hap," was the Kid's reassuring message, "everything's okay."

On March 21, one of Reles' attorneys was at the Tombs at 10 A.M. What was said, no one, of course, knows. It is virtually certain, however, that the beady-eyed boss still pooh-poohed rumors that any of his ranking cohorts had turned informer. Nevertheless, no sooner did the attorney leave than Reles sat down in his cell and wrote a letter to his wife.

"Dear Rose," it began. "Go and see O'Dwyer and tell him I want to talk to him."

Mrs. Reles got off the elevator at the fourth floor of the Brooklyn Municipal Building and entered the District Attorney's offices alone, at 5:30 the next afternoon. A tight-fitting turban, matching the wolf-fur collar of her beige coat, was pressed over her dark, glistening hair. Her eyes seemed worried. But there was no fear in her voice . . . no distraction.

"I want to see the District Attorney, please," she said evenly.

No one in the place even dreamed Reles had sent her. The prosecutor asked me to talk to her.

"My name is Turkus," I introduced myself. "Is there something I can do for you?"

"I want to talk to the District Attorney personally," she insisted. She was carrying out Reles' instructions to the letter. There was more conversation. Then, without warning, she weakened. She was weeping. "I want to save my husband from the electric chair," she cried. "My baby is coming in June."

The potentialities were obvious at once, unbelievable as it sounded. I was in such a hurry getting into O'Dwyer's office that I don't remember now what I told him. It went something like, "You better get her in here in a hurry; this might be something."

Mrs. Reles had recovered her composure quickly. "My husband wants to talk to you," she admitted to the prosecutor.

"He will have to make that request in writing," she was told. "He must ask for permission himself."

"Well, to be truthful, he asked me to come . . . he wants an interview with the Law." She finally had come out with it. It was fantastic. And the thing to do was to get him before he had a chance to change his mind.

Mrs. Reles was dispatched to her home under guard of detectives. We realized what could happen to her and her family, once the grapevine reported that Kid Twist was even thinking of singing. I was already on my way to the Tombs. In my pocket was a Consent Order form. A jail inmate signs it, giving his consent to be taken to the District Attorney's office. No prisoner has to go there unless he asks to.

In the dim and ancient Tombs, where even the air seemed to smell of locked doors, barred windows and hopeless men, Reles signed the consent to be interviewed. He signed it as nonchalantly as a celebrity obliging an autograph fan. It was well along in the evening. The next step was to translate the consent into the required court order for Reles' release. State Supreme Court Justice Philip A. Brennan lived only a few minutes away by car. Luck was with us; the judge was in. Justice Brennan sought to extend the hospitality of his home. He was affable and polite and said, "Have a chair." I was fidgety, and fretting to see if this was the break that would end our frustration over those two hundred baffling murders. The good justice must have gotten the distinct impression that prosecutors should learn to relax more.

Shortly before nine o'clock, two detectives and myself were back at the Tombs with the most priceless piece of paper in the entire investigation of Murder, Inc.—the order that unlocked the prison's ponderous doors to the Law's most invaluable songbird. When the keeper brought Reles out and turned him over, the runty racketeer was wearing that perpetual sneer. I remember distinctly what I thought, because I got the same thought every time I saw him afterward. It was that I could name one thousand and one more delightful companions for a stroll down a lonesome road on a dark night. There was something about Reles' physical bearing, and a look in his eye, that actually made the hair on the back of your neck stand up.

By a minute or two after nine, Kid Twist, the moblord who wouldn't crack, was on the way across the river. For the first time in his life, the cop-hater, the killer who had spent a lifetime of lawlessness, was setting out to an interview with a law officer that he had personally requested.

When a killer under indictment for murder asks to see the District Attorney, it would seem reasonable to anticipate that he is desperate to make any deal to save his skin. The first thing Reles did was to let us know that he was not afraid of a thing.

The Alpert murder indictment? "You think a jury would convict even a cat on what a bug like Harry Rudolph says?" he taunted.

The single overhead light etched his unworried sneer sharply. It was not bravado; he was definitely not a cornered criminal. His whole attitude was the insolent assassin, putting us in our place. We knew how insecure our case against him was, and the Kid was making it plain that he knew we knew. We were at the long desk in the D. A.'s private sanctum, a severe room with wooden chairs. It reminded you of a press headquarters. The District Attorney was in his regular seat. Kid Twist sat at one of the desk corners opposite. I was at the other. Two detectives stood behind us.

This was a master's chess game, tense and suspenseful. Reles wanted something. Otherwise, what was he doing there? We needed something. The crafty killer knew we would not have had him there unless we did. There was no doubt the boss mobster had the more powerful pieces on the board. But he, more even than we, realized that we had the tactical position. The opening move was his. And he made it—by shrugging away any idea that he was even slightly apprehensive.

"That Rudolph," he jibed. "I could make a monkey out of him myself."

No terror, no explanation of why he requested the interview. His manner shouted that he was doing the D. A. a favor by being there. This hoodlum was almost putting us on the defensive! A hole must be punched in that brash bravado. For weeks, we had been studying murders in which he was suspected of having a hand. We tried one on him—a sort of feeler to show we had him in mind on more than just the Alpert job. The Kid stared back. "You can't touch me on that one," he said flatly. "You," he pointed out, "ain't got no corroboration."

From the other corner of the desk, I picked another at random, and fired it at him. "You were in with the Pug Feinstein job," I pointed out, referring to a particularly brutal erasure of the previous September.

Reles swung nonchalantly around. The drama gripping that room had no more outward effect on him than if he were combing his kinky hair.

"On that," he parroted, with supercilious smugness, "on that, you ain't got no corroboration either."

About the best you could say for Reles was that he was an animal in human guise. And here he was, confidently talking of a proposition of law that Appellate Courts have labored on. What made the barb all the more painful was that he was entirely and exactly right.

Section 399 of the Criminal Code of the State of New York says:

"A conviction cannot be had upon the testimony of an accomplice, unless he is corroborated by such other evidence as tends to connect the defendant with the commission of the crime."

In Federal Court, a defendant can be convicted on testimony of accomplices, unsupported. But not in New York. Every prosecutor is as aware of that section of the Code as a builder is of the foundation of a house. He has to be; corroboration is the foundation of the case.

A Kid Twist could say, "Me and Buggsy and Happy did such-and-such a job." He could climb on the witness stand and swear he saw the other two in the actual act of murder. He could tell every detail, and furnish motive. Yet, unless an outside witness— one neither accomplice nor principal—substantiated him, Buggsy and Happy would walk out of court free! That is the Law. In New York, a stoolpigeon can accuse an accomplice in a felony from now until Blackstone and Sherlock Holmes sit down to a canasta game—and there will never be a conviction unless evidence is forthcoming from a nonaccomplice.

Kid Twist, self-praising "expert" at law, sat there and scorned us with, "You ain't got no corroboration." And he was so right.

"But," he added, and he stabbed his stubby thumb at his bantam-rooster chest, "I'm the guy can tell you where you can get it." He had us, and it hurt. He was ready for his master move now.

"I can make you the biggest man in the country," he promised the District Attorney. He said that he had a bomb to explode the size of which law enforcement never had any conception. He said he could break a series of murders that would electrify the nation. Yes, he repeated, the entire country!

"But I got to make a deal," he stipulated. He pointed to the prosecutor. "I want to talk to you alone about it."

The rest of us filed out of the austere room and left gangster and prosecutor to talk. I remember glancing at the calendar. It was one of those with the holidays blocked off in red. This March 22 was one of the red blocks. Here was the last word in incongruity. The boastful badman had picked the anniversary of the Crucifixion, Good Friday, to tell about throat-cutting and murder the country over!

It seemed as if hours passed. Actually it was but a few minutes, when the District Attorney walked out.

"He wants to drive a hard bargain," he revealed. His tone was not optimistic.

"What does he say? Has he got anything?"

"Oh, he can tell plenty all right," the D. A. said. "I'm convinced he can break a lot of murders. But he wants to walk out. Should we deal with him? What do you think?"

Now, there was a sticker: to trade, or to tell Reles, the killer, we did not want to buy what he had to sell. This was not Dukey or Pretty, who knew nothing of motive or corroboration. This was a deliberate, savage assassin, a racket guy. He knew the why and the how, as well as the who about murder. He was a boss.

The problem stirred up a heated debate over dealing with so unsavory a character. This stumpy hoodlum was absolutely immune to all human decency. What would be the public's reaction to a District Attorney making a bargain, in its name, with a murderer? Suddenly, I found myself a minority of one. Granting all his evil, I wanted to let him talk, if some deal could be made. I detested Reles as much as any of them.

"But where will you get without him?" I asked the prosecutor. "I'll be trying these cases in the court; but don't forget, the credit or discredit for results is on you. We can't get convictions on what we have."

I wasn't at all sure that we could even make the electric chair fit Reles on what we might dig up. But if he opened up on the criminals who were his partners, we would have the audited statement; the connection that could give motivation to previously reasonless killings. A break from "inside" was essential.

Fault could hardly be found with a bargain in which, by sparing one, half a dozen killers are sent to the chair. That is good business. The simple truth was that only with the help of Reles could we get anyone at all, or even unfold the bloody pattern. Without his singing and his knowledge of where lay corroboration, it might take years to put the pieces together; worse, the puzzle might never be worked out.

It was a long heated debate, and finally, the District Attorney went back to Kid Twist—to make a bargain. Reles' stipulations were tough.

"I want to walk out 'clean,'" he insisted. How brazen could he get? All he demanded for his story was to be entirely excused by society for committing over a dozen murders and ordering the

Lord only knows how many more, to say nothing of uncounted beatings, robberies, extortions and terrorizing.

A counter-offer was made: "We will let you plead guilty to second degree murder, and ask the court for consideration for you." That way, he would serve a comparatively few years; might even get a suspended sentence. Reles' fist hammered the desk.

"Nothing doing," was his ultimatum. "No plea to murder two, or any other kind of murder."

Another factor was explained to him. He would appear before the grand jury on a number of cases, and would not be required to sign a waiver of immunity. The waiver means just what it says. By not signing, the witness reserves his immunity to prosecution based on the information he provides. Reles could not incriminate himself in murders he revealed to the grand jury. There would, of course, be nothing to prevent our prosecuting him on any other killings—*if* we got the information and corroboration.

At last, the hard-bargaining hoodlum was satisfied. It was 4 A.M. I still feel it was the most valuable deal the Law ever made.

Reles' song was a full-length opera. He started right out on a high note: "I can tell you all about fifty guys that got hit; I was on the inside." He tossed it off with an "I don't want to brag, but . . ." nonchalance; a skilled artisan, proud of his craft. He was, he went on, on the inside of homicide in Los Angeles and New Jersey, Detroit and Sullivan County, Louisville and Kansas City.

In two days, he had taken a trail of triggers and rackets to cities a thousand miles away. In five days, he was wearing out stenographers, and they had to be put on in relays. By the eleventh day, he was going at such a rate that investigation of extortions he exposed had to be set aside in order to keep up with his listing of homicides. At the end of the twelfth day, he had confessed the incredible total of twenty-five notebooks, chock-full of shorthand record. Several stenographers were virtually exhausted. He was a victrola with kinky hair and a nonstop switch.

He had the most amazing memory I have ever encountered. He could recount minutely what he ate at a particular meal years before, or where he was and with whom, and all without a single reference or reminder of any kind. And investigation proved him entirely accurate, down to the last pinpoint check, on every detail he mentioned.

You might argue that when a man commits murder, every incident of the crime would be engraved on his memory. But not with these hoodlums. With them, dealing out death was commonplace. One day, I asked Reles how he ever brought himself to take human life so casually. "Did your conscience ever bother you?" I inquired. "Didn't you feel anything?"

His agate eyes showed no expression. "How did you feel when you tried your first law case?" he countered coldly.

"I was rather nervous," I admitted.

"And how about your second case?"

"It wasn't so bad, but I was still a little nervous."

"And after that?"

"Oh . . . after that, I was all right; I was used to it."

"You answered your own question," the Kid rasped. "It's the same with murder. I got used to it."

No—details of a slaying would not necessarily stamp themselves on the minds of these casual killers. Yet, the Kid rattled off names, places, facts, data of one manslaughter after the other, days on end, without once missing up. He recalled not only the personnel involved, but decent people who had an unwitting part in some angle of a crime. That way, if you please, he kept his promise to uncover corroboration. He pointed out a cigar stand where a man happened to be standing when murderers went by in flight. It provided a witness who placed the killers near the scene of the crime. Again, he mentioned a filling station where the attendant sold a can of gasoline that had been used to burn up a body. The attendant proved a vital link of evidence against the cremators.

Sometimes, telling a story, the Kid even tried to anticipate you—beat you to the punch—to show where corroboration could be found. He thrived on it, too. When he started out, he had 135 pounds packed on his squat frame. Seven weeks later, at his public appearance in the first of the Murder, Inc., trials, he weighed over 160 pounds . . . "fat and sleek as a goose," wrote one newspaperman. An extrovert with an outsized ego, he derived much pleasure from the horror he stirred up with tales of the terrible deeds of himself and his buddies.

There has remained in my mind but one major mystery from the entire probe of Murder, Inc., one provocative question: What made Kid Twist sing? As far as I know, no one ever got the answer. The Kid was the only one who knew—and he is gone.

Viewed from the angle of threatened danger from the Law, it did not make sense. The first thing he had told us was that he had no fear over the Red Alpert murder rap. Nor was it likely that he was affected by the war of nerves—the rumors dropped here and there that this gangster or that was talking. Reles, on the inside of the national organization, certainly appreciated that every mobster high enough in the Syndicate to do him any real damage would also be aware of its power. No one ever had lived who told on the mob.

There were also the romanticists who attributed his singing to conscience finally catching up with him. At first, the Kid himself tried the same chant of home-and-fireside with which his wife had tearfully sought to impress us. His stabbing little eyes opened as wide as they could, trying for an innocent expression. "I was disgusted with the way I was living, killing and all that," he said. "And the new baby is coming."

That was patently the Kid making a grandstand play. Inner conscience—if he ever was endowed with it—had been totally absent from Reles through ten years of the worst crime. Why suddenly start worrying about the baby that was coming? His first child, born during the course of his murdering, never caused him any remorse. Not even the afternoon the youngster came in sobbing, and confronted him with his evil.

"All the kids in the neighborhood are calling you a bogeyman," cried the boy, with bitter accusing tears. That hadn't affected Kid Twist any. No—that love-of-family hokum was just the ham actor coming out.

The reason might, of course, have been our announcement two days before he started his recital. "We expect to pin the murder of Puggy Feinstein on Reles," the statement had said. The Kid knew Dukey, who was a witness to the slaying, was talking. However, no prosecutor could go anywhere on the uncorroborated disclosures of the comic-strip fan. And no one showed a keener appreciation of legal technicalities than Kid Twist.

Then there was the school of thought that held to the old prize ring philosophy of the fighter who "gets the wrinkles out of his belly." A boxer is full of drive and ambition when he is "a hungry fighter"; he loses his incentive with success. Reles admitted he had some $75,000 to $100,000 tucked away. With that, he could take his family to far places—perhaps South America—after clearing himself with the Law first. Here again, however, the power and avenging arm of the Syndicate made the reasoning illogical. Reles himself told me that the Syndicate could find a fugitive anywhere on earth.

Finally, there is the theory that Reles, smarter than all the rest, saw the day approaching when the secrets of the national organization must be uncovered. Dukey sang; Pretty sang. The fix no longer stood up. Maybe, like any rat, he sensed a sinking ship. Or, he may have spotted indications that the party was over for the Brooklyn branch. As a matter of fact, there were signs that the high councils of national gangdom were leaning toward the belief that it was no longer conducive to the best interests to maintain the enforcement branch.

By talking, Kid Twist could beat them to the punch, and, marked finis anyway, he would scuttle the entire ship. This possibility of retributive justice is the hardest idea of all to knock down. The Kid's likely analysis would have been that, with himself and his enforcers slated to go, the Law offered at least a temporary haven to an opportunist. Significantly, he suffered no self-incrimination.

"I am not a stoolpigeon," he shouted. "Every one of those guys wanted to talk. Only I beat them to the bandwagon. They would be hanging me right now, if they had the chance."

Kid Twist's aria reached its crescendo in the incredible disclosure that there actually existed in America an organized underworld, and that it controlled lawlessness across the United States.

For the first time in any investigation anywhere, the lid was lifted to lay bare a government-within-government, in which the killings and the rackets worked hand in hand in a national combine of crime. Law enforcement had hardly any concept even of what a national combination meant. A lot of officialdom, it would appear, still remains in the dark about this danger from within. Only now has a United States Senate Investigating Committee at last discovered the very setup Reles exposed a decade ago. Unfortunately, however, Senator Estes Kefauver's Committee appears to have made up its mind that the Syndicate is something less firmly put together than Reles' genuine picture of a cartel. There is no doubt, though, that Reles, as an insider, spoke authoritatively.

Then and now, it is just as real as any fifth column of totalitarianism. Where, when you come right down to it, could enemies of Democracy find a more convenient ally than the ready-made existing organization of gangdom? Their ambitions, in fact, are virtually identical.

At the very outset of his encyclopedia of crime, Reles put the finger on just about every mob that amounted to anything in the entire underworld.

"We got connections," he tossed off. "It wasn't easy at the start. But now," he held up two fingers, close together, "now we are like this with the Purple Mob. We work with Buggsy Siegel in California, and with Lepke and the troops he's got. (Other mobs were generally "troops" to Reles—"like the boy scouts, only different.") We are with Charley Lucky. With the Jersey troop, too, and Chicago and Cleveland."

He explained that Lepke and his associates on the high level financed, directed and organized Syndicate groups in New Orleans, Florida, even Havana. In fact, Reles had you spinning with all the ways and means these thugs had dug up to turn a dollar—as long as it was illicit—and the area they covered doing it.

It was—and it is today—big business, with all the appurtenances of big business, except, possibly, formal incorporation papers and a department for advertising and publicity. Had it been a registered corporation, the Federal Trade Commission would long since have investigated it for monopoly and general unfair trade practice.

No one—not even the insiders or their auditors—can tell, with any precision, just how many billions the Syndicate grabs from the people of the nation. Back in 1931, a New York State Crime Commission reported to the legislature that racketeering was costing the United States between twelve and eighteen billion dollars annually. That estimate was made at the height of the nation's worst economic depression, and when alcohol was the dominant illegitimate industry. It was made, too, before the ganglords discovered syndication. By 1940, the moguls of mobdom had perfected, perhaps, fifty new ways to extort, steal and prey in their diversified country-wide commerce. And they have kept on perfecting, as witness the California Crime Study Commission's recent estimate that the yearly national take from slot machines *alone* is two billion dollars.

Truly, the setup had a stranglehold on the pocketbook of America—on the clothes and food and entertainment of almost every citizen. The outfit, Reles related, had key offices in virtually every important city in the nation. The moblords preyed on industry in every community.

Substantiation of the Kid's statements was quickly produced, when Sullivan County District Attorney Bill Deckelman returned from California with Gangy Cohen. On the way, as their train stopped in each city, the mobster-turned-movie-actor took the upstate prosecutor on what amounted to a conducted tour of the underworld.

"He provided information on the relations with gangs in Denver, Kansas City, St. Louis and wherever we stopped, during the ride back," Deckelman disclosed.

Reles recited an astonishing assortment of businesses. In a very brief cross-section of only the Brooklyn takes, he said:

"Me and my partners are in shylocking, the restaurant business, the unions and strike business, the trucking business, the moving-van business, the garment industry—through Lepke—crap games, slot machines, bookmaking, payrolls on a few bookies. . . ."

The connection, of course, was some extortion in regard to each of the industries.

"What were you doing in the union business?" I asked.

"Oh—you know . . . we got the money that comes in," he replied. What he meant, when you pinned him down, were "gimmicks" like kickbacks on wages and union membership fees and dues in a large number of labor organizations into which they had muscled.

There were shakedowns in all shapes, sizes and forms. Every

loan shark, numbers bank, bookmaker and prostitute paid regular tribute. There were robbery and assault for pay. Occasionally there was some dope business. Once (1932), the Kid himself was arrested for handling narcotics. As usual, he was discharged.

Nor is any of this peculiar to Brooklyn alone. The same things —and possibly more—go on in your town. And yours.

On murder, under Reles' recital, the chain reaction which had been touched off, ironically, by Harry Rudolph's unsupported rambling, mushroomed into a huge mass of cold, hard fact. Before he finished, the Kid had recounted the complete detail of some eighty-five killings the Syndicate gunmen had piled up in the City of Churches alone, and he had mapped out the blueprint for as many as a thousand unsolved homicides in every corner of the country.

Early in the recitation, he provided the key—the reason this co-operative system of death on order had managed to survive, despite violent moblord temperaments. These murderers took life only when it was sanctioned and approved by the very top echelon. This was disciplined murder. Not even Pittsburgh Phil would dare try a rub-out unless he got the nod.

While Pep and Happy Maione derived pleasure from murder, Reles thirsted, rather, for knowledge of the how and the why in the operation of the rackets. In his ballooned self-importance, he felt he was as competent as anyone to run the whole show. Through this search for knowledge, he had picked up the great mass of data on national crime that he now unfolded for us.

The Kid got down to specific cases quickly. He was an excellent raconteur, if you like your killings right from the feed bag, with all the grisly detail. The troop, said the Kid, was called on for contracts from various mobs in the Syndicate.

"Like the time we took John the Polack," he cited. "It was a contract for the big guy in Jersey."

Reles was no more familiar with John's last name than he was with common decency. However, the complete data he added to the misty identification enabled Nassau County (Long Island) Police to wipe the slate clean on the case of John Bagdonowitz.

Back in the late twenties, John Bagdonowitz was with the Jersey outfit in Newark. There came a time, however, when John broke away.

"I'm going straight from here on," he announced.

Such an announcement in mobland has an effect similar to jumping from a sixth-story window. The jumper may live—but it is doubtful. The mob holds to the belief that desertion indicates a sign of conscience. A man with a conscience is always a potential threat. However, when John made his announcement, he already had his bag packed and was en route, leaving no forwarding address.

The mob hunted him, but the abdicated torpedo could not be located. John Bagdonowitz had made good his leap to law and order. Some few years passed. Then, one day in 1933, Walter Sage happened to be on Long Island on a business trip. His travel took him to the village of Albertson Square, close by the fruitful fishing grounds of the Island's south shore. In the unhurried hamlet, the visiting gunman saw a familiar face. It took several moments for Walter to recall a one-time business associate. The reformed mobster—for it was John—was living quietly in his mother's home in the tiny seashore community. Unfortunately, he did not see Sage when Sage saw him.

On his return to the more familiar stamping grounds of Brownsville, Sage mentioned his accidental discovery. "Remember John the Polack?" he remarked, merely by way of making conversation. "Well, I bump into him out on the Island. He looks like he's doing all right, but I don't know how he can take it out there. Nothing is doing. I'm glad to be back in civilization."

Word of its long-missing operative was sent to the Jersey mob. The message came back to please take care of John any way at all—as long as it was permanent. The assignments went to oxlike Vito Gurino and Joe Mercaldo, also handy with "the piece." Julie Catalano was to drive the car.

"I went along for the ride," Reles explained.

All the firing squad had to do was follow Sage's simple directions to locate the cozy cottage, with flowers and grass. The carful of killers made two turns around the neighborhood, casing the terrain and setting up a plot. When they were satisfied, they pulled up near the cottage. Reles and Catalano remained in the car and kept the motor running. Gurino and Mercaldo mounted the steps of the front porch and knocked. A lady came to the door.

"We're detectives," they introduced themselves menacingly. "We are looking for John Bagdonowitz."

"Just a minute; I'll get him." The unexpected intrusion of the Law made the lady nervous. She disappeared.

A moment later, John came to the porch door. Two guns fired simultaneously.

Walter Sage was complimented most heartily by the powers in Jersey for his fingering job in this matter. That, of course, was before the mob dumped Walter into the Catskill Mountain lake with the pinball machine tied around his neck.

One of Reles' boasts, in prying open the Syndicate's locked doors was that, "We got connections where they count." He meant protection connections—high connections, on the national level. Concrete evidence of highly placed corruption had been effectively exposed only a short time before our investigation, in the Dewey probe's exposé of services supplied by Tammany Leader Jimmy Hines. That such protection extended even to higher places was clearly indicated—even to high places in the national capital. The further we went, in fact, the more it became evident that there existed an "in" for the national Syndicate—a most important "in." And it is definite, incontrovertible fact that an organization such as this could not and can not exist on a national scale without top-level protection.

The machinations and depredations poured out in a continuous flow by Reles became harder to believe the more he lifted the lid. The most nefarious gangs of the Prohibition era seemed apple-off-the-pushcart crooks compared to the activities of this infamous country-wide cartel. The FBI's Public Enemy outfits in bank robbery and kidnaping looked like mischievous boys tying cans to little dogs' tails against this well-oiled machine working the rackets and murder of the nation. This amounted almost to a national dictatorship. It had levied tribute for almost a decade on virtually every ordinary citizen, and the vast majority never even dreamed it was going on. It bled legitimate business and labor, and they had been too terror-struck to call for help. It operated rackets in gambling and shylocking and narcotics . . . and in bread and suits of clothes and vegetables.

As you listened to Kid Twist's astounding saga, one word kept turning and turning in your mind: How? How could it have been accomplished? How could an empire build up extortion in billions and snuff out life at will without something happening along the road to give it away? Even more mystifying—how were the ganglords ever able to control their traditional jealousies and touchy trigger fingers so they did not dissolve this gigantic industry of infamy themselves, with bullets? In fact, how were the always individualistic mob moguls ever brought together into one huge working organization in the first place? How . . . and when?

Reles could explain that, too. The stumpy stoolpigeon went all the way back to the beginning, to the how and the when of the national Syndicate.

4.

National crime: a cartel

Mafia, Black Hand and Unione; please do not confuse—Joe the Boss dines and dies in Coney Island—Lucky Luciano and the purge of Mafia—Frank Costello, Prime Minister—a sharp little man gives birth to the Syndicate.

FOR all the free-shooting, mad-dog wars of Prohibition's heyday, gang crime was but a suckling in swaddling clothes and diapers through the tempestuous twenties.

There is no doubt bootlegging created an anaconda of crime. Millions were made by mobsters in illicit alcohol. Public officials were corrupted. Small plug-uglies became mob big-shots through guns and the closed-eye attitude—if not outright connivance—of the Law. Those gangs and gangsters, however, dealt for the most part exclusively in alcohol.

When Prohibition was doomed, it was a foregone conclusion that the ganglords were not going into anything so prosaic or peasantlike as earning an honest dollar. So, with repeal, they switched to big business, the magnitude of which they never even dreamed—and which illicit alcohol never produced. Then organized gangsterism grew up. It is ironic, indeed, that by ending the trigger-happy dry era, the Law lent the helping hand which shoved the racketeers into far-flung labor-industrial extortion, into the tremendous narcotics trade, the unbelievable billions in gambling, and, eventually, into national organization.

Actually, the development of *national* crime can be dated from the impeachment of Joe the Boss Masseria as top man of the so-called Italian Society of Crime, and the emergence, in the early thirties, of the ugly, savage Unione Siciliano. For the sake of accuracy—and law enforcement—a few facts are necessary concerning this murderous aggregation.

It has become popular in recent years to "expose" Unione as the single society ruling all crime in these United States. The evidence and recorded history paint a different picture of the facts. No one who really knows anything at all about the sharp clannishness of mob bosses with respect to nationalities and creeds would ever attempt to attribute to any one group the control over the whole. Besides, if one such unit had all crime in this country under its power, is it not reasonable to assume that somewhere along the line, some law agency—federal, state, county or municipal—would have tripped it up long before this? No single man or group ever was so clever, so completely genius, as to foil all of them forever. Powerful, Unione is; murderous, unquestionably. But it always has been just one strong link among the many links in the national chain of crime. Actually, the Syndicate loves to have the theory expounded that there is a supreme irrevocable individual authority. Then, the directors of crime know that not too much heat will generate under their cozy rackets.

Even more serious, however, is the popular pastime of lumping Italian crime groups under one heading with interchangeable names. The most recent example of such misconception was that achieved by the Kefauver Senate Crime Investigating Committee. Mafia, the Committee said officially, is "also known as the Black Hand and the Unione Siciliano." With no attempt to dim the work done by the Senators, I should like to point out that Unione is no more Mafia than man is the ape. In fact, as a factor of power in national crime, Mafia has been virtually extinct for two decades. Unione, meantime, has grown fat on felony. The evidence is incontrovertible. Court records prove it. The chief difference between the two lies in Unione's co-operation with other mobs, a characteristic entirely foreign to the clannish Mafia.

The inclusion of the headline-catching label of Black Hand as a synonym for either or both is even farther afield. In fact, striking evidence of this was found by the New York Police Department—and as far back as forty-four years ago! At the turn of the century, Black Hand was a fashionable form of extortion, aimed at honest, hardworking immigrants. The name grew out of menacing letters, each signed by a crude drawing of a black hand and demanding money, under threat of death, kidnap or mutilation of the selected victim's children. The letters became so prevalent that Police Commissioner William McAdoo assigned a squad to investigate.

Heading this squad was one of law enforcement's great policemen, Lieutenant Joe Petrosino, a swarthy, two-hundred-pound detective in a derby hat. He spent half a lifetime digging into Italian criminal societies, and sent dozens of killers to the chair. A secretive man who rarely smiled, Lieutenant Petrosino won the confidence of the honest immigrants, and gathered information from them.

As his effectiveness increased, he became the target of many threatening letters himself—and most of those he received bore the insidious black hand. Eventually, these very missives provided the key that cleared up the mystery of what it is popular to term the Black Hand "Society." By checking and probing and analyzing, the lieutenant found that such letters were not the work of any single group. Anyone who wanted to capitalize on the accepted terror, he discovered, simply wrote a letter, drew a black hand on it, and sent it along. In fact, Lieutenant Petrosino proved that no central Black Hand organization even existed! Black Hand, he demonstrated, was a myth, deliberately perpetuated by Neapolitan Camorra and Sicilian Mafia who were, at that time, flocking to the United States. And his report to the police department said so.

Eventually, Petrosino was a martyr to his career. In 1907, on a police mission to Sicily, he was ambushed and slain in Plaza Marina in Palermo. A plaque, placed on the plaza by grateful Italians and Italian-Americans, commemorates the spot.

The story of Italian criminal societies in this country begins shortly before the turn of the century, when old-world gangsters of Mafia and Camorra crept into America. Picking up where they left off at home, these brutal bandits preyed primarily on their decent newly-arrived countrymen, to whom tales of the dread Camorra and Mafia were still very real.

As the years passed, the infants who had migrated with their families grew up. So did the first generation spawned in the new world. They went to American schools and learned American ways—particularly the ways of the environment in which they grew. Many rose to eminence. Others followed the easier way. These fledgling felons differed from their older criminal countrymen in that the new world taught them it was possible to work together with others, even if they were not of the same blood. Eventually, they began to resent the elders. A contemptuous hatred was born. They referred to the elders of Mafia as "The Handlebar Guys" and "The Moustache Petes," because most of them were adorned with flowing moustaches that were reasonable facsimiles of coat hangers. The resentment stemmed, mostly, from the clannishness of the elders, their adamant refusal to associate with any but their own Sicilian-born tribesmen, and their continued preying on their own immigrant countrymen. Those were the ways of Mafia.

As they grew up, the new element—this Americanized faction—acquired sufficient strength to set up its own version of a mob, dealing not in comparatively puny extortions from immigrants with limited resources, but pointing toward bigger money crime. It was the first spark of Unione. All—old and new—were, however, generally grouped for descriptive purposes as "The Italian Society."

Ruling over the oldsters of Mafia in the early days was a greedy, sadistic character widely known as Lupo the Wolf, or just plain Lupo, since that means Wolf in his native tongue. Born Ignazio Saietta, he crossed the Atlantic after murdering a man in Italy, and here he found new fields of endeavor. In the late teens and very early twenties, his organization had a hand in such juicy pies as the Italian lottery, narcotics and extortions from immigrants—all accompanied by assorted bombings, blackmail and murder. But the money did not come fast enough for Lupo the Wolf. So, he took to paying off with money he manufactured himself. For that, the Government sentenced him to thirty years. President Harding commuted his sentence after a few years, but when Lupo showed virtually no signs of having reformed, he was sent back to finish out the full term. Many men died trying to move in as his successor.

In early Prohibition days, bootleggers hijacked their liquor from bonded government warehouses or acquired it from these same warehouses through official medicinal permits which they had the foresight to steal or obtain from "friendly" connections.

Like any business catering to the public taste, they ran into the normal problem of supply and demand. One man might get ten cases of bourbon, for example, and have a good customer who insisted on Scotch. Another might have Scotch, but need bourbon for a steady-paying speakeasy client. The businessmen set up an exchange on the street curbs of a certain neighborhood in lower New York to barter for their requirements. Trading stolen government whiskey right out in the open was not, however, the height of their audacity. They actually set up their curb exchange on the very streets surrounding police headquarters!

It was here, on the scene of the bootleggers' curb exchange, that Guiseppe Masseria entered the picture. He was short and chunky and a gunman dating back to 1907. He just walked in, and declared himself the downtown boss, succeeding Lupo the Wolf. Through the next two years, Guiseppe proceeded, by conquest, to back up his claim. Since the head man of the Society is always "the boss," he soon took to calling himself "Joe the Boss." However, one Umberto Valenti, a bootlegger, was ambitious for the leadership, himself. He oiled up his pistol and sallied forth, abetted by aides and associates. Many shooting matches followed.

On a bright, hot August day in 1922, a sedan pulled up opposite the lower East Side flats in which Joe the Boss lived. Two men got out, entered a small eating place, and took a window table, with a clear view of the entrance to the Masseria domicile. For an hour, they dawdled. Finally, through the door opposite, Joe emerged. For a moment, he poised, breathing in the heat, his new straw hat glistening in the sun. Then he bounded briskly down the steps.

The coffee-and-cake watchers hustled out. One mounted the stairs Joe had just left, thus sealing off an avenue of flight. The other torpedo opened fire from the middle of the street. Joe realized at once that the only haven lay in a row of stores close at hand. His short legs churning, the ambushed boss charged through the doorway of the neighborhood milliner's shop, owned by Fritz Heiney. The gunman was right behind him. Mr. Heiney knew at a glance that the racing arrivals were not there to buy hats. If he had not been an entirely neutral observer, no one would ever have believed what happened.

"The man with the gun come right up to the other fellow," the milliner recounted afterward, shuddering. "Just as he fires, the little fellow jumped to one side. The bullet went right through the window of my store. The man fires again, and the little man ducks his head forward. I don't know where that bullet went, except it didn't hit him. The man shoots again. The other man ducks again. This one made another hole in the window."

His pistol finally empty, the gunman fled the shop and leaped into the car. It roared away. And Joe the Boss was untouched!

Just looking at him, you would never have imagined this agility of the squat Guiseppe. Nevertheless, to the superstitious followers of the secret society, any man who could move faster than bullets fired at close range bore a supernatural charm and was marked for high places. It virtually clinched his command.

This had been such a close call, however, that Joe the Boss took immediate steps to prevent recurrence. He called a peace conference in an East Side spaghetti house. Joe did not advise Valenti that he had two aides stationed a block away. The huddle over, the enemies strolled out together, like long-time friends. Masseria's hired hands joined them at the corner, and the shooting began. They chased Valenti across the street. One of them fired the entire clip from his pistol at the ambitious bootlegger's fleeing back. Valenti made it to a taxicab; even got the door open. Then he fell on his face.

Unopposed now as The Boss, the little man who could dodge bullets ruled for the next nine years. Joe was just as clannish as his predecessors—still for Mafia supreme—but he was not entirely averse to having his assistants form friendships with outside outfits. He was still a loner in principle, but his ideas were sufficiently modified, so that during his regime, the groundwork for Unione was laid.

He picked wisely for his aides-de-camp. In Brooklyn, he put most of the enterprises under Frankie Uale, an expert torpedo known through the underworld as Frankie Yale. Frankie was Pittsburgh Phil's earlier counterpart both as the Beau Brummell of the Brooklyn underworld and as a killer the country over. To this day, Chicago police insist he murdered Big Jim Colisimo in 1920, paving the way for his old school chum, Johnny Torrio, to take command of The Loop. And they credit him with killing Dion O'Banion there, in Dion's flower shop, in 1924, to line things up for Al Capone. Frankie handled the Brooklyn business until 1928. One Sunday afternoon, as he was driving in his bullet-proof sedan, another car ranged alongside and let go a barrage that blew the life out of him. The pilotless limousine plowed across the sidewalk, through a hedge—and ruined Mr. and Mrs. Sol Kaffman's garden party, just then at its merry height.

With Frankie's departure, much of his Brooklyn business, particularly in alcohol and industrials, was taken over by Anthony Carfano, whose mob cognomen is Li'l Augie Pisano. Li'l Augie not only had contacts in Tammany Hall; he had relatives. It was generally understood, too, that Li'l Augie's senior associate was Joey Adonis, who has been very well fixed politically for a long time.

As carefully as he had selected the Brooklyn manager, Joe the Boss was even more particular in his choice for downtown Manhattan. Here he placed a hard-jawed soft-eyed hoodlum whose name, after various syllabic alterations from its native Sicilian, was Charles Lucania. As a boy, young Lucania got a job in a hat factory. It was the only job he ever held in his life. He quit it in a matter of months.

"Who wants to wind up being a crum?" he remarked.

By the time he was eighteen, he was in the reformatory for peddling heroin and morphine. Having served this apprenticeship, he was ready to take a managerial post under Joe the Boss. He made further modifications in his name—and he emerged as Charley Luciano.

With his enterprises in most capable hands, Joe the Boss Masseria went into seclusion. Like the modern moblords later, he recognized that it was not good business for the executive to appear on the firing line or otherwise to acquire notoriety. He moved from the East Side squalor to the splendor of a penthouse over-looking Central Park, close to where Lepke lived later—and Frank Costello does today. He became the perfect host.

It is an axiom as old as history itself, though, that small men become ambitious to be big men. In fact, it is history. As time passed, Charley Luciano got growing pains. More important, Charley knew what to do about them. He had vision. He per-formed extra-special service, and worked his way up to the right-hand chair in the councils of Masseria's organization. He got to know the right people.

For a time, Charley worked for the Diamond Brothers—Legs and Eddie—in alcohol, and for George Uffner, whose dope opera-tions were backed by the gang gambler, Arnold Rothstein. (Inci-dentally, in November, 1950, when bookmaker Frank Erickson's Park Avenue office was raided, among his papers were sev-eral dealing with oil leases in Texas and Oklahoma, in which Erickson and Frank Costello were associated with one George Uffner of New York City. Not a newspaper or a law enforcement officer mentioned such a remarkable coincidence.)

Luciano grew chummy, too, with Lepke and his muscle-bound partner, Gurrah, as they snatched complete control of entire in-dustries, and with Buggsy Siegel and Meyer Lansky, whose Bug & Meyer Mob was, at that time, the most efficient enforcement arm in the business. Along about then, too, Luciano acquired the nickname that became known the world over.

Usually, the gangster cries that his label is the invention of a newspaperman with a too colorful typewriter or a law enforce-ment agent with overactive imagination, and that this should not be allowed. This plaint is for sound effect only. Almost invari-ably, the mob itself pins on these tags, and with a far more apropos touch than any composer of deathless journalistic prose. Thou-sands of gangsters are known almost solely by nicknames tagged onto them by their own co-workers. In the Brooklyn troop, some of the hoods were actually unknown to the gang except by these mob-given names. They had no payroll receipt to sign, remember. Other hoodlums gave Waxey Gordon, biggest of all bootleggers, his tag, it is said, because, as a youthful "dip," his fingers slid into and out of a pocket as if coated with tallow. Legs Diamond, as a young thief, could outleg the police. Scarface Al was a natural for Capone's carved features. In the case of Luciano, it was a simple, sincere selection, with a touch of the picturesque that smacked of Runyon.

Another mob boss wanted to learn the location of a batch of narcotics that Luciano had carefully put away. The rival hood had his strongarms pick Charley up and take him out to Staten Island, across New York harbor from Manhattan. There, on a road that saw little of traffic, they hung Charley up by his fingers. They sliced him up somewhat. They used the handy plug-ugly's trick of applying cigarettes to the soles of his feet, and here and there. The cigarettes were lit. Charley wouldn't talk, even if it killed him —which it very nearly did. After a while, they left him hanging there, and departed. They assumed that what was left of Charles Luciano would be found sooner or later.

But Charley came back. His left eye had a permanent droop and there were assorted cuts and bruises he never lost. But he was alive. So, the boys simply named him Lucky—Lucky Luciano. As his gang stature grew, this was universally altered to Charley Lucky.

Guiseppe Masseria came to count more and more on Lucky's mob know-how. Luciano blossomed out as racketeer, trigger and first assistant to the head man of the secret society. But Lucky did not think in Guiseppe's old-country way—the way of the "Moustache Petes." He became allied with a group that ruled the rum-running of the Atlantic Coast, from Maine to Virginia. There were associations with Frank Costello and his good right arm, Dandy Phil Kastel, a bucket shop and securities thief who still handles Frank C.'s tremendous New Orleans operations. And there was Charley (King) Solomon, the Boston boss, and Longy Zwillman, the New Jersey nabob. From these alone, it is obvious there were other gangs and other ganglords besides Mafia on the scene.

As the unpopularity of Prohibition brought louder public cry for repeal, a new type of businessman boss rose to power. This new order was realistic. It recognized the danger in indiscriminate shooting and gang warfare, and the limitations in the clannish every-man-for-himself mode of doing business. The idea began to spread among the sub-leaders who, like Lucky, had grown up in

American ways. With Joe the Boss dealing entirely on the executive level, these moderns were the operational bosses, and they instituted changes. The trend was all toward less inter-gang rivalry and attendant blood-letting. Joe the Boss couldn't see it. He was not against friendships, but "combinations" did not appeal to Joe. He was still old school enough to be basically isolationist.

"An outfit runs on its own and knocks off anybody in the way," was his set credo.

Nevertheless, crime was moving toward co-operation, if not yet organization. Lepke and Gurrah already had a co-op of sorts going—an association with Buggsy Siegel's murderers. Lepke and Gurrah did the extortion and the organization stuff in industry; the Bug & Meyer Mob handled the enforcement.

Now, to Joe the Boss, Lucky was chum as well as hired hand. Charley was always helping a friend out, and Joe liked that. As a matter of fact, to digress momentarily, Lucky evidently is still helping out friends today, though he has long since been exiled from the United States to Italy. In the spring of 1950, a million-dollar narcotics ring was broken up and thirty-one persons were indicted in New Jersey, after a six-month Federal investigation that took in Los Angeles, Kansas City, Miami and a dozen more cities. At the time, assistant U. S. Attorney Charles J. Tyne discovered this mob had sent an emissary to Lucky to set up the pipeline for the importation of the "powder." In May, 1951, the key figures in the ring were convicted and sentenced to prison. Among them was William Margo, a night club owner, who was described during his trial as the ring's transatlantic ambassador. It was brought out that he had made the trip to Italy to contact Luciano. Always helping out his pals—that is Lucky.

Joe the Boss enjoyed Lucky's company. Although modern in his ideas on crime, Charley had an old world flair for living. He still has. So, when he invited Joe to Coney Island for dinner one unseasonably warm April day in 1931, The Boss looked forward to it.

"We'll go over to Scarpato's," Lucky suggested. "Scarpato fixes the sauce like the old country, with the clams and the garlic and the good olive oil. And the fish is great."

"That's good, Charley," agreed The Boss.

"I'll pick you up in the afternoon, and we'll have a nice drive over in the sun." It would, Lucky pointed out, do The Boss good.

Guiseppe liked the easy, pleasant things. The songs of Sorrento he appreciated; the rich olives from the Sicilian hillsides—the old country ways. Everything at Scarpato's was just as Charley had promised. Joe the Boss pushed back his chair and lazily wiped his chin. The lobster had been sweet and meaty. The clam sauce for the pasta reminded him of Civita Vecchia, the ancient seaport above Rome, where you discover with the first meal that you have never really tasted seafood anywhere else. The chianti had that exact half-bitter bouquet which makes it the meal-time ideal. Joe sat back to savor to the full the satisfaction of a perfect dinner.

The restaurant was thinning out now. The food and the wine left Joe with that post-feast inertia which calls for relaxation.

"A little cards, Guisepp'?" Lucky proposed pleasantly. "Some three sevens, maybe . . . or brisco?"

"Good . . . for an hour or so; then I must go." It was, Masseria contemplated, just the touch to round out an enjoyable evening.

Lucky called for a deck from the house. They played and they talked for about forty-five minutes. Scarpato's was completely empty now, except for the help sweeping up in the kitchen. It was then Lucky excused himself. He walked slowly between the rows of white cloths, and disappeared into the men's room.

It is too bad he took so long washing his hands, he explained. He missed it when impeachment proceedings were carried out against Joe the Boss. It seemed there must have been three voters. They came in while Lucky was away washing his hands—as he explained—and he missed it all. More than twenty bullets were sprayed around the premises. The passing years and the easy life must have robbed Joe of his agility, for five of them were buried in him.

The Boss (ex) was slumped over. His right arm was pushed out straight, as if it had been his play of the cards. His hand lay frozen on the gleaming cloth. The lone bright red spot of the ace of diamonds sparkled up from his lifeless palm. Ever since that night, it has not been considered good manners to mention the ace of diamonds in certain circles—such as Mafia.

Lucky said sure, he heard the shooting. "As soon as I finished drying my hands, I hurried out and walked back to see what it is about," he related. He was too late to see who the impeachers were. Thus, he is unable to confirm the report, as mentioned in Case No. 133-31 of New York law enforcement files, that among those present may have been such stalwarts as Albert Anastasia, Joey Adonis and Buggsy Siegel. And since Lucky was the only witness who might have seen, the report has never been confirmed.

The car the impeachers used was eventually uncovered. The license plates on it had been made at Auburn State Prison, and were stolen from a batch shipped to the Motor Vehicle Bureau office in Brooklyn.

Charley Lucky no doubt hated to do it, what with the untimely end of his friend and sponsor, but he was prevailed upon to move in as president of the Italian Society in the United States. He did not, however, jump into the driver's seat at once. Perhaps it was out of respect for the dead. A more practical reason concerned a few details of old business, to pave the way for his administration.

Two factions still remained in the Society, despite Masseria's demise. They were still the old and the new; opposite poles in their ways of thinking. The so-called "Greaser" crowd—the Handlebar Guys—would not see the modern trend. With Lucky now the top man, though, the new held the upper hand. For the first time, Unione emerged as the dominant factor. Still, Mafia had to be reckoned with. Even with Joe the Boss gone, there was capable leadership, notably Salvatore Marrizano, or Maranzano. He headed the "Moustache Petes"—the oldsters—who were not yet convinced.

Now, at about this time, civil war broke out in the clothing industry. The vast Amalgamated Clothing Workers, parent organization of labor devoted to the manufacture of some seventy-five percent of the nation's garments for men, was torn by internal strife. Sidney Hillman, as Amalgamated's president, headed one faction. Philip Orlofsky, executive of the key clothing cutters' union in Amalgamated, commanded a group opposed to Hillman and aiming at assuming control. To accomplish this, the Orlofsky faction had organized a rival parent body. In addition, Lepke and his mob turned up as enforcers for this faction. The danger was obvious to the Hillman group leaders, who included Bruno Belea, General Organizer for Amalgamated and Hillman's chief expediter. To meet this threat, a counter-enforcement gang was necessary. Lucky was thought of at once.

"I'd like to take it, but Lepke and Buggsy and Lansky are friends of mine," replied the moblord who is loyal to his friends.

With the new Unione unavailable, the remnants of the old Greaser gang were approached. Marrizano accepted. His first official act, however, was to look Lucky up.

"I'm going to take the contract, Charley," he explained to the new power in the Society. "But there's nothing to worry about. We won't make any trouble. We're just going on for a payday."

"Okay," nodded Lucky. "Just remember—those other guys are my pals."

Labor slugging was not Marrizano's principal activity. He had a modern office high in the Grand Central Building, which straddles Park Avenue in Manhattan, towering over Grand Central Station. The sign on the door said "Real Estate." Marrizano's major business, however, was in smuggling alien criminals who had been chased from Sicily and lower Italy.

In spite of Marrizano's pledge, some shootings did result in the ensuing weeks of the clothing labor strife. Eventually, after a man was killed, a crisis was reached. Lepke saw that steps would have to be taken, since such untoward developments would do the Orlofsky faction's plans no good. These plans, by this time, had become Lepke's own ambition to control the industry. The rackets czar sought out his friend Lucky. Always one of the more respected counsels in the national underworld, Lepke had a plan all thought out. Lucky, he asserted, was blind to reality in this matter.

"You think this is a fight in the clothing business?" he challenged. "Open your eyes, Charley. Marrizano is out to take over the Italian Society again."

A most persuasive salesman was Lepke, with soft cow-eyes and a smooth, modulated voice. He convinced Lucky. Luciano decided it was time to settle this intra-mural rivalry once and for all. All the Greaser crowd would have to go. Not only in New York, either—but all over the country. And Marrizano was the

No. 1 candidate. The day for the cleanup was set for September 11, 1931. It has long been known as "Purge Day" in Unione. All of the mob leaders in and around New York, in and out of the Society, pledged Lucky shooting co-operation.

An unusually mixed group of five men strode into Marrizano's office suite in the Grand Central Building that September afternoon. Leader of the party was Bo Weinberg, ace of Dutch Schultz's crack crew of killers. Police files say that those with him included a top assassin of the Bug & Meyer Mob; a fellow named Murphy and another named Allie, who were known as friends of Longy Zwillman, the Jersey magnate, and an unidentified fifth man. Incidentally, this Allie was later found full of bullets on a road leading to Troy, N. Y.

Twelve men were in Marrizano's outer office. The five flashed police badges and mumbled something about a raid. Almost docilely, the twelve who were there permitted themselves to be lined up against a wall. Then, while part of the invading party stood guard, the others barged into Marrizano's private inner office, shot him and cut his throat. Its mission accomplished, the quintet departed.

Somehow, Bo Weinberg lost his way, and was still trying to get out of the building when the police arrived. Bo saw a door near the end of a corridor. He dashed inside, slammed it behind him. It was most fortunate that was the sort of slow, quiet afternoon when people did not stir much. Otherwise, there might have been some most unusual incidents, to say the least. For, the place Bo had picked as a refuge was the ladies' room.

The day Marrizano got it was the end of the line for the Greaser Crowd in the Italian Society—the finish of "The Moustache Petes" —and a definite windup to Mafia as an entity and a power in national crime. For, in line with Lucky's edict—which had been inspired by Lepke's persuasiveness—some thirty to forty leaders of Mafia's older group all over the United States were murdered that day and in the next forty-eight hours! It was a remarkable example of planning and accomplishment that this mass extermination of Mafia executives across the country has never, as far as I have been able to learn, been linked, one with another. Had the connection been established then, in 1931, and Unione's position uncovered, there would now be none of the erroneous conception, grown so popular through the years, of classifying Mafia and Unione as one and the same.

They are, actually, no more the same than are the Democratic and Republican Parties. There is strong evidence on the subject. It was a matter of sworn court testimony during the Dewey rackets investigations in the late thirties. J. Richard (Dixie) Davis, the notorious attorney for Dutch Schultz and so many moblords, turned State's evidence and revealed that Bo Weinberg told him of the Purge in the Italian Society which left Mafia dead and Unione and Lucky as the surviving might and strength in every sense of the word.

Even more irrefutable evidence was provided as recently as 1944, directly from an insider—an eagle-beaked one-eyed thug named Ernest Rupolo, who is known as The Hawk and who describes his trade as an assassin for hire. Only out of prison a year, after doing nine years for one shooting, The Hawk was arrested for another. Almost eagerly, he pleaded guilty, stating that he had been hired for $500 for the job. Stubbornly, he refused to name his employers—until the Court threatened him with a sentence of forty to eighty years. That changed his mind. He supplied information that broke four murder cases. He involved Vito Genovese, then and now accredited with being a national power in Unione.

The Hawk went into the background and modernization of the Italian Society of crime, and supplied the clincher to the exploded myth. Unione, he declared flatly, is the self-appointed successor to Mafia. Since 1931, any similarity has been purely imaginative.

With its opposition and their antiquated methods erased, Unione spread like a high tide of scum to all corners of the country. The moderns who took over even accepted as blood brothers some members not of the same nationality or extraction. This must be final proof of the schism between Mafia, with its deadly code of Omerta and its clannish ways, and Unione, with its modern-day methods of co-operative endeavor in crime. The old order would as soon have a polecat as a non-Sicilian on its rolls.

Like all heads of Unione, Lucky acquired the emblematic title: The Boss. And from far off Italy, in spite of his exile, he continues a powerful factor—if not absolute ruler of the order—to this day.

These early developments have been chronicled, since it is from Masseria's demise and the purge of Mafia, and Lucky's resultant coronation, that modern gangdom—Murder, Inc., the national crime organization—may be traced. When Joe the Boss bowed out, the old order packed up and went with him.

Mobdom did not like the approaching demise of Prohibition. Alcohol always was a good buck, as they say. The hoods wondered which way to turn for new and lucrative illegalities.

It presented a serious problem to the suave underworld millionaire who operates under the name of Frank Costello—except when the boys call him the Prime Minister, as they do. Prohibition had been good to Frank C. On the stepping stone of alcohol, the little paisan climbed out of the tenements of Harlem and the slums of Greenwich Village, where the Bohemian idealist mingles with the practical politician, to a swank seven-room apartment overlooking Central Park. He advanced to ownership of Wall Street skyscrapers, to oil lands in Texas and Oklahoma, to plush gambling operations heaven only knows where, and to remarkably close association with many ranking political figures in various parts of the country.

Costello had early realized the opportunities in alcohol. He was chummy with Bill Dwyer and Big French Lemange, Owney Madden's pal. They had put together as lavish an alcohol operation as the era produced. There had been a mix-up with the Law in 1927. Several coast guardsmen, admitting their guilt, called Costello the payoff man. The jury did not believe that of Frank. Not all the jurors, anyway, and nothing came of the charge. That occurred only a short time after Costello became a citizen, too. (Incidentally, the "Prime Minister's" application for citizenship carefully avoided any reference to a 1915 conviction, with its one-year sentence, for possessing a pistol.)

Like Costello, most of the boys had problems, with repeal on the way in 1931 and 1932. A man has to keep busy. As the recently-appointed ruler of Unione, Charley Lucky had some investments with excellent returns. He had become acquainted with the numbers, for instance, and moved into dope on a wide scale, and launched an occasional foray into industrial stuff. But alcohol was still the big revenue-producer.

Lepke already had a neat "gimmick." He was developing labor and industrial extortion in the garment trade, in flour and trucking, from all of which he exacted tribute. Most of the boys, however, were in the same boat as Costello. In New Jersey, Longy Zwillman and his first lieutenant, Willie (Moretti) Moore, had made fortunes during Prohibition. They were now at liberty, too, and could use something to keep the pot boiling.

Dutch Schultz, who had been in beer, found an answer faster than most of them, in the everyday institution of the restaurant.

"Those places need protection," The Dutchman told his cabinet solicitously. "There's hundreds of them in New York alone. A stink bomb in the rush hour, or a worm in a batch of bread dough . . . anything could ruin a restaurant."

The Galahad in the Dutchman came out. "We gotta protect them." Only Dutch said "pertect." To executives of fashionable food establishments and successful eating chains, he explained how he realized their success was dependent on public whim. He pointed up their potential disaster, in case they did not get the point themselves.

"Now, I'm the guy to pertect you," Dutch reassured them. The fee? A bagatelle, compared to the service offered. He would not take "no" for an answer: the restaurateurs did not dare offer a "no." Before 1932 was out, the restaurant racket was a $2,000,-000-a-year extortion for Dutch in New York alone. Added to his take from Harlem numbers banks, it kept the wolf from the Dutchman's door.

Frank C., though, was the direct antithesis of Dutch Schultz. The "Prime Minister" deplores violence. Such things as mob wars and gang shootings cause him to shudder. Indeed, violence has been so abhorrent to him that in 1929 Costello even called a convention in Atlantic City to talk about cutting down on the rough stuff, and similar economic improvements. Al Capone came to that one. After it was over, Al took the train home. In Philadelphia, almost before the train came to a stop, police hauled him off to the station house for toting a gun among his belongings. The scar-faced thug got a year in jail. No one has ever been certain whether it was Al's own gun that put him behind bars—or, as was whispered, someone else's gun looking for Al. Such as Bugs Moran, for instance—Al's chief business rival in Chicago. Capone was simply placed "on ice" for safe-keeping.

Dignity—that is the way of life, insists Costello. So, Frank C. vetoed this and that proposition, back there when repeal was causing so many changes. Then gambling was brought up. Perhaps Frank Erickson mentioned it, because the notorious roly poly bookie was just then beginning to forget all about his bus boy days in a Coney Island eatery. A couple of hundred thousand a year from as soft a touch as making book can cause anyone to forget practically anything, even hustling dirty dishes, was the way Erickson looked at it. Gambling had a ring of class to Costello. Several years later, he was to tell Bob Considine, the versatile New York newspaperman, about it.

"If you say that I am a gambler, you will be right," the Prime Minister confessed. "But I am an uncommon gambler. An uncommon gambler is a man who accommodates common gamblers."

You may not believe this, but Costello really moved into gambling legitimately. Before the legalization of pari-mutuel machine betting in 1939, bookmaking at New York race tracks was as lawful as going to church. One of the leading bookies in the sanctioned betting ring at the tracks was Johnny Ferrone. Costello simply bought a piece of Johnny's play, and was a bona-fide partner—all on the level. Of course, that doesn't mean the boys got out of bookmaking after 1939. In fact, fellows like Frank Erickson, who is probably the biggest bookmaker of our time, have handled handsome action since then, what with clients who bet as much as $10,000 a day.

In 1945, New York City Investigations Commissioner Edgar Bromberger looked over Erickson's interests and found that the flabby-faced bookie had made bank deposits of over $30,000,000 in a twelve-year period. And in 1950, Erickson told a U. S. Senate Gambling Investigating Committee—preceding the Kefauver Committee—that his office in Cliffside Park, N. J., took "layoff" bets from customers in all forty-eight states daily, handled some

$12,500,00 yearly, and that he paid one man $20,000 annually just to put the money in the bank.

The prospects were so excellent that even before 1932 ended, Costello and the other big bosses already were in gambling, and branching to all fields of the many-sided industry of chance. There was the policy game—the numbers, with mountains of profits. And so simple to handle—especially with the protection of Jimmy Hines, the benign and supreme political power in New York City. Next, in the conversion from rum, came slot machines. Costello had the rich New York play exclusively—until Mayor Fiorello LaGuardia began removing the slots. It did not nettle LaGuardia when the courts held that the "one-armed bandits" were legal. The Little Flower simply had the police go out and chop them up with axes, anyway, and sink them off Sandy Hook by the scowload.

Frank C. saw the light then. He packed up and moved to New Orleans. The welcome mat was out there. Huey Long, in fact, personally extended the invitation to him. The story is that the Louisiana Kingfish's State fund for widows, orphans and the blind was to share in the profits. Costello set up his machines by the thousand. At the height of the operation, there were five thousand in New Orleans alone. The story is, too, that through the first year Huey's widows, orphans and blind netted exactly $600 from them.

As recently as the spring of 1950, Chicago and California crime study groups reported that the slot machine racket is "headed by" Costello nationally. The California Crime Study Commission put the yearly national take from the one-armed bandits alone at two-billion dollars, and baldly asserted that $400,000,000 of it goes for "protection." Even if this were over-optimistic by as much as fifty percent, a billion a year still puts it in the Big Business class. All that—and dignity, too.

The largest investments by far in the switch of the boss mob-sters to dignified gambling were in swank saloons, roadhouses and plush eating places—with roulette, craps or name-your-game, behind the velvet draperies, in the back rooms or upstairs. Cos-tello's fancy Beverly Club, a few minutes from downtown New Orleans, was a $1,000,000 investment alone. The topper, though.

was the flamboyant Flamingo Club in Las Vegas, Nev., which cost a mere $6,000,000 to put up.

The gold mine for gambling operations has been Florida, although Saratoga, during the racing season each August, has been, by no means, penny ante. In Broward County, Fla., alone, fifty-two of the flashiest dives anywhere have been in full swing every season, wide open and no holds barred, with high-priced floor shows for the come-on. The play in the bankrolls of tourists and gamblers from the North and West is high in the millions. In secret testimony in the fall of 1950, George Patton, a deputy sheriff of Dade County (Miami), admitted he was a bagman or collector in the payoff under which gambling was permitted to operate. He told of one almost unbelievable dice game of which he had been informed.

"A big, well-known gambler named Ryan steered Harry Sinclair, the oil man, to the casino, and Sinclair lost $800,000 in two nights," Patton testified. "Sinclair settled for $500,000."

Law enforcement officials agree Costello has been high up in Broward County and Dade County operations for years; yet his name never appears on any partnerships. The names which do, however, include men long identified as "interested" in Costello's interests. Some of these partnership lists were uncovered when Erickson's Park Avenue bookmaking domain, in New York, was cleaned out in 1950. One, for the colorful Colonial Inn, a short distance up the highway from the heart of the Miami Beach tourist belt, showed a profit of $685,537.26 for the 1948 winter season of three months. Put fifty-two such traps together, and it takes no slide rule to compute that this is quite an industry. And that is only one section of the gambling industry, which reaches into every village and hamlet!

Among the Colonial Inn partners was Meyer Lansky, long-time Costello lieutenant, one-time mob associate of Buggsy Siegel, and a ranking member, in his own right, in the national ring. Meyer and his brother, Jack, cut in for a sizeable twenty percent, or nearly $140,000. Then there was Joey Adonis. This time, Joey A. went under his formal tag of Joseph Doto, it being a business statement. And there was Vincent Alo, an old hand at running gambling spots. Alo has one bright distinction: his nickname, Jimmy Blue Eyes.

Now that Moey Dimples is no more, it is the prettiest tag in gang-dom. Before his demise, Dimples, otherwise Wolinsky, was well up in the Florida gambling mob, particularly in partnership arrange-ments with Game Boy Miller, the Cleveland gang's leading traveling delegate.

The largest individual take in the Colonial "split," according to Erickson's list, went to men identified with the elite of the Detroit underworld. The financial statement showed that "Mert Wert-heimer, Eben Mathers, et al.," of Detroit received thirty-three and a third percent, for take home pay of $222,800.10 for their winter's work.

Other well-known westerners are always on hand, too, soaking up the southern sun and keeping an extremely close eye on op-erations. The Cleveland, Chicago, Philadelphia, Detroit, Kansas City and New York mobs have headquarters in hotels which they own, in the region. One regular visitor to the winter playground through the years, until his death in the spring of 1951, was Charley Fischetti. Charley and his brother, Rocco, picked up where their cousin, Al Capone, left off in Chicago. In 1949, the Chicago Crime Commission looked over the Broward County gambling and insisted that "Charles Fischetti, top-ranking mem-ber of the Capone syndicate, is affiliated (with) Costello and his mob."

By the time Prohibition was ready for burial, the new lineup was already in the game. The batting order in the East looked something like this:

Frank Costello—gambling (Frank Erickson, bookie boss and Florida representative; Dandy Phil Kastel, bucketshop specialist, as New Orleans general manager; section chiefs in other places).

Lucky Luciano—narcotics, numbers, prostitution (although he set up a mighty cry that the latter was a wrong rap, even after he was convicted of it).

Joey Adonis—bail bond, arbitration and "contacts" for above groups; political connection specialist; Brooklyn waterfront enter-prises.

Lepke and Gurrah—industrial and labor extortions in flour, clothing, trucking, bakeries, fur, motion picture theaters, ad inf.

Buggsy Siegel & Meyer Lansky (Bug & Meyer Mob)—dirty work and enforcement specialties, particularly for Lepke; varied Philadelphia enterprises.

Abner (Longy) Zwillman—assorted New Jersey operations. (Willie Moretti, or Moore, chief deputy, and Florida operative.)

Dutch Schultz—restaurant racket; Harlem numbers banks; general protection extortion; beer. (Bo Weinberg, chief assistant and trigger.)

For group purposes, this set was known as the Big Six, since Dutch Schultz, an insane individualist, had little in common with the others. But the entire set-up was still practically isolationist in form—"every man for theirself," as the boys sometimes put it. In spite of the modern trend toward lessening violence, each had his own organization, lined up his own protection and declared mob war when he felt like it. It was, largely, the horse-and-buggy way of the Al Capones, the Legs Diamonds. Across the river, too, Reles told me afterward, he and Happy and Pittsburgh Phil and Louis Capone lived in a crime world of their own. It was the same celluloid collar isolationism.

Nevertheless, 1932 was a big year all around. Except, perhaps, toward the end, for Dutch Schultz. The Treasury Department detected an odor about The Dutchman's income tax returns. Schultz left rapidly. "Bo Weinberg is the boss while I'm away," he stipulated, as he tossed his other shirt into a bag.

In spite of Schultz's absence—or because of it, since Dutch was strictly a hothead—things went along swimmingly, as they say. The new rackets brought out such profits that the bosses hardly had to reach out to pick them up. Then the natural reaction set in. Human nature is easily the most unfathomable of all phenomena. The bosses became eager for power and insured security to go with their plunder. What they wanted was some development to guarantee their edge—to prevent any slip-up.

Actually, the "gimmick" was so obvious that it is amazing it took until 1934 for someone to finally come up with it. It was there all the time—the blueprint which converted the scattered mess of unconnected mobs in New York and Chicago and Kansas City and here and there into a smooth-going, tightly-bound business.

According to the mob's most reliable "recording secretaries," Lepke had the germ of the idea as early as the end of 1931, and Lucky saw the possibilities even before Joe the Boss was impeached. But credit for really pointing out the way goes to Johnny Torrio, a round little man who started out as a saloon-keeper.

Johnny Torrio always was a sharp guy. 'Way back, even before Prohibition, Johnny showed how sharp he was. That was when the Italian Society was expanding onto the Brooklyn waterfront. Johnny closed up his Manhattan saloon and opened one in Brooklyn, just to be near the center of business.

There, he hooked up with Paolo Vaccarelli, who was known to the underworld as Paul Kelly and was one of the first to combine a position as an official of the longshoremen's union with manipulation of dock control. When Prohibition came, though, Johnny Torrio headed west and took over Chicago from Big Jim Colisimo. En route, of course, he called on his old school chum, Frankie Yale, to come out and remove Big Jim. When half a dozen bodies were found on a railroad track, Johnny imported another old buddy from Brooklyn as his bodyguard, a hoodlum with a scar on his face, name of Al Capone.

Prohibition took hold, and the first thing you know a man couldn't even go out in his garden to pick a rose, without someone with an unfriendly implement, like a sawed-off shotgun, blowing holes in him. Then Johnny really demonstrated his astuteness. He could not see the fun in living in a shooting gallery. He had all the money he needed. So, he said, "Here you are, Al—I'm handing it over to you and I'm getting out." And he "delivered" Chicago to Capone.

Johnny took a trip to Italy, stayed for several years. When he came home, he bought real estate in Miami and Maryland. At this writing, he is still in real estate. His most recent recorded transaction, in fact, was with the sheriff of Hillsborough County (Tampa), in Florida. As for Capone and Yale and the rest who stayed to pick the roses—they wound up being buried under them.

By 1933, Johnny was dealing in millions. He ranked with Lucky and Joey A. They said he was the biggest thing since Arnold Rothstein, the gambler-boss, as a bankroll man for underworld enterprises. After repeal, Johnny acquired a strictly legal and legitimate licensed liquor concern—one of the largest ones in the field.

You might say, in fact, that the only time Johnny Torrio wasn't on his toes was when he tried some flim-flam with fake stamps and juggled books in his liquor business. The Government asked a lot of questions about $68,000 in unpaid taxes. Ironically, the same Al Capone to whom Torrio handed Chicago as a gift, helped send the round little ganglord up. Al was a doddering has-been by then, serving time himself for tax evasion. He had fallen so far, by underworld standard, that he pleaded to turn stoolpigeon. That made them laugh—mighty Al Capone, who used to shoot guys for the same thing, begging with tears in his eyes for permission to sing. He thought it would make him look good to his keepers, and win privileges. In his babbling, Al mentioned Torrio's income. Uncle Sam already had been checking on Johnny's books.

When they sprang it on Torrio, he was still quick on the pick-up. He knew they had him, and that a trial and accompanying legal loop-the-loops would only waste time. Besides, testimony often involves friends. So, Johnny pleaded guilty. He served two and a half years, and was out and around again in 1941.

It was long before that—back in 1934, actually—that Torrio got the brainstorm for streamlining crime. The idea had to be presented first to the East's Big Six. The reaction of Lucky was required, and of Lepke and Buggsy Siegel and his partner, Meyer Lansky, Frank Costello's friend. New Jersey's rackets ruler would have to be consulted, too. The stoolpigeons told us the first discussion meeting was held in a fashionable New York hotel, with all mobs represented.

"See what you think of this," Johnny was quoted as saying, and he proceeded to outline the method that would not only provide the sought for power, but would guarantee security of the mob bosses, with it. There is, of course, no verbatim report on the conclave. No one was keeping the minutes. But according to the mobsters who talked, the following is close enough to exhibit the proposition:

"Why don't all you guys work up one big outfit?" the mob moguls were asked. Immediately, the old antipathy to "hooking up" could be felt. "Wait now," they were advised. "That doesn't mean throwing everything into one pot. Let each guy keep what he's got now. But make one big combination to work with."

The new ventures, it was pointed out, would involve far more risk than the well-oiled machinery of bootlegging. In planning for the future, a prime item must be proper recognition and evaluation of the common foe: Law enforcement. It would be different than during Prohibition's happy heyday, when every mob had its individual protection and connections. A lot of the contacts would die with repeal. Why not pool surviving connections, then?

First and most important factor to be faced was the fighting among themselves—the gang warfare that marked every difference of opinion.

"One guy gets hit, and his troop hits the outfit that did it," the protagonist went on. Reprisal in mob murder always cost valuable manpower. But more: it exposed the underworld's most vulnerable spot—it brought heat from the Law. In the end, it helped no gang, for good men were being lost continually. Why not an organization, then, which could eliminate this weakness, simply by dealing with such matters to the interests of all?

There was sudden interest among the magnates at that. Each had been plagued by—and participated in—such costly clashes. These, remember, were the new order moguls. In spite of envies and ego, they were administrators and businessmen. There is no intent here to hand them unwarranted credit; these are simply the facts as our investigation found them. These gang leaders appreciated prospects never admitted by the isolationist torpedo of the Joe the Boss ilk.

It was quickly realized, of course, that no one of them would ever stand for one single boss—one czar over all. Each regarded himself a big shot, and was fanatically jealous of his position. But it was explained how there could be central control based on co-operation, without sacrifice of individuality. A board, or panel, of all the bosses themselves—that was the gimmick Johnny Torrio had in mind. Such a board could arbitrate inter-mob disputes by meeting and talking and deciding who was right and who was wrong. That was the key that finally convinced them.

Enthusiastically, the ganglords agreed on this board of directors, to include all the individual mob leaders, each with equal say, each with equal power. The board would dictate policy, handle all negotiations on the inter-mob level. And on that principle, they organized. On that conception, the Syndicate was born.

Each boss remained czar in his own territory, his rackets unmolested, his local authority uncontested. In murder, no one—local or imported—could be killed in his territory without his approval. He would have the right to do the job himself or permit an outsider to come in—but only at his invitation. In fact, no lawlessness, on an organized scale, could take place in his domain without his sanction and entire consent, unless he was overruled by the board of governors. And even then, he would have a say in the discussion. It was State's rights in crime!

Basically, it was a gilt-edged insurance policy. Every mob leader now had behind him not just his own hoods, but a powerful amalgamation of all mobs. Every gang chieftain was guaranteed against being interfered with in his own area—and against being killed by a rival mobster. The structure was definitely not a corporation. Had any of them known the word, he might have called it a cartel —a confederation of independent business concerns working toward the common goal of insured crime, and profits from same.

Soon, the criminal bands from beyond the East saw the strength in the union. The Brooklyn stoolpigeons told us a second meeting was called in Kansas City, to hear from the Western executives. The Capone crowd from Chicago and the Kansas City mob liked the idea. Reports came from Cleveland and Detroit that the Mayfield Gang and the Purple Mob wanted in. Boston and Miami, New Orleans and Baltimore, St. Paul and St. Louis— all flocked to the confederacy of crime, until it was nation-wide.

Thus, the Syndicate came into being. And, incredible as it may sound, the incessant, indiscriminate toll of gangsters lost through mob rivalries came to an abrupt end almost immediately!

A century and a half before, men of noble purpose had gathered

from separate colonies to form a more perfect union. Here, a handful of evil delegates met, inspired by no nobility at all, but just as
intent on a more perfect union—for crime. In each case, the
result achieved a sovereign government made up of several sovereign "states." Perhaps no other analogy more closely fits the
national Syndicate and its thriving organization to this day.

The Law never had or ever will have insurmountable difficulty
with unorganized crime. Some cases are always bound to go unsolved, certainly. But graveyards hold uncounted headstones
heralding the quick dispatch by law and order of unattached criminals.

Up to 1934, with mobs separate and individual, no matter how
swiftly the underworld traveled, the Law overtook it sooner or
later. But when the gangster discovered organization, when he
converted from unorganized crime to Syndicate operations on the
national scale, he developed an edge that law and order has not
entirely matched, even yet.

The vast majority of lawbreaking, from burglary to murder, is
against local law—state, county and municipal. All are bounded
by jurisdictional limits. On the other hand, nationally-organized
crime knows no limitations of boundary. It has a chain store in
virtually every city and town in the country. A county or state
prosecutor, hemmed by jurisdictional boundaries, can hardly turn
up an organization functioning in forty-eight states. A District Attorney, armed with just ordinary crime fighting weapons, has no
means of penetrating this tightly-knit body. He can get lowly
members of the mob; the higher-ups who pull the strings are always well covered.

The confederation of the mobs resulted in so powerful an an-
tagonist that, until the Brooklyn informers enabled us to attack
Murder, Inc., from within, not a single top-notcher in the Syndicate ever had been harmed. And, except for that one temporary
break, not a single top-notcher has sat in the electric chair before
or since. It remains today the same mighty adversary. If Kid
Twist had not turned a light on it, there is no telling how long it
would have been before the Law could even have surmised the
existence of such a set-up. No one would have believed that

these self-exalted cut-throats would ever cede even the smallest scrap of personal power to a syndicate.

Once it was agreed, back there in 1934, the government of crime was quick to get its machinery under way. Already established gang territorial lines became kingdoms inviolate against murder or muscling. And for seventeen years now, this national ring has governed the underworld through that policy.

Whenever a body is found in the gutter or a doorway today, it is still more or less casually dismissed by press and public as the result of a difference of mob opinion, just as it was in the trigger-happy twenties. It doesn't work that way any more. Not one top boss in the underworld has been slain since 1934, unless the execution was sanctioned, approved and, in fact, directed by the ganglords of the nation. That goes—from Dutch Schultz in 1935 to Buggsy Siegel in 1947 and Charlie Binaggio in 1950.

There has been virtually no internecine warfare in gangland in that period, other than that ordered by the Syndicate itself. This is exactly what the organizers had in mind when they combined to eliminate the economically unsound flare-ups in which gang had difference with gang, and settled it with guns. In the statute book of the new order, it was made absolute that there must be arbitration before blood spilled between rival jurisdictions—whether both are in New York or one is in Detroit and the other in Los Angeles. Murder for personal reasons is flatly banned. Majority rule decides all issues, and all gang moguls are charged with responsibility for seeing that the code is lived up to —to the letter and the punctuation.

Each member of the board of directors, at the top of the new government, was a boss of a member mob—the head hoods in the major cities. The succession has followed that form. They hear all business disputes, decide all policy and operational methods after listening to all sides.

"That is the democratic way," they said then. It never has been a one-man decision.

Along with the legislative and executive branches of crime, the gang planners also set up a judiciary, just as in any "democratic" government. They devised the Kangaroo Court of the underworld, with "justices" from the board of governors.

Charges serious enough to warrant the death penalty for any high echelon gangster are called before it—cases which, in the deadly non-co-operating days of gang vs. gang, would have meant imme-mediate no-questions-asked mob warfare. Like the Supreme Court of the United States, the Kangaroo Court is a court of last resort. Its word is final; its decisions irrevocable. Thus, when the court ruled, in 1935, that Joey Amberg, extortionist and dope peddler, must die, die he did, although he was a protégé of Buggsy Siegel and his cause was pleaded by the highly-placed Joey Adonis.

Even such prominent powers as Dutch Schultz and Buggsy Siegel had no appeal from the verdicts. When each of these char-acters was rubbed out, it was the formal execution of a death sentence officially decreed by the kangaroo court—and after regular trial, at that. Nor does the kangaroo court know no other verdict than "guilty." Reles told me of at least two acquit-tals, in cases in which conviction would have carried the death penalty with as much enforcement power as any duly constituted court of criminal jurisprudence.

Hand in hand with the new set-up, too, came an accent on "connections"—political, protection connections. One of the sug-gestions for co-operation at the original organization meeting, at which Johnny Torrio had outlined the whole idea, had been for interchangeable use of each mob's contacts. Under the Syndicate, such protection worked perfectly, right from the start.

There are various methods of accomplishing this end. On the basic level, is the prosaic paying of "ice." Then, too, top-ranked bosses are always on the lookout for friendships that produce valued contacts. They weasel themselves into political campaigns and into close association with public officials wherever and when-ever possible. Corruption is a cancer that spreads all too easily under the careful nurture of criminal chiefs avid for power.

One snatch of testimony during the Kefauver Committee hear-ings in New York in March, 1951, expressed it especially succinctly, even though protection or corruption were not mentioned. O'Dwyer was on the stand at the time, telling of a visit he made to Frank Costello's apartment, and of seeing several top political leaders of the city there:

Q—A funny thing what magnetism that man (Costello) had.
How can you analyze it; what is the attraction he has?

A—It doesn't matter whether it is a banker, a businessman or
a gangster; his pocketbook is always attractive.

The racketeer regards himself as a businessman, with policies
every bit as sound as those in legitimate enterprise. Take good
will, for instance. The grocer, the manufacturer, the mail order
house build up good will in order to keep customers coming back,
to prevent a competitor from taking customers and to convince
potential customers to deal with them. That, says the mobster,
is exactly what murder does. Assassination, therefore, has always
been given as careful consideration by the gang magnate as good
will ever has received from the decent businessman.

With the advent of the national organization, and the banning
of "unnecessary" killing, sanctioned eliminations became a matter
for experts, strictly. It took more than just pulling a trigger to
carry out the purpose of the Syndicate—the furtherance of the
new national rackets business.

Each outfit had always taken care of its own eliminations. A
few of the gang bosses, whose multiple activities required it and
whose affluence could afford it, sometimes hired special slayers
at so much the throat-cutting. But mostly, each mob used its
own triggermen.

When the Syndicate opened for business, however, it became
vital that there be no slip-ups, no loose ends, in such matters.
There were occasions when one or another mob had a job to
be done which, for security reasons, could not be efficaciously
handled by its own members. The local boys, for instance, might
be so placed that such a slaying would point directly toward them,
or, perhaps, the selected victim was wary of them. That made
it desirable to bring in a new face to do the work. As time passed,
this custom became more popular. In a businesslike manner, it
advanced to importation of killers from a mob in another city
or state, with the approval of the boss of that outfit.

Early in the growth of this practice, the Brooklyn executioners
were summoned, like any others, for, through Joey Adonis, Brooklyn was on the Syndicate's national map. It was soon noted that

the Brooklyn killers always were proficient. The precision-like technique they had perfected came to be looked upon with great respect and approbation by mob moguls the country over, for its painstaking attention to detail and its neat finality of accomplishment.

"Those kids in Brooklyn got it taped real good," said one gang boss. And another praised: "That Reles and Pittsburgh Phil, and that Maione know how to cover up a job so nobody can find a thing."

No matter what the assignment, their talents functioned with art and skill—even to labor disputes and eliminations, which were the most hazardous. Hence, since every mob, the country over, had the right to call on any other for co-operation and assistance, gang bosses far and near took to inviting the Brooklyn assassins more and more frequently. It was no more the duty of the Brooklyn troop than of any other mob in the cartel. But so adept were the Brownsville thugs that, before very long, they were being used almost invariably from the Atlantic to the Pacific, from Florida to the Canadian border. Eventually, they were recognized as the more-or-less official execution squad for the Syndicate, on call at any time. They worked so many contracts so successfully that Lepke, before long, practically adopted them en masse.

"Lepke would send in $12,000 flat a year for his work," Reles revealed to us. The Kid had but one complaint about the set-up. "Their accountant came with the proposition," he related ruefully. "His name is Simon Lepasco. He would bring the money down to us. He's no accountant. He's a shakedown artist."

The Brooklyn experts were not for hire. Their outside work was solely on contract service for other Syndicate gangs—the same as a garbage disposal company contracts to haul off the refuse from a suburban block every day; not just one garbage can from one house that summons it on one particular day.

That put the last nail in the Syndicate's construction. It completed Murder, Inc., a coast-to-coast crime co-operative, dealing in everything from nickel-and-dime thievery to murder, and comprising every mob that meant anything in the underworld of the United States. It was a going concern, and for the next six years, it went where it pleased. All in all, it was the biggest thing to hit crime since Cain invented murder and used it on Abel.

The new lineup, with the Brooklyn troop as enforcement squad, proved a huge success immediately. The upper echelon mobsters were openly and audibly appreciative.

"Lepke was satisfied real good," Reles preened to us in 1940. "Lep give us eleven contracts for witnesses when he was on the lam. We knocked off seven of them before Dewey put him on trial last year."

Lucky, too, took to the set-up at once. In fact, one of the first Syndicate contracts the Brooklyn troop undertook was at the behest of the notorious dope-peddler with the droopy eye.

Muddy Kasoff, a small-time narcotics hustler from lower Manhattan, was meddling with Lucky's territory, and he was granted permission to take the proper reprisal. He contacted the Brooklyn firing squad.

"This bum is cutting in on my play with the stuff," Lucky briefed them. "You guys take him."

The boys learned that Muddy had some good friends—and the friends had money. They figured here was a golden opportunity. They "snatched" Muddy. (Kidnaping was popular back there in 1934.) They took him to a hideout and they bound him and stood guard over him.

"Get your pals to get up five thousand, or we knock you off," they demanded. Muddy was impressed, naturally. With no quibbling, he told his captors how to contact his friends. Two or three days later, the return contact was made.

"We can only get up twenty-seven hundred," the friends reported sorrowfully. "Here it is. If you hold off a little while, we can dig up the rest."

To the hoodlums, though, the request for time sounded like an obvious stall. Besides, $2,700 was a fair night's pay, anyway. Muddy was blindfolded. His hands were roped behind his back. He was loaded into a car. Muddy felt relieved. Evidently, his kidnapers were preparing to release him. They drove him far out on Long Island—to Island Park, a pretty seaside spot, where the fishing is good not too far offshore. The car was stopped. Muddy was led to the edge of a vacant lot, and his hands were freed.

"We're turning you loose, punk," the captive was informed. "Take a hundred steps before you touch the blindfold. If you touch it before, we'll grab you again. Now get!"

Muddy walked nine paces. He could feel the grass under his soles. He took ten strides more, into the weeds. He heard no sound, and he wondered if his abductors had gone. He counted off half the distance, with stumbling unseeing steps. As he got that far, the hoods raised their pistols and blasted away. Next morning, what was left of the dope peddler who meddled with Charley Lucky was found at the foot of a billboard—which pleaded for motorists to drive safely.

"Sure . . . all the big shots was satisfied," sneered Reles, when he told of the Syndicate, and Brooklyn's death-dealing function in it.

The national network rooted deep. It has been subject to devastating attack since 1934. The industrial and numbers extortions of the 1930's were throttled by Governor (then Prosecutor) Dewey when he nailed Lucky and Jimmy Hines, the Tammany boss. In 1940 and 1941, our convictions of the murderers who made the rackets click eliminated some of the highly ranked operatives. But the organization remained. The blueprint, the methods of the rackets, the gang killings—these are the signs that it is still with us.

As a matter of fact, our convictions could not even completely obliterate the Brooklyn branch, despite the loss of the seven killers I had the pleasure of putting into the electric chair. The troop had dug in for too long to be altogether uprooted. Just how long, Reles related next, after he had completed painting the picture of the national organization. He went all the way back, to the flowering of the Brownsville branch—and its birth in blood.

5. Out of a rape, a murder mob

The boss brothers—honor of fair damsel starts mob war—Kid Twist takes over—a bag job and the last of the brothers—the State Street game: big business on a dice table—Shylocking: 3,000%, or schlammin with a lead pipe.

In the twenties, the Shapiro brothers were the tough guys around Brownsville and East New York, which were very tough neighborhoods, indeed.

Meyer was the toughest—the head hoodlum. He had a hard face, and eyes that were as small and cruel as his character. He bragged that, among other things, he had fifteen houses of prostitution "going for" himself, alone.

"I'm the boss of Brownsville," he proclaimed. And he put together a collection of toughs and hoodlums to prove it to any doubters.

Irv was the heir apparent—not quite as tough as his brother. His tangles with the Law were small stuff mostly—minor-league lawlessness. Willie was the court jester—a little man with a low forehead and a high collar and a dimple. He was not very tough at all.

The brothers built up a good thing in alcohol and slot machines and prostitution. They limited their reign strictly to their own domain—Brownsville and East New York, the pestholes where breeding hoodlums was a major industry. Once in a while, they sauntered forth for a quick fling at Coney Island, to cash in on the rich pickings in slot machines. They paid regular protection, and they took care of the higher-ups to insure continued unmolested operations.

"We got everything straightened out our way," Meyer smirked.

"As long as we stay in our own back yard, we ain't got a thing to worry about."

Occasionally, they thought of expansion; a branch, perhaps, in Manhattan, where there were so many more ways to pick up a loose dollar. But that, Meyer said, "would just be sticking our necks out." No tough kids from Brooklyn were going to make the likes of Big Bill Dwyer and Frank Costello, or Lepke and Lucky move over. In their home borough, on the other hand, the brothers had absolute rule. Helping to keep it that way was the fact that manpower presented no problem in Brownsville, where young punks sprouted and dreamed of becoming successful hoodlums, and even bosses, on the underworld social ladder.

The punks gladly did any assignment, just to be seen with the boss brothers. "Here's a fin," one of the brothers would say, tossing a five-dollar bill for a job that could have meant prison for the punk. (The local juvenile attitude toward being sent "up" for the first time was akin to that of a debutante at her coming-out party. It was a long step up the social ladder.) Many times, it did not even require the "fin." Just a, "Hey, Tony, do this-or-that," would suffice. The worshipful punk thrills at recognition by name from the big shot. He only hopes his friends are within earshot.

The brothers swaggered and strutted. But their own self-importance and tyranny blinded them to the one detail they should never have overlooked. Punks grow up; sometimes punks get ideas. Brooklyn in general, and Brownsville in particular, have legends about its sons who did. The deeds of Johnny Torrio and Al Capone, who went West, are oft-recalled. The memory of Buggsy Siegel, too, is ever green. The Bug rose to rank high on the national directorate of gangland. Mickey Cohen, the loudmouth ex-pug who likes to think he succeeded Buggsy in California, is still another who graduated.

Then there was flashy, ruthless Kid Twist Reles. The Kid was just a punk then, but he was ambitious and cunning behind his flamboyant front. And he had no more regard for law and order than he had for human life—which was none at all. The Shapiros should have spotted him as something different than the usual pathetic and psychopathic punk they pushed around. Instead, they threw the Kid the same patronizing bone. It was their big mistake; especially when Reles got a bullet in the back protecting their slot-machine interests one night.

Reles was twenty when he began to get ideas of lese majesty. He could see no reason why, if he took the risks, he should not also enjoy a proportionate share of the money and influence the boss brothers monopolized.

"Why do we got to take the left-overs?" he asked his pal, Buggsy Goldstein, one day as the frenzied twenties dragged toward an end. "We should cut a piece. The hell with them guys."

Buggsy would follow anywhere Kid Twist led. They had gone to school together; done their first stealing together; worked their first extortions together. Reles did the thinking; Buggsy flexed the muscles. When Reles suggested breaking away, the Bug went along with the theory of free enterprise, mob style. At first, all they wanted was "a piece"—a block or two of slot-machine territory, a house for the prostitution take. They sought something more than just the crumbs, while the brothers enjoyed the icing from the cake.

Reles got a few things started for himself and his brash buddy. He set up a few girls to work for him. Then he looked up the Dasher. Frank Abbandando was a powerfully built bully who might have gone somewhere in baseball if he hadn't sneered at the Law. In fact, he won his nickname through his hustle and dash on the field. They dubbed him the Dasher when he was the classy infielder of the Elmira (N.Y.) team. The Elmira Reformatory, that is.

When Reles looked him up, the husky hoodlum and his pal, Happy Maione, were running the loan-sharking and bookmaking and similar activities in Ocean Hill, adjoining Brownsville. Happy was the older and the more ruthless; Abbandando was still in his teens.

"How about getting together on a little booking?" suggested the Kid. "We could handle some betting—you here and me and Buggsy in Brownsville."

"I don't know . . . me and Happy are okay here." The Dasher was practical. "And what about the Shapiros? They won't like it."

"Let me worry about those bums." Reles' revolt was in the open now. "I'm for Kid Reles from here on."

The Dasher took the suggestion to his partner. Happy's Ocean Hill hooligans were ranked second only to the brothers in the entire area. Happy did not like second best. So, an unofficial alliance in bookmaking on a minor scale was born on the Brownsville-Ocean Hill axis, in defiance of existing authority.

Revolution was new to the reigning royalty of Brownsville. The clan Shapiro was furious. If they let Kid Twist get away with this, other punks might get ideas, too.

"Brownsville belongs to us; nobody moves in here," Meyer decreed. It was a declaration of war.

Through his entire hoodlum life, Reles reveled in rough stuff —when the odds were right. Right now, however, they were not right. The Kid was not yet ready to expose his outnumbered forces. He laid plans designed to keep the brothers too busy to bother his small enterprise. He hired Joey Silvers, one of the neighborhood punks, to tip him off whenever an opportunity might arise to throw a blow—in any form of violence—at the big shots. As one of the kids used by the brothers, Joey was in an excellent spot to obtain such information.

One night, not long afterward, Joey got word to Reles that the brothers' cars were parked in a certain easily accessible spot, vulnerable to attack. Reles and Buggsy showed up at the lonesome corner. They brought with them a neighborhood ally, George DeFeo. The cars were exactly where Joey had said they would be. Reles had an ice pick, and he set to work slashing away at the tires of the enemy's automobiles. The others stood guard. Then the ambush opened up.

Buggsy stopped a bullet with his nose. Another slug hit Reles in the stomach. DeFeo was killed. It was the neatest double cross they ever ran into. The Kid had never anticipated, naturally, that Joey Silvers would dare take a salary from him, and still work undercover for the brothers. Espionage and counterespionage were not part of day-by-day Brownsville diplomacy.

The business rivalry flamed into a vendetta after that. The ambush aroused Kid Twist, not only because of his own wound or Buggsy's, but also because the death of DeFeo took away one of his guns, of which he had far too few. However, the craving for vengeance did not blind the Kid's cunning. He would still not be lured into the open.

Meyer, meantime, racked his twisted mind on ways and means to wipe out the uprising. He was obsessed with devising some scheme to get Reles to expose himself. One day, the answer came to him.

That evening, the leader of the brothers got into his car and began to drive through the area. Up this street of noisy saloons and coffee pots, he prowled; down that avenue of tenements and delicatessens. He peered at every pedestrian, examined closely every front stoop holding its quota of Brownsville youth. Finally, he spotted his quarry.

The girl was just ambling along in the cool of the evening. Occasionally she dawdled, window shopping at a display of cheap frocks which had one quality in common: loud color. She was young—just eighteen—with dark eyes and dark glistening hair. She was pretty, in spite of the hard look she was already acquiring. And she was Reles' sweetheart.

To Meyer, this ripe and luscious Brownsville peach was the lure to smoke out Kid Twist. He swerved his car to the curb. The strolling girl was so startled that he had grabbed her, heaved her onto the front seat and was once more behind the wheel himself before she realized she was his target.

The girl fought, as only Kid Twist's girl might be expected to fight. She struggled and she scratched and she kicked. Once, she even managed to get the door partly open. She was up against a mob-hardened hoodlum, though. With one hand, he pinned her to the seat; with the other, he navigated the car. He headed for a secluded spot he knew, just beyond the edge of Brownsville. In those days and in that neighborhood, chance passers-by did not generally stop to investigate comparatively minor disturbances or private arguments. It was not conducive to good health.

There, in that quiet, lonely place, Meyer raped Reles' sweetheart. Then he beat her. Methodically, with fat, flailing fists, he clubbed her head and her face and neck, so the bruises, the discolored eyes and the split lips showed plainly. As one brutal blow piled on another, the girl's screams became whimpers; her fierce struggles, subconscious cringes. For an unmerciful time, the boss brother kept it up. Then, calmly, he opened the door and kicked her out onto the pavement.

"Now," he sneered, as he threw the car into gear, "go back and tell that dirty rat what happened. And who made it happen. And tell him this is only the start."

For a long time, the girl was too hurt to move. Eventually, she managed to pull herself to her feet. She dragged herself back to Brownsville and found the Kid. And she delivered the message.

Reles grew up in a hurry. He threw off his punkdom like a snake crawling out of its skin. Meyer, disliked only for his dictatorial power before, was a marked man now—and his brothers with him. Joey Silvers, the double-crosser, too. Reles' hatred was a cold, hard thing that plotted shrewdly. It told him he and Buggsy did not have a chance, even with their new gunmate, Pittsburgh Phil. The foppish slayer had thrown in with the punks by this time, and was a tremendous addition.

"The way Pep went, it was like we put on a whole new troop," Reles related to us later.

Reles and Buggsy and Pittsburgh Phil were an imposing army, but not enough. The brothers had been building for years, and this was total war. Allies were needed.

The chief thing Reles did not like about Happy Maione was that the sour-faced plug-ugly wanted to be the boss. The Kid regarded himself as No. 1 man. Two twenty-year-old temperaments gave off sparks when they brushed.

Happy was left-handed and completely ruthless. He was the kind of sadist who smashed a meat cleaver into the skull of a victim "just for luck"—after the man already had been strangled.

Reles' vow of vengeance for the bruises and honor of his sweetheart was too important, however, to let personal dislike prejudice necessity. Happy's guns would give him an army at full strength. They were close by, too, to form a united front. Reles outlined his proposition. The Kid had great powers of persuasion when he wanted something.

"Those bums can be taken," he asserted, opening the conference. Then, not to appear too eager, he added, "Of course, me and Buggsy are going all right on our own."

"What's on your mind?" Happy was quickly impatient. "What's the deal?"

"Well, if we put a mob together, we could take everything over."

"Look . . . I'm the boss in Ocean Hill, and I get left alone," Happy pointed out. "Why should I stick my neck out?"

"You throw together with us, and we'll all move in."

"Where do I fit if I do?"

Reles had figured that one, too. "We take care of the Shapiros; then we take over. Everything goes into the pot . . . Brownsville, East New York, Ocean Hill—everything. Then we cut down the middle."

Sour Happy was never one to show unnecessary enthusiasm. But Louis Capone cast a strong ballot for the plan. "It sounds real good, Hap," he assured his protégé. Both of these rising plug-uglies, in fact, were Louis' protégés. Vito Gurino was very strong for it, too. But then, Socko, vicious and conscienceless, was strong for any kind of violence. Gurino was probably as savage as any of that band who would commit any crime. He was five feet eight and 265 pounds, and he looked older than his twenty-three years in those days when he became one of Happy's most competent torpedoes.

Gurino was a pistol expert. He maintained his sharpshooting eye with sessions of popping the heads off chickens as they raced around a yard. All told, he was a principal in at least eight murders. Ownership of five bakeries provided him with a legitimate front for all sorts of operations. He was, moreover, a figure in the bakers' union. Our murder investigation disclosed that the secretary of the attorney for the bakers' union council had made out a number of checks to Vito at one time or another.

His heft—his neck was nearly the size of a water main—made Socko look like anything but a ladies' man. Therefore, it came as a pronounced shock to the boys the day he showed up squiring a tall, gorgeous seventeen-year-old redhead.

"Meet the wife," he said, practically slobbering. None of the hoods, tough as they were, dared ask an obvious question such as "What has an ape like you got to attract a beauty like this?" It seems Gertrude had been working in a beauty parlor and had met Gurino on a blind date. Four months later, they were married. It was a perfect mating of Beauty and the Beast. Gurino, who had the manners of a wallowing animal and the habits of an oaf, was particularly proud of this most beautiful of his possessions. He also liked to show off the diamond ring he presented to her.

"Wow!" exclaimed one wide-eyed detective, interviewing Gertrude during our probe, "that rock is as big as the headlights on my prowl car."

With his co-workers unanimously in favor of the amalgamation with Reles' growing troop, Happy grudgingly agreed. "Now what happens?" he asked.

The Kid knew just what he wanted. "Well," he replied, "the Shapiros got to be hit. We can't just muscle them out; they got to go. And remember, the first one is Meyer. I got something to square him for."

So, Brooklyn, Inc., two gangs, with twenty-year-old bosses who hated each other, went into business in 1930. It was the Brooklyn "combination." To its members, the combination it always remained.

It did not take long for the Shapiros to realize they were no longer the hunters. For all of the next year, the combined regiment tried to corner the brothers. Once, Reles ran into Meyer on a busy East New York street. Meyer was the prime target—the must. The Kid whipped out his pistol and commenced firing. He wounded the boss brother—and two complete strangers who happened to be passing.

All told, the upstart rebels had eighteen shooting opportunities at Meyer between June, 1930 and July, 1931. And eighteen times, they missed! It was a humiliating record, indeed, for the gunmen who were later to win far-flung fame as the most able assassins in gangland.

Up in Sullivan County, in the rustic reaches of the Catskill Mountains, Jack Siegal, friend of Brownsville's boss brothers, was the slot-machine czar. Near the end of July, in 1931, Jack went on trial for his transgressions in the county seat at Monticello.

"Let's get out of town today," Irv proposed to his brother in

Brooklyn that morning. "You're a little jumpy, Meyer. We can run up and see can we do anything for Jack. The ride will do you good."

The pressure of thirteen months as a clay pigeon for a set of wild killers was telling on Meyer. He was glad of a reason to leave town, even for a few hours. The departure and destination were reported to Kid Twist in short order. He knew this tip was accurate. By this time, he had learned to check sources of information. Hastily, he summoned the troop.

From espionage over the past year, Reles could anticipate the brothers' usual movements. "There's a card game at the Democratic Club on Sheffield Avenue tonight," he outlined, scheming. "Those rats are sure to be back for it. Let's see now . . . they figure to leave Monticello about four-five o'clock. That would get them down here about eight. They'll eat and be at the club, say, ten-eleven o'clock. We'll be there when they come out."

Almost as if Reles had written the itinerary, the brothers returned and headed for the club and the card game. The July night was especially warm. The lights over the table were hot. After only an hour or two, they tossed in their hands. Two or three others had the same idea, simultaneously.

As the brothers emerged, fingers tightened on five triggers in ambush across the street. But before the guns could fire, the rest of the retiring card players followed closely through the doorway. Two couples also picked that precise moment to stroll by, homeward bound from the neighborhood movie house. Before the unsuspecting shield dispersed, the brothers were in their car and gone —driving away from their own murder!

"Quick," ordered Reles, resourceful as usual. "Over to their house. They'll head there."

The five torpedoes bolted to their automobile and sped to a block of modern, middle-class apartments on Blake Avenue. A glance along the street showed that the brothers had not yet parked.

"Good . . . we beat them," said the Kid. "Now we go in the hall and wait. Remember, Meyer goes first."

Inside, they unscrewed the single overhead light bulb. In after-midnight darkness, they pressed against the wall. The late hour was on their side. No residents entered or left, who might complicate the plan. The brothers, however, were not co-operating.

"I don't think I'll go home," Meyer decided as they pulled away from the club. "I'm still jumpy. Drop me off at the Cleveland Baths. I'll stay there overnight. Maybe it will loosen me up."

"Okay," his brother agreed. "I'd stay with you, only I got to be around early tomorrow. Something doing with that new alky."

Thus, when their car turned into Blake Avenue, the one Reles had ruled "must be first" was trying to relax in a Turkish bath a mile away. Had they known that, Reles calmly related during his recital, the anxious assassins would have barged right into the place and blasted him there.

The younger Shapiro parked the car and entered the darkened vestibule. The latch clicked behind him. The shadow of his head was vaguely etched in the faint moonlight seeping through the crack of the door. It was just enough to tell the triggermen this was not their prime target. Reles felt a pang of disappointment. The Kid longed for the satisfaction of disposing first of the man who had raped his love. The rest of them, though, were not weighed down by chivalry. They fired, anyway. Two bullets hit Irv in the face. The impact jerked his head back, like the end of a bull whip, and spun him around. Sixteen more bullets hemstitched his spine before he hit the floor. The reigning clan had suffered its first loss.

One week later, Meyer was walking on a street, and three men shot at him from a car. Wounded for perhaps the tenth time in a year, he staggered into an automobile and fled. The gunmen roared after him. A police car, showing a perfectly natural curiosity, gave chase. The officers caught the automobile that was doing the pursuing. In it were the Dasher and Reles and Pittsburgh Phil.

The ensuing questioning centered more around the car than the shooting. (It seemed the vehicle was stolen.) Strange things like that were always happening for Reles and his troop in the thirties. At any rate, the trio, benefiting once more from its astonishing "luck" with the Law, was back on the street in a matter of hours.

For the nineteenth time, Meyer had escaped the death sentence. For a prime target, he was carrying a remarkable charm. For Joey

Silvers, too, the dice had been rolling well, although he was not nearly as sought after as Meyer. For a year, he escaped the penalty for his double cross. But he was neither as clever nor as powerful as his boss, and one evening, Reles and Maione caught up with him on a street corner. They backed Joey close to a building and blew his head off.

It was obvious, as the pursuit became more desperate, that time was running out for Meyer. A good-luck charm can stand off a bullet for just so long. Finally, sixty-nine days after Irv wound up with eighteen slugs in the apartment hallway—and a mere fortnight after Joey Silvers was paid off for counterespionage—three gunmen caught the boss brother alone one night as he left a bar. They forced him into a car and sped away.

As dawn uncovered the East Side tenements in Manhattan the following morning, the first rays of the September sun poked into the dingy hallway of a poor, paintless building and picked out two five-gallon alcohol cans. A trickle of red spattered their bases. It dripped from Meyer's body. The tough guy had a bullet neatly through the left ear. It had been a ride job. The police were able to pick up nothing more than that. The finger pointed to Reles, Maione and Buggsy. They were brought in. And once more a case went "out the window" against the three thugs.

The grown-up punks were the top guys now. Of course, Willie was still left, and the last of the brothers pledged himself to revenge. But little Willie did not have the tools—the "savvy," the mob instinct. The combination was too busy setting up and improving the new organization to take care of Willie, who was not considered particularly dangerous, anyway. By 1934—at the end of three futile years—Willie gave up. A week before the third anniversary of Irv's assassination, he saw his sister Rose.

"What's the use?" shrugged the little man with the high collar. "I can't make it alone. I'm out of the rackets; I'm going to forget about those bums."

It was too bad Willie waited so long before making up his mind. The very next day, Vito Gurino, joining the boys on a Brownsville corner, dropped a bit of casual information. "I just spot Willie going into a place over near Herkimer," the pistol marksman mentioned. Pittsburgh Phil always had his eye out for a chance to practice.

"Y'know, we got nothing to do right now," he pointed out. "Why don't we take him tonight and be done with it."

There was general agreement. A couple of hours later, Willie was picked up. He was dragged into the basement of a bar and grill on Rockaway Avenue that Gurino ran with Happy and Happy's brother-in-law, Joe Daddonna. (Daddonna, it might be explained, kept the memory of Brooklyn, Inc., green until the spring of 1950, when he was shot to death in an Ocean Hill saloon.)

Willie was definitely overmatched that night in 1934. There were Vito and Happy and Pittsburgh Phil and husky Dasher Abbandando. The 265-pound Gurino, alone, would have made almost two of Willie. They proceeded to give the smallest of the brothers a barbarous beating. They battered him about the head and broke his left arm and committed assorted savage mayhem.

"The bum is done for," Maione called a halt at last. Willie was trussed up by Pittsburgh Phil, the specialist with the rope, and was shoved into a laundry bag for convenience in handling. The murderers tossed the sack into the back of a car, and drove out among the sand dunes of the Canarsie Flats with it.

A resident of Canarsie was having trouble sleeping that night. He tossed and turned for hours, and finally decided that a walk among the dunes might induce elusive slumber. He was strolling along when, off to his left, he detected movement atop one of the dunes. He had to look twice to believe his eyes. Silhouetted on the hummock, four men were digging in the sand. Grown men, he knew, do not go digging in sandpiles, especially in the middle of the night.

Suddenly, one of the four lifted his head. Happy—it was he—spied the solitary witness. With only a gasped, "Somebody made us," he fled into the night. The rest were right on his heels. The witness was certain now that something was peculiar about the entire performance.

Hurrying to the spot, he kicked away at the disturbed sand. A twisted cord was uncovered. The witness took a firm hold and yanked. It did not budge. Eagerly, he set to scraping with his bare hands. Soon, he had cleared enough to see what appeared to be a large bag. He pulled the top open. It is, he explained a few moments later to the police he fled to summon, a shock to open a laundry bag buried in a sandpile and have the top of a man's head push its way out. The police quickly finished the excavating and found the battered body of Willie Shapiro, last of the racket brothers.

The killers had believed they were giving little Willie a burial after beating him to death. They had, however, overlooked one detail. The Medical Examiner found sand in Willie's lungs. Obviously, the killers had buried him alive.

The new order in Brooklyn took over with Meyer's extermination in 1931. It was an evil mob, ruthless and cunning.

Reles and his pal, Buggsy, and the kill-crazy Pittsburgh Phil ruled Brownsville and East New York—the rackets, the homicide, the protection. Maione and Abbandando and Vito Gurino conducted identical operations in Ocean Hill. It was all one combination, with, of course, the supervisory and executive guidance of Albert Anastasia. This was Brooklyn, Inc., at its formal unveiling.

Almost immediately, Louis Capone was added to the local board of directors. Actually, the restaurant keeper had been close to the Brownsville boys for some time.

"A couple of years before," Reles recalled for us, "Louis asks me to do the first job for him. Happy and him drive me to one of them little streets near Pleasant Place, over in Ocean Hill. Louis points to the house, and tells me what room this bum lives in. I go in and shoot the guy five times. One of the slugs goes in the back of his head and takes one of his eyes out. After that, I do a lot of jobs for Louis when he tells me . . . Louis was always very nice to me."

Reles explained why Anastasia put Capone into the troop's directorate. Albert, who often held business and social meetings with Joey Adonis (and continues to hold them) had noted that the Brownsville-Ocean Hill alliance was bound to end in open warfare between Reles and Happy. A strong hand, respected by both, was required to keep the two explosive commanders from each other's throat. Of course, the fact that they committed murder after murder as a team had nothing to do with personal enmity. That was business. Louis and Albert A. were early aware that these wild-eyed kids could be valuable, once their talents had proper leadership. Through Capone's diplomacy, Kid Twist and Maione, in spite of their unharmonious relationship, had even been thrown together frequently over a bowl of pasta or a plate of creamy pastry. Louis, then, was just the man to maintain the status quo. The graying restaurant owner simultaneously soothed the ruffled Reles and kept the inflammable Maione in line. He was, simply, Anastasia's front man.

Prohibition's hastening doom, which caused concern in the underworld generally, did not, oddly enough, upset the new enterprise in Brooklyn. By that time, the combination had discovered loan-sharking. "Shylocking," it is called. There was, too, extensive commerce in bookmaking and in crap games. Happy and Vito had one handbook that took in an area from Brooklyn to Union City, N. J. Another, belonging to Reles, Capone and Pittsburgh Phil, covered a territory from the Hudson River, clear across New Jersey and into Pennsylvania. Between them, they handled millions of gambling dollars annually.

Crap games sprang up on street corners and behind fences fronting vacant lots. Bigger games were run in the rear of public garages or other buildings. Wherever there was room to roll a pair of ivory cubes, there a game was opened. All were mob-sponsored. All territories were assigned.

Many lesser members could not live on what the bosses grudgingly tossed to them. So, they were granted small territories for crap games, loan-shark operations or pinball machines. Even in these scraps, the bosses were not altogether open-hearted. They insisted that the original financing for any assigned territory must come from them—at regular shylock interest.

There was also a stolen-car department, mostly for "the kids," like Dukey and Pretty. For a while, Blue Jaw Magoon was in that, too. As a matter of fact, the rugged gangster with the uncontrollable beard growth prepared for membership in Murder, Inc., by stealing cars while still a student in grade school. The most extensive stolen car operation, though, was Sholem Bernstein's. He was invaluable in procuring transportation rapidly and circumspectly, when required for use in a contract.

"I stole maybe seventy-five, a hundred cars . . . whenever I got orders," he recounted afterward. Yet, he was arrested exactly once for car theft. He pleaded guilty and drew a probationary sentence—although, when he was found in the "hot" car, three guns and two known holdup men were in it with him. Later, Sholem said, yes, they were on the way to a robbery when they were picked up. It was, he insisted, most inconvenient.

Along with its varied activities, the combination soon made labor and industry a big business. It muscled in on any side: union, management, strikers, strikebreakers. Such labor groups as the plasterers' union (in which Louis Capone and his brother were powers), the painters' union (in which several murders were done during a war in the early thirties) and the longshoremen (playtoy of Anastasia, the dock czar) felt the impact especially forcefully.

Many operators of large trucking fleets and bakers who supplied the city with its daily bread had to pay tribute. Few independent shopkeepers—from department stores to corner delicatessens— were free from protection rackets.

Shylocking, though, was the big profit-maker. The interest from gang loan-sharking can multiply money faster, almost, than a government printing press. The gang term is "the six-for-five," because the rate of repayment is six dollars for each five borrowed for one week. Before long, through Louis Capone's friends in Detroit, the combination and the Purple Mob promulgated the working agreement by which they controlled the lush interstate shylocking across half the nation.

Practically anyone, with proper identification and sponsorship, was eligible to obtain a loan, with virtually none of the red tape of normal borrowing channels. The average transaction was for six weeks; the borrower repaying eleven dollars for the use of each five. A mere 120 per cent in 42 days!

"Sometimes it's as good as 3,000 per cent," one of the shylocks once explained to a new member, just granted a small territory. "If the guy wants the dough over six weeks, he still pays the buck on every five every week . . . but he gotta get the okay to hold it over."

Neighborhood businessmen, strapped for quick cash and with

bank credit overextended, made much use of the shylocks. These better-class clients, however, were not asked to submit to the usual street-corner dealings. The mob's office for this branch was the candy store at the Corner. This hole was run by the Dapper, an agent for the boys, and his mother, who, as introduced earlier, was called Midnight Rose because the shop never closed. Midnight Rose had some interesting logic when we questioned her concerning the goings on in her sweet shop.

"Why did you allow hoodlums to hang out in your store?" she was asked.

"Why don't the police keep them out?" was her argument—a none-too-easy one to rebut, at that. "Can I help it who comes into my store?"

"Do you know Pittsburgh Phil?" inquired another questioner.

"Pittsburgh, Chicago, San Francisco . . . what do I know about them?" she demanded. "I was never out of Brooklyn in my life. All I know is I got 'syracuse' veins. I'm a sick woman."

The businessman, seeking a loan from the shylocks, would drop in at the candy store, where the Dapper was empowered to handle the transaction. This portion of the business was no small-change operation. In thirteen months, to the end of 1938, some $400,000 was handled in Midnight Rose's account alone. In his 1942 report to Governor Herbert Lehman on official corruption in Brooklyn in the thirties, Special Assistant Attorney General John Harlan Amen touched on the workings of this particular department:

"The businessman borrower would invariably be given a check for the amount of the loan, drawn on the account of Midnight Rose in the Bank of the Manhattan Company, Brownsville Branch. It was the practice of Dapper to have his mother sign blank checks and leave them in the tobacco humidor in the store.

"To get a loan, the borrower had to give the Dapper postdated checks for six successive weeks, which totaled the amount of the loan plus the illegal interest."

As each instalment fell due, one of the checks was deposited. Thus, a delinquent borrower left himself open to a charge of passing worthless checks. Delinquencies, however, were rare for a much stronger reason; slow pay would bring a "schlammin" for a reminder. "Schlammin" is pure mob-ese. It is a beating, customarily administered with a lead pipe wrapped in newspaper. It was popular in labor slugging, witness intimidating and shylock reminding—and very effective.

Shylocking and the crap games went hand in hand. It is human nature for a man who has been cleaned at a dice table to believe that his luck will change on one more roll. The shylocks made themselves available for just such emergencies.

As a boss, Reles was thoughtful—and powerful—enough to declare himself the official shylock of the State Street Crap Game. This notorious daily dice-shooting was ideally located in a building just off the busy corner of State and Court Streets in the heart of downtown Brooklyn. The accessibility was its lure. Men of prominence and reputation were always dropping in. The State Street action, as a result, was no nickel-and-dime "floating game." This was a major operation.

Kid Twist's representative was Louis Benson. They called Louis "Tiny," although he was the average five feet eight when pulled to his full height. This was rare, however, for Tiny toted 420 pounds on his frame, and hauling 420 pounds erect, shoulders back, stomach in, is a bit of a chore. They also called Tiny "the Blimp." Tiny had been a cabdriver. Reles rescued him just in time. Otherwise it might have been necessary to build the cab around him.

Each day, Tiny would report to the Kid. They would settle up accounts of the night before. Then Reles would toss his outsized operative a bundle of bills with a, "Here's the cash." Benson never carried less than $10,000 at the State Street game. The play often was rough. As a player would "tap out," Tiny would sidle over and sympathize.

"Y'know, I bet if you hung around a while, you'd get even," he would coo. "I can let you have what you need."

It rarely failed. Every dice thrower is convinced the next toss will change his luck from "snake-eyes" to "naturals."

Responsible and respected citizens lost life savings to the State Street soiree—and to the shylocks who made it so convenient. A successful druggist of the neighborhood dropped $12,000 in a year or so—mostly borrowed from Tiny Benson. A dentist went for $5,000, at the usual rate of interest. A prosperous shoe manufacturer, a clothing merchant, a liquor store proprietor—all lost large sums. They admitted it when the Law finally descended. More than one man of standing in the community went completely broke seeking diversion in this trap.

As their reputation spread, the gunmen of Brooklyn, Inc., were kept consistently busy on murder contracts for outside mobs in the Syndicate across the country. However, they never neglected their own work.

There were bound to be rash "musclers" cutting in on the business of the new organization. They had to be taught it did not pay. A labor leader would not listen to reason—the mob's reason. A mobster would want to go straight. Someone got ideas about singing to the Law. The death sentence was mandatory for all these transgressions. Actually, no one will ever know the exact number of assassinations they performed, any more than anyone will ever find the bodies of all the victims.

The system they worked up was foolproof for more than ten years. They knew the law of corroboration, these specialists—and they planned accordingly. The bosses would scatter the assignments for any contract so that the fewest possible number working on it would be aware of all the details. Those who had to know were brought in so deeply that they would be accomplices, thereby rendering their unsupported testimony of little value under New York law. The car thief procuring the stolen automobile for the getaway; the "gun man" who obtained the pistols; the triggerman, the finger who pointed out the victim, the one who delivered the contract, the wheelmen piloting the getaway car and the "crash car" . . . each was permitted to learn as little as possible of the whole. Unless there was a break from high on the inside, law enforcement had no real chance to uncover a case. It was a theory of murder by accomplice, plus intimidation.

As a matter of fact, the general membership was totally unaware that the organization had been responsible for seven of the first eight executions Reles disclosed to us. That is how fine they worked out detail. But the Kid ranked high enough to know how contracts were relayed from outside, through the boss of Brooklyn, down to the executives of the troop, like himself.

On local murder, he got down to specific cases at once, that first night, and produced immediate results. He spoke of the assassination of Spider Murtha, a neighborhood tough kid who defied the mob. In this, he brought a new member of the troop into the picture, one Max Golob. This pasty-faced plug-ugly is not often remembered on the roster of the Syndicate's Brooklyn chapter. But he was a handy man; not too smart, but willing. He had to be guided carefully or he was as likely as not to complicate a contract. The boys had tagged him "the Jerk," thereby demonstrating once again their remarkable knack for picking nicknames to fit.

"The Jerk always was a handy guy," said Reles, recommending Golob's talents. "He pulled me out of a bad hole one night."

That occasion had to do with a youngster named Rube Smith. He was the son of Joe Litvin, who had opened one of the first supermarkets in the area, and also owned a large parking lot. There came a time when Litvin apparently found himself in need of cash beyond his credit. In East New York, there was one way to get it. He went to the loan-shark "corporation."

"I want to take five thousand dollars," he requested of Reles. The Kid looked up his credit rating, and found the repayment potential excellent. The $1,000 a week shylock interest was pleasant to contemplate. He approved the loan.

Joe had, no doubt, every good intention of repaying on the due date. But the shylocks' extortionate interest frequently had the harassing habit of eating up amortization funds. That Litvin was rated a good risk was evident in the fact that Sholem Bernstein later revealed he personally tried to raise the money in his own name from a bank.

"I wanted to get it to make good for Joe with the shylocks," he explained when I questioned him. The hope—and the loan application—fell through, though.

With Reles' agents pressing, Litvin, it seems, decided to try a bit of special financing. "Even though he owes me," related Reles, "he goes to Pittsburgh Phil for more, without telling him. Then he sees Midnight Rose, too."

Kid Twist was irked. On the night of October 17, 1939, he and the Jerk piled into a car and Pittsburgh Phil's brother, Alex, drove them to the corner near Joe's parking lot.

Joe's son, Rube, who was on duty that night, had chosen that particular moment to step over to the eatery close by for a cup of coffee. Reles and the Jerk stealthily moved in among the orderly rows of cars. They snapped open long, sharp-bladed knives. Each took an aisle, and they set to work ripping at the hundreds of tires. The Kid figured the resultant embarrassment would cause Joe to see the light about double financing.

Returning from his brief repast, Rube Smith took a routine turn about the lot. In the dark, he almost stumbled over a bent figure, intent on sabotage and unaware that the guardian of the automobiles was at hand.

"What the hell is going on?" cried Smith. His answer, from Reles, was a blow at his face. They wrestled desperately in the dark.

"I was having a helluva time with him," Reles recalled. In the next aisle, however, the Jerk sensed that the scuffling indicated all was not well.

"The Jerk jumps in to help me out," concluded the Kid, "and it is all over in a minute."

The finishing touches were applied with the very knife that had been chopping tires only a moment before.

"The Jerk is a good man," Reles repeated his recommendation.

If Reles was uncertain at all about any background detail, as he continued spouting of the combination and the Syndicate, it was only in names. He could recite the entire story, from plot to icepick, of erasures in which he had a hand—except that in a number of cases, he did not know the name of a man whose life he had taken. "Names don't mean nothing," he said with a shrug. Generally, the vagueness on identity was on a contract handed him by his boss. There was, therefore, no reason for him to have known the victim well enough to call him by his first name—or be able to spell his second.

Nevertheless, sooner or later we managed to identify each and every corpse he brought up—by both first and last name—even though the slaying was anywhere from four months to ten years or more old. You couldn't miss, in fact, with all the details he provided of how these master murderers mapped out a contract with the minute pains of a D-day landing. They even held full-dress rehearsals on killings. The only item missing would be the victim. On one job, the complete operation was rehearsed for two straight days. On another, the "wheelman" had to drive the entire getaway route eight times to assure his familiarity with it. It was only natural, then, that word of these perfectionists spread far through the underworld.

"That," said Reles smugly, "is how we got to be a big outfit . . . handling the contracts for the Syndicate."

He left Brooklyn now, and turned to these outside contracts. The first stop was in New Jersey, and the Kid hadn't spoken three minutes, before he threw the profound findings of a federal, state and local investigation into a complete state of confusion.

For five years, the much-publicized murder of Dutch Schultz, the beer baron and numbers king, had been officially listed as reprisal by a vengeful gang rival for some of the treachery which made the insane Dutchman infamous. That, said Kid Twist, "is cockeyed."

6. The almost-assassination of Thomas E. Dewey

Dutch Schultz beats a rap—gangdom and politics hookup in New York's most shocking killing—proud father and son "case" a prosecutor for murder—Dutch defies the Syndicate—Dewey is 36 hours from death—shooting match in the chophouse—ultra vires: a point of law beats the kangaroo court.

No ONE expected Dutch Schultz was ever coming back when he took off running at the start of 1933, about a step and a half in front of the Internal Revenue men.

The Dutchman had tried everything, before he took flight. No amount of pressure from his political connections, however, had been able to soften Uncle Sam. After all, Schultz's income then was something more than just loose change. His return from beer alone, from 1929 through 1931, was a matter of $481,000, with all overhead paid. Then there were such other remunerative grabs as the protection racket and the numbers.

Even Dutch's sincerest supporters could see only certain conviction and a long stretch as guest of the government, if he so much as poked his face out of his hole. Gangland didn't especially care. When the boss mobsters voted the national Syndicate into existence in 1934, the absent Dutch was not wanted. He was isolationist—antagonistic to the new aim toward amalgamation. The bosses knew that, at heart, he was a mad dog whose maniacal outbursts and twitching trigger finger would get everyone associated with him into serious trouble sooner or later.

For most of his thirty-three years, he had been that way—this hoodlum scion of a Bronx saloonkeeper and a pious, patient woman whose great grief it was that the son she adored turned out as he did. Born Arthur Flegenheimer, he had a brief exposure

128

to education in P. S. 12, where the principal was Dr. J. H. Condon, who was to achieve international notoriety as the "Jafsie" ransom man of the Lindbergh baby kidnaping.

At seventeen, Arthur was already serving fifteen months for burglary. When he emerged, his playmates nicknamed him Dutch Schultz, after an infamous member of the old Frog Hollow Gang of the Bronx. He began to put together a gang of his own. Notable among his early hired hands was Joey Rao, a character who is prominent to this day in assorted affairs in New York, not the least of which is politics.

Rao's police record goes back to 1920. It includes sixteen arrests, and convictions for burglary and felonious assault. Once, while spending some time in New York City's House of Correction on Welfare Island, Rao was the "prisoner boss," handling matters such as kangaroo justice and distribution of assorted drugs. Since his earlier days, he has been tied up with the uptown end of Unione.

At present, Rao remains under $40,000 bail as a material witness in one of the most shocking murders in New York history—the savage slaying of Joseph Scottoriggio, a Republican election captain. Scottoriggio was beaten to death in broad daylight on a lower Harlem Street on election morning in 1946. He had been especially active in combatting Vito Marcantonio, whose long run as a pro-Communist Congressman was finally brought to an end in the 1950 elections—to the regret of practically no one at all.

New York District Attorney Frank S. Hogan had Rao placed under bond, he explained, because "this notorious racketeer" attended a meeting at the home of one Trigger Mike Coppola the night before the murder. At that conclave, the prosecutor said, "the fate of" Scottoriggio was discussed.

In recent years, Rao suddenly has acquired entrée to many and unexpected places. In November of 1950, a probe of politico-crime tie-ups was launched in New York, after Samuel Kantor, a district leader, charged that "underworld characters are exerting influence on City Hall." Almost the first names to pop up were Joey Rao and his brother-in-law, Joe Stracci, who is more notorious as Joe Stretch.

The probe uncovered a drive by Tammany Hall to oust former

General Sessions Court Judge Francis X. Mancuso from his post as Democratic leader of the 16th Assembly District. For this purpose, a meeting of election captains, district leaders and officials of prominence in Tammany Hall and in the city government, was held next door to Rao's home in East Harlem. The District Attorney described the meeting as a "gangster-controlled" political session. He said that Rao and Stretch showed up at the meeting and "laid down the law in strong-arm language."

"The presence of Rao and Stracci," declared Hogan, "had the same effect as if they had leveled a gun at the heads of the persons at the meeting."

Rao's explanation was novel, anyway. "I went over and looked into the house because I thought it was a crap game," he reported innocently. "It was a political meeting. So, I ain't interested . . . I go home."

For Dutch Schultz, back in the late twenties and early thirties, Rao advanced to the post of manager of Harlem for slot machines. Dutch had aligned himself with the leading moguls of the one-armed bandits—Dandy Phil Kastel, the bucket-shop impresario, and Phil's boss, Frank Costello.

As repeal neared, Schultz moved into the restaurant racket, snatched control of a window cleaners' union and grabbed the $20,000,000 numbers racket in Harlem. The profit in a single numbers bank ran as high as $4,000 in one week. He had a stable of prize fighters; raced his own horses and owned pieces of various night clubs. His gang of gunmen was the envy of mobdom.

When it came to principle, Dutch hit new lows, even for a mobster. He was a cheating guy always. His beer was the worst. His liquor was cut horribly. Even the 1,000-to-1 odds against the player in the numbers game didn't satisfy him. He hired Abbadabba Berman, a mathematical wizard, to make it absolutely foolproof—for Schultz. The daily winning number was based on the total of mutuel odds at certain race tracks, such as Coney Island, in Cincinnati, and Tropical Park, in Florida, both racket-controlled then, and the New Orleans track, in which Mayor Robert Maestri, who was Huey Long's political heir, had more than a passing interest. Abbadabba was a human comptometer, and was able to rig the final odds so that it would bring out the most lightly played policy number for that day. It mulcted the players of millions.

Now, there has always been a suspicion that something more than just the insane Schultz violence was behind his omission from the national Syndicate. Dutch's comparatively new restaurant racket, which had mushroomed into a $2,000,000 annual extortion, caught the eye of Lepke—an eye easily caught by profitable "gimmicks" in industrial extortion. With the explosive hoodlum left out of the cartel, Lepke could embrace this racket without violating Syndicate law against muscling. He simply moved in and took over while Schultz was in flight. Nor was Lepke the only one who made hay while the Dutchman had his back turned. Charley Lucky's Unione did the same with a major portion of the lush Harlem numbers banks Dutch had developed.

"He won't be back, anyway," was the gangland excuse.

The bosses also summoned Bo Weinberg, whom Dutch had named acting commander-in-chief of his crack cadre of killers.

"You deliver the mob to us, and we'll take care of you," they suggested persuasively. "The Dutchman ain't coming back, ever."

Bo was not only a good gunman; he was an adroit businessman. There would be little percentage in holding out for something as nebulous as the return of Schultz. Nor did it smack of sharp business to buck the Syndicate. The moguls just reached out and took what they wanted, anyway. Bo made a wholesale delivery of the troop. The torpedoes were adopted en masse, and spread among the Syndicate's various subsidiary branches. The annexation of the Schultz empire was then complete.

And then—Dutch beat the rap!

From the moment he had started his flight, his former associates had buried the Dutchman. The interment turned out now to have been grossly exaggerated.

For a while it had looked very bad. However, with Dutch safely out of sight, his lawyers had continued plugging away. Their chief goal was to defeat the government's demand to try him (as, if and when he exposed himself) in Metropolitan New York, where his reputation and record would be a serious handicap with any jury.

In spite of the government's determined efforts, the attorneys finally succeeded in winning a change of venue. When he came out of hiding, the trial would be taken upstate, to Syracuse, where Dutch Schultz was a name known only through the newspapers.

With that guarantee, the Dutchman emerged after eighteen months under cover. Out on bail pending trial, the conniving mobster moved into Syracuse early, and craftily set out to achieve a notoriety completely new and different from that to which he was accustomed. He did a great deal of socializing with the townsfolk. He took up charity—making sure that word of his noble gestures reached the newspapers, so the citizens who might serve on the jury would be apprised of what a lovely fellow he really was. The result was that, when the trial was held, Schultz escaped, temporarily anyway, on a hung jury—a disagreement.

Much to his satisfaction, and his lawyer's efforts, the retrial was moved even farther upstate—to the tiny border town of Malone, N. Y. Once more, Schultz arrived early, and slyly plotted his "defense." He spent money all around the place. He sent gifts to hospitalized children. He entertained expansively and expensively. He was, as a result, thought of most sympathetically among the citizenry of Malone. And the jury acquitted him. It drew a blistering denunciation from Judge Frederick Bryant.

"The verdict was dictated by other considerations than the evidence," the jurist charged.

Dutch dropped out of the clouds on the mob. No one, however, was particularly perturbed. The Syndicate was a going concern by then. New York still had a number of embarrassing matters to take up with him. So, the Dutchman had to settle in Newark, N. J. He called in Bo Weinberg immediately, and demanded an accounting of his staff.

Bo was forthright and no longer in awe at talking up to the boss. He advised his deposed employer it would not be healthy to try a comeback in the New York rackets. Perhaps he was too blunt. At any rate, that turned out to be Bo's last recorded appearance. The better gangland society has always maintained, over its teacups, that he got a gift of a cement overcoat shortly thereafter, and that he is still wearing it—on the bottom of the East River.

It was soon clear to the Dutchman that, during his vacation, a new era in gangdom had risen, based on an organized, concretely knit front. No single mob could crack it. Schultz could no more blast this efficient system out of his way than he could recoup the empire it had purloined from him. As touchy a torpedo as he was, Dutch still was not sufficiently bereft of his reason to try it. There was enough room left, anyway, for him to maneuver. He was able to save some of his numbers, and he managed to dig up assorted action in New Jersey without drawing rude stares from Longy Zwillman.

He had no particular financial worries, anyway. Dutch's personal bankroll was estimated in the millions—sometimes as high as seven million dollars.

Early in 1935, a Manhattan grand jury was investigating the numbers racket in New York, when some shenanigans began to take place.

An assistant District Attorney had been presenting the evidence —and doing an excellent job that was rapidly nearing indictments against "important" people. Suddenly, the assistant D. A. was called off the case. In his place, the District Attorney, personally, appeared. At once the investigation began to sag badly. The District Attorney then was William C. Dodge. Later, it was to be revealed that Dodge's election campaign had enjoyed contributions of some $30,000 from Dutch Schultz's organization.

The grand jury took the bit in its teeth. It demanded removal of the District Attorney from the investigation on the ground that he was not supplying the evidence it wanted. It became, in fact, one of the few "runaway" grand juries in New York history. (Grand jurors rarely realize they have the power to order before them any witnesses they wish to hear and to pursue any inquiry they deem necessary. Both the District Attorney and the court are subservient to the grand jury. Actually, a "runaway" jury is nothing more than a jury aware of its authority—especially when a prosecutor is unaware of his obligations.)

The grand jury that ran away in 1935 demanded that Dodge be superseded by a special prosecutor who would really dig into the rackets. The suggestion was made that the appointment go to a young lawyer named Thomas E. Dewey, who had compiled a hard-hitting record in the Federal Attorney's office. Immediately there were indications that Dewey would not be welcomed in certain quarters. The newspapers, however, picked up the jury's demands, and Governor Herbert Lehman designated Dewey, in a wide-sweeping mandate, to delve into the rackets in New York City.

Excitable even when normal, Dutch blew up completely at this. He got his current lawyer on the telephone.

"Hey, mouthpiece," he bellowed, "what does the word nemesis mean?"

"Why, Arthur," replied the attorney, who insisted on complete formality with his client at all times, "it means a hoodoo, a jinx."

"Just what I thought." Schultz nodded dolefully as he hung up.

It affected him most morbidly. Night after night, he wept in his cups about it.

"That Dewey," he would moan. "He is my nemesis."

Dutch had something there, at that. As an assistant Federal Attorney, Dewey had obtained the indictment for income-tax evasion which had started all of Schultz's woes. Now the same Dewey was looking into the numbers, which was one of the very few lines of business Dutch had left. For many days, The Dutchman brooded. The mad dog began to froth; the nemesis became an obsession. One night, it got him.

"Dewey's gotta go," Schultz slammed the table and screamed. "He has gotta be hit in the head."

In the old days, such a pronunciamento would have had an official ring to it. Now, though, it was no longer the ultimatum of the Boss with one hundred of the top triggermen of the era to back his play. Now he was just one gangster—and at the fringe of the cartel, at that. However, Dutch was not the only mobster who wanted Dewey removed. Others—accredited members of the Syndicate—felt his elimination was called for; but for business, rather than personal reasons. That made it a subject for the board of governors, like any murder matter involving inter-mob affairs. A meeting was called in New York to consider the case. Schultz was so beside himself that he slipped over from his home base in Newark, despite the standing order for his arrest on sight if he ever set foot in Manhattan. Although not part of the cartel, he was permitted to sit in as an interested party in a similar line of business.

Following protocol and procedure very carefully, the new democratic order limited discussion to the question of whether Dewey should be stopped and if so, the extent of the stopping. This was not a meeting held in desperation or dread. The bosses sat down as coolly and methodically as any board of directors considering important business policy. These ganglords had seen investigations come and go. No one was panicky. In fact, no one—except Schultz—was even very excited. Everyone had his say.

There was no unanimity of judgment at the conclave. The division of opinion ranged from outright assassination of the prosecutor as the sound means of ending the investigation, all the way to, "forget about him." The discussion dragged on. Finally, some of the wiser heads felt more time should be taken to weigh so important a problem. After all, murdering a prosecutor was not just any mob job. Eventually, in order to allow for profound thought, it was decided to adjourn for one week, and meet again.

"But suppose next week we vote to take him?" interposed the single-track-minded Dutchman. "We should be ready to do the job quick."

That was logical. It would be wise to blueprint in advance the mechanical details of so delicate a matter, in the event the ultimate decision favored assassination. The directorate agreed to have Dewey cased between sessions. His movements, his comings and his goings (and his stops) were to be thoroughly checked and clocked. All necessary details for the execution were to be prepared. It was Murder, Inc.'s, customary painstaking and studied preparation, by which risks of failure due to carelessness were eliminated.

Obviously, this assignment would require utmost subtlety and finesse. The job was, in fact, so top priority that no less an individual than Albert Anastasia, czar of the Brooklyn waterfront and boss of the Syndicate's newly added death squad, was proposed as the ideal man to do the casing and take charge of preparatory details, such as the getaway car and murder weapons. No one opposed the nomination. It was an important piece of work and required an important man. Albert A. was important enough to be officially described as "the overlord of organized crime" in Brooklyn.

In those days, Dewey never moved without his two bodyguards. The caser would have to be especially adroit to avoid attaching suspicion to himself. Someone got the idea for the perfect subterfuge. A child was borrowed from a friend to accompany the caser. What could be less sinister than a devoted father romping with his offspring?

For four straight mornings, this "proud parent," with his decoy child pedaling a velocipede, took up an innocent stand in front of Dewey's apartment building. Each morning, they were already there when the prosecutor and his guards emerged. It must have been a fine show of parental devotion to Dewey and his companions—this man willing to rise early enough to spend a bit of time with his heir before heading off for the daily toil.

For the inoffensive "father," the setup was ideal. Given four mornings of uninterrupted observation, he noted that Dewey's daily routine followed a pattern. The prosecutor and his guards left the apartment at practically the same minute each day. They headed for the same drugstore a couple of blocks away. There, the guards took up a stand outside the door, while Dewey went inside. He remained for several minutes, then reappeared, and the trio would be off.

The pharmacist could hardly be suspicious of the proud parent and his child who dropped in on two different mornings just after Mr. Dewey left. The man was very disarming; seemed interested, mostly, in seeing that the tot did not ride his tricycle into a floor display of beauty soap. It was no trouble for the man to learn that the prosecutor's regular stop in the drugstore was to make the first phone call to his office each day. Later, when someone mentioned it, Dewey recalled that morning call.

"I did not want to disturb Mrs. Dewey by using the phone in our room at the apartment so early," he explained. Besides, it was very likely that his home phone was tapped, once his probe began.

By the fourth morning, the caser felt he had established that Dewey's actions were regular habit. The prosecutor could be counted on to do the same thing every day. Meantime, the other necessary details were being handled with the same efficiency.

From a public garage, the Brownsville troop stole a black four-door sedan, especially selected for inconspicuous color and high-speed power. This would be the getaway car for the killer, if the decision was to proceed with the assassination. The car was stored carefully away in a prepared "drop," to remain under cover until needed. License plates were stolen from another car, and transferred to the "hot" or stolen vehicle, completing the almost impenetrable disguise. Guns for the job were secured by rifling one of a number of crates of weapons, waiting on a pier for shipment to some European government. Even if their absence were eventually noted—which was unlikely—it would be months, and thousands of miles away.

Not even that insurance satisfied the combination's sticklers, however. The guns were also specially treated. The usual precaution against tracing a pistol is to file off the numbers. Crime-fighting science has discovered, though, that the metal beneath the number on a weapon is compressed when the numerals are stamped in. Thus, when the number is simply filed away, an application of acid—nitric, hydrochloric or glycerine—will bring out the ghostlike imprint of the figures. The Brooklyn hoods, well aware of this, had a gunsmith who could circumvent it. He merely gouged out the metal completely—and an acid bath produced nothing but blank steel. Finally, the business end of each weapon was threaded so that silencers could be attached. With that flourish, everything was ready to carry out the mandate, if the decision of the adjourned meeting of the board of governors dictated the assassination of Dewey.

The report of the "caser" showed exactly how it would be done. On the day selected, the gunman would get to the drugstore a few minutes before the regular time for Dewey's arrival. He would be inside and waiting and the bodyguards, who always remained outside, would not know there was a stranger even in the neighborhood. Keeping his back to Dewey, the triggerman would be "buying" a tube of toothpaste or a box of cornplasters, or something, until the prosecutor went into the phone booth, as usual.

"Dewey'll be a sitting duck in there," it was pointed out.

Out would come the gun—equipped with silencer. That was a must. The flat crack of the silencer would never carry enough to be audible to the guards through the closed door of the store, above the street noises. The assassin would turn and blast Dewey, cornered there in the booth. The druggist would be drilled where he stood, behind the counter. There would be no outcry, no sound of gunfire, no alarm—and no identification later.

Having completed the contract, the killer would ease out. The guards, having heard nothing, would barely look his way as he ambled past. Casually, he would turn the corner to the waiting getaway car, which he would abandon with the untraceable guns wherever convenient. Before the bodyguards grew perturbed enough to investigate, there would be ample time for a smooth, easy disappearance.

All of this was before the board of governors as the adjourned meeting opened. Dutch Schultz was on hand again, as anxious as ever for the elimination of his nemesis. The debate was resumed. However, this time the Syndicate's cooler heads dominated. The new-order mob moguls balanced the necessity for any killing against the consequences it might stir up. Besides, Lepke and Lucky were firmly convinced they knew the technique with which to meet the danger that threatened.

"All investigations collapse when no witnesses are around," argued the czar of industrial extortion. Lepke always maintained the same philosophy. He had learned it through probe after probe that had died slow deaths in the past.

"We are bombproof when all the right people are out of the way," he pointed out. "We get them out of the way now—then this investigation collapses, too."

Lepke's logic was deadly. Under our system of jurisprudence, witnesses before a grand jury must make out a prima facie case of crime before law enforcement can secure an indictment. Without the essential witnesses, a prosecutor cannot muster such a case.

The other directors of crime respected Lepke's judgment. His record was excellent. On the basis of his "success" alone, he must have the right answers.

"Besides," both he and Lucky propounded another powerful point, "the best Dewey can do is try to go after the New York rackets; he can't touch anything outside of New York."

No one in the Syndicate could ignore as particularly pertinent a

consideration as that. Dewey was bound to Manhattan by jurisdictional limits. The take from the New York rackets was important, but it was a drop compared to the businesses the cartel
was operating across the nation. And assassinating a prosecutor
would stir up such righteous indignation throughout the country
that it could very well dam up the financial flood from the lucrative rackets in all other places.

"If we knock him off," cautioned another of the ganglords in
support of this view, "even the Federals will jump on the rackets.
We'll be chased out of the country."

The proposed assassination, then, was potentially disastrous
enough to blow up the entire national empire of crime. Sacrificing
the whole chain-store system to halt an as yet embryo threat solely
against New York was not sound business. That was the main
concern of the directors: good business. They saw the light.
Lepke's sage and forceful persuasion, backed by Lucky, won out.
They took a vote, and the directors decided to permit Dewey to
live.

The decision was not unanimous. Dutch Schultz did not approve. Nor did Gurrah, Lepke's snarling partner. This might have
been expected. Of the entire group, these were the two strong-
arms famed for doing most of their thinking with their muscles.
All the rest, however, turned thumbs down on the idea of murdering the special prosecutor. They were not inspired by any humani-
tarian motives. The executives of national crime spared Dewey's
life solely for the sake of—national crime.

Dutch Schultz was of that era and ilk of power-mad paranoics
so pampered and fawned upon by favor-seeking punks that they
came to believe their orders were royal decrees· and their wishes
ordained commandments.

Dutch was neither satisfied nor happy with the edict sparing
Dewey's life. He made no secret about it.

"I still say he ought to be hit," the mad dog barked defiance. "And if nobody else is gonna do it, I'm gonna hit him
myself."

Anyway, he contemplated, it would be a shame to waste all
that valuable data gathered by the "proud parent."

"That drugstore phone booth is a natural," thought the outlaw hoodlum, beaming. So, in defiance of the board of governors, Schultz set out to murder Dewey on his own—using the very scheme the board had discarded. It looked foolproof.

Dutch Schultz was a blowhard. Like all blowhards, he talked too much. He couldn't keep this one to himself. To an associate, he whispered that he was not only going to do it—but he even said when. He boasted that he was going to get the big rackets-buster in forty-eight hours!

No such startling undertaking could be kept off the grapevine for long. Anyone who heard such a whisper must realize it was guilty knowledge, much too hot to keep. In short order, the Syndicate buzzed with the report that the Dutchman was going to "take" Dewey on his own. The ganglords were shocked—not so much at the assassination plot as at the defi.

"That Dutchman is just daffy enough to do it, too," Lepke warned the others. "This is no good."

Obviously, Schultz's insane plot would bring on the cartel the entire heat of the Law that the leaders had always avoided. It would wreck the rackets and launch the biggest war on crime in history. Or, as one informer told us:

"They got scared that rubbing out Dewey would hit them where it hurt the most—in their pocketbooks."

Having ordained that Dewey should live, the chiefs of crime now had to insure his life. And since Dutch was rushing the demise of his nemesis, the insuring would have to be done in a hurry. The fact that Schultz was plotting to defy Syndicate decree for personal reasons made this a matter of prime importance. It was especially significant in that this was the first real challenge to and test of Syndicate law.

The directors discussed it—and ruled that the Dutchman himself must die to guarantee Dewey's life. The mob actually ordained that it would rub out a mobster—to save a prosecutor!

Schultz was a veteran of gang gun fights, tough to corner. Over in Newark, his guard was always up. For public appearances, his favorite spot was the Palace Chophouse in downtown Newark, and things were so arranged there that he could transact business and social obligations in a sort of back room niche, easily guarded at its one entrance.

This was a special job; it would take special men. Without a word of palaver on personnel, each of the bosses immediately picked, mentally, the exact men called for. Lepke had two operatives on his staff made to order for it. Lepke knew it, too. He designated both for this all-important mission—Charlie the Bug Workman, one of gangland's most deadly executioners, and Mendy Weiss, a hulking, snarling murderer with a touch of directional ability.

Mendy was a strangler and a strong-arm veteran of the labor wars. He was an operational boss on Lepke's staff—although perhaps not quite as important as he liked to have others believe. He fancied getups like one flashy all-green outfit that practically blinded an entire courtroom one day. It was Mendy who reveled as acting boss when Lepke was in hiding in 1939, and ordered murder done as far away as California.

Bug Workman, one of the most valuable gunmen in the entire underworld, was a curly-haired completely casual killer, customtailored from head to foot. Because of his ability at assassination, his place in gangdom was high, for a gunman. Although not a member of the directorate, he sat in council chamber with the executives and did only important work for the boss. Detectives called him the Powerhouse. When it came to doing a job of slaying, gang style, the Bug was practically a mob all by himself.

"A guy has to be a bug to do what Charlie does," his admiring gunmates used to say, shaking their heads in awe over the score of contracts he had handled.

For the Dutch Schultz expedition, a third party would be needed, someone who knew his way around Newark to pilot the getaway car for the two New Yorkers. The story is that this third man was supplied by the Jersey mob, and was especially familiar with the best routes. He is identified to this day only as Piggy; there are, however, suspicions as to who he is.

On the night of October 23, 1935, one of the hundreds of cars rolling through the Holland Tunnel, outbound from New York, was an inconspicuous black sedan, carrying three inconspicuous-appearing men. Their talk was equally inconspicuous, idle chatter of fights and baseball and maybe a bit of politics, like any three men thrown together in an automobile.

Their mission, however, was not so innocuous. They were on their way to beat a deadline—on assassination. Dutch Schultz was just thirty-six hours away from murdering Thomas E. Dewey, special rackets prosecutor, and the trio had strict orders from the overlords of the underworld to stop the Dutchman—for keeps!

The car slid swiftly through the aromas from the slaughter-houses and glue works which make automobiling across the Jersey meadows more comfortable with the windows rolled up, even on hot days. In Newark, Piggy, the driver, found the Palace Chop-house easily enough. They pulled up in front of the place not long after ten o'clock.

Mendy was designated as "cover" for the getaway. He stayed at the door. Piggy, as wheelman, remained in the car, ready to pull away. Charlie the Bug barged right into the place.

There was a bar in the long front room, and beyond it this sort of back-room niche, which the Dutchman used as a combination office and cozy nook. The "finger" had reported that Dutch would be there that night.

The Bug strolled the length of the bar, breezily and completely carefree, like a man on his way to the free-lunch counter in the better days. Just off the end of the bar was the men's room. Workman flipped open the door to it. Even the bold Bug would not overlook an uncovered quarter, from which a flanking attack might be launched. Inside, a fellow, his back to the door, was washing his hands. Something about him looked familiar.

"One of the bodyguards, I guess," thought Workman. And he pulled out his pistol and fired. The handwasher toppled without even turning off the faucet.

The Bug, gun ready, now advanced on the boys in the back room. The bar had emptied in a hurry. The bartender, with admirable presence of mind, disappeared behind the mahogany. A World War I veteran, he knew the advantages of defilade under fire.

In the rear room sat three Schultz aides. A business meeting had been in progress. Before them, papers were piled on the table

—apparently the monthly accounting of Dutch's enterprises. One strip of adding-machine tape carried a long list of figures, among them entries of $313,711.99 and $236,295.95. Obviously, the Dutchman had reorganized well. The three lieutenants, however, were no longer interested in financial statements. As Workman appeared, they opened fire. The Bug fired back. He kept banging away, and pretty soon, Lulu Rosenkrantz, who was Dutch's chauffeur and bodyguard, and Ab (Misfit) Landau, one of his torpedoes, and Abbadabba Berman, the human comptometer who fixed the daily number, were all dead.

Workman was troubled, though, as he retired once more to the empty bar. The word had been that Dutch was to be there. The Bug had not seen Schultz. And there was no one else in sight.

"Funny," thought the Bug. "The Dutchman ought to be around. I got to take him."

Then, it dawned on him:

"Why, sure . . . that guy in the toilet. No wonder he looked familiar."

He was right. The man in the men's room had been Dutch Schultz. The first to go had been the mob magnate whose extermination the Syndicate had ordered to save the life of a law-enforcement officer. Almost simultaneously with the realization, a recollection hit Charlie the Bug of an incident in the Dutchman's life which is legend among New York's police. One June night in 1931, Dutch and his torpedo, Danny Iamascia, had just slipped out of Schultz's hideout on upper Fifth Avenue when they noted two vague figures detach themselves from the shadow of a building across the street.

"The Mick," snapped Schultz in warning, presuming they were representatives of his sworn enemy, Vincent Coll, the maddest mobster New York ever saw. Dutch and Danny went for their guns. The two figures made no threatening move, though, until the hoodlum and his stooge started shooting. For, the two figures were not the Mad Mick's men. They were Detectives Julius Salke and Steve DiRosa. The battle did not last long. Detective Salke put a bullet through Iamascia. Dutch, seeing his triggerman fall, threw his own gun away and started running. Detective DiRosa could have shot him right then. Instead, he took off after the speeding

Schultz, caught him in a matter of yards and dropped him with a superb bit of tackling, that would undoubtedly have warmed the heart of George Halas, who coaches Chicago's mighty professional football Bears.

The police legend is that Dutch reached into his pocket after his arrest, brought out all the cash he had on him and offered it as a bribe for his release. And all the cash he had on him was a mere $18,600! The officer was so incensed at the bribe attempt, the legend runs, that he roared, "You miserable bum, I'll shove that dough down your throat." And, the legend concludes, the officer had the Dutchman down and had one end of this king-size roll of bills in the Dutchman's mouth, and was doing just that, when a fellow officer persuaded him it was not a nice way to treat money.

All of this ran through Charlie the Bug's mind as he stood in the middle of that Newark saloon that night in 1935, with Dutch on the toilet floor, mortally wounded. Now it may have dawned on him that all the pistol-popping was going to bring a lot of curious policemen rapidly. But the threat was not nearly strong enough to outweigh the possibility—and the hope—that maybe lightning could strike twice in the same place. Back into the gents' room barged the Bug, and he gave Dutch's pockets a thorough and total frisk. He never mentioned to anyone afterward whether it proved worth while.

Mendy was supposed to be at the door of the chophouse covering the getaway when Charlie the Bug started out, leaving Dutch Schultz and his trio of hired hands fatally wounded. But Mendy was not there.

The Bug did not think that was right. Suppose he had needed cover for his escape. Outside, there was no Piggy at the wheel of the getaway car, either. In fact, there was no getaway car. And right then was neither the time nor the place to be on foot in Newark, in the vicinity of the Palace Chophouse.

The hue and cry was going up all over the neighborhood by now—and no wonder, with all that gunfire. The Bug could see any number of curious citizens bearing down rapidly, from all directions. He slid into an alley, and from there he had to dash across back yards, slip through vacant lots and leap over fences, before he finally made his getaway back to New York. Those guys, he pondered in annoyance, must have run out on him. What irked the Bug was that they had taken the car with them. Not only did he have to run practically all the way home, but it had made him late for a date, besides. Charlie the Bug was fit to be tied.

The incident raised hob in the underworld. Mendy and Piggy had a lot of explaining to do—especially Mendy, because he was a staff gunman. Under the Syndicate's law, abandoning a post and a mobmate, while on organization business, is fatal. Not even the fact that he was a trusted lieutenant of the mighty Lepke could ease Mendy out of this one. Unless he had a perfect explanation, the bull-shouldered strangler would have to stand trial before the kangaroo court.

The supreme court of crime was made ready for Mendy. The mere fact that he was not there when the Bug came out of the chophouse made it an open-and-shut case. The situation looked bad. Mendy foresaw his danger, and immediately reported his side to his boss, in a desperate move to avoid a trial. Surprisingly, he maintained that he had definitely remained at his post until the contract was all finished. The bulky badman admitted he wasn't at the chophouse door when Workman finally came through it. That, however, was no contradiction, he held.

"I claim," Mendy concluded, "that hitting the Dutchman was mob business, and I stayed there till it was over. But then the Bug went back in the toilet to give the Dutchman a 'heist.' I claim that was not mob business any more—that was personal business."

That being the case, Mendy maintained, he had a perfect right to depart forthwith, before the Law arrived, and to take Piggy and the getaway car with him. On a point of law, the Bug's act was simply *ultra vires*—it was not in furtherance of the purposes for which the corporate mission was organized.

There was no argument against such logic. Not even the Bug would dispute the point. Mendy was discharged without even standing trial.

Dutch Schultz did not bow out immediately the night Bug Workman blew a big hole in him with his .45.

The dying Dutchman lingered, in fact, for close to twenty-four hours, with Police Stenographer John Long glued to his bedside in a Newark hospital, shorthanding his every gasp, and Police Sergeant Luke Conlon asking him questions in his few conscious moments. Mostly, though, it was delirious babbling, interspersed with an occasional lucid word or phrase or paragraph, as Schultz struggled for life. For only about two hours, on the afternoon following the shooting, did any of his garbled ramblings have any coherency at all.

Apparently the violent gangster never knew what hit him, there in the men's room of the saloon. At least, that was the impression he left in the brief chances Sergeant Conlon had to put any questions to him through his coma.

Q—What did they shoot you for?
A—I don't know, sir . . . honest . . . I don't even know who was with me, honestly . . . I went to the toilet . . . I was in the toilet. When I reached the can, the boy came at me.
Q—The big fellow gave it to you?
A—Yes . . . he gave it to me.
Q—Do you know who this big fellow was?
A—No.

Once, in reply to another query about who shot him, the writhing hoodlum groaned:
"The boss himself."

Both FBI agents and police investigators grabbed at the babbled phrase as pointing directly to Lucky Luciano. Wasn't Lucky head of Unione Siciliano, they reasoned? Wasn't the head of Unione always known as the Boss?

Later, The Dutchman brought in another name, and sent the investigators off on another tangent:

Q—What did the big fellow shoot you for?
A—Him . . . John? . . . Over a million—five million dollars.

"John," FBI and police figured, could be Johnny Torrio, the sharp little gangster who had turned Chicago over to Al Capone. No one knew then, of course, that he had given gangland the recipe for national organization. In fact, no one even dreamed a national organization existed. But they did know that in underworld stature, John was a "big fellow." As for the "five million dollars," that probably was Dutch's estimate of his loss through the mob's snatch of his rackets.

Mostly, Schultz just lay there gasping and raving. From his wandering snatches came few, if any, pieces to fit the puzzle.

"If we wanted to break the ring . . . no, please . . . I get a month," he stammered once, through teeth clenched with pain. And again:

"My gilt-edge stuff . . . and those dirty rats have tuned in."

And still again: "No . . . no . . . there are only ten of us and there are ten million of you fighting somewhere. . . . So get your onions up and we will throw up the truce flag."

The thread through all this was that the muscling of his rich rackets by Lepke and Lucky preyed on Schultz's distorted brain. The "I get a month" may have referred to a time limit given him by the Syndicate to clear up his business. He may have tried to get paid off—"get your onions up"—for agreeing to pull out of the rackets entirely.

Later, there was:

"Please crack down on the Chinaman's friends."

One of Dutch's bitter enemies was Charles Sherman, a Waxey Gordon strong-arm and narcotics executive known to the underworld as the Chinaman, or Chink. Schultz's "crack down" request was followed to the letter within a couple of months, incidentally. Sherman's body was found buried in quicklime on the Sullivan County (N. Y.) farm of Jack Drucker, a Brooklyn boy who was Murder, Inc.'s, Sullivan County manager for a time. It was Drucker, remember, who emerged from the car, carrying an ice pick, the night Walter Sage was stabbed to death and dropped into a lake with a slot machine tied around his neck.

Off and on during that twenty-four hours on his deathbed, Schultz stammered parts of other names that only added to the mystery.

"Now listen, Phil . . . Fun is fun . . . What happened to the other sixteen?" was one bit of incoherency. Phil, in this case, could have meant Dandy Phil Kastel, Frank Costello's general field manager (then and now), with whom Schultz had been in deals over slot machines.

He failed to mention his wife directly at any time, but at one point, a request to "get the doll a roofing" was taken as a plea to his mobmates, in his delirium, to see that she was cared for. His wife, however, never saw any of his millions. Dutch's pals and underlings, who were generally understood to be holding his money for him (since he never did trust banks), demonstrated exactly how much honor there is among thieves by making off with his fortune as soon as his trigger was no longer there to defend it.

On the other hand, there were half a dozen occasions when he cried out for "mama." Once, toward the very end, tossing with pain, he sobbed:

"Mother is the best bet . . . And don't let Satan draw you too fast."

Perhaps the quiet, churchgoing woman who tried so hard to make her son respectable could take some solace, at last, from that.

The most puzzling development of the Dutchman's last hours, however—even more puzzling than trying to make sense out of his deathbed delirium—were the antics and verbal ambulations of his twenty-one-year-old, hatcheck girl-wife, Frances.

Frances has frequently been pictured, and especially in one recently published book, as a shy, shrinking violet, brought up on that block of West Forty-seventh Street which Damon Runyon dubbed Dream Street. The romance of Frances and the cheating, conniving criminal flowered in a couple of hours one night in a restaurant on Dream Street where she was a combination hat-check-cigarette girl. Dutch came into the place and promptly went "on the make" for her. Sweet Frances would have nothing to do with this miserable plug-ugly—for at least an hour after she first set eyes on him. Then he told her he was *the* Dutch Schultz. From that moment, it was a beautiful romance.

The day after Dutch was shot, Deputy Police Chief John Haller of Newark, plunging into the investigation, thought he ought to ask her a few questions. That was only natural. Frances told him, explained the deputy chief with a mystified air, that the wedlock joining her and her mobster mate operated under a "legal contract." The usual satisfactory results were achieved evidently. The legal contract had produced two children.

Deputy Chief Haller said that, at first, Frances told him she had not been near the Palace Chophouse the night the love of her life was murdered. Then police had an employe confront her, and the employe said, sure, she was there only two hours before the fireworks.

Frances, the deputy chief stated, now did a neat verbal flip-flop. She explained that she had left Dutch two days before, had gone to New York and had stayed there until the evening of the shooting. On the murder night, she stopped in to see Dutch at the saloon about 8:30, on her return from her New York visit. She refused to tell the police official, he said, with whom she had stayed in New York for those two days and two nights, or whom she had seen there. She left the chophouse on the murder night, after visiting with Dutch for about half an hour, and she went to a nearby movie.

"I got out about eleven o'clock, and there was a crowd in front of the tavern [chophouse]," the deputy chief quoted her. "I thought it was a saloon raid, so I walked right by."

She walked to the tube station, and took a train back to New York, evidently preferring the bright lights of Manhattan, at that moment, to the company of the mobster with whom she shared such a great and abiding love that it was written about in books, like Romeo and Juliet. Reaching New York about midnight, she bought a newspaper. It was then she learned that the "saloon raid" actually had been the slaughter of her husband and his chums.

Did Frances now hurry back to Newark to be at the bedside of her mate, who was near death? Did she run—her pure little heart thumping in panic—to the nearest phone to try to learn the very latest word of his condition? Deputy Chief Haller said she told him she went in the opposite direction, to the apartment she maintained in Jackson Heights—a short subway trip to Long Island—

and she went to sleep. Some time the following afternoon, Frances finally got back to Newark.

This was all very interesting, the deputy chief agreed. It left him still wondering, however, who had fingered Dutch; who had let the mob know that he would be in the chophouse that night when the killers arrived?

Not long after Dutch Schultz ended up in the gents' room, Kid Twist Reles gave a party at his home. It was a strictly social evening—no business. (No one to be shot, slugged or strangled, that is.)

A lot of the boys were there, relaxing from the everyday toil. It was noted, though, that Charlie the Bug Workman was not getting into the swing of things as merrily as the rest, and this was surprising. As the evening wore on, the curly-haired hoodlum loosened up some. Finally, he leaned forward in his easy chair and brought his pet peeve onto the floor. He hadn't believed Mendy's excuse.

"Nice thing, huh," he was hurt and bitter. "Here I go on a job with two guys and they're supposed to be good. I do all the work. That's okay. But these two bums run out on me. You know what those bums did? . . . That Mendy and Piggy—they 'pigged' it!"

And out popped the story. It showed how worked up the Bug really was, when he got as eloquent as that. It was the costliest conversation of his life. Two of his listeners were his host, Kid Twist, and Allie Tannenbaum—who was called Tick-Tock by the mob because he talked with the easy regularity of a clock at work. Of course, the Kid, being an individual who got around in the gang, already knew many of the details from other sources.

And when the Kid began to sing for us that Good Friday night five years later, he included the story of the Dutch Schultz slaughter, and the Bug's bitter and voluble monologue at the party. Only then did the startling motive for the quadruple blood bath come out for the first time anywhere, except in the innermost sanctums of crime.

As might have been expected, the assassination of the Dutchman had stirred up all manner of furore. For five years, the possible motives advanced had almost outnumbered the suspects.

When Reles talked and the "inside" cracked, the actual reason finally leaked through gangland's forbidding silence. The mad-dog Dutchman was hit, not by a New York mob, but a national Syndicate. He was hit, not because he stood in the way of the rackets—the mob already had taken over his major operations—but simply because he insisted on murdering Dewey in defiance of this Syndicate, and the ganglords believed that would hurt their business. Only then did it come to light: Thomas E. Dewey had been within thirty-six hours of never living to be almost President of the United States and a three-time Governor of New York State!

A long time later, I related the story to Dewey. I was tremendously impressed by his obvious personal courage. Through all the details, step by step, he said not a word, gave never a sign of the slightest shock at learning he was mere hours away from certain death. But when I mentioned the baby on the velocipede—the decoy for the man casing him—Dewey's eyes widened a fraction. It was a barely perceptible flicker; hardly any motion at all. It gave me the idea, though, that he had recalled the tot—and its "proud parent."

And what ironical justice developed! Organized crime had saved Dewey's life in 1935. Four years later, Dewey dealt organized crime the most severe blow it ever had been hit up to that time. He convicted Lucky for his rackets and Lepke for industrial extortion. And Lepke and Lucky had led the campaign to save him, when Dutch wanted him murdered.

It took four more years for the touch that rounded it all out. Then, Lepke, doomed for murder in our Brooklyn probe, made one last desperate plea for executive clemency. That is a right enjoyed by every man, even a Lepke, under American justice.

Nine years before, Lepke had the life-or-death say over Thomas E. Dewey—and Lepke had said life. Now Lepke was begging for his own life for the crimes he had committed. And the man who now had the life-or-death say over Lepke was—the very same Thomas E. Dewey!

7. A war of extermination backfires

Charlie the Bug gets his—the Syndicate sets up sabotage—Defense and Lamming Fund; everybody chips in—imported triggermen hunt songbirds—"cross Joey Adonis and you cross the national combination"—fortress for bric-a-brac, and witnesses.

IT WAS roundup time in Brooklyn, once Kid Twist started talking in 1940, and the dragnet spread wide. Some of the characters had to be dug up out of their holes; some fled to the Law, in terrified realization that they were marked for murder merely because they knew too much.

Some got into the act by mistake, like little Frankie Galluccio. Back in the early twenties, there was a dance one night and Frankie took his sister to it. Another young tough guy was attracted, and made some remark to her which he should not have made. Frankie whipped out his knife, and right there, he carved his name on the records of mobdom for all time. For, the other tough guy was Al Capone, just then building up a hoodlum reputation, and that night Frankie put the scar on Scarface Al that became probably the most widely known trade-mark in the history of crime.

During those early days of the roundup, any number like Frankie popped up in the net, were held until it was clear they were not involved in the business at hand—which was organized mob murder—and then were released. Of those we retained, all had one thing in common. Each and every one knew something more about assassination than how to spell the word—even the few who could spell it.

Early in his aria, Reles broke the five-year-old Dutch Schultz mystery. As a result, Charlie the Bug Workman, who wiped out

the Dutchman's mob, and Allie Tannenbaum, who had heard the
Bug boast of it, were high on the list the District Attorney's office
was eager to entertain. True, the target area of the Schultz shooting match was not in our jurisdiction, but that was a mere technicality. It was the handiwork of the same Syndicate we had on
our hands. The Bug was the trigger in many other murders. And
Allie was present and accounted for in half a dozen executions.

Allie had gone far in the mob. The story of how this tall, dapper
individual, with the continually harassed look, had fallen in with
the thugs and become a staff specialist on Lepke's personal payroll
is an object lesson in the development of a criminal. Born in Nan-
ticoke, Pa., deep in the anthracite country, he was brought to
Brownsville as a baby. He reached the third year in high school
by the time he was sixteen—an age when most of his later co-
workers were still baffled by the mystery of grade school.

Allie's father became a hotel owner in the Catskill resort area,
and each summer Allie worked in his father's hotel, first the one
at Rock Hill and then at the more lavish Loch Sheldrake Country
Club.

"It was a big place," he described it afterward, "with a cabaret
and casino, a bar and a lake for boating or swimming." (It was
to develop that some of the bathers were not breathing when immersed.)

The Catskills are a paradise of mountains and lakes and trees,
annually attracting a cross-section of society . . . athletes, indus-
trialists, show people, politicians, the girl with an eye out for
a husband—and the criminal, as in any resort. The criminal insists he needs relaxation just like the next fellow.

About 1925, a guest at Allie's father's place was one Jake
Shapiro, a lumbering gorilla who growled orders in snarling bursts
of sound. His stock command when annoyed was, "Get out of
here," only it came out, "Gurra dahere." So, his friends took to
calling him "Gurrah." Through Gurrah, Allie became acquainted
with other visitors, like Shimmy Salles, who was a bagman, or
collection agent, for the rackets, and Curly Holtz, expert on labor
organization—and Lepke. Naturally, Gurrah did not introduce
them by trade. They spent freely in the cabaret or at the games
of chance in the casino. And they made the hotel owner's son

welcome at their parties. Allie received no salary until summer's end; he had very little money in his pocket. Any youngster with an empty purse, "adopted" by men who toss large bills around as if they were used paper napkins, can very easily be impressed. Summer after summer, they flaunted their affluence in the face of Allie's empty purse. And pretty soon, Allie was ripe.

After the season ended in 1931, he was strolling along Broadway one day, and he ran into Big Harry Schacter, one of his friends from the mountains. By that time, Allie, naturally, had more than a hazy idea of the trade in which these characters were engaged. But by then, he didn't care. Allie and Big Harry started talking.

"Do you want a job?" asked the hoodlum, coming to the point.

"I could use one, if it pays," Allie replied.

"This one is for Lepke. You know what kind of a job it will be."

Allie shrugged. What difference did it make? Besides everything else, the Great Depression was just then hitting bottom.

"Go and see Lepke at his office," Big Harry advised.

Allie began at $35 a week on "general assignments—sluggings, strikebreaking and throwing stinkbombs," he explained afterward. He was promoted to "specific assignments." He took part in half a hundred schlammins, in strong-arm strikebreaking and labor-union grabs. And he had a hand in six murder contracts, from New York to California, and helped dispose of the body of a seventh. As evidence that his work was eminently satisfactory, Allie's weekly salary was boosted, bit by bit, to $125. He did Lepke's bidding in everything from extortion to murder. The season dictated the locale. He summered in the Catskills or at Saratoga, and he wintered in Florida, as a strong-arm in gambling joints.

"The first spot I worked there," he swore later, "was at the Deauville in North Miami Beach. Lepke sent me down. I was also sent to work in a joint in Saratoga one summer."

Allie's familiarity with Sullivan County was a valuable asset. He was thoroughly acquainted with the highways and the byways —and deep spots in the lakes where a body might be dumped.

In January of 1940, Allie was in Florida doing nothing. The gambling trap in which he was to work that season had closed.

"What the hell," he had told himself, "I'm getting my pay every week. I might as well take a vacation."

Word of the launching of our offensive in the icy North perturbed him no more, at first, than it had any of them. Then the newspapers reported that Pretty and Dukey had talked, and Kid Twist and Buggsy were "in" for murder. This caused a certain uneasiness among the brotherhood of bandits who annually flock to Florida. Leaving his wife and five-year-old son, Allie boarded the northbound train. When he arrived in Brooklyn, most of the ranking mobsters were either scattered or in custody. Bug Workman was serving as bagman and fund distributor. Allie looked him up immediately. He sought financing to depart for the hideout the Purple Mob kept open in Detroit.

By coincidence, that was the very day Kid Twist began to sing, and Allie was one of those the Kid had in mind when he had sneered, "You ain't got no corroboration, but I can tell you where to find it." It was the same day, too, that Detective Abraham Belsky went to Workman's home in Brooklyn—not far, fittingly enough, from Washington cemetery—to get the Bug. And he found Allie right there with him. It was most convenient.

If we needed any proof that we had bagged big game, the immediate reaction furnished it. "The legal machinery of the gang, dormant for many days, leaped to life," said the *Brooklyn Eagle*. A move was begun at once toward habeas corpus freedom for Allie.

"The District Attorney's office will not oppose this writ," we told the court, "because state troopers are here in court to arrest this man for a murder in Sullivan County for a crime overlord."

It was surprising how quickly Allie changed his mind about demanding his freedom. But he was most wary.

"I refuse to answer on the grounds of my constitutional rights," he intoned to one question after another over the next three days, with the monotony and monotone of a wound-up music box. As a result, at his hearing, we did not press charges. Allie's smirk all but shouted, "Well, I sure handled that just right." We had, however, made certain that Sergeant Quinn, Corporal Lawson and Trooper Driscoll of New York State Police were in the courtroom. They caught him before he reached the exit and hustled him up to Sullivan County. District Attorney Deckelman had a welcome ready: an indictment charging Allie, Pittsburgh Phil and Gangy, the movie actor, with the 1936 murder of Irv Ashkenaz, details of which had been supplied by Dukey and Pretty and Kid Twist.

Ashkenaz was a taxicab owner who was telling Dewey investigators about the mob's cab racket in Manhattan. The Lithuanian-American taxi man apparently had become overly ambitious. He had run up to the Catskills to do a little investigating on his own. His body was found near the entrance to a resort hotel. It had slumped through the open door of his hack and was draped across the running board. The feet were still inside; the head was in the dust of the mountain road. Sixteen bullets had torn the life out of him. And over the dusty, bloody corpse, a sign swung, with an incongruous message:

HOTEL OF HAPPINESS

For six more weeks, Allie kept his mouth as tightly locked as his cell door. One Sunday morning in May, when the hillsides were bursting into green, Bill Deckelman walked into Allie's cell.

"We've got enough on you to put you in the chair," the District Attorney warned the unco-operative thug.

The weeks of no one to talk with but himself had taken all the self-assurance out of Allie. All of a sudden, the no-longer-dapper hoodlum was scared. He came out from behind his "constitutional immunity" chant, and in no time at all he had babbled of half a dozen jobs done in the mountain precincts. Then he said, "I want to see somebody from Brooklyn."

For us, he expanded Reles' coverage of many murders. He filled out the Dutch Schultz story, and that was a relief, because just about then Bug Workman had us bordering on frustration.

One morning in late March, the door to the office opened and a pleasant young fellow, completely at ease, was ushered in, custom-tailored from hand-painted cravat to hand-stitched brogans.

The snowballing murder investigation was a day-and-night job just then. A procession of characters paraded through our offices, most of whom I had never seen . . . hoodlums and punks and murderers and respectable men, too.

"Must be a lawyer," I assumed, as this smartly dressed citizen was pointed through the door. "Come right in, counsellor," I invited, pulling up a chair. "Sit down here."

Before he could, the detective who had followed him charged across the room. "This bum ain't no counsellor," he snapped. He kicked the chair clear across the office. "This is Charlie the Bug."

Bug Workman, the enigma of Murder, Inc., fooled you completely. With fairly well-modeled features and short, curly hair, he looked like anything but a killer. His score, however, was about twenty "hits" for the Syndicate.

For thirteen months, I worked to open one little crack in him. He was so highly placed in the councils of crime that if he talked, his superiors—the men who pulled the strings on murder—would be a long step nearer where they belonged. I tried persuasion, coaxing, cajolery, threat. Through hours of grilling, he remained poised, completely contained, with a lack of emotion so maddening, I felt, at times, like hitting him with a chair. He was always polite, always very careful not to rumple his tailor-made suit. But never once in that thirteen months did he so much as admit that he knew what day it was.

The Bug was cute enough not to parry with a questioner, ever. The thug who tries that is easy prey for an investigator, for one reply always leads to another question. The Bug simply said nothing at all. He would sit there hour after hour and just look at you in deadpan speechlessness as you asked questions. He carried it to extremes that sometimes were downright ridiculous. Take the day of one of his hearings. Court Clerk Steve Higgins began running through the usual "pedigree"—name, date of birth, address. . . .

"Ever been arrested before?" was the next question.

"I believe I was—I just don't recall at the moment." The Bug gave it his best I'm-trying-my-darnedest-to-remember look.

"How many times?"

"I don't remember. . . . I think maybe once."

Even while he was thus straining his recollection, the Bug could see the "Yellow Sheet" court clerk Higgins was holding in his hand. No one knew better than the Bug that this transcript record from the Police Bureau of Criminal Identification would give the accurate count. For Charles Workman, who couldn't recall if he had ever been arrested—it showed nine previous arrests.

For no other torpedo did the Syndicate go so all out as it did in seeking to "spring" the Bug. Move after move was made to free him. The efforts were so determined that we were convinced he would be silenced forever if he were bailed, because he knew too much.

After a few days, the vagrancy charge was dropped, but we promptly rearrested him as a material witness. We asked bail of $100,000. It was our way of telling the underworld that the Bug would stay in jail—that any attempt to post such high bond would invite application for even higher. Besides, whoever put up a bond that size would come in for uncomfortably close scrutiny.

Workman's aplomb, outwardly, anyway, was startling. This unruffled thug knew we had evidence that he represented big-shot racketeers in several cities and that he, personally, had a hand in a number of murders. He was alert enough to appreciate that he would not for long have the choice between being a witness or a defendant in murder. Yet, he coolly declined to utter one word that might spare himself.

A week after the high bail was set, he was back, seeking habeas corpus, demanding that we show why we were holding him; in short, a put-up-or-shut-up ultimatum. The Bug knew that if there was even a suspicion he was singing, he would be killed, even in jail. Undoubtedly, this move was a frantic signal to the mob that he was keeping the faith. The time had come to show the Bug that the string had run all the way out for him.

"This man is the key to Dutch Schultz," we finally revealed. A gasp of astonishment swept the courtroom. It was the first time the Bug had been linked to the five-year mystery, or, in fact, that it had even been mentioned in our probe. Workman knew where he stood now.

Naturally, we had turned over our information to Prosecutor William Wachenfeld of Newark. Early in 1941, he obtained a warrant against Workman. The gang immediately redoubled efforts in his behalf.

Two weeks later, Benny (the Boss) Tannenbaum (no relation to Allie) was blown apart—while baby-sitting for some friends on Featherbed Lane in the Bronx. For several weeks, there was no connection between Benny's demise and matters at hand. Then, one of our informants brought out some interesting data. It seems that, unknown to most of his associates, the Bug had hired himself a helper: Benny the Boss. When the Law started to close in on the Bug, someone recalled that Benny, as his right-hand man, knew a great deal. As Blue Jaw Magoon related afterward, "Benny was probably one guy could tell enough to put the Bug in the hot seat."

This, remember, was fourteen months after the murder ring had been exposed, its members arrested or dispersed and its activities placed under the strongest light. Yet, even then, this brazen combine went on with its death-dealing. Nor was it the finale when Benny was silenced on Featherbed Lane. The gang tried several more even later, and did succeed in committing at least one more assassination.

Early in April, we loaned out Kid Twist and Allie to speak their pieces before the grand jury in Newark. Workman was indicted for murder in the first degree, and extradition proceedings were launched. Then the battle really started. The showdown came before Supreme Court Justice Peter B. Smith in Brooklyn. The Bug was resplendent in chocolate sport shirt and sky-blue sweater. No chances were being taken that the mob might get ideas. More than a score of detectives guarded courtroom and corridors, and double-checked identification of those entering.

The Bug claimed that everything, including his arrest, was illegal—in effect, demanding to be turned loose so the whole thing could start all over again. Then he took another tack.

"A man whose testimony is vital to Workman's case is out West," his attorney pleaded. "He cannot get back for three weeks. His testimony will clearly implicate someone else."

That topped everything. Here was a killer who for thirteen months would not admit the time of day. Now he stood in open court and declared that, *pro bono publico,* no less, he would produce a Lochinvar who would put the finger on the real slayer of Dutch Schultz—for which he himself was indicted and identified! No wonder they called him the Bug.

"Just who is this mystery witness out West?" I countered.

"We won't reveal him," the Bug's attorney insisted. "He would be molested by police."

"Workman," I turned to the bench, "is one of the most valuable triggermen on earth. Each day he remains out of the jurisdiction of New Jersey, danger exists for witnesses against him and for their families."

Justice Smith ordered the extradition. The Bug went on trial early in June, with Reles and Allie again on loan to the State. Still the Bug clung to his nonsense about a mystery witness.

"This witness will be produced at the trial," his lawyers insisted in a pretrial statement.

The Bug kept it up—up to the moment when Kid Twist was called to the stand. Then he got the idea. The Kid's corroborative story would mean a sure-fire first-degree conviction—and the death sentence. The Bug promptly stood up and changed his plea to "no defense." That meant life imprisonment, instead. Up to today, his witness has not yet come out of the West. Workman is still in New Jersey State Prison. In the spring of 1951, he applied for parole, but the chances are slim that it will be considered before, perhaps, 1955.

Of the participants in the Dutch Schultz slaughter, only Piggy is unaccounted for. Rumors have it that he is still alive and not too far from the scene of the shooting match, either—and that he has climbed quite a way up the gangland social ladder.

Reles had said that the ganglords would try to kill witnesses. He had said they would fight with all the ferocity of cornered animals. He had said they would import triggermen we didn't even know. He had said they would stop at nothing to scuttle our probe. And he was entirely and exactly right.

The investigation had barely started before we were hit by real evidence of a determined organized opposition. Man after man we wanted suddenly faded from sight . . . Albert Anastasia and his boys, Vito Gurino, Dirty Jimmy Feraco, Dandy Jack Parisi,

Tony Romeo—the most competent killers in crime. Some, we learned later, were killed. Most, though, had fled.

When a man is "on the lam," the cost is enormous. Heavy sums are required to keep his presence from being "tipped," and to keep his information coming, fresh and accurate. Yet, from somewhere, the money was available now, to finance not only the lammisters, but the defenses of those caught in our net, as well. The most highly rated criminal attorneys were sought as counsel. The roster read like a Who's Who of criminal law, locally and nationally. Sam Leibowitz, who had successfully defended Albert Anastasia, the killers' boss, against three earlier charges of murder, was offered $100,000 in cash to represent some of them now. The finances, therefore, had to be more than casual donations. The answer, eventually, was uncovered.

So sensitive is the national ring that it reacted immediately to word that Reles was talking. A number of ranking moblords rushed to New York. Leading the way was Buggsy Siegel, who had migrated to California a few years before. On the way East, Buggsy picked up an ace of the Detroit Purple Mob. They set themselves up in one of the best Park Avenue hotels for conferences on the crisis. From all corners of the Syndicate, the gang moguls responded.

For eight days, the high executives of crime held secret sessions. They were appreciative of the fact that peril threatened the industry nationally. Kid Twist had been so strategically placed that they were positive he was exposing the most top-secret information of all—that a national Syndicate did exist. Therefore, it was the unanimous agreement, our probe must be sabotaged. There was no panic among the plotters. Again, it was a board of directors in serious session on business policy. Quickly and efficiently, they mounted a co-ordinated two-pronged offensive based on:

(a) The raising of a "Defense and Lamming Fund" through contributions from all mobmen, and,

(b) A War of Extermination against witnesses already in custody and mob hirelings still at large who might consider their information valuable for trading with authorities.

The defense fund was not deemed a local project. Nor were collections left to chance or charitable inclination. The mob bosses set themselves up as a Committee of the Whole to see that all hands contributed fully. As a result, the mobsters in flight and their families at home were lavishly financed, as if they suddenly were beneficiaries of a rich aunt's will. The sources were many and varied. There were reports of kickbacks imposed on members of labor unions for mobdom's war chest. Even those unions in which honest workers already were forced to kick back part of each day's pay to the rackets—like the local hod-carriers' organization, in which Louis Capone and his brother were moving spirits—now raised the extortion ante. For decent hard-working men, it was pay—or no work. Maybe even worse.

The very fact that Buggsy Siegel, in person, led the planning sessions disclosed the gravity with which the combine regarded the situation. "Buggsy is here because the Brooklyn bosses either lammed or were nailed," we were informed. "He's the best guy to get things going and to cool off the jitters till the heat's off."

Our real worry, more than the financing, was the all-out War of Extermination inside the mob. The sole reason the Syndicate had waxed so fat was that the mob magnates had been able to keep its very being from discovery. Now, however, there was danger that the whole country would be alerted. A coast-to-coast alarm went out to get anyone and everyone who was already aiding the District Attorney or who might know something that would aid him.

"Triggermen are here from out of town," the D. A.'s office cautioned publicly. "They are here to shoot down those who stand in the way. Buggsy Siegel is the field director, and will mark those who must go."

There was method in our alarm ringing. This was dog-eat-dog. These master murderers were pledged to dispose of one and all of whom there might be the slightest doubt—loyal or not, in or out of jail. Terror-struck hoodlums, still on the outside, realized they were marked for death simply for knowledge they had. That was the mob's strongest strategy; we took it and used it, too. We played it up to the thugs in announcements, starting them wondering if they would be more valuable dead or alive. It was apparent from the word go that the key was corroboration. We were seeking it; they were seeking to exterminate it. The race was often close—too close.

On the local scene, Happy Maione, snarling defiance from his cell in the Tombs, went wild at news that Reles was talking.

"So those guys in the D. A.'s office want to keep busy, eh?" he repeated his threat of weeks before. "Okay—we'll keep them busy. We'll drop 'packages' all over Brooklyn for them."

He sent out orders to gunmen still loose. The commands were relayed through the prison grapevine to City Prison, where his brother, Duke Maione, was serving a ninety-day sentence for vagrancy. It was interesting to note that, although Duke had been in prison for five weeks, no attempt had been made to get him out. Yet, any time one of the hoods was locked up, his release always had been sought immediately. Happy saw to it that such efforts were not made in Duke's behalf. Free to receive visitors without suspicion, Duke made an excellent relay point for messages. In addition, Happy did not want Duke blamed if and when the jobs he was ordering came off. In jail, Duke had a perfect alibi. When efforts were made, finally, to gain his release, his attorney insisted Duke was a legitimate businessman, with three flourishing florist shops. He made no reference to Duke's eleven previous arrests.

"Flower shops could be an excellent cover for other activities," State Supreme Court Justice (then assistant District Attorney) Vincent Keogh reminded both counsel and the court. Duke stayed in his cell.

Shortly after Reles started to talk, Vito Gurino twice visited Duke in jail. We were not yet aware that we would want Socko for half a dozen murders and as beastly a rape case as was ever encountered. Reles could not talk about everything at once. He just hadn't gotten around to Gurino yet. Gurino received Happy's pointed commands to dispose at once of the several eyewitnesses who could put him on the spot for murder. As a result, for a while there, Joe the Baker was having nothing but one narrow escape after another.

Joe Liberito—or Liberto, to give it the Americanized version—was known as Joe the Baker, because he had once been one, although at this time he hadn't turned out a loaf of bread or a cupcake for perhaps ten years. The Baker was not a mobster, but he knew all the boys. For some years, he was night attendant at the Sunrise Garage, of which Gurino was part owner. This was just a step from the Atlantic Avenue and Eastern Parkway corner that served as GHQ for the Ocean Hill hooligans. As the night man, Joe the Baker saw some things which, since he was not an accredited member of the fraternity, caused him to be one of the first Happy mentioned when he issued death sentences from his cell. The Baker was first-class corroboration against Maione.

Joe had shifted to another garage—but Joe Daddonna, Happy's brother-in-law, was able to find him, all right. He invited the Baker into his car "because we got to go somewhere." They drove far out on Long Island.

Daddonna locked Joe the Baker in a vacant house, and mounted guard, apparently awaiting someone. The Baker realized now that the end result spelled no good for him. He kept his eye peeled for opportunity. After a while, Daddonna reached into his pocket for a cigarette, and found his pack empty. As minutes passed, his desire for a smoke grew stronger. Suppose he just ducked out for a few minutes to get some; his hostage would keep, he felt. He'd be back before the Baker even realized he was gone. Daddonna slipped through the door—and the Baker promptly went through a rear window. Our report was that he did not even bother to open it first.

Liberito just ran, blindly, for a while. Then he stopped a passer-by, and explained that he found himself far from home and without funds. Fortunately, he had selected an understanding individual—understanding to the extent of forty cents, anyway. Joe was on the next train out. The forty cents would not get him all the way back to Brooklyn; but it did take him to Jamaica, a section of New York City on nearby Long Island. Joe's mother lived there. The frightened Baker knew the mob would be hot after him. He stayed with his mother only overnight. Someone suggested he go to Yonkers, in Westchester County, at the other end of the city.

"I never was there and I don't know nobody there," reasoned Joe. "Maybe it'll be a good hideout."

For a week or so, he was tucked away in a two-by-four furnished room. But Daddonna showed up then. It had not been cricket of the Baker, leaving Long Island through a window like that, said Maione's in-law. Before he left, he said he would be back, and Joe had better stay put this time.

Apparently someone else was afraid of the same thing. Just at that time, we were tipped off to Joe's hideaway. Four detectives found him in his hole in the wall, and brought him back. All the Baker could think of was that if he talked, the mob would track him down. He kept quiet.

Meantime, Happy became more and more impatient over failure of his agents to report progress. Over his prison lines of communication, he ordered Gurino to get on the job.

Liberito was placed in the Queens County Civil Jail in Long Island City. Civil jails, not to be confused with criminal lockups, ordinarily house only alimony defaulters, debtors and the like. Inmates are so few, they usually operate with skeleton staffs. In the Queens jail, the cells were not even locked. The night after Joe the Baker was put in, the only official on duty was deputy sheriff William Cassell. At about 11:30, as Joe was lying on his cot, Cassell appeared at his cell door.

"He asks me do I want to see Vito Gurino, and I say no," Joe explained afterward. Nevertheless, keeper Cassell brought Joe into the jail kitchen. And there was Gurino, sitting on the edge of a table.

"What did you say?" Vito came right to the point. The mob was having trouble getting inside information by this time. The boys hadn't been able to find out if Joe had talked.

"I didn't say nothing," the Baker reassured him.

There wasn't much more on that visit. Gurino was not ready to move yet. Three or four nights later, he was back in the jail kitchen.

"Did you say anything?" he challenged again.

"I kept my mouth shut," Liberito repeated. "Hap got nothing to worry about me."

Vito seemed satisfied. More likely, he wanted to put the Baker at ease.

"Anything you want, ask the keeper," he invited pleasantly— or as pleasantly as Socko ever could get. The Baker recognized opportunity. He turned to Cassell.

"Buy me two pairs of socks and some shorts, and gimme a couple dollars for cigarettes," he ordered. Gurino nodded an "okay."

"In case you want to go for a ride, the keeper will take you out after one o'clock in the morning," the mobster went on. That was what upset Joe—that mention of "ride." Vito was able to get inside the jail at will. Then what was to prevent Vito, himself, from taking Joe for that 1 A. M. "ride"? Joe knew what that meant.

He waited until Cassell brought him the socks and the other things he had asked for. Then he told the keeper flatly, "I don't want to see Vito no more." As a civil prison, the Queens jail permitted benefits strange to a criminal pen, even to ice cream, made in the jail kitchen. A baseball bat was used to stir the rock salt and ice. Somehow, Joe got hold of the bat. He slipped the sturdy length of ash into the space between the window of his cell and the bars outside. He was going to be ready for any predawn rides.

Gurino, meantime, rounded out his plans. Realizing his face was now too familiar at the jail, he recruited a helper, and gave him $100 to handle the matter. The idea was to appear at the jail, carrying forged papers calling for the delivery of Liberito— a method employed more than once by the underworld. If that didn't work, the keeper would simply be overpowered—anything to get the Baker out where he could be finished off. The helper, however, got cold feet over this frolic. He took the $100—and then headed straight for the District Attorney's office.

That was the mob's last chance at Joe Liberito. He had remained faithful to the code, but now he saw that the ultimate reward for protecting these thugs was permanent silence. The mob itself had unlocked the lips of the Baker.

Killers ranged from coast to coast in the war of extermination, and when the torpedoes were on the prowl, there was no place on the face of the earth for the hunted men to hide; no hole to cower in.

Each lammister realized, in stark terror, that his continued existence now rested precariously, not so much on his loyalty to the combination as on whether the combination would take out "insurance" in spite of that loyalty. Each frantically began to wonder if he were the next marked to go. That was when the War of Extermination backfired. It was laughable, really. Not one of them had any intention of informing—until that became the only way to save his life.

In the next weeks, there was a life-and-death race between the Law and the gang's guns to get each of the lammisters. Every time we scored, the man we won was only a short step in front of assassination. They were an astounding collection. Their stories were even more so. Here are some who became key witnesses:

JULIE CATALANO

Angelo (Julie) Catalano was barely able to write his own name, and barely able to read it when he did write it, but words poured from him like water down a rainpipe in a heavy storm.

Julie was tall and lean, and when he spoke, it was with shrugs, gestures and facial grimaces as well as words. Even in pantomime, Julie was eloquent. He had a fluid loquacity that was to win for him the label of "Kings County Canary" in capital letters in the public prints.

He had gone to school with Happy Maione and admired the sour-faced hood with the punk's open admiration for the big shot. He had been a cabdriver, but his hacking career came to an abrupt end, when, as Julie always explained it, "I got into some trouble with some burglar tools." This difficulty cost him eleven months on vacation with the State. After that, Happy put him to work as a $30-a-week pay-off and collection man for the hand-book from which Maione and Gurino and Dasher Abbandando netted $40,000 a year.

From bookmaking, the smooth-faced extrovert drifted naturally to varied activities. His art as a driver, developed as a taxicab jockey in the huffle-scuffle of New York traffic, made him the official wheelman in six of the mob's contract killings. And he bragged that he never left a fingerprint.

Julie had been one of those we landed in our original campaign against the hoodlums on the street corners. He had drawn sixty days for vagrancy. However, his brother had appeared with deeds in his father's name, and some cash, and mysteriously bailed him out.

Three weeks passed before we learned that Julie's corroborative knowledge would make him far more valuable dead than alive to the mob. Where, then, was Julie? Had the War of Extermination claimed him—or was he still able to talk?

Detectives Johnny McDonough and Babe Werner rushed to the Catalano home. As they walked in, Julie was not only there, but he practically fell into their arms in sheer joy. This was novel, indeed. No one in the mob was glad to see a policeman, ever—and especially not just at that period.

"Take me in," Julie almost babbled in his glee. "I was praying for the Law to come and get me." It came out then that only by the sheerest good luck—and a matter of minutes—was Julie still able to babble.

When he had been sentenced for vagrancy, the hoodlums had ordered his brother to bail him out. The brother did not want to. In jail, Julie could not get into trouble. The gangsters advised Julie's brother, though, that he had better do as they said. Julie was out only one day when Vito Gurino looked him up.

"Happy wants to see you," Vito said. So, Julie took the subway under the river and walked into the Tombs, just like any other visitor come to cheer an inmate. Happy had wanted to see Julie, as Gurino said, but that was before the murder probe exploded. Now, the very last thing he wanted was a visit from a man under suspicion.

"What the hell are you doing here?" he demanded. "Don't you know Pretty and Dukey squawked? You'll get pinched."

"What the hell do I care?" Julie talked right up. "Socko says you want to see me."

"You should never take a chance to come here now. What I want to say is: don't go home. Make yourself scarce from the neighborhood. Evaporate yourself. And when you get a couple blocks from here, send me a wire, so I know you got away okay."

Julie saw no reason to leave the comforts of home. He waited until he reached the Western Union office near his home, then sent a message informing Happy he had no intention of "evaporating."

"I'm all right and I'm going home," he wired. He spelled it "I'n" instead of "I'm," a natural mistake for Julie.

The defiance aroused Happy's suspicions. Julie's inside knowledge could, if revealed, be dangerous, particularly concerning a double murder the previous year. This twin assassination had been touched off during a hod-carriers' war in February, 1939, in which at least three plasterers were killed. The bloodletting had stemmed from an attempt by Louis Capone and his brother, controlling the local hod carriers and builders union, to impose a new kickback of one dollar a day on each member.

Some workers took exception to the extortion. One Cologero Veruso was so strenuously opposed that Capone decided it would best serve his ends if the opposition were out of the way —permanently. Apparently Louis felt this was strictly a union matter and that plasterers should do the job. The command was given to Cesare Lattaro and Antonio Siciliano. Since they were plasterers and not murderers, they refused flatly. Capone would not stand for that. He directed his fellow torpedoes from Ocean Hill and Brownsville to "take" the two plasterers.

Lattaro and Siciliano not only worked together; they also lived together. They maintained bachelor quarters, with their pet bulldog, in a cozy basement apartment on Bergen Street, a few blocks west of the corner headquarters of the Ocean Hill hooligans. This cellar flat would be an ideal spot to knock them off, except that since they told off Louis Capone, Lattaro and Siciliano were keeping their eyes peeled.

On the night of February 6, there was a light knock on the door of the basement quarters. The roommates asked who it was, and a soft feminine voice answered familiarly. Now, Cesare and Antonio, like any bachelors, occasionally entertained lady guests. They peeped out and saw a curvaceous charmer in white blouse and a black hat with jaunty red feather. The charmer's face was half turned away. The bachelor buddies were satisfied it was one of the companions of their lonely hours. They opened the door.

From the shadows a bulky figure suddenly joined the young lady. The couple pulled out guns and blasted the life out of the two plasterers. Deliberately, they turned their pistols on the barking bulldog pup and fired several shots into it. Then the lady and her escort stepped out to the street and into a car, waiting there with motor running and driver at the wheel, and were whisked away.

Another waiting car picked up their trail. After proceeding for some distance, the caravan stopped. The driver and the murder couple abandoned the getaway car, and disappeared in the second vehicle. Anyone close enough could have identified the party. The wheelman of the second automobile was Dasher Abbandando. Driving the getaway car had been good-looking Julie Catalano. The bulky gunman who was the lady's escort was easily spotted as Vito Gurino. And the lady—well, by then she had removed the feathered headpiece and the "falsies" that had provided necessary glamour. "She" was Happy Maione.

Sitting there in his Tombs cell, Happy considered Julie's close association with that job, and with others in which he was involved. Unable to check for himself, Happy's suspicions magnified quickly. Through his grapevine, he transmitted orders.

"Hit Julie on the head," he commanded.

The edict traveled from the surly hoodlum's cell to Rikers Island, and was passed on to Vito Gurino, who visited Happy's brother, Duke, there. Adept as Socko was, however, no opportunity arose on that day, Friday, or on Saturday. As the hours passed, and no word seeped through, Happy grew more and more fretful. Late Saturday night, the prison grapevine crackled with another message:

"What's holding up that job?" it demanded.

That night, Julie's brother-in-law got married, and he was mildly surprised to see the bull neck of Vito Gurino at the nuptials. The ponderous plug-ugly drew Julie aside.

"Things are too hot around here," Gurino began. "You and me are going to take a little ride down on Long Island."

A cold shiver shot up Julie's spine. The invitation had an unmistakable ring. He had neither suspected nor expected this.

"I know a nice place where we can hide out until this thing cools off," the apelike killer went on pleasantly. "It should be all over in two-three months."

Julie needed no college degree to recognize a "ride" setup. He had to get away from Gurino without exciting suspicion.

"I'll go home and tell my wife I'm going," was all he could

offer. He did it disarmingly as if he hadn't a worry in the world.

"No," cautioned the torpedo. "Don't tell her. Don't let her know who you're going with. I know a couple of dames we can take down there—so don't say nothing. We'll have a helluva time."

"Okay," agreed Julie, his mind still whirling desperately. "But first, I gotta go home and get some clothes."

Julie had hidden his distraction well. "Get them," Socko approved, "and meet me in an hour on the Corner."

All the way home, Julie frantically contemplated how to get out with a whole skin. It was like the nightmare of being stuck on a treadmill, with a two-headed dragon chasing him. Run and hide? "But they'll dig me up," he rejected. Go to the cops and talk? "They can reach me in jail, too." He was trapped. And as he pondered his predicament, his long admiration for his "old pal Hap" died. In its place, hatred blazed—hatred and a mortal dread.

"That man is crazy enough to kill me," he suddenly realized.

He was still debating feverishly when he reached home. The idea of flight had a bit the upper hand. It was early Sunday morning; with luck and a head start, he might make a getaway. He was still in a panic ten minutes later when Johnny McDonough and Babe Werner, the detectives, arrived.

"What a favor you guys did for me!" Julie broke down almost in ecstasy. "What a spot I was in. It is either a rubout for me, or the hot seat for those bums. Well . . . they're on their own, now."

SHOLEM BERNSTEIN

The eyes of Sholem Bernstein bore a dreamy look. Those sleepy eyes, set off by the long thin face, gave the distinct impression that Sholem was in endless philosophical reverie, far from the cold facts of life.

But there was nothing out-of-this-world about Sholem. No man is a dreamer who can borrow $50,000 from a bank by saying he is single, when he isn't, and by saying he is a real estate salesman, when he actually is up to his eyes in crime.

As a matter of fact, you would say Sholem was a very sharp character, indeed—except for one thing. He could not resist cold dice and slow horses. He started gambling when he was sixteen, and he kept it up through a considerable stretch as a shill with carnivals in Maryland, New Jersey and Pennsylvania. And he got over his head in debt. A Brooklyn boy, born and bred, he naturally knew of the shylocks. So, Sholem went to the coffee pot where Pittsburgh Phil and Louis Capone maintained one of their offices.

"I'd like to get a little," Sholem requested, and after the usual examination of credit and character rating, the loan was granted.

For a long time, Sholem borrowed, paid back, borrowed again. He was always one who could figure things out for himself, though. Eventually, he saw that paying six dollars for each five he borrowed was sure-thing gambling only for the shylocks. He established his credit at a bank called the Food Dealers Association.

"That is the ace in the hole," he used to grin. "I guess it is close to $50,000, or maybe more, that I borrowed there."

From time to time, in his loan applications, he identified himself as a real estate operator, as a $5,000-a-year salesman and as a single man. Sholem felt his wife would understand about that.

"It is easier to get a loan that way," he explained.

One day it came to him that the only advantageous connection with the shylocks was to be one himself—so Sholem became a shylock. It put him on the verge of affluence. He even moved across Brooklyn, to the Bensonhurst section. He felt a better class of people could be found there. He took one Al Glass, known as Cherry, as a partner. They opened a candy store as an office (with the combination's approval, of course). For a time, Sholem was proud of this little enterprise—the neat, legitimate look about it. After a while, though, he became somewhat irked.

"It's turning out to be a big hangout," he complained. "All kinds of guys—burglars and stick-up aces and everything else."

Sholem's repugnance was not personal, mind you. "Dreamy-eyes" could match the record of virtually any character there. Besides shylocking, he was in wholesale car-stealing, bookmaking, burglary, safecracking, strong-arming in Florida gambling joints and specialization in assorted phases of assassination for Murder, Inc. Once, a law enforcement officer, startled at how many pies Sholem's fingers dipped into, gasped:

"He is a one-man finance company, with muscles and guns."

He began this well-rounded career before he was twenty, setting out with a couple of neighborhood kids one night with intentions somewhat less than honest. Sholem was caught, and indicted for burglary. Almost miraculously, "it was straightened out," as he explained it, just as he was brought into court. He was told that if he pleaded guilty to unlawful entry, a misdemeanor, the more serious felony charge would be dropped. Sholem got off with a suspended sentence. To a Brownsville tough guy, it was the same as an acquittal.

"This," said Sholem, as the court door closed behind him, "is easy."

After that, he was caught twice more—but he never went to prison. Apprehended in a stolen car with two known stick-up men, all with guns, he pleaded guilty to automobile theft, and was placed on probation. Six months later, he was up for larceny, pleaded guilty—and again drew nothing harsher than probation. Sholem never did find out that there was any penalty—as long as he walked in and said, "I'm sorry and I won't do it again."

Sholem never really belonged to the mob. He did all sorts of work for and with its members, but he was a loner in underworld society. Of course, he cut the combination in on some of his loner jobs. That way, he never had to worry about interference.

As a one-man finance company, with accouterments, he lived comfortably. There were annual trips to Florida, half a dozen visits to California, and relaxation each summer in the Catskills.

"Those California trips are a vacation," he sighed. "I go there to get away from murders. That is what I call a vacation." And he would add, with that dreamy, preoccupied look, "Don't you think so?"

There was one thing Sholem never could figure out. He just did not see how a virtually innocent bystander—meaning himself —could be accused of participation in a murder, if he didn't pull a trigger. There was one contract, in which he stole the getaway car and drove the killers from the scene.

"I had nothing to do with that job," he always insisted, because he did not know the car was to be used for a killing, and when the three torpedoes leaped in and he whisked them to safety, he didn't even know the victim's name.

Speaking of murder, things were always happening to friends

of Sholem. There was Fatty Cooperman, for instance. In the early thirties, Fatty was in the middle of the feud between the Shapiro Brothers and Kid Twist. In the shooting match in which a bullet went through Buggsy Goldstein's nose, Fatty was an interested party. Just three months after Willie, the last of the brothers, was buried alive, Sholem bumped into Fatty in a cafeteria early one morning. They chatted over a cup of coffee.

"I got the car; I'll drop you at your house," offered Sholem. It was 4 A.M. when Fatty dismounted with a, "see you later," in front of his apartment, and Sholem drove off. The killers apparently were waiting for Fatty in the foyer, just like the time his co-worker, Irv Shapiro, was eliminated. Happy and the Dasher and Blue Jaw Magoon were picked up and held for a while, but as usual, it ended in a "turnout."

In 1940, Sholem had planned to forego his Florida migration. Suddenly, he began to notice a certain uncomfortable change in the Brooklyn air.

"All of a sudden, there is too much law activity," Sholem said. He changed his mind, and left for the South.

After checking into the modern Miami Beach hotel he favored, he proceeded to move around, acquainting friends and associates of his presence. Every place he went, however, he kept running into detectives from New York. Now, a few New York detectives are in Miami every year, keeping up on things, because the mobsters flock to the winter playground annually. But this time, there were so many detectives from home that Sholem began to suspect Miami Beach was nothing but Brooklyn with palm trees. He did not even finish unpacking his bag; he just got back into his car and pointed it for home. When he arrived, it took only a few minutes for him to discover that, for him, Brooklyn was hotter than Miami. The mob had marked him as one of those who knew too much.

Sholem took to the road again, and he did not stop until he had put the entire continent between himself and mob headquarters. As the miles tolled off, the awful thought ran over and over in his mind—that he was as hot as three feet inside a furnace; that the enforcers would be looking for him.

In Los Angeles, he put up at a hotel on Olympic Avenue. He had friends and connections. But connections, no matter how powerful, meant nothing for a man marked in the War of Extermination. In less than a week, the whisper came, "certain people are around asking about you." Sholem was positive they did not want to wish him the time of day. He fled once more. At San Francisco, he realized he must get rid of his car. It marked him. And besides, he was already feeling the high cost of being "on the lam." The deal was completed only a matter of hours before the hunters discovered his whereabouts again.

A cross-country chase for Sholem's life was in full cry now. He followed no special pattern of flight. Yet, the Syndicate was organized so nationally that it rarely took more than a day or two for the killers to have him spotted. In fact, only through friends who apprised him of the approach of the enforcers did he manage to stay a jump in front. He took a bus to Dallas. They caught up in nine hours. In St. Louis, they stalked him down in two days. He hopped to Chicago and buried himself in a hotel on Winthrop Avenue, where he was a stranger.

Meantime, Reles, Allie and Catalano all had mentioned Sholem. Now we joined the chase. We learned that killers had left for Chicago to finish him. Frantically, we phoned Chicago police to pry into the dark corners for his hideout. Two detectives were rushed west to join the hunt. We waited—and sweated it out with Sholem.

An anxious week later, we received a long-distance call. "The body and legs of a man were just found in a bag in Chicago," was the message. "The fingers were cut off, so prints can't be checked."

It was a bitter break to all of us in the District Attorney's office—to hope for Sholem and get a headless torso. And just then, the door opened and Detective Johnny McDonough walked in—with a very live, although somewhat harried, Sholem!

Holed up in Chicago, Sholem had sensed that he was at the end of the line. There was no place else to go. Then it came to him: "They can't get me if I am with the Law." Most of his remaining funds went for a ticket east.

Once home, however, he did not dash to the nearest station house. He watched and he waited, until he saw Johnny McDonough. Then he walked up and said, "Take me in where those guys can't get me." Sholem knew what he was doing. Johnny McDonough was a cop to be respected—as tough as poison on hoodlums, but a square-shooter. Every underworld citizen knew Johnny kept his word. There were some cops, Sholem insisted, who might even tip off the mob that he was back. But if Johnny McDonough said he would take him in—that is where he would go.

Actually, Johnny was added to the District Attorney's staff for the investigation on the recommendation of a mobster! Johnny's beat had been Brownsville, a rough territory to cover. When Reles began to talk, he also began to act as if he was running the investigation. He probably thought he was, at that. Johnny, he proposed, should surely be brought in on the probe.

"The guys in the combination know he's level, and he knows what's going on," the Kid advised the District Attorney. "Nobody ever could square him ten cents' worth."

Since all of Reles' information had rung the bell, McDonough was transferred. Again Reles was "on target." Sholem would have surrendered to no other.

At first Sholem would not talk, even though he knew the gangsters had ordered his assassination. In this respect, a peculiar thread is woven inexplicably through the mental processes of virtually all of these characters in organized crime. Every one of them understands all too clearly that the Syndicate would seal the lips of any member it deems necessary, with no compunction about personality or past services. Yet, each, in his heart, is sure it can't happen to him. He will cling to that conviction in spite of all evidence to the contrary. "They know I can be counted on," he will tell himself.

Thus, even a sharp plug-ugly like Sholem, after being inexorably hunted across the nation, still embraced the belief that perhaps it was all a rectifiable mistake. I am positive that a lot of those who have lost in the War of Extermination, by which mobdom has purged itself for years, died with a surprised look on their faces, when they finally did realize that it could happen to them.

After Sholem held out for a while, we had a notion that it might, perhaps, do some good if he came face to face with Reles. Sholem knew Reles had never before given away any information. So we brought the reluctant prisoner and the garrulous songbird together in a room. In fifteen minutes, Sholem had an announcement.

"I will become a rat and tell everything," he said, precisely.

Once more, the combination itself had chased in a witness—to tell the very secrets it wanted to kill the witness to preserve.

Perhaps Sholem's most notable contribution was in elaborating on the execution of Hy Yuran. Yuran was a dress manufacturer of some affluence. Lepke, invading the garment industry, "used" Yuran to such an extent that the manufacturer was almost as involved as the mob boss. When Lepke's extortion trial was approaching in 1939, Yuran was recognized as a prime source of information against the nation's czar of industrial rackets. Yuran was vacationing in the Catskills at the time. Lepke ordered a "varsity" firing squad to the spot immediately. Sholem was in the area, and the staff specialists looked him up.

"Come over to our hotel in Fallsburg three nights from now," Pittsburgh Phil directed. "We got something to do."

In the late afternoon of August 6, Sholem toured the eight miles to the hoods' hotel.

Jack Drucker proposed a ride to Sholem. They drove perhaps half an hour, when Drucker pulled up. "Come on—take a walk," he invited pleasantly.

Meantime, the others had learned that Yuran was relaxing at a cabaret that night. They took him out of that cabaret, and they treated him to a development that was unusual, if not actually brand new. He was taken for a ride in his own car!

Sholem and Drucker, walking slowly, had come to a sort of alley, or narrow street. "Then this car happens to come along," related Sholem, "with Pep and Allie and a guy named Simey. They stop and shove a body out."

All of them bent to the task of digging a grave. They had, however, selected a rough cemetery. The spades glanced off rocks and thudded into shrub roots.

"This is no good," gasped Pittsburgh Phil, mopping his brow. "Tell you what . . . the rest of you go find another spot, and then come back with a truck. Me and Sholem will stick here and watch."

No sooner were the others gone—with only the uncomplaining

Sholem remaining—than Pittsburgh Phil coolly and methodically went through the pockets of the corpse.

"He found a lot of money on the stiff," Sholem charged.

Soon a small bakery truck drove up, with Allie and Drucker aboard. Yuran's remains were loaded into the back. The quartet sped to nearby Loch Sheldrake. The new grave site was close to the new swimming pool of a prominent inn.

One of the thugs picked up a vacationing girl en route. He had been designated to serve as the lookout, from a tennis court hard by the grave. A fellow out alone under the Catskill moon is conspicuous in the mountain vacationland. So, here was the lookout petting away with all the fervor of young love with a charming young lady. Afterward, they often speculated curiously how she would have reacted to romance had she known that fifty feet away, her Romeo's co-workers were lining a hole with quick-lime and dumping therein a corpse.

The grisly job finished, Pittsburgh Phil had one more chore for Sholem. "Take Yuran's car and give it to Oscar," he ordered. Sholem was not too enthusiastic, as he started out. Brooklyn was three or four hours away by the fastest driving. It was dawn before he completed the trip. The hot car was stored away for the day. The next night, Sholem turned it over—with a great deal of relief —to Oscar, as ordered.

"You'll find Oscar in the park with a book," Reles directed us as he reached this point in his singing. "He's a skinny guy, with hair that hangs down on his collar and his clothes look like he rolls around in them."

Oscar was a bizarre character, indeed. His long bushy hair was brushed back, à la Byron. You might have called him the François Villon of Brownsville. He carried an anthology of poetry around with him, and spent his time sitting in the park, absorbed in its pages. He had been labeled, appropriately, Oscar the Poet. A penchant for poetry was not, however, Oscar's outstanding distinction. He was the only man who ever outsmarted these gangsters—and he did it consistently!

Instead of abandoning the hot cars used on contracts, the combination, as time went on, saw the advantage in having the vehicles simply evaporate whenever possible. Or, say the legitimate automobile owned by one of the hoods became outmoded. If it could disappear, he could collect the insurance and buy a new one. In both cases, Oscar was the "evaporater." For years, the mobsters had paid him $50 for each car they turned over to him. They understood that he worked over each with blow torch and acid until not a traceable bolt or scrap of fender was left.

But Oscar the romanticist had never unscrewed a single screw. He simply sold the cars for $5 apiece to a junkman he knew, and left any disguising to the junkman. Had the shrewd hoodlums ever suspected it, rest assured they would have cut Oscar up into so many pieces, he would have resembled a tray of canapés.

BLUE JAW MAGOON

Blue Jaw Magoon gave off an aura of power like a collie dog sheds its hair—all over the place.

All the words ever said about such a character fitted Blue Jaw. (They may still fit him; he was still around when last heard from.) Built like a Russian peasant, he was a one-man army. His pals in the combination vouched for that.

He had close-cropped hair on a large head, with a flat nose, steady penetrating eyes, and a sinister look. Nor did his practically permanent · five-o'clock shadow—from whence sprang his nickname—make the general effect any more angelic. There was a hesitancy in his speech, a kind of internal stutter. Words came out slowly, as if after great thought and determination, creating a picture of the strong silent type. The mobsters always said, "When Blue Jaw is with you, he sticks till the game is over." It was one unholy shock to them when Blue Jaw jumped over to the Law.

Nothing fazed this flat-nosed felon. Once, he was cheerfully willing to take on the entire gang of killers, when they blandly decreed they were going to muscle in on his business. When he was still just a car-stealing youngster, he squared off against a policeman one night, waved his pals back, and knocked the officer out cold.

"I can take care of myself," was his pet philosophy. But he insisted he should not be classed as a chronic strong-arm. "Only for a fight or an argument or something like that," he explained, by way of setting the record straight.

He was one of the very few audacious enough to stand up to Pittsburgh Phil. Not even Reles and Happy had a taste for any such boldness with the killer whose delight in murder was that of a miser fondling his gold. But when Blue Jaw and Pittsburgh Phil became involved in a harsh argument over a killing, Blue Jaw challenged the Beau Brummell badman with, "You can't talk like that to me." And Pittsburgh Phil was the one who made peace. When Blue Jaw thought he had law—mob law, that is—on his side, he even faced Albert Anastasia, the big boss, and said so.

When the fireworks of our investigation started, Blue Jaw was serving sixty days for vagrancy. He had no idea that this was the end of the line for Brooklyn, Inc.

"After all," he reasoned, "I been pinched twenty-five times, and this rap for vagrancy is only the first I ever got nailed."

This remarkable record began with a boyhood so incorrigible that the Brownsville schools could not hold him. He left school when he was sixteen, or, maybe, fourteen. "I am not sure," he would explain, in his careful way. "You see, I was not interested in school much." By 1933, he already was mixed up in gunplay —shooting two men. "But they were only wounded," he tossed off.

Actually, Blue Jaw was glad to be in jail at the start of the probe. He was away from where fingers were pointing uncomfortably at his friends and co-workers on the outside. He just sat tight, on the theory that as long as the fingers did not swing his way, he was out of the line of fire. He could no more have been overlooked than the tax man on March 15.

It was obvious he had no idea of talking. So, we played 'possum. He served out his full sixty day term, and as he entered the warden's office for his discharge, detectives took him in tow immediately. For more than two weeks, then, he just sat and stewed in his own silence—and we let him stew. Then he saw in the papers that he had been identified in the theft of a murder car. And he read where his closest friend, Buggsy, was indicted for murder, and his second-best buddy, Kid Twist, was telling everything.

"It looks like I'm on my way unless I get into the act," Blue Jaw told himself. "I better find a peg to hang my hat on, too."

He was sharp enough to comprehend that he would need something special and brand new, or the District Attorney wouldn't even listen to him, what with Kid Twist chirping away. He combed his memory, and he recalled several exclusive items concerning Lepke, Anastasia and others among the commandants. The other stoolpigeons would not have the same items, simply because they were not on hand when the incidents happened. Then, Blue Jaw joined the chorus.

Blue Jaw was a student of human nature. He provided down-to-earth insight on the personalities and habits of the hoodlums that lent a touch of low-class comedy to the probe.

"I went out social with all those guys," he pointed out. "When Pittsburgh Phil, who I call Pep, is with the big shots in the mob, he wines and dines them and makes a big show. But with his equals or with the little guys, he argues about a nickel when it comes his time to pay.

"Reles is ungenerous, too, but he puts on no airs. No matter who he is with, he is slow to pay—and he makes no bones about it.

"When Pep and me went out social," he added, "we would meet, at times, Shimmy Salles and Charlie the Bug Workman and Mendy. I rate them as follows: Mendy, kind of tight; the Bug, a nice fellow; Shimmy, all right—only slow to put money up. And he was one of the main men in the Lepke mob.

"Joe Adonis is supposed to be tight in money matters, too, which is why the boys don't like him too good."

Mention of Joey A. brought additional pertinent information on the sinister Syndicate executive, whose status in the national set-up has not changed up to the present.

"Joey A. is like one with Albert Anastasia," Blue Jaw revealed. "And Albert is the boss of Brooklyn. He is part of the national combination. In other words, if he got crossed, the guy who crossed him has the whole combination on his back.

"If Joey A. got into trouble or there was a war, he could always depend on Albert and Vince (Vince Mangano, an Anastasia associate, sometimes considered an Anastasia partner). The time the war is on with Waxey Gordon's mob, Happy Maione and Pep were bodyguards for Joey A."

Blue Jaw's revelations of other fertile facets of the bewildering band included even a racket in labor on the contracts for painting the public-school buildings of New York City—a racket, it might be pointed out, that still pops up from time to time! (Or a reasonable facsimile thereof.) It all began, Blue Jaw recounted, in the early thirties when he took unto himself a shylock partner— "Bobby Burns, the prize fighter."

"Along in 1935, Bobby gets this proposition to be the strong-arm for the boss painters who got the contracts for painting the schools in the city," related Blue Jaw. "The deal was to keep the unions off these contractors so they could hire and fire like they pleased—keep the unions out and let the contractors have open shop. That way, they could keep wages 'way under the scale, meaning they could put in low bids and get all the contracts."

The partners were handed $1,000 by the boss contractors as a down payment for their services.

"It is a big thing," Blue Jaw admitted. "Then the combination hears about it. They send for me and Bobby. There is Buggsy and Pep and Louis Capone. Reles was away (at Elmira Penitentiary). They tell us they had the school thing before us, and they are going to cut back in on us now. I know they never have it before.

"Bobby and me go into a huddle. I say, 'It is your thing, and you took me into it.' I say, 'If you want to fight them, we'll fight —whatever you want, we do.' Bobby leaves it up to me. I tell him that I know these guys all my life, and if he is satisfied, it is okay with me. So, we make a deal to split with them. That is how I hook up with the combination."

Only a few months later, however, Blue Jaw and Bobby dissolved their partnership, because of romance and finances and the two-timing heart of a lady.

"Bobby went with a girl, who, I suppose, he was giving a few dollars every once in a while," Blue Jaw related. "But she is going with a fellow called Leo the Turk—a high-pressure fellow—on the side, and he is clipping her. In other words, Bobby is a sucker. This Leo clips the girl for eight or nine hundred dollars. Well, it starts to cool off with her and him, and she wants her money back. There is an argument, and she comes to Bobby. She does not say Leo is her sweetheart. She says it is a loan, and Leo is a friend of the family. Bobby gets in it—and gets me in it. So, Bobby is mixing partnership with private business, involving women. I tell him, 'You and me are through.' "

The assets of the firm were divided by mutual agreement. "Bobby takes the poolrooms we got, and I get his end of the school-painting thing," Blue Jaw explained. "From then on, Buggsy Goldstein and me work together, hand in hand, on the school contractors. Buggsy is there to watch the combination's end."

For over a year things rolled along smoothly. Then, about Labor Day, in 1936, the Law came looking for Buggsy and Blue Jaw for the school-painting racket.

"We lam," Blue Jaw recited. "I turn over my shylock business to my friend, Manzo. I got to take my chances with him. I am in a hurry."

The fugitives set out on a cross-country motoring trip. "We got a car from Matty Moscowitz, the safe-cracker," he explained. "Matty was a hard-luck guy for real. He gets convicted on a wrong rap, about a dame. He wins the appeal, and a couple weeks after he is on the street, he gets knocked off sitting in a barber chair getting a shave."

"In California," Blue Jaw drifted into a travelogue, "we met a movie actor on small parts, who is a brother of a friend of mine. And we know Bug Siegel and Meyer Lansky—from the big Syndicate. While we are there, though, Pep sends us a letter to get out. He says to go to the tomato farm of Menici in Milton, N. Y., near Newburgh and lay low. I hear Lepke is afraid we will be nailed out in California."

The tomato farm, up the Hudson from New York, was both hangout and hideout. The owner would accept no payment for keeping the mob's lammisters. "So," Blue Jaw explained, "every day we play pinochle and purposely lose a dollar or two. That way, we pay for our stay."

Financing for the cross-country tour had been accomplished by contacting Pittsburgh Phil through an attorney. The two tourists would tell him at what Western Union office they would stop next to pick up needed cash.

"From the tomato farm, Buggsy makes the contact to have the money sent to Newburgh," Blue Jaw disclosed. "But the wires are tapped. When Buggsy goes to the Western Union, he is snatched."

In jail, Buggsy found an inmate just being discharged, and handed him a five-dollar bill. "Get in touch with Menici's tomato farm," he requested, "and just say, 'Evaporate.' That's all—just 'evaporate.' " The man kept the five dollars—and delivered the message to the police.

"That night, I am wondering where Buggsy is," Blue Jaw continued. "I see headlights coming. I don't think it is Buggsy, so I go to a back window to leave—and I find a gun pointed at me. They put me in with Buggsy. We got out, though."

On his return to his old haunts, Blue Jaw found his shylock business virtually wiped out. In his predicament, he sought Reles. The Kid let him have $1,100 to pay his debts, and then bought his dead business for $2,300 more.

"I sold him on the proposition it is a prosperous concern," Blue Jaw smiled. He was to receive a $40 weekly salary to handle it for the combination.

"I put all my time into it," he said, "and in about a year, it is back making $500 a week clear. I pay Reles back. One day he calls me and he says I am getting a raise to $75 a week. I say, 'That is nice—and I am also going to take a piece of the take.' Reles is slow answering, like Reles always is when it comes to giving," Blue Jaw added. "He finally says I could have 25 per cent, but I got to guarantee the combination $150 a week. After that, I am an important man in the eyes of the combination."

Blue Jaw's car-stealing talents reached their peak in 1939. We were able to count five murders between January and July for which he acquired the transportation. On two of them, he drove the murder car. Among these, Magoon and Reles detailed the removal of Whitey Friedman—a remarkably rounded account, for motive, plot and execution.

An important meeting was held at Pittsburgh Phil's home one April Sunday afternoon. Principal speaker was one of Lepke's leading lieutenants, Tom Kutty. (His name really was Cutler, or the variant, Kutler.) Kutty explained that one Whitey Friedman, a labor personality, was suspected of informing on Lepke and that, from his hideout lair, Lepke had dictated Whitey's elimination.

"Let's stage a phony pinch at his house," Reles proposed, the stage manager directing a production. "We make out we are the Law. We take Whitey out—and bury him."

"That's good," Buggsy admired. But then, Buggsy always admired the Kid's gimmicks.

Pittsburgh Phil vetoed it. "This Whitey is sure to balk at a pinch," he said. "Then we'll have to hit him and his wife, both, right in the house."

Eventually, the decision was for orthodox methods—on the street near Whitey's house. The two transportation specialists, Blue Jaw and Sholem, "clipped" the hot car across town, near Ebbets Field. A day or so later, Louis Capone rang the doorbell of Reles' home. He was carrying a package. The Kid's wife and mother-in-law opened the door and said they were sorry, he was asleep, and could they take the package. Capone suppressed a grin, picturing the reaction if these ladies were to open his parcel.

"Will you wake him, please," the suave Capone urged. "It's important."

Reles carried the bundle into the cellar. Inside was a shotgun and a pistol. He picked a hacksaw from among his household tools and went to work cutting down the barrels of the shotgun to a size appropriate for the task. Pittsburgh Phil and Blue Jaw arrived and watched, like a pair of "sidewalk superintendents."

"Afterward, me and Pep take the shotgun out to the lots in Canarsie and try it," Blue Jaw reported. "Both barrels work real good."

Blue Jaw and Pittsburgh Phil then trekked to Manhattan to see what the man they were going to shoot looked like. Allie met them and led the way to a building in the garment district. He pointed to a man coming out and said, "That is Whitey." Pep and Blue Jaw followed Whitey into the subway and rode all the way back to Brooklyn in the same car with him.

"Now we got a good picture of the bum," Pittsburgh Phil nodded.

On the day for the killing, Mikey Syckoff was to park his car at the subway station nearest Whitey's home, then take the train to Manhattan and pick up Whitey's trail when he emerged from his office building, en route home. When Whitey left the subway in Brooklyn, Mikey would leave too, and notify the waiting killers of the approach of their target.

On the afternoon designated, Blue Jaw picked up the hot car at the drop which the combination rented. He drove to the corner at which he was to meet Pep, but the fashion-plate killer was not in sight. Searching for his confederate, from street to street, Magoon spotted Mikey in his car.

"Where's Pep?" he inquired anxiously. "He wasn't at the corner."

"I ain't seen him," Mikey confessed. "But it's too late today, anyway. The bum went home already."

These hoods invariably referred to their victim as "the bum," a peculiarity probably based on a psychology of justification. They thus sought either to soothe a fleeting flicker of conscience on the theory that killing "a bum" was excusable, or to work up a dislike for someone they were about to murder for business reasons, who might otherwise be a very nice fellow.

"Well, I better get this hot car back in the drop," Blue Jaw said to Mikey. "Follow me down, and I can ride back with you."

When they returned, an irate Pittsburgh Phil was pacing the sidewalk, accompanied by Buggsy.

"Where were you?" Magoon took the offensive at once.

"I was here," snarled Pep. "Where the hell was you?"

"Don't give me that," Blue Jaw contradicted. "I was right here."

A noisy argument developed. It upset Buggsy and Mikey. They did not relish being eye and ear witnesses to anyone facing up to the worst killer in the mob, or to what Pep might do about it.

"Don't holler at me when I was here and I know it," Blue Jaw roared finally.

Pittsburgh Phil, who had shot challengers for less, surprised the bystanders by turning and walking away. "He cooled off," the defiant Magoon remembered. "And we set the job up for the next night."

On the following evening, when the victim disembarked from

the subway, Mikey hurried to his parked car and drove it along the street where Whitey lived. As he passed the gunmen waiting in the hot car, he blew two blasts on his horn.

"A couple minutes later, the bum walks past us," Blue Jaw detailed. "Pep steps out with the shotgun. I pick up the pistol from the seat next to me in my right hand and steer with my left. Both of us got silk gloves on. Pep sneaks up and makes a jump a couple feet behind him. Then he blasts away at the back of his head. The bum drops. It sounds like a car backfiring.

"There is an old lady sitting on the stoop of a house. She lets out a scream. No doubt," he concluded, "she sees what happens."

Pittsburgh Phil leaped back into the car, and Blue Jaw sped around the eastern end of nearby Lincoln Terrace Park, where they abandoned the death vehicle and the shotgun. Passing a vacant lot, a block away, Blue Jaw tucked the pistol under a rock.

"About two or three o'clock the next morning," Blue Jaw topped off the recital, "Buggsy and me are coming back from a cabaret with some girls. We walk toward the lot. As we pass by, Buggsy and me excuse ourselves. We go over and get the gun from under the rock. Then we come back to the girls and take them home."

We now had a precious collection of bric-a-brac; like any connoisseur, we needed a place to keep our priceless pieces so they would be both handy to get at, and safe from damage or destruction.

Certainly, Kid Twist and Blue Jaw and Sholem and Julie and the rest were as valuable a set of curios as any prosecutor ever put together. It became obvious all too soon that the worst cutthroats in crime were more determined than ever to wipe them all out—and their families, too.

These were crafty criminals plotting the sabotage. They had unlimited funds as well as boundless personnel on call the country over. They could worm their way inside prisons. They had methods of finding out where a witness or a prisoner would be. The security we needed so vitally must have the answers to meet all potentials.

We had our sights lifted now toward indictment and trials of killers who had hundreds of murders to their credit. Keenly aware that our "glee club" could sing top mob moguls into the death house, the underworld threw the sabotage program into high gear. Efforts were redoubled toward silencing the irreplaceable pieces in our collection before they could be called to testify, in any manner, up to and including group assassination. At least two threats were telephoned to the sheriff's office in the first three weeks of the probe.

"If you think anything of those guys working for you, you better keep them out of the way, because we're gonna knock off all the canaries," was the brazen boast.

Sheriff James V. Mangano was inclined to believe the callers were cranks. But the threats could also have something to do with mob policy of shying from unnecessary killing. Whenever any witnesses—aside from our informers—had to make an appearance in court, before a grand jury or at the District Attorney's office, the sheriff had the responsibility of getting them there and back in one piece. And at the height of the probe, there were twenty-two material witnesses held under total bail of $1,800,000!

Reles and his chorus were in our care. Every one of them was a marked man for every second of the year and a half we held them. With Buggsy Siegel personally directing the picked torpedoes, many of them from out of town and not recognizable to us, only the most extraordinary precautions—and the best of luck— kept the songbirds alive.

After the trials started, two of the imported gunmen were assigned to silence the witnesses as they came out of the courthouse. They stationed themselves in the nearest building, at a window commanding the street along which the stoolpigeons were led. They had rifles equipped with telescopic sights. For days, they trained the high-powered guns on that street, and patiently waited for an open shot—when the detective with each witness would be out of position to intercept the bullet. One day, a gust of wind blew the hat off a detective as he led Allie to a waiting car. As the guard bent to retrieve it, the hotelkeeper's son was squarely in the sights of the guns. But before the shots could be fired, the detective had straightened up. It was that close.

The killers never did stop trying to get Reles. The Kid was the key to the Syndicate's threatened destruction. They cooked up one scheme that, for diabolical cunning, would have been hard to beat. They knew Reles was likely to make a court appearance on a certain day. That was easily ascertained from day-to-day developments in the newspapers. A fake traffic jam was plotted, to halt his car at an intersection along the route his guard would be certain to follow. All the torpedoes wanted was one shot in the open at Kid Twist. We received a tip on the scheme with only moments to spare. Reles was hastily loaded into a steel-sided armored car, as if he were the crown jewels or a Federal Reserve shipment—and with guns to match, inside. He got to court.

A Reles is the greatest asset a prosecutor can have—and the greatest liability. If an "accident" happens to such a key witness, all other witnesses are going to say to themselves, "This guy can't take care of me, either," and they are likely to balk at talking. We had to demonstrate conclusively that we would—and could— protect our informers. The chief worry, then, was how—and where.

Jails are no sanctuaries for canaries. They would be killed inside prison walls as easily as on a deserted street. Easier. Hard men are in jails. That is why the windows have bars and the guards are armed. A large percentage of any prison's population feels it is imprisoned because of stoolpigeons. Thus, the stoolpigeon is a symbol of their incarceration. Any informer placed among these bitter prisoners is a natural target. The shiv or the spoon sharpened down stealthily has been plunged before into the necks of singers inside prison walls. You can keep a prisoner in solitary, but then the chances are you will wind up with a babbling stir-bug character, worth nothing to anyone. Not even informers' jails, which have exclusive facilities for segregating stoolpigeons, were the best choice for our witnesses. Their information, remember, encompassed some of the biggest big shots in national mobdom. Master murderers were after them—organized killers who had pried themselves into more fortified places than an informers' jail.

We had to set up a vault that was entrance-proof and invasion-proof. The result was as elaborate an arrangement, short of a fortress, as human ingenuity could devise. Virtually one entire floor in one of the large downtown Brooklyn hotels was appropriated. It was high enough up so nothing could slip in through the windows except light and air. No one could get off an elevator at that floor unless he had been checked in below. The informers were kept in one large suite, which could only be entered by a single door—and that was backed by strong shiny bolts.

A system of mirrors was aligned, like a huge horizontal periscope, so that all approaches were under observation for the full length of the corridors. Slotted peepholes were set in the door, much as in the approved fashion of the speakeasy of Prohibition. Night and day, a squad of detectives stood guard. They had pistols and rifles and pump guns, and knew to how to use them. They ate with the informers and sat with them when they played cards, and were ready for anything.

The ultra-security precautions even impressed the thugs. "Machine guns and shotguns and what all else they got," an awed Sholem murmured. "When I go to sleep, two detectives sit in the room all night," he reported to his wife on one of her Sunday afternoon visits.

The elaborate setup did not escape the observation of defendants and attorneys during the trials. Defense counsel sardonically dinned into the jurors the verbal picture of gangsters "wined and dined and entertained at the public expense." The inference was that the witnesses were "singing for their supper"—that in return for pampered treatment, they were willing to testify for the State. Counsel also charged that the witnesses, in close confinement, had opportunity for collusion in testimony. The fact that the guarding detectives were under inflexible orders to forbid the witnesses from so much as mentioning any Murder, Inc., case—was casually brushed aside.

Those who listened to such contentions, however, obviously realized there must be a vital necessity for safety measures so careful and detailed. We were on our way to as important a series of criminal prosecutions as probably ever were put together in one investigation, and we were not going to lose our witnesses for any lack of watching over them. The proof of the pudding, finally, was that we brought witnesses into court who were able to point fingers at the deadliest of the murderers and say, "You were there and did it—and I saw you do it." We brought them in, like Frank Buck, alive.

8.

Ladies' night in Murder, Inc.

Odd shapes and sizes in the Ladies' Auxiliary—the strange behavior of Mrs. Tootsie—revenge en masse—body in the swamp —Miss Murder, Inc.: Miss Hotfoot—the "late" boy friends of the Kiss of Death Girl.

WE EXPECTED to find anything but romance in an investigation of assorted assassins and their bloody business. We were looking for murderers, not their amorous adventures. Nevertheless, the adventures kept cropping up, along with throat-cutting and cadavers in quicklime pits, and they provided no end of interesting little touches to the saga.

To myself, I have always labeled this particular facet, "The Ladies' Auxiliary of Murder, Inc." Under this heading, come the love lives of the killers—and some of these were only slightly less remarkable than their maneuvering in murder.

Now, the wives of some of the gangsters seemed to be nice girls, and you felt somewhat sorry for them and the fact that the delusions of grandeur entertained by their homicidal husbands wrecked their lives. Most were completely loyal. Recognition of this fidelity is inescapable. When Reles decided to talk, he trusted neither lawyers nor close male relatives nor anyone else he ever knew—with one exception. The only person in the world in whom he had complete faith was his wife. To her alone, he entrusted the life-and-death mission of going to the District Attorney to ask for the interview that started the avalanche.

The unswerving loyalty of these women, however, was rarely mutual. Wifely fealty was generally repaid with a continuous indulgence in extramarital activities. The exceptions were notable only for their rarity. Thus, when Pretty Levine and his lovely

191

Helen fell into a desperate sobbing embrace, their complete devotion was so obviously real as to be extraordinary among these philandering felons.

Mostly, though, the Ladies' Auxiliary was made up of the girl friends—clinging, curvaceous clotheshorses, generally, with furs and diamonds and the lacquered look of so many store-window mannequins. As a group they came in all sizes, shapes and hair tints. Those we include here were not exceptions, but, rather, representative of a cross-section. They ranged from beautiful flossies to the plain, sometimes even the ugly; from mental pygmies to those who could fit in any set; from hard-looking, vinegar-voiced flowers of the slums to polished pretties with good table manners. The only item they shared in common was their consorts.

They fought for their men, and when any of the gangsters was rubbed out or, later, electrocuted, you could always spot the lady with whom he had been dallying last. The girl friend donned deepest mourning, and wore her widow's weeds even longer than the widow. She felt she thus showed the more heartfelt grief.

A girl friend stuck to her thug as long as the thug would have her, a condition dependent on the old adage that nothing lasts forever. It was considered natural custom in their society for a girl, on ending a romance with one plug-ugly, to take up with another of the same—as often as not, a close friend of the very sweetheart who had just thrown her out. No one felt very uncomfortable; it was the way of life and love.

One mobster's idea of female pulchritude did not always meet with unanimous agreement from his associates. There was, for instance, Renee, who was Happy Maione's minx. Renee was a blonde, about twenty-six. She had most of the necessary assets of her sex—and in their proper places. Happy thought she was gorgeous. Reles, though, always said her eyes had a squint to them. However, Kid Twist and Happy never did see eye to eye.

What these girls could see in the cutthroats, was a riddle as unfathomable as some of their assassinations had been. As the lasses of the Ladies' Auxiliary flitted in and out of our probe, investigator after investigator would ask, "What have these bums got that gets these dolls?" None of the stock arguments—wealth, glamour, even plain animal attraction—held here. That applied not only to the Brooklyn branch, but everywhere in mobdom.

It certainly could not be their looks. Reles wouldn't have looked attractive even to an orang-utan. And the wooing and winning, by the oafish Vito Gurino, of the willowy redhead he met on a blind date remained an unsolved mystery even to the mob. Aside from, at best, three or four, none of the mobsters were likely prospects for screen tests, except, perhaps, for type-casting for a prison sequence. It is impossible, too, to conceive of these characters intriguing the opposite sex by conversational ability or wit. They had neither the romance of the poet in their souls nor the intelligence of the learned in their minds.

The girls did, however, glamourize the gorillas to themselves, and that, probably, was what sold them. Many of the girl friends started as kids, awestruck by the neighborhood big shots. These thugs traveled around the country. They sported flashy cars. They never appeared to work for a dollar. Surface glamour undoubtedly impressed these easily impressed neighborhood girls. To them, places like Hot Springs and Hollywood, Las Vegas and Miami were only names in the Sunday supplements. In their set, the girl was considered well traveled, indeed, who had even made the Catskills.

Whatever the kinship of spirit, it was a strong intersex magnet. Strong and strange. They attracted the hoods; the hoods attracted them. Only in rare instances were any of these lovelies drawn to people in ordinary life.

Connie, who ran a beauty shop in the Williamsburg section, was one who got around. For a time, she was chummy with Dasher Abbandando, proving the Dasher did not spend all his time at baseball and bloodletting. Then Connie became very friendly with Chippy Weiner, who developed from a bit player in Brooklyn, Inc., into a well-known burglar and fence in the late forties.

Chippy used to brag about the fifty suits of clothes he owned. He was equally versatile when it came to women. There was Connie, and there was a lady known widely as "the Red Rose of Williamsburg." This is, however, a horticultural misnomer; she possesses neither the aura nor the aroma of the American Beauty.

Once, the Red Rose had been Chippy's companion—until, that is, he laid eyes on her eighteen-year-old daughter. During our probe, Rose was established as a figure in the Larney Gang, a mob of shylocks and killers with ramifications in the Brownsville combination. The Red Rose, personally, was named in a large role in at least one murder. Then, there was Chippy's wife.

One cold, wet night in the winter of 1948, the telephone rang in Chippy's Manhattan apartment. Not long afterward, Mrs. Chippy donned her soft furs.

"I'm going to the corner for some cigarettes," she murmured as she drifted toward the door. Her mate, absorbed in the television screen before him, barely heard as she walked out into the mid-January slush—wearing open-toed shoes.

Not half an hour later, Chippy was shot full of holes, while he was sitting there viewing the video. It turned out afterward that the first—and last—act he performed after this untoward incident was to telephone Connie and whisper to her the names of the unfriendly individuals who did this to him. She admitted the phone call later.

"But I didn't get the names he said," she told detectives, so very rueful over her inability to help.

Chippy's wife did not return to the apartment until an hour afterward. Police were naturally curious as to how open-toed sandals remained so dry, after an hour and a half on the wet streets.

"I took a cab to the Hotel New Yorker to meet a friend—but I was stood up," she disclosed.

A month later, a jeweler was held up. As the stick-up men fled, the victim reached the window in time to get the license number of their car. Sal Bretagna and Curly Fennessey were picked up, Curly in New York and Sal in Boston, while entertaining two girls in a night club. Curly became panicky and offered to do some talking.

"Me and Sal heisted that joint so Sal could get some dough for a getaway, on account of the Chippy job . . . he's hot," was the unexpected information.

It developed that Sal had murdered Chippy for one Farby, who was somewhat annoyed because Chippy had shortchanged him by

$500 on the spoils of a hijacked truckload of cloth. Farby had been the "friend" who called up Chippy's wife. Farby, who was a ladies' man, probably would have kept the date, too, only he was more anxious to get Mrs. Chippy out of the house so he and Sal could attend to her husband.

Unfortunately, Farby never had a chance to atone for standing up the lady. He and Sal went to the electric chair too soon.

Mrs. Tootsie Feinstein was a curly-haired wide-eyed darling who, as later developed, had nothing to be ashamed of in a bathing suit. Tootsie, her husband, was one of Lepke's most trusted hands, deep in the murder and rackets. Too deep for him, in fact, for, on May 10, 1939, he said he was fed up and he was going straight. He said it loud enough to be heard, and that was a mistake.

That very evening, Tootsie's close pal, Bug Workman, stopped in at the apartment. He nodded a hello to Mrs. Tootsie, then turned to his old chum.

"I got something on my mind," he said. "How about taking a ride?" Tootsie saw no reason not to help a friend with a problem, even though he had renounced the way of life the friend practiced.

Charlie the Bug drove Tootsie to Lyndhurst, N. J. There he was murdered and buried in the lime-lined gang graveyard the mob maintained on the banks of the placid Passaic River. The boys liked Tootsie. They felt sorry he had to go. But when a mob member suffered pangs of honesty, there always was the risk that his conscience might feel like explaining trade secrets to the Law.

Mrs. Tootsie was obliging enough not to make a point of the absence of her helpmeet to the police. The boys felt some solace should be tendered her, both for her loss and the fact that she did not mention the intimate details thereof out loud. Shortly after she had seen the last of Tootsie, the doorbell rang one day. She pressed the buzzer which unlocked the inner door of the apartment's downstairs lobby. But no one came up. Mystified, Mrs. Tootsie went to her living-room window and peered out. On the sidewalk, a man was looking up. As her face appeared, he beckoned. Mrs. Tootsie traipsed downstairs. The man thrust an envelope into her hand, muttered something about, "Tootsie is all right," and meandered off. Imagine Mrs. Tootsie's surprise when she opened the envelope, and found $50 in United States currency!

About a week later, the episode was repeated; and every week thereafter, for a considerable period of time. She always went downstairs to meet the messenger. (An attractive young widow, living alone, can't be too careful about inviting gentleman callers into her apartment.)

Allie recited this tale in detail for us when he started to talk. "I knew Mrs. Tootsie very good," he said. So, Mrs. Tootsie was invited in as a material witness. It was a memorable occasion—the first anniversary of the very day on which Tootsie had disappeared. She wore costly jewelry and tasteful clothing. She spoke in modulated tones. She was, you might say, every inch the lady. And she evinced a complete lack of worry over why Tootsie no longer took his breakfast coffee with her.

"And," she said of her weekly envelope, "I don't know where the fifty dollars comes from. I don't know any of the men who brought it. And I don't know who my husband went out with that night."

Most of all, she denied that she had ever even heard of Bug Workman and Allie and their wives. Allie was brought into the room.

"I," was Mrs. Tootsie's disdainful comment, "never saw him before."

Allie's sensitive nature was affronted. "She's a damned liar," he retorted, his chronic pained expression even more tormented than usual. "I delivered the first fifty to her, and some after that. She knows all the boys." He thought for a moment; then he brightened a bit, and he said, "I can prove it, too."

At his suggestion, a package was dug from among his belongings—a roll of 16 mm. movie film. We ran it off. It was fine, clear action of a group at play on a white beach, swinging golf clubs on a palm-fringed course, and similar pleasant pastimes. Among the cavorters were Charlie the Bug and Mrs. Workman and Allie and his bride, and even Lepke's partner, Gurrah. And, flitting in and out of scenes like a hummingbird in shorts, was a lady who looked remarkably like Mrs. Tootsie! The abridged creation adorned her charms in a manner to indicate she was not one to hide her equipment, of which she possessed better-than-average stock. Evidently, Gurrah noticed it, too. The pictures showed him lighting her cigarette and otherwise being quite the attentive gallant. It was just as well, perhaps, that Mrs. G. was not on hand.

It seems that in order to make it easier to stand Tootsie's absence, Mrs. Tootsie had gone to Florida when the rest of the mob headed south that winter. Allie was there, as usual, and Allie had become an amateur photography fan. He brought his camera to the beach and here and there, and took a lot of pictures of all his pals, their wives and their playmates, rollicking and romping. No wonder Allie felt so hurt over Mrs. Tootsie saying she did not know him.

We ran through the entire film for the "unknowing" lady. From end to end, she evinced no reaction to the lady on the screen cavorting with the hoodlums. When the lights went up, Mrs. Tootsie looked at us as coolly as before.

"I don't know any of those men," she repeated flatly. "I never saw them in my life." And, she added, she was not at all sure that it was even she in that picture.

All in all, Mrs. Tootsie was about as exasperating as any female could be. As a conversational opponent, her "footwork" was as slick as a boxing champion's. She was, in fact, the female Charlie Workman—Charlie the Bug with a hairdo.

"Where is your husband?" I asked.

"I don't know."

"Why did he go? For how long?" Shrugs.

"Did you report his absence to the Missing Persons Bureau?"

"No."

"Why not?"

"I expected him to come back."

"Weren't you worried?"

"Not worried. I was concerned some."

"Where did the money come from every week?"

"I don't know."

"Did you ever ask the man who brought the fifty dollars about your husband?"

"At first. He said, 'Tootsie's okay.' So, I stopped asking."

That was what floored us—that utter lack of normal wifely curiosity about her missing husband, from whom she had heard not a word for one year. There were those of us who were mean enough to suspect that, perhaps, that weekly delivery of U. S. currency had warped her memory, to say nothing of playing tricks on her eyesight.

At any rate, Mrs. Tootsie was the complete antithesis of the usual run of the Ladies' Auxiliary, who mourned their consorts so passionately, with or without benefit of clergy. Here was a widow, complete with marriage license, ring, and, it is assumed, honeymoon, whose grief—or lack of it—so affected her that she could not even recognize herself prancing around in a bathing suit as big as two handkerchiefs, with the very murderers who had made her a widow.

There is nothing new about women and gangsters getting together. The "weaker sex" have long picked cutthroats for partners with no less evident enjoyment than those who lean to school-teachers and librarians. There have been bobbed-hair bandits; pistol-packing deadshot gals smoking cigar for cigar with bank-robber boy friends; women in men's clothes whose ideas on fashion centered more on the built-in shoulder holster than the plunging neckline and strapless bra.

The gunmen of Murder, Inc., however, did not hold with gang girl friends as business partners. They may have been modern in the art of skulduggery, but, for social pleasures, they were of the old-fashioned school which believes woman's place is in the home. Or in a gilded cage, anyway. I don't recall one of the Ladies' Auxiliary pretties who had a hand in the business—whose dainty fingers dipped in the blood. The killers did not mix business and pleasure.

That is what made that brisk fall evening in 1935 all the more memorable. Perhaps there had come a time when the policy of exclusion piqued the girls; or maybe the boys just decided that the girls ought to get a break. At any rate, a gala affair was arranged, a special ceremony. That was Ladies' Night in Murder, Inc.!

Now, this developed from the evening some months before, when Hy Kasner was placed in a burlap bag, tied very attractively at the neck. The sack was dropped into a sewer in lower Brooklyn, obviously on the assumption that by the time the currents had done tossing it about, it might come up in the Azores, if at all. The tides, however, did not co-operate. The bag, and contents, flushed into open water and was spotted while still practically touching the shoreline. It was fished out at the junction of Jamaica Bay and Fresh Creek Basin, a narrow inlet stabbing two miles into southeastern Brooklyn.

This was, understandably, most embarrassing for those who had done in poor Hy. It was even more embarrassing, when, in no time at all, the grapevine reported the identities of the executioners. They were named as Jack Elliott, a tough, dangerous professional bodyguard and burglar; Joey Amberg, a narcotics distributor and somewhat influential racketeer, and Frankie Tietlebaum, a well-known Manhattan thug.

Just what caused the upheaval which resulted in Kasner holding the bag—and winding up in it—is not officially known. It might have been a holdover vendetta from the war between the East's leading alcohol combination and Waxey Gordon in the early thirties. At any rate, each of the killers had served in the pooled army which had been recruited to combat Waxey. Amberg was a Bug & Meyer mobster, Elliott was a loner who had done work for Buggsy Siegel personally, and Tietlebaum was a Lepke killer.

Not long before his death, Kasner had become an associate in the organization of Albert Anastasia and Louis Capone. No matter what he had been before, he was now one of their men. Albert was naturally incensed when his new hand ended up as a bag job in a sewer. The board of governors of the still-new Syndicate was urgently requested to do something about it. The three perpetrators were so very well connected, though, that a near-crisis resulted. It was intensified by the fact that Joey Amberg was an associate of Joey Adonis.

"Joey A. had an interest with Amberg in some lines," was the way Reles put it. These included food markets and a part of the Brooklyn clothing industry.

The kangaroo court studied the case at length. "A lot of pressure was put on Ben Siegel and Joey A.," Reles went on. The Kid himself was "away" at the time—making one of his rare visits to prison. But, he hastened to add, his co-workers kept him abreast of business progress.

"Pep come to see me," he recalled. "He tells me, 'They are putting heat on to hit Amberg, but Joey A. likes him and wants they should leave him alone.' But the heat is too much," the Kid concluded. "They finally get the okay. Ben and the rest got to go along."

The reprisals for Kasner's demise had to be taken one at a time, as convenience and developments dictated. Joey Amberg was first in line, since he spent most of his time around Brooklyn. The other two were intermittent "traveling men." Some two months after Hy Kasner was dropped into a sewer, the program was launched.

Louis Capone summoned Happy, and, along with him, Philly and Red, two of the water front boys. Red, incidentally, was to be awarded a gangland extermination himself within seven months of this incident.

Joey Amberg was lured into a garage a short step from what is now the magnificent four-block-square Brownsville slum-clearance project. In those days, that particular garage was run by a partnership, one-half of which happened to be Pittsburgh Phil. Joey had his chauffeur, Mannie Kessler, with him when he was steered into the place, which was, indeed, unfortunate for Mannie. When Joey was stood up against the wall, there was nothing to do but line the chauffeur up with him. Then the firing squad opened up. The heads of both men were all but blown apart. Three rivulets of blood oozed from holes in Joey and trickled across the garage floor, into the water drain. The gunmen did not even wait for the bodies to hit the floor.

The exhilaration of the occasion apparently overexcited Philly. As the party dashed out into the darkness, he evidently forgot where Happy had parked the getaway car. Later, Happy told Reles about it.

"Hap says Philly takes off the wrong way," the Kid repeated. "Hap gets the car and starts hollering, 'Philly; hey, Philly. Over here.' He is looking around for Philly in the dark. He gotta get out of there, because there is a traffic cop down on the corner.

At the last minute, he finds Philly, and they take off. When they go by the cop, he takes a shot at them. It misses."

Just why Philly should have been upset is a bit obscure, since he was hardly a novice. As far back as 1923 he and Angelo Bacci, a Boston hoodlum, were indicted for murdering John Piccone in a bootlegging battle. The indictment was later dismissed—and two years later, Philly became an American citizen. For Philly, Reles explained, was Philly Mangano, a friend of Anastasia. Philly had business in the laundry, water front and shylock trades, and was a brother of Vince Mangano, who is frequently mentioned as a Syndicate power.

One April day in 1951, Philly's body was found in the ten-foot-high marsh weeds of a desolate swamp, just across Mill Basin from Floyd Bennett Field, the huge Navy and Coast Guard airbase. His black tie was neatly in place under the gold tie clasp. His flashy diamond ring was still on his finger. But he had no pants on. A gun apparently had been placed right against his head, and the trigger pulled three times.

Now, Philly never was hardly more than a staff operative, according to our informers. Nevertheless, the more lurid press immediately indulged in magnifying his importance remarkably. One identified him as a "member of Mafia's Grand Council which hands out orders to such top-flight ganglords as Lucky Luciano and Frank Costello." Even if Mafia was that powerful, it would certainly come as a surprise to the underworld to learn that Philly Mangano ever was handing out orders to Lucky or Frank C. or anyone even close to their rank.

The theories advanced as to why Philly wound up as an obvious gangland extermination, after so many years of serving the Syndicate, have piled high in recent months. One of the most loudly voiced was that he had informed federal authorities, including the Kefauver Committee on Crime, of the whereabouts of his brother Vince, who had departed his usual haunts. This was proved somewhat laughable when Detective Captain William Kimmins said he learned Philly had not even seen a single Kefauver Committee representative. By that time, Philly had been buried—only a few yards, incidentally, from where Charlie Fischetti, Al Capone's cousin and Chicago rackets heir, had been interred a week earlier, after his death in Florida of natural causes.

No one has mentioned one possible motive that has, at least, a basis in precedent. This is the possibility that sudden new pressure early in 1951, applied by law enforcement on top bosses in various places—particularly such Brooklyn executives as Joey A. and Anastasia—might have set off another War of Extermination. Items such as gambling charges would not worry the executives—but investigations of such charges might turn up other matters. Philly knew a great deal concerning a number of sudden deaths, such as the Joey Amberg job—which Reles vowed was a reprisal for the killing of one of Anastasia's men.

Among those questioned about Philly's slaying were Frank Costello, Joey A. and Anastasia. Costello said he did not know Philly from a Labrador Eskimo. Adonis, exhibiting a remarkable memory, recalled Philly as a character, twenty years ago, around his restaurant where many ranking politicians of the city gathered. Anastasia said he had known both Manganos like brothers for thirty years.

Talking to newsmen afterward, Joey A. came up with a theory of his own that was, to say the least, interesting.

"Philly's pants were off," pointed out the national Syndicate executive. "When you're caught with your pants down, it means you're a ladies' man. This must have been a crime of passion." Philly, it should be pointed out, was fifty-one.

Twelve days after Joey Amberg was mowed down in 1935, the revengeful gangsters caught up with the second of Hy Kasner's killers—Frankie Tietlebaum.

It was decided a bag job was in order, so that the motive would not be mistaken as any but the one intended. The mobsters, though, did treat Frankie to a wardrobe trunk instead of a burlap sack, and instead of dumping him into a sewer, they left the trunk under a bridge in Manhattan. It was suspected that the assassins had made a mathematical error—that after getting Frankie into the trunk, they discovered it was too large to stuff into a sewer.

Jack Elliott was, by far, the toughest of Kasner's killers to corner. A swarthy barrel-chested man, Elliott was a cold, methodical criminal who sprang from the Brooklyn waterfront. Although a loner, he was known all over mobdom. Once Al Capone practically begged him to take a job as one of his Chicago gunmen.

"I could use a fellow like you," the scarfaced crime boss of the Midway offered.

"Al," Elliott politely refused, "I work alone. I don't travel with an outfit."

Mostly, Jack's trade was as a hired protector. Sometimes he was a paid guard against holdups of gambling enterprises—either in Brooklyn buildings or aboard excursion boats plying from New York and Brooklyn to New Jersey seashore resorts. Occasionally, he hired out to guard a load of liquor in transit.

He had an excellent reputation for dependability. An affluent bookmaker once received a tip that he was going to be kidnaped. He signed Jack up to see that it did not happen. A day or so after beginning work, Elliott spotted two members of the mob eying him and his client as they walked along a street. Jack walked unhesitantly up to the gunmen.

"If you come within twenty feet of that guy, I'll knock you both off with one slug," he warned. He wasn't belligerent. It was more authoritative, like an umpire drawing a line in the dirt and telling an argumentative batsman, "Cross that, and you're out of the game."

The two hoodlums left at once. The next day, Jack was approached by some more of the boys—thugs he knew.

"Geez, Jack," they pleaded, "we're only trying to snatch the guy and you're in the way."

"That guy is paying me to take care of him, see," they were cautioned. "He's my property, and if you try to take my property, you guys know what'll happen." The mobsters changed their mind.

Respect or no, however, when he bucked the combination by helping to kill Kasner, he had to go. The executioners had to wander far from home base before they accomplished it. Finally, one night, Jack was locked inside his automobile on the Hackensack Flats in New Jersey. Then they set fire to the car—and forgot to let Jack out.

As might be expected, the deaths of the three stalwarts of the gun (with Joey Amberg's chauffeur thrown in for good measure)

.

had repercussions in the underworld. It was generally agreed that it had to be done as a demonstration of the new Syndicate's determination to brook no deviation from its policy and law. However, there were some recalcitrants, and the loudest was Joey Amberg's brother, Pretty.

Pretty's first name was Louis. But his athletic build, his sleek hair and his well-cut features, which had the girls of his set swooning over themselves, made it a foregone conclusion that he would be called, Pretty. He is not to be confused, of course, with Pretty Levine, who would never have dared object to anything the mob did. Not out loud, anyway.

Pretty Amberg was upset, naturally, that his brother had been shot full of holes. More distracting was the fact that Joey had been much the smarter of the two about business, and with Joey gone, it affected Pretty's pocketbook. At one time, Pretty had been one of Dutch Schultz's hired hands. He must have been bitten by the same bug that made the Dutchman a trigger-happy paranoiac. Like the Dutchman, Pretty talked too much. He knew Louis Capone had set up his brother's extermination, with the active directorial asistance of Pittsburgh Phil, in whose garage Joey had been executed. Pretty leveled his revenge at them, rather than at the actual triggermen, who were merely employes under orders. In the best Dutch Schultz manner, Pretty made what amounted to a public proclamation that he was "going to get Capone and Pep." The directors of Brooklyn, Inc., heard about it. Pretty's death warrant was sealed.

The boys realized Pretty would be suspicious of everyone connected in any way with the combination. As a result, it was decided to borrow a man from Lepke to maneuver Pretty into position for the "pop." This was a brand-new switch: the Brownsville killers, contract murderers, asking outside help on an assassination. Up stepped Lepke's staff extermination expert, Mendy, to insist he was the ideal man.

"Pretty won't go with nobody but me—he likes me," the hulking hood volunteered. "I'll steer him; he'll never get wise."

Mendy had just the place, too. Pretty would not go near Brownsville or Ocean Hill. No one knew better than he that those neighborhoods were entirely enemy-held. The site Mendy had in mind was in the vicinity of the plaza leading to the Williamsburg Bridge over the East River. This was as close as you could come to Manhattan and still be in Brooklyn. On the fringe of the plaza was a club run by a friend of Mendy—a character who was not at all particular about the uses made of his premises. The bulky thug got in touch with Pretty one mild evening and suggested a visit to his friend's club. "It's no trip at all," he promised. "Right the other side of the bridge. We're there in ten minutes." That suited Pretty.

At the club, Mendy's friend, the proprietor, invited them into the office for a drink. The libation, however, was never poured. Two of Mendy's confederates were waiting there, and all went to work hacking on Pretty with sharp instruments.

It was decided to dump Pretty's not-so-pretty remains on one of the dark, lightly traveled side streets near the Brooklyn Navy Yard, only a mile or so away. To forestall identification, what was left of the cut-up gangster would be locked in a car over which liberal quantities of gasoline would be poured. A match would then be dropped on the pyre. The cutthroats selected North Elliott Place, narrow and only one block long, which faces on a small patch of green called City Park. Not until the rite was over would it be likely to attract the attention of a curious policeman, who might object to holding a cremation in an automobile on a public street.

It was then that someone got the inspiration. At least, that is what we were told, five years later. At that moment, an undying paragraph was written in the chronicle of crime ·and chivalry. Heretofore, the fair companions of the torpedoes had been summarily shunted from all business matters. Here was the chance to make up to the pretties for it. Why not hold an occasion for them? Why not a Ladies' Night in Murder, Inc.? The idea met with immediate enthusiastic endorsement.

Just how "Miss Murder, Inc.," was chosen, our informants no longer knew. That was relatively unimportant, anyway. And the "Oscar" to the winner? Why . . . the lucky lovely was permitted to touch the match to the gasoline-soaked car containing the well-hacked body of Pretty Amberg! Could she ask more? It went off beautifully, too.

Some of the stoolpigeons advised us that this Queen of Ladies' Night felt so signally honored, she bragged about it for months afterward. Two women still in Brooklyn were mentioned as possible sources of additional details. They had known all the boys well; some intimately. During an eight-hour interrogation, they filled in some of the circumstances of this memorable event.

Both have long since turned in their membership cards in the Ladies' Auxiliary, so there is no reason to identify them by name here. Had the mob known they were talking to us, neither would have lived for very long. One, a beauty-shop proprietress, explained that she had a husband and a son—and a sweetheart. She, therefore, would appreciate as little advertising as possible. The other had become a hospital attendant, and was working seriously at it. Both were brunette, and both were, as they say, well stacked in the matter of feminine accouterment. Yet, both earnestly conceded that, on looks alone, the shellacked blonde who was Miss Murder, Inc., had it all over them.

They explained, too, that the rest of the girls gave the winner the nickname of Hot Foot. When her back was turned, the less sportsmanlike altered this to Hot Tomato.

"They," the brunettes insisted, "were just sore losers."

If the Ladies' Auxiliary had been a Greek letter sorority on some college campus, with secret handshake and, maybe, Friday night pajama parties, Evelyn Mittelman could not have been ignored for high office. Treasurer, perhaps. Any sweet young thing who could round up a collection of jewels like Evelyn did, traveling in the company Evelyn kept, would certainly qualify to handle the exchequer.

They called Evelyn "the Kiss of Death Girl," and that came close to being the understatement of the year. Being her boy friend around that time was like advertising for a violent end.

Evelyn started out as a luscious blonde from Brooklyn's Williamsburg section in the early thirties. Even then she caught the eye and held the memory. Nine years later, when she burst into our investigation, Eddie Zeltner, the *New York Daily Mirror's* veteran columnist, recalled her from those days.

"I knew Evelyn ten years ago, when she was barely sixteen,"

wrote Eddie, "a gorgeous blonde who used to come from Williamsburg to Coney Island to swim, and dance in the cellar clubs which are grammar schools for gangsters."

Evelyn moved quickly from the grammar schools. When she was eighteen, she turned up in California, with a fellow named Hy Miller gaga about her. There came a night when she and Hy were at a dance hall, and another young man came along, took one look at Evelyn, and was smitten. This romantic impulse led to one word, and another, and pretty soon, there was a heated discussion. The newly smitten swain claimed Hy had insulted Evelyn. There was a fight—and Miller became Evelyn's "late" boy friend. Two or three years later, she reappeared in Brooklyn, tall and statuesque, with another consort in tow—one Robert Feurer. One night, at another dance, she caught the eye of Sol Goldstein, who was known through the mobs as Jack, and who had good connections in the lush wholesale fish-market rackets of lower Manhattan. Jack came over to talk to the lovely young thing, and Feurer did not like it. He not only said so to Jack, but to Evelyn as well. Jack said no one could give the lovely young lady a hard time like that while he was around. So, he up and killed Feurer. Exit another boy friend.

Jack took over as "top man." Then Pittsburgh Phil went to a dance one night and he saw Evelyn. He liked what he saw, and said so. And the same old scramble started. Jack complained that was no way for Pittsburgh Phil to behave, and that Evelyn should not act as if she liked it, either. Pittsburgh Phil thought this was an insult to a sweet, defenseless damsel. The two men repaired to a poolroom, and Pittsburgh Phil gave the boy friend a terrible beating with a billiard cue. It had the simultaneous effect of completely altering Jack's features and his romantic notions about the Kiss of Death Girl. To the victor, the spoils; Pittsburgh Phil moved in as the boy friend. Evelyn, who had been making steady progress, had really hit the big leagues this time—being sweetheart to the torpedo ranked as the most zealous killer of them all.

Battered as he was, Jack (or Sol), nevertheless, had managed to elude the usual fate that befell his predecessors who fought to hold Evelyn's favor. Jack's mother was glad he broke off with the Kiss of Death, and was even happier when, a short time later, he stopped running with the mob. The change was affected after he met Helen, who was the daughter of a used-car dealer in Cleveland.

"Sol is away from the tough boys at last," said his mother contentedly to his sister.

That was in the summer of 1936, and one day in July, the pleased parent received word that Sol and Helen were married, and were honeymooning at Glen Wild, a pretty spot in the Catskills, off the beaten path of vacationing crowds. Weeks passed, then months—and there was no further word from the love-birds. Sol's mother began to worry. Eventually, she got in touch with Helen, although the bride was not easy to find.

"What happened—I haven't heard from Sol in months?" asked the anxious mother. Tears came to the eyes of the pretty young wife.

"I don't know," she cried. "We were in our room getting dressed for the Saturday night dance, when the phone rang and he answered it. A little while later, some men drove up. Sol said he'd be back in a few minutes. I haven't seen him since."

Through the ominous silence of the following weeks, the frantic mother went nearly wild. After two months, she set out for the mountains, to do some checking on her own. And the first thing she discovered there was that Sol's bride was not nearly as upset as she expected a bride stranded on her honeymoon would be. In fact, as she reported later, there was Helen entertaining in a cottage practically next door to the honeymoon nest she had shared with her bridegroom. Gone, too, was the broken-hearted front.

"Sol was thrown into a lake," Helen explained in a matter-of-fact recital, when she had pulled herself from the boys and girls at her party.

For four long years, mystery and silence surrounded the disappearance of the son who had made his mother so happy when he stopped running with the tough boys, and took up with a "nice girl." Then, in 1940, Allie and Pretty told the minute details of a contract on a man they knew only as "Jack," and Reles filled in the missing identification. Reles could always be depended on for such incidental intelligence. His fellow felons seemed forever to have been apprising him of the fulfilment of plans and contracts.

The Kid was the "big ear" of the troop into which all of them dumped their autobiographical trash.

What had happened was this:

At the end of July, in 1936, just about the time Sol was starting his honeymoon, his name came up back in Brooklyn. A contract was received from Manhattan. Louis Capone said it was to eliminate Sol for Joe Socks, or Zocks, which is another name for Socks Lanza, a ruthless extortionist who controlled the rackets at the tremendous Fulton Fish Market in downtown Manhattan.

This municipally owned marketplace is the second largest wholesale fish market in the United States. It does more than a quarter of a billion dollars of business each year, distributing denizens of salt and fresh water to retailers as far away as Mississippi and Indiana. Socks Lanza, a vicious overjowled outlaw, was the actual boss of the institution. He had the power to bring its functions to a grinding stop through a czarist control of half a dozen illicit operations. Through the twenties and early thirties, there is no telling how high in six or even seven figures were his extortions from his thousand-member Sea-Food Workers Union, his Fulton Market Watchmen's and Protective Association and assorted other "services" to which fish dealers subscribed in mortal fear of what would happen to them and their legitimate businesses if they didn't. Socks, besides, had helped organize dealers' associations, had a piece of a canning company and controlled the vast retail fish establishment, near the parent Fulton Market.

He had excellent connections, too. Once, a policeman dared to chase some of his "boys" from Fulton Market. Two days later, strangely enough, the policeman found himself pounding a beat in the farthest outlying precincts of Staten Island.

In the mid-thirties, Socks was indicted by a federal grand jury for monopolistic control of fish sent from Minnesota, Illinois, Wisconsin, Michigan, Ohio and Canada. His outfit controlled the market and the prices, the indictment said; his strong-arms beat up buyers, wrecked trucks, dumped fish and threw stink bombs or acid to keep dealers in line. Socks was convicted, appealed, and won a retrial in 1936. In looking about him, he apparently realized that Sol, who had ambitions on the Fulton Market take himself before he stopped running with the tough boys, could be a dangerous witness. That is why Sol's name came up in Brownsville while he was honeymooning in the Catskills.

At the end of July, Louis Capone summoned Pretty to the Corner. "Go up to Loch Sheldrake in the mountains, where Pep is staying, to do some work," he directed. "Pep will tell you."

Pretty and Dukey drove to the Catskills and found not only Pittsburgh Phil, but Mikey Syckoff and Jack Cutler, another of the boys. Pittsburgh Phil briefed his squad. It was necessary to get Sol away from the side of his bride. Pittsburgh Phil was exceptionally appreciative that he himself could not appear in the enticing. His billiard-parlor relations with Sol, or Jack, over Miss Mittelman, were not conducive to such familiarity. However, Jack would not recognize "the kids"—Pretty and Mikey and Cutler.

At 9 P.M., on August 3, the phone rang in the cottage at Glen Wild, just as Jack was tying his silk cravat for the evening dance. Whatever bait the kids used, it drew a bite, for Sol thought the message important enough to warrant leaving the side of his bride. A car with three men in it pulled up in front of the cottage. Sol got in, and the automobile drove off. The bride saw that much from the window.

Sol made one vital mistake, aside, that is, from entering the car at all. He should not have sat in the back seat, between two of the kids. One of them mugged him—grabbed him from behind and held him with forearm gripped around his throat. As Sol squirmed, Pretty brought out a hammer he had concealed, and struck him a hard, but not fatal, blow on the head, rendering him unconscious. Pretty was under very specific—and most unusual—orders not to do any permanent damage.

"Just snatch the bum and bring him here," Pittsburgh Phil had instructed most pointedly. "Don't knock him off."

To Phil, nothing could provide a more delightful situation—a personal score and a contract at the same time. The "kids" delivered their inert package to him at the rear of his hotel. There the master murderer finished what he had started in the poolroom. Perhaps he was thinking of Evelyn. He put special artistry into his roping. He packaged his bound victim in a blanket and toted the bundle to the lake shore, where Allie and Jack Drucker were waiting in a rowboat. They paddled out to the center of the lake and Phil personally threw the blanketed bundle overboard.

Now, there were some who pooh-poohed the influence of romance on this matter; they maintain it was strictly business. But that does not account for Pittsburgh Phil's strange and explicit orders to bring Sol back alive, or his insistence that he rope the victim himself, and personally dump him out where it was nice and deep. He had taken Evelyn from Sol and was now head man in her life. This had heart interest all over it. This was more than a contract for Pep; it was a pleasure. And when he had completed the double-barreled mission, there was another dead ex-boy friend of the Kiss of Death Girl.

For nearly five years after that, the score remained unchanged. In fact, nothing much happened, except that about every time Evelyn went up to Sullivan County's resorts with Pep, by strange coincidence, a murder would follow the visit. Pep always was an unusual fellow that way.

Just to please Phil, Evelyn converted from a golden blonde to a raven brunette. When they walked down the street, the boys and girls would sigh after them. More than one housewife pointed and remarked, "Don't they make a handsome couple?" And her hard-working, and sometimes harried, husband would grunt in reply.

Then, in 1940, Pittsburgh Phil was thrown into jail. He had suffered that indignity before—only this time, he did not come out overnight. We began to get information on so many murders in which he had his homicidal hands, that it struck us it was a wonder Pep had had any time at all for romance.

While he was languishing in the jailhouse, a striking brunette came to visit him on several occasions. She registered as his sister, Eva. None of us knew Eva personally, but it was unanimously agreed there was hardly a family resemblance between the lovely visitor and the kill-hungry hoodlum. So, on her next visit, "Eva" was picked up. She turned out to be none other than Evelyn, the Kiss of Death Girl.

Evelyn came in with three diamond rings and a bracelet blinking like neon lights. "Pep gave them to me," she remarked, and she said there were more such trinkets in the bank vault. We checked on the baubles. As Kid Twist had said, the Brownsville boys had an alliance with the Chicago gorillas on gem business as well as gambling in Florida. Pittsburgh Phil simply could have held out an occasional piece or two from a night's work, and brought them home to his love. Obviously, Pep was well aware that diamonds are a girl's best friend.

Evelyn explained that the reason she visited Pep in jail was because of telephone calls she received, instructing her to do so.

"I don't remember who it was who called," she insisted. "But he told me to deliver some message or get some message from Pep."

We had her held in $50,000 bail as a material witness, and immediate intense efforts were begun to get her out. She not only was close to Pittsburgh Phil, but was friendly with several of his associates—all members of the same club. Love or no love, any number of people might like to see her out of the way. Hadn't a lot of murders just happened when she went holidaying with Pep in the Catskills? Evelyn, however, was no girl to relish confinement. She went quickly into court, seeking to have her bail cut.

"She is a good, decent girl," her counsel contended. She looked it, too, a dashing dark (converted) beauty in her neat blue gown, her red pancake chapeau perched over one plucked eyebrow, black caracul coat tossed nonchalantly over her arm. A large man's-sized handkerchief, pressed demurely to her face, completely foiled the newspaper photographers.

"She knows all there is to know about how this Syndicate worked," I countered her attorney's argument.

"She comes from a good home and fine parents," counsel came right back. "She intended to marry Strauss."

That proved Evelyn was not a girl to be rushed into wedlock. She had been Pittsburgh Phil's sweetheart for five easy years, and now that he was charged with murder and she was in jail as a material witness, she had matrimony on her mind.

"She has fared better," I told the court, "than one seventeen-year-old girl who caught the fancy of these hoodlums."

She had, indeed. The seventeen-year-old had voluntarily come forward and told us her tragic story. She had been a refined child, with ambitions for a career as an entertainer. Her chance for a start came as a singer in a night club in Brooklyn. On her second night there, this trap was, unfortunately, visited by some very exclusive society, consisting of Dasher Abbandando, Happy Maione, and that mental zombie, Vito Gurino. They took one look at this sweet untouched youngster—and they got ideas. The Dasher broached the subject to her, right there during her performance.

"How about stepping out with us after you're through, honey?" he leered, expecting his charms would be irresistible.

The girl didn't even bother to look him or his chums over. The finality and immediacy of her refusal irked them. They waited outside until she finished her singing and emerged, on her way home. They threw her into a car, picked up another of their friends and drove to a parking lot, deserted at that hour. There, all four of these animals forcibly raped the girl. Their viciousness completed, a couple of them suddenly became a little nervous.

"This kid is liable to holler, and we're in trouble," one of them anticipated.

With the terrified girl—already half-mad from the horror she had been through—forced to listen to every word, they argued over whether to "bury her or buy her." The latter course was finally approved. Two of them went to the girl's house and saw her mother. They displayed ugly-looking revolvers.

"Here's $500," they said, tossing some bills onto the table. "Keep your mouth shut, and keep the girl's mouth shut, too. Any squawks and we'll come back and get her and bury her alive."

Yes, Evelyn Mittelman, Kiss of Death Girl, with her diamonds and furs and Pittsburgh Phil to look after her, had fared considerably better than this seventeen-year-old who just wanted to be decent. Evelyn would not concede the point, however.

"Can't your honor conceive," her counsel asked the court, "that this young lady, even though she may be the sweetheart of this man, might be the one person in the whole world who would know nothing at all of what he was doing?"

No, the court admitted frankly, it could not. Bail remained at $50,000. Evelyn stayed in the Women's House of Detention for six weeks, while we rounded up our case against Pittsburgh Phil. During her stay, she fell into the habit of putting down daily notes of her surroundings, experiences and impressions. These were, of course, turned over to the Prosecutor's office. Most of them centered on her complete inability to see why she was held. And she placed the blame for all her troubles entirely on one Burton Turkus, assistant District Attorney. She did not blame Pittsburgh Phil or anyone else in law enforcement—or herself. Through entry after entry, it was always that nasty "Mr. T., who put me here." Here were typical remarks:

Friday—Went to court (on bail reduction hearing). Mr. T. made sure he said things that have no bearing on the case. He's putting me on trial instead of them. They took me in a patrol wagon. If that's protective custody, I'll take vanilla. Other witnesses very ignorant and coarse. Sex and crime main topics. Tell me their affairs, and then ask very personal questions. Resent that I don't answer. Forget that they told me scandalous things about themselves and other witnesses, and think I'm dumb enough to tell them the whys and wherefores of my life. What a morbid pastime.

Monday—Very blue. Mr. T. said I wasn't going to jail . . . but outside of food, no difference from prisoners. Dotty was refused pass to see me. That's the result of all Mr. T.'s promises. [Authors' Note: Mr. T. never heard of Dotty, had nothing to do with passes, and always was careful never to make promises to the ladies.]

Tuesday—3 P.M.; no visit. Nice going Mr. T. Just think of what you are doing to me.

Saturday—It's all so hopeless. Can't think of anything but Mr. T. Just for going out with a fellow, look where I am.

Monday—Finally learned how to make my blankets like a sack so they don't fall off at night. Hope I remember stories I heard in here.

Wednesday—Dotty and mom and pop came to see me. They look worse than I. Nobody forgot about me but Mr. T., and he'll realize some day what a mistake he made.

Thursday—Heard I'll be here 18 months. [Authors' Note: She was there less than six weeks.] Wonder if Mr. T. is human. NO.

Wednesday—No visit . . . no letter . . . thanks for what you are
doing to me, Mr. T.

Thursday—New witnesses are very nice. Learned how to play
coon-can and whist.

All in all, then, it was not a total loss. Evelyn was protected
while she was held. She learned how to make a bed and to play
coon-can. And she heard some stories that were so entertaining
she even wrote herself a reminder to remember them when she
was let loose. In fact, she may still be telling them in her set.

While she was still in custody, though, Evelyn suddenly saw
the light. "Reles did the right thing from the start," she concluded.
"Pep should do the same. He was stupid." She asked for permission to see Pittsburgh Phil, to urge him to open up.

Pep was granted an interview. Assistant D. A. John Rooney
(now Congressman Rooney) talked to him. Pittsburgh Phil was
perfectly willing to sing all right. He even suggested that after he
talked to Reles, he'd recall everything. There was only one little
wrinkle he attached.

"I got to walk out clean," was his demand. For unmitigated
gall, that was a world's record. Here was the most lustful killer
of them all; an assassin who had done a matter of thirty murders
in sixteen cities (and those were only what we had been able to
identify). And all he wanted was to have every one of them condoned and the slate wiped clean! We decided to struggle along
without Pittsburgh Phil's aria.

He did win one point, though. By this time, we were ready to
take the first Murder, Inc., trial into court, and Pep was honored
with a place among the defendants. That was, certainly, the least
he deserved. To pave the way for the interview, however, the case
against him was severed from his co-defendants, so that they
could go on trial as scheduled. It really didn't make much difference. We could have selected any one of half a dozen murders
on which to try him, and the result would have been the same as
it eventually was.

The last visitor Pittsburgh Phil was to receive in the death
house, incidentally, was Evelyn, the Kiss of Death. Then he sat
in the chair—next in the series, From Kisses to Cadaver. . . .

9.

Score one and two
for the law

*Signal 32; all cars proceed with caution—a note from a "freind"
—the Whitey Rudnick trial begins—63 stab wounds, and a
meat-ax "for luck"—a perjuror with a manicure—a mortician
breaks an alibi—Happy and Dasher take the train up the river.*

Patrolman Francis Schneider checked his watch and stretched,
as well as he could, in the tiny police prowl car.

"7:40, Jim," he said, looking across at his partner.

Patrolman Jim Reilly, at the wheel, nodded. He thought how
nice it was that nothing had happened on their overnight tour to
spoil a fine morning like this May 25, 1937. Twenty minutes more,
and they'd be on their way home.

Just then, the radio came alive with the static gurgle that
prefaced every announcement:

"All cars! All cars!" The policemen came alert. "On Jefferson
Avenue, between Evergreen and Central, Brooklyn. Signal 32.
Black sedan. That is all."

Reilly's foot came down on the gas pedal even before the Telegraph Bureau's regular sign-off ended the message. Signal 32—
that could or it couldn't mean trouble. It meant you never knew
what you were going into. Might be only a neighbor's imagination about an automobile parked overlong in front of her house.
It meant—well, you proceed with caution until you find out.

The prowl car slammed into Jefferson Avenue, a pleasant tree-
shaded thoroughfare in the north-central residential district, less
than ten blocks from Cemetery of the Evergreens. Halfway up the
block, the patrolmen spotted the black Buick sedan at the curb.
Schneider was out of the coupe before it had stopped. He couldn't
see anyone in the sedan. Nevertheless, he approached cautiously,

216

and peered inside. Even to a policeman's eye, accustomed to violence, the sight was a ghastly one.

The man crumpled on the rear floor had literally been hacked to death! His forehead was laid open to the bone. A rope was wound so tightly around his neck that the tongue, stiff and dry and purple, had been forced out between his clenched teeth. His neck, and down into his collar and chest, was a mass of round stab wounds, as if skewers had been stabbed into the flesh, one after another.

Schneider dashed for the nearest house. He telephoned the Telegraph Bureau and his own precinct station house. The wheels of law enforcement began to whirl.

Only minutes later, the ambulance screamed up to the scene. The man in the sedan did not need an ambulance. "D. O. A.," the doctor pronounced the traditional symbol—Dead on Arrival. By now, other prowl cars had arrived, and Sergeant Radigan had rushed over from the station house.

"Cut the rope around the neck, Kaminski," he ordered. It was not an easy job, Patrolman Ed Kaminski found. The garrote had been squeezed until it was buried deep in the flesh.

Searching the corpse, Acting Captain George Gallagher found a badly typed note in a rear trousers pocket. It indicated the grim object was all that was left of one George Rudnick. As deputy Chief Medical Examiner for New York City, Dr. Edward Marten made a superficial check at the scene. Then the morgue hearse— the "meatwagon"—rumbled up and carted its grisly load away.

In a little while, Mrs. Dora Rudnick, a worried little mother, appeared at the morgue in response to a telephone summons. She broke down at sight of the carved corpse.

"That's my Georgie," she sobbed the identification. "That's him. Last night, he ate supper and then left the house at eight o'clock." She choked on the words. "Now I see him in the morgue."

Dr. Marten's autopsy report showed the following facts:

"This was a male adult, somewhat undernourished; approximate weight, 140 pounds; six feet in height.

"There were sixty-three stab wounds on the body. On the neck,

I counted thirteen stab wounds, between jaw and collarbone. On the right chest, there were fifty separate circular wounds.

"He had a laceration on the frontal region of the head. The wound gaped, and disclosed the bone underneath.

"His face was intensely cyanic, or blue. The tongue protruded. At the level of the larynx, was a grooving, white and depressed, about the width of the ordinary clothesline.

"When the heart was laid open, the entire wall was found to be penetrated by stab wounds.

"My conclusion," Dr. Marten finished, "was that cause of death was multiple stab wounds, and also that a competent producing cause of death was asphyxia due to strangulation."

Clues were virtually nonexistent. Car, body, the note gave up not a smudge to fingerprint tests. The rope, an ordinary piece of clothesline, was of no help. Finding the one spot where the butchery had been committed, before the body was "dumped," was all but impossible. Murder weapons? There was no telling, even, what it was that had stabbed George Rudnick sixty-three times or had smashed open his skull like cracking a walnut. Any number of needle-pointed tools could have done the piercing—a shoemaker's awl, a knitting needle, an ice pick. The head might have been split by a hatchet, a woodsman's ax, a butcher's meat cleaver.

The black Buick belonged to Cedric Marks, sales manager of a liquor concern, and had been reported stolen four days previously from a public garage in East New York. One odd point was that the license plates on the hearse were not those that belonged on it. Oddest of all, they had been stolen in the Bay Ridge section, clear across Brooklyn from where the body was found or where the Buick was pilfered. How had a set of stolen plates become attached to a smart sedan (also stolen) eight miles away? And what of the licenses that belonged on the sedan?

The note gave a hint of possible tie-in with the rackets probe in Manhattan. But it was an obvious phony. Lines ran off the end of the paper, and there was a notable misspelling in the word "freind." It read:

Freind George: Will you please meet me in N.Y. some day
—same place and time—in reference to what you told me

last week. Also, I will have that certain powder that I promised you the last time I seen you.

PS. I hope you find this in your letterbox still sealed.

I remain your freind, you know, from DEWEYS office.

No one in Dewey's office had ever heard of Rudnick. However, mention of "that certain powder" could mean only narcotics. Then, too, the mere fact that the note was signed "from DEWEYS office" would indicate a mob affair.

Tracing the dead man's background, detectives learned that his nickname was "Whitey" and that he had been an addict to "that certain powder." The writer of the note, at any rate, was evidently well acquainted with him. Whitey had been a small-time—very small—shylock operator in Brownsville and Ocean Hill. But everybody apparently had liked the skinny hophead.

All of the bizarre details, except one, were given thorough headline coverage. Some clever police mind reasoned that the note probably was left in Whitey's hip pocket to throw the Law off, or, perhaps, as a tip-off of some kind, when revealed. A top-secret classification was placed on it. That might help smoke out something.

For three years, the case stood there—"unsolvable." Then, starting off our investigation, Dukey and Pretty mentioned a black car. And when Reles spoke his piece, the black car fell into place.

Judge Franklin W. Taylor sounded the battle cry for the war on the mob. "The skull and crossbones of the underworld must come down," the judge commanded.

The mushrooming probe had piled up such a mountain of material that a special grand jury had become necessary. Judge Taylor, deadly serious, was setting forth its duties and obligations. With the battle cry ringing in their ears, the jurors began their deliberations. That same afternoon, an indictment was ready. It charged Happy Maione, Dasher Abbandando and Pittsburgh Phil with murder in the first degree. They, it said, "wilfully, feloniously and of malice aforethought, killed George Rudnick, by stabbing him and strangling him."

We soon had other indictments, but as we began to look ahead to trials, the one that offered the best opportunities was the Rudnick case. This first prosecution would be the acid test. The entire investigation lived or died on it. Our case rested entirely on the testimony of killers and the corroboration of those killers by more killers. Since Kid Twist and his ilk were accomplices in the murders we were prosecuting, large numbers of skeptics, in the Syndicate and in law enforcement, did not give us a chance. Some laughed out loud. And what they were all saying was:

The police department may mark cases "solved," but can you make a jury believe Kid Twist—enough to send defendants to the chair on his say-so, even corroborated? And even if you do, what will happen in the appeals courts? Can you make a conviction stick?

No prosecutor ever had dared bring into a court a murder case against a gangster, based entirely on other gangsters as witnesses. If we could not satisfy a jury in this first trial, organized crime would go on to even more far-flung racketeering and bloodshed and corruption. And the witnesses who had agreed to talk would be in mortal terror ever to talk again—if they lived, that is. We had a powerful case in the Rudnick murder. So, we led with our ace.

The trial was set for early in May, 1940, less than six weeks after the indictment was returned. The defense turned over to us details of any alibi to be offered. The state legislature had only recently granted prosecutors permission to obtain this information, after it had been demonstrated time and again that when an alibi is suddenly sprung in a courtroom, a D.A. has no way at all of checking its truth or falsity. Happy, alone, had an alibi. His eighty-two-year-old grandmother had died the very night Whitey Rudnick was cut up. Happy listed various brothers, sisters and aunts who would prove he was there all night long, weeping and wailing in the bosom of his family.

As the trial neared, it became menacingly evident that the Syndicate had stepped up its sabotage for this first case. Killers were imported from California and the Midwest. The orders were brief and explicit: "Get those stoolpigeons!" Police and prosecutor's office received a tip that a series of shootings and kidnapings were planned to begin the night the trial started.

Coincidentally, the grapevine also said no effort would be made for the time being to post bail for Joey Adonis. "Mr. A." had given himself up only a few days earlier to an indictment accusing him of kidnap and extortion on one Ike Juffe, who had been the State's chief witness in an investigation of a fur swindle not long before. These charges were explained in a report in 1942 to Governor Herbert Lehman by Special Prosecutor John Harlan Amen.

This report also related, incidentally, that Adonis' "most profitable legitimate business was the Automatic Conveying Company," a trucking concern devoted to hauling automobiles.

(Apparently no particular attention was paid to this revelation then. In March of 1951—nine years later—though, a considerable storm was produced over the fact that, to this day, Automatic Conveying Company enjoys a federal government monopoly which nets a handsome profit—although Joey Adonis, a ranking member of the directorate of national crime, still was a principal stockholder. The company hauls more than 50,000 new cars a year from Ford Motor Company's Edgewater, N. J. plant. It is, in fact, the *only* trucker to which the Interstate Commerce Commission has granted a license in the Edgewater area.

(The attendant publicity caused William T. Gossett, Ford's general counsel, to confer with Interstate Commerce Commission officials. Gossett said afterward they advised him that as long as Automatic Conveying Company performed efficiently, its ICC license and its profitable monopoly would not be disturbed. Thus does the federal government protect a member of the board of governors of the crime Syndicate! The question left unanswered, of course, is how a company largely owned by a high executive of national crime was able to get a government license in the first place. Would not a government agency presumably check on the financial structure of an organization applying for a license?)

The indictment against Adonis, back there in 1940, accused him and one Sam Gasberg of kidnaping Juffe and another man and extorting $5,000 from their womenfolk. Gasberg was tried first, alone. The jury came up with an amazing "split decision"—

acquitting him of kidnaping and disagreeing on extortion. Joey A. has never even been tried on either charge.

It was in this case, however, that Adonis had given up, just about the time the grapevine reported that a mob shooting sabotage would coincide with the start of the Rudnick murder trial. As the grapevine had said, no immediate effort was made to get his release. In fact, not until the day after the trial ended was Joey A. bailed out. As long as he was in jail, he had a perfect alibi if anything "happened." And when his $50,000 bond finally was posted, much of it was supplied in cash by one Pete Savio, also known as Petey O'Brien, a one-time associate of Albert Anastasia.

Not even a desperado attempt to free the defendants or silence our witnesses in the very hall of justice itself could be put past the Syndicate's magnates, long sated with their protective connections. The results of the forewarning were most noticeable when the trial for Rudnick's murder began. Not only Judge Taylor's courtroom, but the entire floor was guarded like the Fort Knox gold pile. Sergeant Joe Leary commanded twenty patrolmen in the corridors. Twenty detectives ringed the courtroom. At the door, a police roadblock checked the special passes issued only to those with business in the court. The 150 talesmen of the Blue Ribbon jury panel were personally passed in by Chief Clerk John Madigan. Inside, guards were at each window and door. Detectives sat, unostentatiously, among the talesmen, for the resourceful mobsters might somehow have contrived to slip agents in as prospective jurors.

As in all mob trials, the defense boasted some of the most able minds in the practice of criminal law. Happy was represented by William Kleinman, who was regarded so highly that he had represented Lepke and other ranking racketeers—and they never retained any but the best. His associate was David Price, who not long before had won acquittal for a judge on bribery charges in an outstanding display of trial talent. Incidentally, Kleinman is a former assistant District Attorney, and once convicted Reles for assault. Thus he was one of the very few ever to win a courtroom decision over the elusive Kid Twist. For the Dasher, chief counsel was Alfred I. Rosner, brilliant at cross-examination, master at spotting the crack in a witness' story.

The first move was to obtain severance of Pittsburgh Phil from the case, for the interview for which his Kiss of Death girl friend had so earnestly pleaded. That left the spotlight exclusively on surly, savage Happy Maione, and his bulky long-time business and criminal partner, Dasher Abbandando. They were on trial for their lives, at last, after too many years of swaggering indifference to law and order.

They were models of sartorial splendor as they were led in. Maione was a symphony in blue, from serge suit and two-tone tie to striped socks. The Dasher sported a blue suit with a wide stripe, and a flaming red tie and plaid socks. Both of them exuded confidence.

Selection of the jury moved rapidly. By the third day, the panel of twelve men and two alternates was completed with a group of representative American businessmen: a manufacturer, a salesman, a telephone engineer, an insurance underwriter.

At 10 A.M. on Monday, May 13, 1940, the Law and Murder, Inc., came face to face at last, with the chips down. The jury was sworn in, preliminary details were ironed out and the court announced:

"The District Attorney will open in behalf of the People."

The tenseness hit me as I began to set forth to the jury the essential details the State intended to establish about the slaughter of Whitey Rudnick. The manner in which the slaying was done was depicted—the "triple insurance" of sixty-three stab wounds, a shattered skull, and a groove, white and deep, in Whitey's neck. The Dasher sneered, as if thinking, "Try and prove it."

The first fourteen witnesses provided the background—the corpus delicti, the mystifying misspelled note, the probable cause of death, the thefts of the black Buick and the license plates. Then Frank Peraino, the night attendant at the garage from which the sedan was stolen, was called. It developed he had more than a nodding acquaintance with any number of the Brownsville hoodlums. They called him Geech. His story was that, at about two o'clock on the morning of May 21, he checked the garage. Everything was shipshape, so Geech slipped outside and into a car parked on the gasoline station fronting the garage, and dozed off for "a while." The "while" stretched into a lengthy two hours.

"About 4:30," he recalled, "I went inside to wash cars. The black Buick wasn't there."

The first problem I faced now was to establish the existence of a criminal conspiracy, and prove that Maione and Abbandando were in it. Ironically, the same weakling who had started the ball rolling three months before was once more cast as the bell cow. Dukey the punk, the first to sing, was the lead-off batter. And as he walked in now, something happened in that courtroom. Abbandando stiffened, fingers clawing the arms of the chair. Happy tensed, a jungle cat ready to leap. You could read his thought: that the punk dare do this to him, the big shot!

Dukey's part in Whitey's execution, actually, had been an innocent one. On the evening of May 20, 1937, he and his shylock partner, Pretty, were standing with Pittsburgh Phil (whom he called Big Harry) on the Corner. Any attempt, at this point, to introduce what they said was barred. Maione and Dasher hadn't been there; the conversation could not be presented unless they were linked to it.

"As a result of what Pittsburgh Phil told you, what did you do?" I started him off.

"We went to garages," he explained, his frightened voice little more than a whisper. "Then we went over to the garage on New Jersey and Liberty, about 2:30 A.M. We left my car around the corner."

As they approached, they saw a man sleeping in a car outside. "So, I went inside," Dukey continued. "I saw a black car like I was supposed to steal. Me and Pretty started pushing the car. We pushed it out in the street, so when we started up, the fellow would not hear it. I got in the car and drove. Pretty got in my car and followed me. I drove it to the garage in back of Big Harry's house."

The next night, Big Harry gave them further instructions. "Me and Pretty took the black car out of his garage," Dukey related, "and brought it to Atlantic Avenue and Eastern Parkway—to the garage there. Happy and Dasher was there."

"Here is the car Big Harry told us to bring down," reported Pretty, as leader of the delivery party.

"Okay," Maione acknowledged receipt.

Dukey and Pretty returned to the Corner. Big Harry was waiting. "Did you bring the car there?" he demanded.

"Everything is okay," they reported.

Counsel objected strenuously to placing this bit of dialogue into the record, but now there was a difference.

"It is sufficiently connected," ruled Judge Taylor, allowing the testimony. "Not because of evidence of conspiracy to commit the major crime [the murder]. But there is sufficient evidence on the conspiracy to steal a car and deliver it to the defendants."

That opened the door for Dukey to go back again to the night Pittsburgh Phil gave him and Pretty the original orders. "Go and clip a black car," the mobster had commanded. "But be sure and go out of the neighborhood to clip it. Put it in my garage."

"Clip?" Judge Taylor raised an inquiring eyebrow.

"Yeah . . . clip. To take," Dukey obliged.

Pretty felt important as leader of the expedition, personally designated by Pittsburgh Phil. Important—and impatient.

"To hell with Big Harry," he said finally. "I know a place we won't get in trouble, even if it is in the neighborhood. I know the guy that works there. He is okay, in case we get caught." And he directed Dukey to Geech's garage.

Obviously, the kids (as Big Harry called them) had a lot to learn about the trade. There were very real reasons for the order to "go out of the neighborhood." An automobile stolen from another section would be unlikely to draw suspicion to Brownsville, especially if the thugs disposed of it outside of Brownsville afterward. Dukey recalled that because the black sedan was taken from "in the neighborhood," Pittsburgh Phil was particularly irate when he and Pretty reported.

"Next time I tell you, do it—or something will happen," Pittsburgh Phil had roared menacingly.

"Did you refuse to clip the car or deliver it?" I asked.

Dukey gave a do-you-think-I-am-crazy toss of his head. "I did not want to get myself killed," was his graphic response.

Counsel were on their feet at once. "That remark is so prejudicial that it is impossible now for the defendants to receive a fair trial," asserted Attorney Price. It was the first of about twenty defense attempts to have a mistrial called. None was successful.

As might have been expected, Pretty was more at ease on the stand than his friend, although still far from comfortable, what with the savage eyes of the two torpedoes glaring murder at him from a few feet away. Pretty told exactly the same story as Dukey, plus supplemental angles, picking up with the night after the car was delivered to Happy and the Dasher. He met Pittsburgh Phil on the Corner. Dukey wasn't there.

"There's some license plates in the toilet inside," said the murder master, pointing a thumb toward the candy store. "Go in and take them to Happy and the Dasher, where you took the car yesterday."

Pretty found the licenses in the lavatory, in a folded newspaper lying in back of the bowl.

"I took them to Happy and Dasher," he recounted. "Happy tells me to take the old plates off the car that we stole and put these on. So, I did. Then, Happy brings over a flatiron, and me and Abby (Abbandando) break up the old plates into little pieces with the flatiron. Then Abby gets in the black Buick and drives it about three blocks away, and puts it in a little garage."

No one ever did find out how license plates stolen in Bay Ridge got into the toilet of the Brownsville mob's "night office." But at least we had now established how they had become attached to the hearse.

Counsel gave both Dukey and Pretty a thorough going over on cross-examination. If the defense could make it appear that the punks had foreknowledge that the car was to be used for a killing, they would be accomplices, and rendered worthless as corroboration for Reles' revelations to come.

As they did through the trial, the attorneys also began now to pound incessantly on an alternative theory of the murder—a theory that Reles and these very witnesses had cut up Whitey, and connived to blame Happy and the Dasher for it! After all, if testimony in a trial becomes confused—through a calculated "campaign of confusion" or by any other means—then it leaves a doubt with a juror. And then the defendant is freed. Dukey denied all with a shudder. Nevertheless, the questions were on the record for the jury to think about.

The most pointed and persistent of all counsel's dagger-like lines of questioning, however, seemed to aim toward determining where our witnesses were being kept.

"Have you been up in the same hotel Reles was?" Dukey was asked.

"Just a minute," the court interrupted at once. "There must be no fishing expedition for the whereabouts of the People's witnesses."

The last thing in the world we wanted, of course, was a public announcement of where we had managed to keep the songbirds safe up to then. In spite of the order, however, counsel dug into the same subject only a few moments later. Again Judge Taylor sternly cautioned against it. Yet, with Pretty, the cross-examination for the third time tiptoed onto the same touchy ground:

Q—Where were you first taken?
A—To a hotel.
Q—Where?

"I want no more inquiry as to where any witness is kept," the court admonished. "It might be something that should be kept secret. And," he concluded, "you are not a bit surprised at the ruling."

"I am not only surprised," Attorney Price made the grand gesture, "I am horrified."

"Pull yourself together," soothed Judge Taylor. There was a faint trace of a smile on his lips.

Apparently anticipating that Pretty would be more effective than Dukey, Happy and Dasher must have pondered on how to "louse him up with the jury," as they put it. Their devious reasoning probably went this way: We're charged with murder; let's charge him with murder. Then we're all a bunch of murderers. The jury will think, "Who can you believe in such a mob—who did what murder?" So, they probably suggested various slayings with which their attorneys might accuse Pretty—whether he committed them or not. Counsel knew the answers they wanted, but they did not seem to have the right questions to produce those answers:

Q—While a man held him, did you stab Walter Sage with an ice pick?
A—No, sir.

"Did you wait in ambush?" was another.

No one ever did ask Pretty a question like, "Were you with Pittsburgh Phil in a car trailing the one in which Sage was ice-picked, and from which Big Gangy leaped to start the trip that landed him in the movies?" If Happy and the Dasher had told their lawyers the truth, in fact, they could easily have developed that Pretty had a peculiar habit of popping up where murders happened.

By the time Dukey and Pretty finished their testimony, Maione and Abbandando had been placed squarely into the conspiracy leading to Whitey Rudnick's slaughter. The stage was all set then for the grisly bloodletting itself—and for the central character to tell of it.

No one in gangland ever thought he'd live to see this day. Kid Twist spilling everything he knew? Never!

But here he was, in front of a judge and jury, no less—and blowing the roof off. He was reciting chapter and verse. And putting in the punctuation, too.

Reles had them gasping, those who knew him, the moment he shuffled in. As the boss of Brownsville, he had always looked the part—hard and mean. But now he was round—almost pudgy. And that funny step was missing—the step someone said looked like a guy kicking field goals in a phone booth. Now it was the short confined shuffle of a man who hadn't had much freedom lately. He was the star of the show, though—and how he knew it! He was Kid Twist, the ham. He loved that spotlight.

The only sign that might have betrayed any inner tension was the way he kept wiping sweaty palms on a dirty red bandanna. Only once in six hours or more on the stand did he drop his cool collected front. He was being put through the wringer on cross-examination then, and counsel brought up the rape of his sweetheart during his feud with the Shapiro Brothers.

"Your fight with the Shapiros—didn't it have something to do with your wife?" The attorney dug the barb deep. The Kid's veneer vanished and the animal poked out. The reply came in a teeth-bared snarl.

"No, it didn't." He spit it out as if he would have welcomed a few minutes—outside and alone—with his interrogator. Happy's face wore a sly grin at that.

Reles' glance shot this way and that continuously. He had spotted the guards, all right, but Kid Twist knew the mob. He was not going to be satisfied until he'd looked things over personally to see that the courtroom held no one who did not belong.

Quickly, in his rasping, grating voice, he got down to the intimate details of the Rudnick job. In fact, there was not an intimate detail he missed, including the footnote that, "Whitey was my friend for fifteen years."

Q—Who first spoke to you about George Rudnick?
A—Pep (Pittsburgh Phil). We were on the Corner.

"I got info George Rudnick is talking to the Law," Pep said. "We got to take him. Let's go up and see Happy and the Dasher. The Dasher," explained Pittsburgh Phil en route to Ocean Hill, "is pally with Rudnick. He would come with Dasher faster than any of us."

They met in Sally's Bar & Grill, a step from the Sunrise Garage where Pretty and Dukey were to deliver the hot Buick later. They ordered a drink all around. Reles, who had committed the better part of two dozen murders, settled for a cream soda.

"George Rudnick is a stoolpigeon for that Detective Browser," reported Pittsburgh Phil. "I seen him come out of Browser's automobile. We got to hit him."

Q—Did the defendants say anything?
A—Maione said, "We'll take care of him up here, if he comes to the garage." And Pep says, "When he comes to the Corner, we'll take him down there."

"We'll leave a note in Rudnick's pocket when we take him to show he is giving information, and at the same time, we're doing Lep a favor," Pep added.

Q—Who is Lep?
A—His name is Lepke.

(The first injection into the trial of the name of the notorious rackets czar brought belligerent demands for a mistrial. The judge remained unperturbed.)

About a week later, a typewriter was delivered to Reles' home by Sholem. The Kid and Pittsburgh Phil set to work on it.

"The ribbon was out of the typewriter," Reles testified. "We didn't know how to fix it. So, I held the ribbon while he typed. We had a rhubarb about the word 'friend.' I spelled it 'f-r-i-e-n-d.' He says it is 'f-r-e-i-n-d.' We tore the first note up. Then we type-writed it my way—'f-r-i-e-n-d.' He says that is wrong, and he tore it up. He put it 'f-r-e-i-n-d.' That was the third note."

"This will do a lot of good for Lep, when they find a dead man with a note," Pittsburgh Phil pointed out.

The note taken from Whitey's corpse was identified now as the one Reles and Pep had labored with, over the hot typewriter. It was publicly apparent, at last, that this misspelled missive had had a dual purpose—to show that a stoolpigeon had been killed, and to frighten off potential witnesses against Lepke, already embroiled in Manhattan. Only, the Law hadn't co-operated. No whisper of the note had been revealed. The uninhibited Pittsburgh Phil, preening himself for having thought this one up, took it as a personal affront.

"Them God-damned cops," he complained savagely to Reles one day. "The letter didn't get in the papers."

There was no progress on Whitey's demise for several days. "Let's go up," suggested Pittsburgh Phil finally, "and see what is holding up that job." Perhaps the homicide specialist suspected the allies were not as zealous as they might be. "Me and Happy will stay here in the garage and lay for him," he announced revised tactics. "You, Dasher—you go down on the Corner with Reles. If he comes there, you two nail him."

The double vigil was maintained daily from midnight until

5 A.M. On the fourth morning, the underfed figure of the suspected stoolpigeon was seen approaching the Corner.

"It's about four-thirty," Reles recalled. "I spot him, walking close to the buildings. I says to Abby, 'There he comes.' Abby starts the car he's got there. With that, Rudnick turns around and starts to go backward. Abby says, 'Don't worry—I'll get him, if I have to drag him in the car.' When he reaches near Dumont (one block north), I seen Rudnick walk to the car and get in."

Q—What did you do?
A—I wait about ten minutes, and I get in my car and I go to Atlantic Avenue and Eastern Parkway, where the garage is. I park at the Sinclair station, across the way.

The Kid crossed to the same Sunrise Garage where Dukey and Pretty had delivered the black sedan. He knocked. After several seconds, the door opened and disclosed Happy's sour countenance.

"I walk in," Reles related, slowly now, for full dramatic effect. "Over there on the floor, Rudnick is laying. Abby is holding him around the shoulders, and Big Harry is putting a rope around his neck."

The brazenness was breathtaking. These killers sought no out-of-the-way execution chamber. They picked a public garage a step from one of the most heavily trafficked intersections in town, where a car might drive up at any time. Yet, the very bravado proved the perfection of the plot. This was the last place any investigator would have suspected.

Reles did not remain in the garage long. He crossed the street and posted himself as a lookout, in the shadow of a building.

Q—How long did you stay there?
A—Maybe five minutes. Then the Dasher comes out. He hollers for Julie Catalano. Julie comes out of the gas station. So I cross the street with him.
Q—When you entered the garage, what was happening?
A—Rudnick is laying there. Pep has an ice pick. Happy has a meat cleaver. It is the kind you chop with . . . you know —a butcher cleaver. Abby sends Julie out. In about five

minutes, he is back with a black Buick. He pulls right into the garage.

"Then," Reles proceeded, "Abby grabs Rudnick by the feet and drags him over to the car. Pep and Happy grab it by the head. They put it in the car. Somebody says, 'The bum don't fit.' So, Abby pushes . . . he buckles it up to make it fit. He bent the feet up."

"You mean the legs?" broke in Judge Taylor incredulously.

"Yeah—he bent up the legs." Reles was thoroughly enjoying the sensation he was creating. He continued, grandly—Hamlet at the grave, pondering the skull:

"Just as they push the body in, it gives a little cough or something." Apparently Abbandando's "buckling" had forced air from Whitey's lifeless lungs. "With that, Pep starts with the ice pick and begins punching away at Whitey. And Maione, over here [pointing with his head toward the defendant], he says, 'Let me hit this bastard one for luck,' and he hits him with the cleaver, someplace on the head."

Eventually, the body was accordioned into the car. "Let's clean the floor up from the blood," Happy directed. He drew a bucket of water. The Dasher procured a broom. As Happy sloshed about, his first lieutenant swept the traces of the butchery into the drain set in the concrete floor.

Q—After the blood was swept away, what happened?
A—Happy tells Julie to drive out of the precinct. The garage is in the Liberty Avenue precinct; he says to dump the car in the Wilson Avenue precinct. He says to me, "Me and you will follow and pick Julie up."

It was nearing daybreak, the Kid remembered, as he trailed the black hearse across the precinct boundary. When Julie stopped, the Kid drove past and rounded the next corner to wait for him.

"I had my own car . . . legitimate . . . in my name," he explained. "In case somebody happened to come along or looked out a window, I didn't want nobody to see my car near the hearse." (This caution, mind you, although it was 5 A.M., and the area was deserted in the pre-dawn stillness.)

Reles thus concluded what was as remarkable a detailed account of the inside of a gang murder, as was ever given from a witness stand. He moved along now to the current year and his stay in the Tombs, before he decided to turn informer. He was there but a few days when Happy, too, was escorted in. "They move him to the sixth tier up, so we couldn't talk," he went on. Nevertheless, the thugs found a way.

"On Sundays, they got religious services for an hour," the Kid explained. He confessed that he had never been to a religious meeting of this particular creed before.

"If he had," observed the court dryly, "it didn't do him any good."

Both of the hoods attended the services, Reles remembered. "Me and Hap sit together on the bench. When the singing starts, we talk. The louder they sing, the more we talk."

Maione told the Kid of his apprehension concerning Julie and Joe the Baker, because of their knowledge of the Rudnick job. "The Baker is more important, because he's an outside witness," he said. "If the Baker talks, I'm cooked." Like Reles, his awareness of what constituted corroboration was as keen as any prosecutor's.

Q—Who is Joe the Baker?
A—That's the night man at the garage where Rudnick was hit.

"The next time Hap spoke to me," Reles continued, "he told me he seen Vito, and Vito is going to take care of the Baker."

Still later, Happy reported that Gurino had made "contact" in Queens jail, just as Liberito told us. He pointed a finger at Reles. "Now you're okay, too," he added.

"I didn't get it," the Kid testified. "So, Hap says, 'Remember—me and you picked Julie up that night; you're in it, too.' "

"Gee . . . I forgot all about it," Reles admitted.

The Kid now faced a cross-examination barrage from three courtroom specialists noted for probing at witnesses. I confess, I was not particularly concerned, having been exposed to his card-index memory and his contemptible self-satisfaction. Before long, he was even catching counsel in errors, with the biting nastiness that was his chief characteristic. He was challenged when he explained that he, Maione and Abbandando were business partners, originally, from 1931 to 1934.

"Abbandando was in Elmira prison during that time." The lawyer shot the point home as if the Kid had been caught with his hand in the cookie jar. "You never came in contact with him."

"I did so come in contact with him," Reles came right back. "And it was not Elmira. He was in Attica. I visited him."

By all odds, the most startling portion of his day-long stay on the stand was a conducted tour through his career of lawlessness, crime by crime. It is not often a man swears, with no trace of self-consciousness, to half a dozen murders he has committed. And that number was all counsel asked him about. His amazing admissions came with a staccato ABC effect that was easy to follow:

Q—Did you kill one Jake the Painter?

A—Yes, sir, in 1933 or '34, I think.

Q—Did you kill a labor delegate named Greenblatt?

A—Yes; with somebody else.

Q—Do you know a man named Rocco who was killed?

A—I don't recall the name. (This was one Rocco Morganti. During the painters' labor war in the early thirties, he was lured to a card game in a third-floor apartment. Reles shot him there, on contract. As frequently happened with the Kid, the circumstances, more than the name, were the key.)

Q—Did you kill a man on Columbia Street?

A—I was a party in it. There was two of us pulled triggers.

Q—When Puggy Feinstein was killed, you killed him, didn't you?

A—I helped; I was part of it.

Q—Did you shoot any of the Shapiro Brothers?

A—Not alone; I was one of the party.

The court—Did you pull the trigger?

Reles—I was one of them pulled the trigger. And if he (indicating counsel) wants to know the other men, I'll tell him.

The offer was not accepted.

As was expected, the defense went over every word of his story of the Rudnick job, right up to the moment he dropped Happy and Julie off, after dumping the body, and went home . . . "to sleep," he explained, entirely undisturbed by the sight of a meat cleaver buried in a man's skull. Before the session ended, he was sparring adroitly with the attorneys. For example, when he re-peated that Pittsburgh Phil had typed the note left in Rudnick's pocket:

"But you took a hand in the letter," insisted counsel.

"Now, how could I take a hand?" he asked, sympathetically. "I was holding the ribbon."

He admitted the black death car was no different than hundreds of the same model on the highways. But, he said, he had a way of identifying this particular one:

"By the body . . . the dead body that was in it." He all but stood up and took a bow on that.

Q—Did any of the defendants have blood on their clothes?
A—I don't know. I didn't inspect them.
Q—Maione was in the car with you; didn't you inspect him?

"Now, how, sir," was the bland response, "could I drive the car and inspect him at the same time?"

Then he stepped down, grandly, sweepingly. And court was adjourned for the day.

As Reles was led out, he came face to face with the defendants, on the way back to their cells. The fresh memory of the co-worker he never had liked, swearing him on the way to the death house, snapped Happy's control. Before the guard to whom he was shackled could brace himself, the savage thug lunged for the Kid.

"You stoolpigeon son of a bitch," his voice broke into a crazy shriek. "I'm gonna kill you . . . I'm gonna tear your throat out."

For a moment, everyone froze. Happy was within inches of Reles' neck, screaming and cursing, before his keeper brought him up. His fingers curled and his eyes bulged with hate, and he had assassination in his heart. And that is exactly what it would have been, right there in the hall of justice, had the morose mur-derer managed to get that few inches closer.

It was unanimously agreed that, for pure dramatics alone, after Reles hair-raiser, anything else was going to be strictly a weak anticlimax. Then Julie Catalano came on—and they took it all back.

Julie was a man with a mission—and the mission was hate. His voice was a whip of hate. He spat out words, and venom dripped from them. His eyes gave off sparks. Julie and Happy Maione had grown up together, gone to school together. The less blood-lusting Julie always was Hap's loudest booster. And then, Hap hadn't trusted him enough to know they could cut Julie's arm off before he would rat on his old friend. Hap had sent out orders to kill him. Julie was paying off now—with interest. The handsome ex-cabdriver wanted to be on that witness stand.

Julie leveled a mocking glare full on the man he still called "my old pal, Hap," and he kept it there, as if not another soul was in the room. He did not so much as glance at the Dasher. Sometimes a slow smile touched his lips, and seemed to sneer, "How'm I doin', Hap?"

Only one person could provide substantiation for Reles concerning the doings inside the Sunrise Garage on that murder night, because only one other person, besides the murderers, had seen them. That person was Julie Catalano. His desire to get on with the testimony was evident. Sometimes, when questions were slow coming, his fingertips would drum impatiently on the arm of the chair. His disdain toward the attorneys—especially Maione's —was so obvious that, on one occasion, counsel made a point of it.

"You are not angry at me, are you?" asked Kleinman.

"No; I am not," Julie barked back.

"You don't mind if I ask questions?"

"It makes no difference to me. You can go all day long."

Julie began with Happy hiring him to pay off and collect on horse-race bets. The job kept him hustling, so it was not unusual that at about ten o'clock on the night of May 24, 1937, he wanted to get home and to bed. He was in a bookies' "drop" on busy Rockaway Avenue. As Julie started for the exit, Happy beckoned.

"Wait a minute; I want to see you," the boss directed, motioning him through the door. "Where you going?" he inquired.

"Home to sleep," yawned Julie. "There's nothing doing here."

"Hang around tonight, in case I need you," Happy changed his hired hand's mind.

"For what?" Julie wanted to know.

As a mob boss, Maione was a Mussolini. He blew up at the help questioning his command. "What the hell!" he stormed. "Do you want to know everything?"

They strolled on, to the Eastern Parkway-Atlantic Avenue base of Happy's hoodlum operations. "What time do you want me?" Julie sighed. "I want to go over to the Greek's for coffee."

"Okay . . . but be back before twelve o'clock. If I'm not here on the corner, I'll be in Kaiser Bill's garage." Kaiser Bill, Julie interpolated, was another name for Joe the Baker.

Julie dawdled over his coffee, and did not return until 12:15. There was no sign of his hot-tempered employer.

Q—What did you do then?

A—I hear hollering and crying across from the garage. Happy's grandmother lives there, upstairs from the oil-burner store. So, I go up. I see Hap and his mother and his mother's sisters. Hap says, "My grandmother is dying."

Q—Did Maione stay in the place?

A—For about an hour. Then he says his grandmother is dead. I says, "Jesus, I feel sorry, Hap." He says, "Come on; let's go down." Me and him walk across to Kaiser Bill's garage.

Q—What did Maione say?

A—I says, "How long will I hang around?" He says, "Go in Sally's bar next door and get a drink. But make sure you don't go away," he says.

Julie glanced into the garage office and saw Pittsburgh Phil. As he turned toward Sally's, the saloon in which the plot for Whitey's extermination had been laid out, Julie passed the garage's tow truck. In it was Kaiser Bill. The garage attendant invited him to sit down. Julie declined.

"This suit I got on now," he held out the lapel, as he sat in the witness chair. "I had this same suit on then."

Q—Was it new at that time?

A—Sure it was new. So, Kaiser Bill tells me sit in the truck . . .

I don't want to get my new suit dirty. He says, "Let's go over and play some cards then." I say it's a good idea.

They crossed to the Sinclair station, and entered the office. "The night man, Trucchio, is there," Julie continued. "We sit down and play some cards . . . some rummy."

Julie took the seat facing the window, in order not to miss the expected signal from his petulant employer.

Q—In the early hours of the morning, did something take place?
A—We played for a couple hours. Then a tan car pulls up on the station across the street, right in front of the door of the garage. Kaiser Bill thinks it's a customer. He runs across; he comes back. I seen the Dasher and Whitey get out of the car, and they walk into the garage office.

In a few moments, the four men came out of the office and entered the main part of the garage. The tan car was driven inside. The doors closed. Julie and the Baker and Trucchio went on with their playing. Another half hour passed. Then Abbandando poked his head cautiously out of the garage opposite and called out, "Hey, Julie," just loud enough to be heard a few yards away.

Q—What did you do?
A—I get up and start across the street. When I reach about the middle, I meet Reles. I didn't see where he come from. I says, "What the hell is going on?" He does not say nothing.
Q—Was the door to the garage open or closed?
A—Closed. It opened from the inside, and we go in . . . me and Reles. There's a guy laying out on the floor. There's a rope all knotted up on his neck. I walk over; I seen it is Whitey. I figure the guy is dead.

Up to this point, Julie had no idea what the proceedings concerned. "But when I see the guy laying there—then I know what it's all about," he acknowledged.

Abbandando motioned him to the door and pushed a key into his hand. "You know the little garage on Sherlock Place?" he said.

Julie nodded. "There's a car in it," the Dasher went on. "Get it and come right back." Julie quickly found the black Buick.

Q—What did you do with it?
A—I get it and go back. What do you think I done with it?

That was typically Catalano. From start to finish, the operation of his mind was almost audible, as though declaring, "Why are you wasting time? I was there; I saw everything what went on. Don't give me no dumb questions. Just let me tell you."

"Before I get in the car," he recalled, "I wrap two handkerchiefs around my hands, so as not to leave no prints."

Q—Was there any difficulty putting Rudnick's body in the car?
A—I'm telling you! He's too long. Dasher crumples his legs up . . . you know what I mean. That makes the guy shorter. With that, he gives a little cough . . . he goes "hem." And Big Harry says, "This goddam bum ain't dead yet." They pull the guy out a little bit—with his head leaning out. Big Harry, with an ice pick—he begins punching the guy with the ice pick. The blood comes out. Then Hap and Big Harry pick him up, and they situate him with his head against the back seat, so you couldn't see him from the window while the car is driving. Then Hap says, "Let me hit this son of a bitch for luck." He leans in and hits him with a cleaver . . . one of them butcher things, like you hit bones or meat with. I don't know where he hit him. All I know, I hear a dull noise.
Q—You know Maione since school. Is he right-handed or left-handed?
A—Left-handed.

It was an important point. From the way the body was placed and the slant of the wound, only a man accustomed to using his left hand could have leaned in and swung the meat ax with sufficient force to crack open Whitey's head.

Julie told how the killers went about sweeping away the bloody signs, just as Reles had said. The housework completed, Happy gave Julie his orders to dump the car in the next precinct.

"Take your time," Maione advised. "Take it easy. Don't worry. Me and Reles will be right behind."

In direct testimony, Julie omitted one interesting illustration of the perfectionist technique. Thanks, ironically enough, to the thoroughness of defense counsel, the omission was filled on cross-examination.

"When you got behind the wheel," counsel challenged, "you put your gloves on to make sure you didn't leave any fingerprints; isn't that right?"

"Yes, sir—because Hap told me to put gloves on." Julie's triumph was a wide-eyed glare at the glowering Maione.

Here was corroboration as damning as the entire trial produced. The question had not been inquisitorial—not, "Did you put gloves on?"—but leading, suggestive: "You put gloves on; isn't that right?" Only someone who was there would have known that Julie wore gloves. Unless a client suggested that he mention gloves, counsel would hardly be likely to ask the leading query.

"Was it from your pants pocket or your coat pocket that you took the gloves?" inquired the attorney.

"I didn't take them out of my pockets," snapped Julie. "There's the box [glove compartment] on the dashboard. Hap says, 'The gloves are in the box.' "

"When I questioned you first," charged the attorney, "you didn't say that Maione said where they were."

Julie smiled pleasantly. "You," he reminded, "did not ask me."

The line of inquiry had been a desperate gamble, and would have paid handsomely—had it worked. Had Julie been shown with prepared gloves, the "innocence of ignorance" he claimed would have been shattered, he would have been destroyed as the only corroboration for Reles of what occurred inside the execution chamber itself.

Piloting the hearse that night, Julie had no particular preference concerning which street to dump the body on.

"When I see I am far enough," he testified, "I stop. I'm looking to get out of that car. While I'm walking to where Reles is waiting, there are yards. I drop the gloves in a yard."

His head gave a self-satisfied toss, and he leered balefully at Maione as he concluded direct testimony.

"I done the whole thing through fear," he had said earlier to us. "They had the cleaver in their hands and they had the ice pick. If I would refuse to drive that car, I would be dead with the guy in the same car."

As cross-examination opened, Happy's former hired hand showed an expressive, gesticulating delight in discomfiting the defense with facts. Before he finished, the defendants were probably a bit rueful that they even started certain lines of inquiry.

Q—Isn't it a fact that you are changing the actual time of Rudnick's death because you know Maione's grandmother did not die until a quarter of two that morning?

A—I don't know what time she died. When I went up there, whether she was dead or she was not dead, I don't know.

Q—If she was dying, she was not dead? (Julie was not gaited for the trick question. It irked him.)

A—Jesus, a man could be dying and take three hours to die, for Christ's sake!

Q—When Happy Maione told you to stick around the night of the Rudnick killing, you did not ask any questions, did you?

A—What am I going to do—answer back?

Any way you looked at it, Julie's long stretch on the stand was quite a show. The hating hoodlum had fully substantiated Reles' gruesome account of the ice-picking and meat-axing and accordioning of the body, and the final disposal. As corroboration for Kid Twist, he would come close to clinching the State's case. It had been emphasized on direct examination and fortified on cross that he was not an accomplice. Under the law, he could be charged with nothing more than driving a dead body through the streets of Brooklyn without a permit for same—and that is simply a misdemeanor by statute.

Aside from Kid Twist and Julie, only one other man living saw the murderers and their victim walk into the Sunrise Garage that predawn. He was Joseph Liberito, otherwise Joe Liberto, otherwise Joe the Baker, otherwise Kaiser Bill, the night attendant at the Sunrise. He had kept his eye on the place all night.

You might say, Kaiser Bill was not quick to grasp the spoken word. It was noted early in his testimony that more than two syllables affected him much as a bucking rodeo horse affects a rider. "Previous" and "subsequent," which keep the time element clear in any interrogation, were a total loss on the Baker. At one point, he was asked if there had been a stenographer present, taking down his statement to the District Attorney.

"Who," was Joe's reply, "is the District Attorney?"

Yet, undramatic and dull as he was, Joe was as vital as any witness to our case—because the Baker was not of the mob. Among the various things he remembered, was that the door between the office and the garage proper could not be opened. That cast a ray of light on a clouded point. Why, after Abbandando arrived with Rudnick on the murder morning, had the killers chanced being seen with their victim by emerging from the office and entering the garage from the outside? That, the Baker revealed, was the only way they could get in.

It was a few minutes short of midnight that night, he recited, when Dasher called out, "Hey, Joe, how about getting me a container of coffee?" The Baker obliged, but just as he returned, there was a shriek from across the street. Happy and Abbandando took off running, and disappeared into the building where Hap's grandmother lived.

"So, I brought the coffee into the office to leave it," the Baker recalled. To his surprise, Pittsburgh Phil was there—with a rope in his hands. Kaiser Bill's sudden entrance momentarily startled the master of homicide. He dropped the rope. Perhaps he was annoyed at being seen in the place this night. The Baker, though, saw no reason to make a fuss about a friend of the owner playing lasso in the place. He set the coffee down and went outside again. He was sitting there, in the tow car, when Julie came along. Joe liked Julie.

"What are you doing here?" asked Julie, leaning into the vehicle.

"I'm sitting," was Joe's enlightening response. "Come and sit down," he invited. Julie declined, and, as he had testified, they adjourned to the Sinclair station for their rummy game with Frank Trucchio.

"Frank was the night man," Joe explained. "Now he is in jail."

They had played perhaps three and a half hours, by Joe's estimate, when, through the window, he saw the tan Ford drive up to the garage. He had run across the street before he recognized the car. It belonged to a "fellow named Gus" who worked in a necktie factory around the corner. He saw Abbandando and "a fellow named Whitey I know" leave the car and join Pittsburgh Phil and Happy.

"Then they all go in the garage," he added. "I went across the street and played cards some more."

Q—How long did you play?

A—About ten minutes. Then I hear Abby call Julie. Julie went. I kept playing. A little while later, I seen Julie backing up a black car out of my garage. Happy and Big Harry come out of the garage, too. I seen Abby backing out the tan Ford.

Something nibbled at the back of Joe's mind. It took several minutes to register.

"Four went in," he figured it out finally, "and only three went out." (Reles had entered and left without catching the Baker's eye.)

"I went looking in the cars and the trucks and all over," Joe testified. "I was looking for Whitey, but I didn't find him." Mystified, Joe counted off on his fingers: Happy, Pittsburgh Phil, the Dasher and Whitey went in; the Dasher, Pittsburgh Phil and Happy came out. The Baker was one man short. Where was Whitey— where was the fourth man? It was still bothering him the following night when he strolled over to the Sinclair station to see his good friend Trucchio.

"There's a newspaper laying there," the Baker recalled. "I pick it up. I look at the jokes. All of a sudden, I seen Whitey's picture. I happen to look at the picture. There's a rope on it."

The rope rang a bell. Joe kept a length of line under the desk in the garage office—"to tie a headlight or a bumper or something, when I tow a smashup." Joe remembered Pittsburgh Phil standing there with a rope in his hand the previous night. He put two and two together. The way the Baker practiced addition, there could be but one answer to Rudnick's murder.

"This was the same rope that was in my garage," Joe deduced.

He was positive and obstinate. "I know the rope," he insisted stubbornly. The murder rope and the clothesline he used to tie broken headlights had to be one and the same.

The Baker concluded direct testimony with details of his arrest during our investigation, of how, for seventeen days, he adamantly insisted he knew nothing—had not even seen Happy at the garage during May of 1937. He told of Vito Gurino's sinister midnight visits to the Queens jail, which convinced him to change his mind.

The most persistent drive on Joe under cross-examination centered on a charge he had made some weeks earlier—that he had been badly beaten by detectives after his arrest. The implication now was that his singing, after seventeen days of silence, must have been punched out of him.

"The detectives didn't beat me," Joe killed the point. "I tried to run out of the room."

Q—You tried to escape from three detectives in a room?
A—I tried to escape from four of them. I made a break for the door. One of them—Joe the Bull—he grabbed me by the hair and I swung for him, and he give me a kick. That was the end of the fight.
Q—Did you receive any medical treatment since your arrest?
A—For my stomach.

"I could not go to the bathroom," Joe explained it.

Counsel leaped on that expectantly. "Were you kicked in the stomach?" he inquired.

"The witness said that he could not go to the toilet," Judge Taylor broke in. "I assume he was just constipated."

The Baker's appearance was worth all the struggle to wrest information from him. He could be given no consideration as an accomplice himself. And his bewilderment about seeing "four men go in and only three come out," until a newspaper photograph of the hacked corpse caught his eye while he was perusing the comics, was an indelibly graphic highlight.

We wound up our case with Faustino Satriale, which was the euphonious name of the man the Baker identified as "Gus with the tan car." Satriale explained he knew Abbandando from school and ballplaying days, and was only too glad to oblige whenever the Dasher asked to borrow his car. It had occurred "maybe three-four nights a week in the spring of 1937," Gus testified. The proof that, in May of 1937, Abbandando had driven the tan car which brought poor Whitey to his windup, was the final nail in the construction. It was a mob murder case such as few prosecutors ever had the opportunity to present, pictured by the mobsters themselves, step-by-step, from motive to "dumping" the body.

Some day, I would like to meet up with the man who has had a piano drop on him from about five stories up—and lived. I would like to compare notes on a kindred feeling.

We had built what we were confident was an uncrackable case, solidly based on what the eager extrovert, Julie Catalano, and the linguistically lost Joe the Baker had seen around the murder garage while playing cards with Trucchio. They were the corroboration the Law demands before the say-so of an accomplice such as Kid Twist means anything toward a conviction.

And now, up stepped a wolf-faced young man to lead off for the defense, and he set off a bomb under the entire case. In an assured, matter-of-fact manner, he threw the lie at both of the vital witnesses. His name was Carmine Scaffo, and we had not had the faintest idea that such a character even existed.

About that card game that night—well, he said, he was in the Sinclair station from 11 P.M. until 5:30 A.M. So was the Baker. But, he coolly declared, Julie Catalano was not there at all! Not for one minute; not even kibitzing! That is when the piano dropped from five stories up.

One informer after another had told us their stories, and the details all matched and dovetailed, and convinced us. But this smooth-talking defense bombshell was blowing them all up at once.

We had suspected a shocker was coming as soon as he took the oath.

"In May of 1937," was the first question, "where did you reside?"

"I was playing cards." The answer was out even before the query was completed. That was a tip-off. Still, we never had any notion of what it was. Not after all those weeks my trial aides,

Louis Joseph and Sol Klein, and Detective Frank Gray and myself had spent fitting in the pieces.

The defense delivered the "Sunday punch" quickly:

Q—Did Catalano enter that place at all that night?
A—No, sir.
Q—Did Liberto leave the game and go across the street to his garage at any time?
A—No, sir. Positive.

His manner was straightforward and simple—and impressive to a jury. Yet, there had to be something that did not add up. Reles and Julie and the Baker had agreed on too many of the minute details. And Scaffo had been just a little too anxious to get out that first response—that "I was playing cards."

But how attack a statement like that on cross-examination? Study the man; try to figure out what was out of place. Very little, in fact. He was smooth-shaven, neat, hair combed. I approached, with no cross-examination yet formulated. I still had not pinned down what it was that did not jell. Carmine Scaffo, twenty-nine, he'd testified; never been convicted of a crime. By trade, a-a-a . . . a what? Funny—the defense had not asked him. Usually, that's almost the first thing put on the record, after name, age and address. This fellow's poor clothing told of an honest workman. It never hurts to bring that to a jury's attention. Then, a glimmer began to come.

Q—What is your business?
A—I am a laborer—a track layer in the railroad. A pick-and-shovel man.

A man may be able to hide every emotion from his face; may keep his eyes dead and inscrutable. But rare is the man who does not make some motion of the hands, some gesture. Scaffo had, and his hand had caught the eye—and it gave him away.

"Hold your hands up so we can see the palms," I asked.

Scaffo held up two hands that were soft and white and smooth. There wasn't a callus on a square inch of skin.

"Turn them the other way."

He flipped them over. A perfectly manicured set of fingernails sparkled up—not a cuticle out of place. Pick-and-shovel man, eh?

Carmine was no longer self-assured. His mouth opened. He swallowed hard. My back was to the defendants, but Louis Joseph told me later that they suddenly developed very sour expressions. Happy, more sour than usual, must have been something to see.

"How long are your fingernails?" I asked.

"Well," Scaffo looked at his betraying hands. "There is a long one here," he pointed. A titter trickled through the spectators.

Objections cascaded from counsel table. The court took care of them. "He said he was a laborer. The jury has a right . . . " The judge left it there.

However, although his aplomb was gone, Scaffo still had damage to do. He'd heard screams from Happy's grandmother's apartment that murder night, he stammered. So, he'd "hurried" in to pay his respects—five hours later, when the card game ended. And, he vowed, Happy was there!

The deflating of Carmine was completed with one final stab. "Please step in front of the jury and hold up your hands so that the jury can see them," he was directed, as he stepped down. The jurors not only looked; they also felt the smooth, soft skin of a pick-and-shovel man.

This had, naturally, greatly damaged Carmine's believability. But, still on the record, unchanged, were his statements that Julie had not been near that card game and that Happy was grieving at his grandmother's at the hour the witnesses claimed he was helping dump Whitey's cadaver. That was damaging testimony to the State's case.

Grandmother Selenga's clan was a large one, and after Scaffo finished displaying his manicure, its members paraded up, one by one, for hours, to swear that Happy could not have had a hand in wiping out Whitey Rudnick. From 9 P.M. to 9 A.M., that murder night, they swore, he was in the tiny flat over the oil-burner store, grieving. Aunts, uncles, cousins, friends of the aged woman in life trooped up and told how Happy had been her favorite grandson.

To have a defendant's entire clan bathe him in innocence by putting him alongside a loved one's deathbed, is about as stout an alibi as can be produced in a courtroom. Occasionally, one kin contradicted another, but never on the basic fact that Happy was at that wake through the murder night. I asked each if an undertaker had been there. Half of them had not seen one. The other half were just as positive they had. Two testified an embalmer came in; the rest said they never saw an embalmer. There was one light touch when Uncle Donato Selenga identified himself as a butcher.

"You never gave Harry a meat cleaver, did you?" counsel hurriedly sought reassurance. Donato said no, he hadn't. On that note, Happy was called to testify for himself.

Happy Maione stretched all of five feet, four and a half inches in height, and his foot was a dainty size five and a half. He denied that this is what made his disguise so successful the night he dressed up, all painted and powdered like a party girl looking for a party, and wangled his way into the basement apartment of the romantically inclined plasterers, Lattaro and Siciliano, to murder them.

The runty ruler of the Ocean Hill hooligans was pale, and testified in a strange, high-pitched voice, but he had lost none of his confidence. He was a potential threat to the defense every minute, for a few judiciously applied "needles" would have him lashing out, snarling and oblivious to a contradiction or semi-admission of some point he had denied maybe ten minutes before. He declared flatly, for instance, that he knew nothing of the killings of the Shapiro Brothers. I harped on the subject a while.

"Did you hear Reles testify he killed one of the Shapiro Brothers, but not alone?" I asked.

That kindled the fire. "Did he tell you Shapiro was going out with his wife?" sneered Happy bitterly. "Did he tell you that?" The jury gathered that Happy was not quite as ignorant of the case as he had so vehemently maintained.

He said that Julie never worked for him, as Julie had testified. "He was a bookmaker for himself," Happy snapped. Later, he forgot, and said Julie worked for Reles. He played down his own handbook as anything but the interstate operation of which Reles had told us.

One day—"between 1936 and 1937," he went on, Julie drove up and said, "Reles wants to see you."

Q—What did you do?
A—I went to see him. Reles says, "How is business?" I says, "No good." I know what is coming. So, he says, "You been bookmaking too long. Turn your book over." I had to turn it over to him.

It was an hilarious picture—the hothead of the troop, second only to Pittsburgh Phil among eager killers, explaining how he had been muscled right out of business and had not even put up an argument. It was even finer comic fantasy when Hap vowed that, shorn of his livelihood, he entered the florist business with his brother. Happy Maione, hoodlum, among the petunias and the marigolds!

As for the Rudnick job, Happy simply said "no" to everything. He hadn't even heard about Whitey's going-away party, he swore, until "a couple of days afterward." He must have been deep in the woods or at the bottom of a well, then, for Ocean Hill had been abuzz with it. He spent the murder night, he said, weeping copiously over the passing of his very favorite grandmother.

"I walked into the bedroom; I sat down—close to the bed. And I stayed there." He was sad-faced and vehement.

Q—Didn't you leave the bedroom even to go to the bathroom?
A—I did not.

And the big thing he wanted to get off his chest was that this was all one huge frame-up against two decent young men. He reiterated it when I cross-questioned him.

Q—All this has been one monstrous conspiracy?
A—That's right.
Q—You are familiar with the machinations of these witnesses and the District Attorney?
A—To save themselves, them people put somebody against me.

Why, he declared, he had never even held a firearm in his hands in his life. A meat cleaver, either. And as for Julie saying he was left-handed—he was as right-handed as the next fellow. "It's only, I can use both hands," he supplemented.

Questioned about several visitors he had at the Tombs, Happy displayed a skill at putting his foot in his mouth. He was sure, twice over, that he did not know one Anthony Cantore, otherwise Anthony Bruno. Then it came out: he not only knew the gentleman, but, in 1928, he and Cantore, together with the Dasher, had ganged up on a policeman. They had felled Patrolman Hampton Ferguson and while he was down, they kicked and beat him. Happy managed to flee. The Dasher and Cantore were arrested and sent to Elmira by Judge Taylor—the same judge now hearing the Dasher's and Happy's trial for murder. Happy was caught weeks later. As so frequently happened for these plug-uglies, the charge against him was reduced, from second to third-degree assault, and he received a suspended sentence. Not much, Happy didn't know Anthony Cantore!

He remained in his denying mood throughout. Nevertheless, I took him through the entries the informers had filled in on him in the crime ledger, and listened to the mobster's stock "Who—me? Not me!" routine:

"On June 25, 1933, in a borrowed Cadillac, did you, Gurino and Pittsburgh Phil shoot and kill Joe Kennedy and dump his body out, with a strap from the car in his death grip?" (Kennedy had been an associate of Maione. Reles brought this one up at the point in his recital of Syndicate affairs when he said, "Joey Adonis is in the picture." He explained, "Happy was going to take this guy, and I loan him my Cadillac." Kennedy put up a bitter struggle. No one noticed that, during the battle, he tore loose one of the rear-seat guide straps. It was still in his dead hand when he was dumped. Reles, however, spotted the damage at once, and raised quite a fuss. It would not look nice to have police match up a strap in a murdered man's hand with a hole in the upholstery of Kid Twist's automobile. "Talk to Albert A. over at the City Democratic Club," Happy suggested, mentioning a favorite rendezvous for Anastasia and his chums. "Albert," Reles recalled, "tells me, 'Go see Joey A. and he will pay you.'" Reles went to the automobile agency which Joey A. ran in those days. "Adonis gives me a car with not much mileage," he went on. "I drive it a few days, but it is not the same as my Caddy. I tell him it is a rattletrap. So, Joey A. says, 'Okay; I will pay you the money and you can go out and buy a new car.' He gives me $800.")

"On October 23, 1934, did you and Abbandando kill Joseph Cooperman, in retaliation for shooting your partners?" (This one was Sholem's friend, Fatty, and dated back to the feud with the Shapiros.)

"On October 18, 1936, did you and Pittsburgh Phil shoot and kill one August Justriano, a tailor in Canarsie, over a woman?"

"On October 16, 1939, did you and Gurino kill Harry Schober around the corner from where Rudnick was killed?" (Julie had told us he was the wheelman on this job, but he had no idea of the motive.)

"On February 9, 1939, did you, Gurino and Abbandando shoot and kill Felice Esposito in the doorway of his home?" (Reles' story was that 'way back in 1922, one Vicenzo Manzi had been killed by a gangster named Anthony Catone. Esposito was a witness and offered to appear. Catone was not rounded up until 1938 —sixteen years later. He was permitted to plead guilty to second-degree murder, and thus no witnesses were necessary. A year afterward, when Lattaro and Siciliano were shot down, police sought the aid of Esposito, who knew nothing of the double slaying but was a plasterer, like the victims. The mob reasoned that since he had been ready to talk on the Manzi job, he would be ready to talk about anything. Esposito was caught in the doorway of his house and cut down. His slaying had been laid to the plasterers' war of early 1939—until Reles started to sing.)

Just as he brushed off all murder, Happy carried his routine denials right on into the collection of other crimes against his name. His ledger was chock-full, and as versatile as vice:

"Did you and Abbandando take a girl from Sally's bar by force to the Palace Hotel and there, with your friends, rape her? . . .

"On August 23, 1939, did you, Gurino, Abbandando and Leo Tocci kidnap a seventeen-year-old girl outside the Parkway Casino, where she had worked for two nights, and rape her, one after another?" (Tocci, also known as Massi and Dacci, was a figure of Manhattan water-front operations, after an early career in Pittsburgh and Erie, Pa. Late in 1940, he was murdered some fifty miles from Miami, Fla.)

"Did you, Gurino and Abbandando organize the East New York

Bakers Association and extort money from it under the guise of withdrawals to officers of the union?

"On Thanksgiving Day, 1939, in Tony Muscarelle's candy store, did you receive $2,000 from Ally the Wop as a split of an extortion from Local 138, Teamsters Union?" (Reles and Abbandando also were in the back-room kitchen of Tony's store that day to get their "cut." The extortion was the result of an earlier meeting attended by Mendy and Shimmy, representing Lepke; Tocci, representing the Manhattan water-front outfit; Maione, Abbandando and Reles from the combination, and the host, Max Becker, reputed close friend of Joe Adonis. The meeting set a minimum charge of $100 against each truck operator to renew contracts with Local 138. This was purely a "bonus" for the mobsters, payment of which merely granted a truck operator permission to enter contract negotiations with the Union.)

"In October, 1939, did you plan and assist the theft of an $18,000 carload of cigarettes, then cheat the actual thieves out of their share, cut it up with Gurino, and threaten to kill the thieves?

"Reles testified he shot three people on Sutter Avenue trying to get one of the Shapiros. Didn't you supply the pistol and drive the car?"

The not-so-happy Happy had been growing more savage as each succeeding question demonstrated how completely his activities had been exposed by Reles. He went off like a stepped-on booby trap at this reminder that he had actually helped Kid Twist rise from punk to gang powerhouse.

"Me supply to Reles?" he shrieked. "To the boss! Me supply to him?" Once again, he had shown clearly that he knew much more than he admitted about the combination and its business.

All of this, mind you, could be charged to the undersized assassin—who had spent a grand total of six months in jail in his lifetime up to that moment!

Abbandando's defense opened and closed with the Dasher his own principal and sole witness. The Dasher simply disapproved of the whole thing. He had been disapproving gradually as the trial progressed. When Happy's kinfolk took half a day parading up to swear to his alibi, Abbandando sat, slumped and motionless, like a thick-shouldered alligator sunning itself. He even forgot how he felt about blue uniforms with brass buttons. He turned to his two guards and announced:

"Why should we put up a case, me and Hap? Who's gonna believe those murdering bastards talking about us."

And then, so dolefully that one policeman thought tears were imminent, the ballplaying badman revealed that his particular grievance really wasn't the prospect of the electric chair, or his wife and family already on relief. "I'm gonna miss the first night ball game of the season," he mourned.

Things definitely had changed. Looking at them now, no one would believe the morose Maione, his surly còntempt conveniently softened, was the blustering boss, and Abbandando the tail to his kite. The Dasher was doing all the swaggering. His testimony came in a contemptuous jeer, a ridiculing singsong that was a slap in the face to the dignity of the court. Occasionally his voice was a strong confident boom, with all his two hundred pounds back of it, such as when he announced, "I never killed anybody in my life." Sometimes it assumed a raucous rasp, as when he was asked if he had heard Reles' testimony.

"I didn't hear Reles say nothing," he lashed out. "I paid no mind to him." No man could be that unconcerned for his life.

With that exaggerated singsong of a seven-year-old reciting Mother Goose, he ran through his vital statistics . . . thirty years old; three trips to the protectory as a juvenile delinquent; a stay at Elmira Penitentiary, and his baseball activities there.

For Judge Taylor, he reserved special, scornful contempt. Perhaps the disdain was a holdover from the time the judge had sent him to prison for assault, when he was eighteen. He had almost made it at seventeen, when he was hauled in for raping a sixteen-year-old girl.

"But I married her," he would explain often, as if that made everything lovely. The incident must have slipped his mind while he was on the stand now, however.

"Did you ever rape any girl or woman?" his attorney asked.

"I did not," he boomed. Surely, the Dasher must have put his wife in one or the other category—girl or woman.

As for what he knew about the butchery of Whitey Rudnick,

it was nothing, he vowed—and he could "prove" it. He never sent Joe the Baker for coffee that night—"because I never drink coffee when I'm outside," was his "proof." Pretty and Dukey never delivered a car to him—because "I didn't know Pretty and Dukey at that time." He did not sweep blood down a drain in the Sunrise Garage, "because," he proclaimed triumphantly, "I never worked in a garage."

Q—Where were you that night?

That was where the Dasher ran out of counterarguments.

"I don't remember; I don't know where I was. I wish I knew," he said, and, for the only time, he neither screamed nor sneered.

He couldn't have been there when Whitey was ice-picked and meat-axed, however, the Dasher maintained . . . "I don't think I would be able to stand that." And this bloodthirsty bandit actually produced a shudder!

But he had borrowed the tan car from Gus, it was pointed out, and he drove it during May of 1937. "Gus loaned me his car in 1935-6-7-8 and 1939—right up until today," Abbandando brayed. "I still know he has the tan car." That was a slip. Didn't he hear Gus testify that he'd disposed of that car two weeks after the murder? The Dasher was stumped for a moment only. Then: "I don't hear so good," he offered. "I'm not deaf . . . It's just I don't hear so good."

He raised his voice another notch, to just below a bellow, to declare, "I never heard of Albert Anastasia." That probably even made Maione feel like chuckling. "How," he concluded, a mildly recriminatory note in his tone, "how could you couple my name in the same breath."

The Dasher was not as cunning as Happy. Sometimes, when a query was repeated, he did not remember his previous answer. Where Happy had to be prodded into contradiction, the Dasher fell flat on his face all by himself. As time went along, he felt the pressure piling up, and he reacted violently.

It reached white heat, oddly enough, over the same item that brought one of Happy's embarrassing moments—the gang-up of the two mobmates and Anthony Cantore on Patrolman Ferguson in 1928. The whole thing had been dastardly, he stormed. There he was, a poor boy, ignorant in the devious ways of jurisprudence. And what happened?

"My lawyer was not in there the whole trial. I was forced on trial by the judge," he alleged contemptuously. He had, however, overlooked one point. He was telling this to the very same judge.

"Walter Hart, the present city councilman, was there and represented you throughout the trial," Judge Taylor retorted. "Furthermore, this court never tried a case without the attorney in court." Abbandando squirmed. His fists clenched and the knuckles were white.

"The court's statement is not an accurate one," his lawyer flung at the bench. The judge's eyes opened wide at the charge.

"Counsel is disorderly," he leveled a finger at the attorney. "You sit down and behave yourself."

Momentarily, all eyes had left Abbandando—and that was when he blew up. Half-rising, he leaned toward the judge, murder in his eye. He snarled a short sentence, low and pointed, like a dagger. Only Judge Taylor heard it. It brought him around sharply.

In this courtroom, in the badly planned Criminal Courts Building, the witness chair was on the same level as the bench, within a yard or two of the judge himself. An inflamed witness might easily leap over and attack the jurist before anyone could move. Judge Taylor summoned a guard now and directed him to stand between the bench and the witness while Abbandando remained on the stand.

Thus, when the Dasher blew up, it was with a loud blast. On trial for his life, he had threatened the court, just as if the judge were some slow-paying shylock customer or a contract from the mob! This athletic assassin had suddenly decided he would blossom into a "personality." He had pointed up most notably the fact that while he may have been a star around second base, he was not nearly so nimble fielding hot verbal grounders.

The criminal mind is enveloped by a psychosis that believes firmly it is genius.

Criminals are willing to pay legal fees running into fancy figures, presumably because they believe the attorneys they retain can handle their problems better than they can themselves. Then they proceed on the theory that what the lawyer doesn't know won't hurt him. The specie forgets entirely that a prosecutor digs into a case night and day, and, more often than not, will come up with something the accused has hidden from his attorney.

Happy Maione had given his lawyers the names of thirteen relatives and friends as the mourners at his grandmother's wake. Infected by that psychosis of omniscience, he had not even bothered to inquire whether an outsider might have visited the tiny apartment over the oil-burner store that night. His attorneys had no reason not to accept his story. They interviewed the thirteen witnesses, and all agreed on Happy's presence.

Meantime, our informers—Julie and the Baker and Kid Twist —all had mentioned that Whitey Rudnick was cut up the same night Happy's grandmother died. Reles, who fancied himself an adept psychologist, submitted, too, a mountain of information on what made these mobsters click—the mannerisms, quirks and peculiarities of Happy and the Dasher. The known normal mental gymnastics of Happy made it obvious that he surely would summon just about every mourner on Ocean Hill to swear him out of that death garage and put him at the bier.

The problem was to destroy his perfect alibi before it was aired. But who, of all the people at the obsequies, would be apt to tell the truth? Relatives were out; friends, too. The doctor had not paid a visit that night. Who, then? It was just possible—just barely possible—that. . . .

"Call Nicholas Blanda to the stand."

Happy did a double take as the dignified, solidly built man walked through the courtroom. His mouth fell open and his eyes popped. Nicholas Blanda had buried Happy's father. And he had buried Happy's grandmother, too. He was the outsider Happy hadn't checked on. Accustomed to killings without benefit of mortician, Happy probably had never even thought of an undertaker.

It had struck us early that, in spite of the late hour of Grandmother Selenga's demise, the undertaker might have been notified, and might have gone to the flat. The day I received the case file, I had Nick Blanda, the mortician, and Thomas Gilmore, embalmer, in the District Attorney's office. We had their sworn statements in hand sixteen days before we even served the defense with the demand for a list of alibi witnesses, from which, we noted with considerable pleasure, their names were conspicuously absent. We had sat through the parade of Happy's kinfolk and let the defense fire every round of its alibi ammunition. And we had saved Nick Blanda for rebuttal now.

Every alibi witness had been asked, almost casually, if an undertaker or an embalmer had been at the wake. Recollection of the wide divergence of responses was no solace at the defense table just now. Happy's own statement had been that he never left the bedroom the entire night, that the mortician walked in, merely looked at the body and walked out, and that no embalmer came at all. It turned out Happy was the most fanciful of the lot.

"About 2:15 on the morning of May 25, 1937," Blanda began, "I received a phone call that Mrs. Selenga was dead. I phoned the embalmer and then went to Mrs. Selenga's house. I went into the bedroom and prepared the body for the embalmer. He came shortly afterward."

Q—How long were you in that bedroom?
A—About an hour and a half. I left just about daybreak.
Q—In that time, who was in Mrs. Selenga's bedroom?
A—There was no one there but me and the embalmer.
Q—Between the time you arrived and daybreak, did you see this defendant, Harry Maione, in that bedroom?
A—Not in the bedroom.
Q—Did you see him anywhere in the apartment?
A—I don't think so.

Gilmore, whose presence at the flat had been remembered by only two of the thirteen witnesses, was even more emphatic:

Q—Did you see this defendant, Maione, at any time in Anna Selenga's premises that night?
A—No, sir.

The desperation of the cross-examination indicated just how flabbergasted was the defense. Counsel came back one after another—sometimes even two at a time—to hammer at Blanda. They resorted to such bizarre questions as:

"Isn't it a fact that you have a horror of touching bodies, and that you yourself never touch a body?"

"I, sir," was Blanda's dignified, and crushing, reply, "have been an undertaker for twenty-seven years."

Blanda knew the mob by repute; now he learned first hand. He barely reached home that evening after testifying, when a telephone caller, presuming to be a friend, sought to arrange a meeting with him at a certain garage. This was, indeed, a fine suggestion to make to a man who had just appeared against a killer accused of meat-axing his victim—in a garage. Nick Blanda went to the police, instead, and got himself a bodyguard.

Originally, that was to have been our case. But something new had been added after trial started. Now I had one more witness to put on. That is, I had him—and I didn't have him.

When Carmine Scaffo had been called as the first witness for the defense, we knew not a thing about him. As a result, even before he reached the stand, Detective Frank Gray was on his way to the Bureau of Criminal Identification.

The BCI has some information on every man in New York, dead or alive, who ever was convicted of a crime. An individual's record is a "Yellow Sheet," because it is roughly the size and color of a telegram. Frank Gray looked for a yellow sheet on Carmine Scaffo. Time went by, but no word came back to the courtroom that he had found one.

The defense did not require very long to have Scaffo drop his bombshell. We felt positive that there was something downright peculiar about the laborer with the lily-white hands, but I could not gamble on detaining him with unduly prolonged cross-examination, especially after he swore he had never been convicted of a crime. I had to let him go, too.

Before he reached the door, though, detectives in the courtroom had the signal. When he left, there was a tail on him. We wanted to know a little more about this pick-and-shovel man with a manicure, who had thrown our clear-cut case out of focus.

He had been gone only a few minutes, when the BCI report finally came in. There was no Yellow Sheet on Scaffo, Carmine— but there was one on Scaff*a*, Carmine," and it was the same man.

The slight difference apparently had gone unnoticed; no cross-index had been made. But Scaffa or Scaffo had pleaded guilty in 1930 to breaking into a laundry with larceny in mind. That was enough for us to want him back. It was enough, too, to hold him for perjury. The word went out to bring him in.

The Criminal Courts Building is in the heart of downtown Brooklyn, not far from the perpetually busy Brooklyn Bridge. The jam of traffic that afternoon, somehow, came between Scaffo and the detectives tailing him. They lost the trail.

About a half-mile east of the Ocean Hill mob's base of operations was Scaffo's favorite beer garden. Leaving the court, he had gone directly there. And there, a short time later, a relative came to him. "There's some dicks hanging around the neighborhood, Carmine," he warned. "I ducked away to tip you off."

Carmine knew what he had done on that witness stand. He headed for the Palace Hotel. Off and on, the boys used this nearby hostelry for sundry unpleasant purposes. However, to a fellow like Carmine, the solitude of four walls, especially at night, is a rapid morale wrecker. By 1 A.M., his fears had become panic. Desperate, he slipped out of the hotel, and headed back to his beer-garden corner. He managed to get a furnished room upstairs. Thus, when he was lonesome, he merely had to skip downstairs, briefly, for relief, then duck back up to his hideaway. All the rest of that night, all the following day and into the next night, he holed up while detectives scoured Ocean Hill for him.

Eventually, they were informed of his favorite hangout. This led to the furnished room. They went up and got him—on the stroke of midnight.

I was still in the office at 12:30, my mind about half made up to close the case the next morning without Scaffo. We didn't really need him for a conviction. It was just that it would be best to demonstrate to the mob now—in this first trial—that it could not get away with anything. Then the door opened—and there he was.

At first, he made a half-hearted attempt to stand by his testimony, including the fact that he had never been convicted. "Everything I said was true," he cried. I took out the Yellow Sheet on Carmine Scaffa. He realized that he was in a dilemma.

"I'm scared of what you'll do to me," he wailed. "And I'm

scared of the Maiones." It was pitifully clear he did not know which to fear more. In the end, since we had him at the moment and the Maiones didn't, he chose to eliminate the fear that was present in front of him.

He made a clean breast of everything. This thoroughly frightened creature, it turned out, had lied in just about every word he had sworn to on the stand. Someone had to be behind his perjury though. Even a man with the unpromising nickname of Fuggie—as Scaffo had—could not be so completely unintelligent as to believe he could give false testimony in a case as "hot" as this without being checked.

When court opened the next morning, Scaffo was not the same smooth, straightforward individual who had given us such a shock only two days before. He was a mongrel pup who's been kicked and takes off down the street, his tail between his legs. But he came as a high voltage charge to the defense when he started to testify:

Q—You told this court that you have never been convicted of a crime. Were you convicted of larceny on April 11, 1930?
A—That's right.
Q—You testified that you were playing cards with Joe Liberto and Frank Trucchio on the night of May 25, 1937, in the Sinclair Gas station. Who told you to testify to that?
A—Carl Maione.
Q—Who is Carl Maione?
A—Carl Maione is Harry Maione's—the defendant's—brother.

Happy was taking it like a fighter on the verge of a knockout, reeling from rope to rope in the ring.

"I was at the beer garden last Saturday night," Scaffo related. "I was told to meet somebody on Monday. I met Carl Maione. He told me to say in court that I was playing cards with Joe the Baker and Frank Trucchio, the night Hap's grandmother died."

Q—Were you told to say Joe the Baker did not leave the game?
A—That's right.
Q—Were you told to say you saw Harry Maione at the wake?
A—Right.

Q—Did you go up to the wake?

A—No, sir.

Q—Were you playing cards with Joe the Baker and Trucchio?

A—I was not.

Q—You were fully conscious that you testified falsely here on Monday, weren't you?

A—I was.

That wrapped up the case—and Scaffo, too. The plaintive perjuror, who had gotten into a lot of trouble because of a manicure, was held without bail. And the trial went on to final summations.

For four hours and forty minutes, the defense attorneys "analyzed" the testimony as conclusive proof of a monstrous frame-up —which no one had detected except themselves. Every one of our witnesses undoubtedly had perjured himself, they charged time and again. There were broad grins at that. The only perjury uncovered was by Carmine Scaffo—and the defense had brought him in solely to commit perjury. Of almost touching beauty was Attorney Rosner's plea for the Dasher, in the fair name of baseball.

"Ballplayers don't kill people," he argued. "In all my experience, I cannot think of a single baseball player who ever killed anybody—at least so viciously as in this case."

Through most of the state's sum-up, which followed, Maione and Abbandando stared stone-faced, concentrating on showing unconcern. I was just reviewing the testimony about the murder orders Happy sent from the Tombs, when a hoarse growl roared out:

"Reles told you everything!"

My back had been to the defense table. I swung around. Happy hung there, half in, half out of his seat. He looked as if he was coming right over the table at me. Then it came again—but a scream this time—"Reles told you everything." Evidently the fact had just dawned on him, although Reles had spent six hours in the courtroom weeks before, baring those very secrets in person.

For one weird moment, the room was a shocked still life. Then everything happened at once. Voices clattered like breaking crockery. Guards jumped. An attorney plucked Maione's sleeve and whispered, "Keep quiet; please, Harry." That snapped him out of it. He settled back, slowly. He looked like a large beetle that has been stepped on. Abbandando blinked once. He blinked a dozen times more, rapidly. Obviously, the Dasher could not reconcile this collapsed balloon with the iron-nerved boss he'd obeyed so long.

Judge Taylor, in his charge, called special attention to Scaffo's perjury. "A defendant," he pointed directly at Happy, "accepts responsibility for witnesses in his behalf. If a witness fabricates evidence, you have the right to infer that the defendant, Maione, knew it was untrue and authorized it."

He turned to the vital point of corroboration and ruled that Reles' testimony would need "independent proof." He came then to Julie, whom the defense had sought, all the way, to involve as a participant.

"I charge you," he let each word sink in, "that Catalano has not been shown, as a matter of law, to be an accomplice. Catalano's testimony of the acts in that garage need not be corroborated."

"Truth is sometimes found in strange places," he philosophized as he turned the case over to the jury.

Ordinarily, accused murderers suffer while they sweat it out, waiting for a verdict. Not these two, though. Happy, recovered from his brief seizure, and the Dasher were as cocky as ever. Even that morning—with all the evidence in—they had been almost blithe about it.

"Don't worry about me," Happy had remarked in the prison van bringing them from their cells. "The worst I'll get is murder two [second degree]." Beating the chair would be a victory to Happy.

The Dasher had frankly predicted acquittal. "I'll have spaghetti home on Sunday," he had gaily asserted.

The jury filed back into the courtroom after only two hours and two minutes. The defendants stood and faced the twelve men.

"We find both defendants guilty of murder in the first degree!" declared Frank Graham, the foreman. It was May 23. It lacked two days of being the third anniversary of the butchering of Whitey Rudnick.

Conviction for murder one, as the boys call it, carries a mandatory death penalty. On the morning of May 27, Happy and his muscled stooge stood at the bar and heard it pronounced officially. Neither of them showed the slightest emotion. Twenty-four hours later, they did, though, when they were shackled together and vanned over to Grand Central Station in Manhattan. As they were urged through the rotunda toward the train gate, it hit them: At the other end of that train ride is the death house. And the chair. They whimpered, and they hid their faces from the photographers.

"All I can tell you is I'm innocent," squealed Happy to the reporters. "I never saw Reles in my life." Everyone laughed at that.

"What do you think of the D. A.'s drive to stop crime at the source?" one enterprising newsman finally managed to say to them.

"I guess it's a good idea," Maione said. We could not have asked for more "official" approval.

We were, of course, greatly heartened by the result of this all-important first prosecution, for we were already pointing our guns at bigger game—and not only in Brooklyn, either. As a matter of fact, the very next murder business took me clear across the country . . . to California, where Buggsy Siegel, who was as big as they come in national crime, was king.

10.   Horace Greeley never meant this

Buggsy Siegel plots murder in a hospital—crime comes to California—movie stars pay off—enter Virginia Hill—California Law falls down—Kid Twist, defense counsel, wins a case—war for the Wire Service—Lucky sneaks back from exile, and Buggsy draws the death sentence—cross-country narcotics tie-ups—who is Buggsy's real heir?

ONE afternoon in the fall of 1932, Buggsy Siegel, most arrogant of gangsters, was checked into a New York hospital as a patient.

"I'm awful sick," said the dapper killer, and he smiled a tired smile. "It's my nerves, I guess. I need some rest and quiet, and a kind nurse to look after me."

The Bug got into bed, and for forty-eight hours or so, he relaxed, like any sick man in a hospital. On the third night, the nurse on the floor looked in, as usual, on her after-supper rounds.

"Honey," cooed Buggsy, "willya kind of fix the blankets and tuck me in? I'm so tired, I'm going right to sleep."

The nurse would, indeed. The patients' call buzzers had been sounding off like crickets in a cornfield. She was, she sighed, glad to be rid of one patient this early. As she shut the door behind her, the Bug became remarkably spry for a tired man. He dressed quickly. He stuffed the pillows under the blankets, so the half-light from the hall would reveal a "sleeping" figure. He slipped downstairs and out of the hospital unseen.

Two friends in a waiting car whisked him off. They knew just where to go—to a house on Fort Hamilton Parkway, near the Government Reservation in southwest Brooklyn. They knocked on the door, and an elderly gentleman opened.

"Where's Tony?" they demanded. "We're detectives."

"I'm Tony's father," replied the elderly gentleman, at once apprehensive in the face of the Law. "Wait . . . I'll get him."

He hurried into the kitchen, where Tony was having dinner, and he delivered the message. Tony strode up the hallway, his family trailing. He swung open the door—and three bullets hit him in the chest, in full view of his horrified clan.

Tony's full name was Francis Anthony Fabrizzo, and he had spent a large part of his forty years in the mobs. So had his brothers. One of them, Andy, had been found stuffed in a sack, over in New Jersey. Another, Louis, had been shot down on Manhattan's East Side. Their fate, among other things, had finally convinced Tony that the trade he was in had no future. He had recently decided that he'd worked on his last murder. That one, incidentally, was as an assistant the night Vincent Coll, the maddest of the mad-dog killers, was caught in a phone booth by an unfriendly individual with a tommy gun.

Realizing that he just couldn't walk out on the mob, Tony evolved a plan to make himself murder-proof. He began to write his memoirs, intending to tuck them in a safe place and then let the mob know that if anything happened to him, they would be turned over to the Law. This treatise was to tell, among other things, how $27,000,000 had been raised by what he called "the 400"—an exclusive group of bootleggers—as a war chest against the end of Prohibition. In this set were such people as Lucky Luciano and Ciro Terranova, the uptown "Artichoke King" and branch manager of Mafia when it was still active, and Li'l Augie Pisano, who had the best political contacts in town. The war chest, Francis Anthony would explain, in his literary work, was to be used to set up a legal brewery for "the 400" after repeal. They would then prevail upon saloonkeepers to purchase their product—at a price they would insist was right, of course. Tony was going to tell, too, of a professional gun troop hiring out to the underworld chiefs, and of the selection of Buggsy Siegel, then the brazen co-commander of the infamous Bug & Meyer Mob, as its leader.

Unfortunately, however, one or two of Tony's closest "friends" heard of his literary intentions—and thus the reforming mobster wound up with three bullets in his chest, at his front door.

Quickly, now, Buggsy got back to the hospital and into bed. In the dark, he stretched, beaming. Buggsy's greatest obsession was himself, from his dark and handsome profile and his wavy hair down to his manicured toenails.

"Pal, you are so smart," he gave himself a mental pat on the back. "Who else would think to set up an alibi with a hospital? They can't blow holes in this one with a cannon."

Through the years has come a tale, however, that before that night was out, Buggsy was not fooling about his hospital stay. His head began to hurt, and he would not have been surprised if his skull was fractured. It seems that a few days before, some rival mobsters had crawled from an adjoining building onto the roof of his social club on the East Side, had lowered a bomb down the chimney on a piece of twine—and had blown the place apart. A piece of timber, or, perhaps, a moosehead souvenir on the wall, landed on Buggsy's skull. So, thinking the effects were just beginning to make themselves felt, he remained in the hospital for two days after the institution had served its purpose as a murder alibi. On the third evening, however, he suddenly dressed, signed a release and checked out with a great deal of speed. Later, much later, the reason was disclosed. Two of his buddies, nearing the hospital to visit him, spotted four enemy mobsters on the street corner opposite. They gathered that an attempt was imminent to hit Buggsy—right in his hospital room. They prevailed upon him to regain his health at once, and leave.

Buggsy's hospital alibi is presented here solely for its relation to national crime. Actually, these carefully covered antics were going to be responsible, in large measure, for singling him out for the doubtful distinction of bringing crime to California—organized, gang-style crime.

Gangdom in the mid-thirties already had organized on a cross-country scale in New York and Chicago and practically everywhere else. If you were an Easterner, you were paying tribute to gangsters on almost everything you ate and wore. But organized crime had not yet discovered the gold in the Golden West.

Perhaps there was a hood here and there on his own around Los Angeles and its environs. Or an outfit taking horse bets, or unorganized narcotics importing and gambling and prostitution.

Even stick-ups and murder, now and then. But of organized stuff Southern California had none. It was, however, en route.

Kid Twist and Allie, singing for all they were worth, mentioned a California killing to us in 1940. So, that summer, with Happy and the Dasher in the death house at Sing Sing, I made a business trip to Los Angeles. A portion of the story back of the western invasion of the Syndicate was unfolded for me.

Some three years after Buggsy played sick for a murder alibi, the board of directors of the then newly formed Syndicate was in serious session. Frank Costello's slot machines in Louisiana and Florida and New York and Lucky's numbers and narcotics, backed by high political connections, were mints. Lepke had a golden pile of industry-labor grabs. But sudden affluence had made greedy ganglords greedier. They wanted more, and looking around, they discovered the one territory still untouched—Southern California. For two years, they studied it. Early in 1937, it was time to move in.

"That money is all around . . . and loose," they agreed. "Not a real racket is going."

"There's labor outfits to snatch," one reported. "And those nice movie people—why should they have to go all the way to Las Vegas to make a bet?"

The project sounded good all around. The Capone gang of Chicago, under Scarface Al's cunning cousins, the Fischetti Boys (ex-Brooklyn), was already preparing for its struggle over the racing "wire service," in which California was a key. A branch office on the scene would be useful.

The talk advanced to choice of a general manager for a Los Angeles office and immediately Buggsy's name was solidly supported.

"Benny is a natural," proposed Lepke. "He knows the angles. And since we got the Brooklyn troop now to handle contracts, Ben is loose to take care of big stuff like this."

It was not all mere coincidence, however. Just about then, the gangland grapevine reported that Buggsy's long-secure hospital alibi had suddenly become a great deal less airtight than he was taking bows for. That clinched it.

"It's getting too hot here . . . Benny should get out of town," announced Lepke, voicing the consensus.

So, financed by Lepke and Lucky, and with the blessing of the rest of the powerful Eastern and Midwestern bosses, Buggsy packed his bag and headed West—because an alibi had developed a puncture. It was not what Mr. Greeley had in mind at all.

A completely uninhibited criminal, the Bug knew all about "organization." He'd been at it since 1925, when he and Meyer Lansky put their racketeering mob together. Operations had been launched by preying on New York cabaret owners. One, Mike Albert, objected—and suddenly was taken dead. There were no more objections. The mob branched to Philadelphia and struck gold.

Buggsy had learned the trade at the feet of the master—Lepke. Meyer Lansky has been a long-time associate of Costello and is a director of the Syndicate himself. He has "cut" as much as 10 per cent or more of Florida gambling joints, some of which enjoy profits of more than half a million dollars a season.

Buggsy Siegel's ego was the most incredible part of this fantastic bum. Charges that would make honest men fight had him throwing out his chest. Yet, he would tear apart anyone who dared call him "Buggsy" out loud, although the gang had pinned the label on him as a compliment, denoting a torpedo who would walk contemptuously into a shooting match that might cause a platoon to reconnoiter.

He insisted on being addressed with the dignity befitting his station—which he firmly believed was the highest in mobdom. If you knew him well enough, you were permitted to call him Ben. Otherwise . . .

"Call me Mr. Siegel," he once demanded threateningly of another hood who was uncertain. "That's my name, isn't it?"

This unrestrained thug established the beachhead of organized crime in California in 1937. Arriving, the Bug cased the layout thoroughly, and decided that the quickest "earnings" lay in the motion pictures. Buggsy's organizational upbringing told him, however, that film company executives had the power and the money to fight a direct, cold grab—something previous musclers had not appreciated. The big-name stars—now there, Buggsy figured, was the immediate target at which to aim.

The Bug was a natural for Hollywood. Handsome as a romantic star himself, smooth-talking, *bon vivant,* he had a brashness, built around his well-padded ego, that was made to order to fit film society. He was soon hob-nobbing with top-name stars. That made his first California collection all the easier. Just what this i:.volved, I learned while looking into the California murder our Brooklyn informers mentioned in 1940.

They involved Buggsy in their singing so there was a visit to his cozy thirty-five-room Holmby Hills hut, a $200,000 pile of white brick, complete with swimming pool, in which he had set up his uncomplaining Brooklyn wife and their two daughters. His particular delight in this palace was his own private bath, done in maroon marble. The master was not at home when we got there. Word of my visit apparently had leaked, although we took every precaution, even to an incognito.

We admired the lavish taste displayed by the connoisseur from the slums. Most noteworthy was a pair of priceless pistols carefully tucked away in a wall safe. They were matchless masterpieces to a man in Buggsy's position; a check showed they had no connection with any criminal deed. But we especially admired the Bug's account books that were found upstairs. Some of the very top film idols had been "loaning" him sums in four and five figures since shortly after his arrival—and no record indicated they ever were repaid! The only deduction possible was that Buggsy did not have to pay back—that here was his first neat dividend in the California territory.

It seems he somehow had managed to achieve considerable power in the organization, at that time, of the movie extras, the army of faceless performers so vital as a backdrop for the stars' talents. Bit by bit—as he had seen Lepke do it in the garment unions—he gained control. Then he showed his hand. He used the silk glove approach, rather than the schlammin, or lead-pipe, technique.

"Look, George," he would confide to a high-salaried star, as if offering a great favor, "I'm putting you down for $10,000 for the extras."

"What kind of a bite is this?" was George's immediate reaction.

"What have I got to do with the extras?" He would shrug Buggsy off.

"Tsk, tsk," the Bug countered. "I guess you just don't understand. Take your next picture, now: script written, director named, scenes set, stagehands drawing pay. The producer says, 'Go.' Then what happens? The extras walk out—just like that. You can't get more, because they're all in the same outfit. So—no picture."

This, George could easily understand. Every star knows that precarious public whim demands films he or she appears in. Many made "loans" to Buggsy. For one year alone, they totaled $400,000. What made it so nice for the Bug was that they were all the same one-way loans. Even more remarkable, many of the stars were socializing with Buggsy at the same time they were paying!

A raconteur extraordinary, the hood from the East became the darling of the very screen society he was muscling—while he was muscling it. Local papers referred to him as "the Hollywood socialite." An Italian countess, whose calling list included titled heads of Europe, introduced him to the best people. He was pointed out as "that wealthy Hollywood sportsman." It was not too inexplicable when you consider that the Bug had never been convicted of any serious crime. In fact, when we were after him and looked for rogue's gallery photographs, the only picture on record, as I recall, was an ancient likeness in the files of the Philadelphia police. His personality could charm the elite of any circle he entered.

Buggsy fancied two-hundred-dollar suits, of which he always had twenty-five or thirty. He was proudest, though, of his handmade twenty-five-dollar silk shirts. He kept them in a specially lighted dresser to admire them the more. His name was linked romantically with a star still established in film and television to this day. That, of course, was before Virginia Hill discovered California—and vice versa.

Virginia arrived in Chicago not long before Buggsy opened the West for the Syndicate. Her first recorded northern appearance was on the Midway at the Chicago World's Fair in a show called "Elephants and Fleas," in which she played the part of neither. She was a wide-eyed seventeen-year-old then, with mouse-colored hair that soon acquired gorgeous auburn tints.

From an Alabama steel town, one of the ten children of a marble-polisher, she had left home and headed for the Fair with a young gentleman. Her father thought of putting the law on the young man, but Virginia herself remarked as how it was all her idea, just so she'd have an escort from 'Bama to the honky-tonk. She made many friends while cavorting on the Midway.

Minus the "spread" which has been added, willy-nilly, since she reached her thirties, Virginia was laden with (a) sex and (b) a remarkable talent for acquiring coin of the realm. Her accomplishments in both fields cannot be challenged. In a matter of sixteen years, she has managed to take on four husbands, including a Mexican rhumba dancer and, currently, a combination Austrian skier and fire extinguisher salesman. In between she developed precious friendships with some of the hottest mobsters *not* in captivity. As Longy Zwillman, the New Jersey representative on the board of governors, once put it, "Virginia didn't look too hard to know." She has been, from time to time, a favorite of the Fischettis of Chicago and Joey Adonis of the Brooklyn set. She has had her associations, too, with Lucky and Frank Costello and Frank's New Orleans operative, Dandy Phil Kastel, and Meyer Lansky. A friend once said Virginia seemed to have a Geiger counter for finding hoodlums to be chummy with.

At one time, reports were rife that she was the mob's cross-country "bagman," or money messenger.

"The only cash I ever carry is mine," Virginia vows most vehemently. Such reports, moreover, have left her with a dim view of newspapermen, whom she lumps, along with photographers, as "God-damn bums."

Usually, she has maintained herself in simple style, such as at Sun Valley in 1950, when she ran through a mere $12,000 in a six-week stay. In cash, too—no bank deposits or checking accounts or anything that means records will be kept. She acquired a reputation as a party-tosser in bistros from New York to Hollywood—with way stops at Chicago, Miami, Havana, Saratoga and Las Vegas—that might have taught Bacchus a thing or two, if the old boy were still around. Some of her $5,000 to $10,000 a night galas are legend in café society. Head waiters and bus boys will never forget "that happy-go-lucky girl"—or her hundred-dollar tips.

The money? . . . Oh, that, says Virginia. That came from two sources: (1) "The men I was around with gave me things," and (2) betting on horses. Certain friends were always tipping her off when certain horses were going to co-operate.

Eventually, the little Dixie maid found her way to California, which is a long haul from the steel mills, at that. She and Buggsy gazed deep into each other's eyes, and the first thing you know, the Bug insisted that she give up Falcon's Lair, which was once Rudolph Valentino's palace and which she had rented. He established her in a lavish Beverly Hills nest. Romance set in. Buggsy even gave her a wedding ring—not, it is assumed, to be confused with the one his wife wore.

With those "loans" from the movie stars, Buggsy could afford it. And they were only the starter. From there, Buggsy proceeded to put California in the Syndicate's country-wide chain-store system.

His first mission accomplished, the Bug's next thought was toward securing his beachhead. It is an old crime credo that you only keep what you can hold on to. He began assembling a troop of his own and laying political pipelines, backed by underworld personnel and cash. His philosophy on politics—in fact, the Syndicate's philosophy—is simple.

"We don't run for office," the Bug would say. "We own the politicians."

The Murder, Inc., branches in Cleveland and Chicago and New York, interested in making a go of the new office, sent torpedoes to build up Buggsy's staff. Usually, these characters were too hot with the Law where they were. One of the Eastern boys was a flamboyant ex-featherweight fighter named Mickey Cohen, loud and somewhat ludicrous—and a product of Brooklyn. Mickey was not a very good fighter. He mixed lawlessness with ineffective left hooks from California to New York, but mostly around Cleveland, where he once did a bit of embezzling on the side, and Chicago, where he was in gambling until things got very warm, and he headed west for a cooler climate.

Actually, Mickey has all the earmarks of the small-shot who

goes for the sandwiches when the big boys have their hotel-room sessions. But he came to Buggsy well recommended from the "best people." In California, Mickey has continued knowing the best people—like Arthur H. Samish, the influential lobbyist. A meaty individual of some three hundred pounds, Samish has an interesting political credo himself, which he once expressed as, "To hell with the governor of the state; I am the governor of the legislature."

From the sparse local talent, however, came Buggsy's most valuable asset—Jack I. Dragna. This largely unpublicized plug-ugly is a survivor of the 1931 purge of Mafia. The California Crime Study Commission confirms that when James Ragan lay dying in Chicago in 1946, murdered for his race wire "service," he gasped,

"Dragna is the Capone of Los Angeles."

Dragna was especially handy when Buggsy set out to organize the bookmakers. He was a local gambling power. Twenty years ago, he had a hand in one of the widely publicized gambling ships that mocked the Law from three miles off the California shore.

Buggsy chose this pair—noisy Mickey and the sinister Dragna— for his assistant commanders. Having financed his original operational costs through his movie-star loans, the Bug now began an expansion program. But before he could get this phase well under way, Buggsy had to drop everything for some high-priority interdepartmental Syndicate business.

Through all the years when corpses were being left around in gutters, in automobiles or in cement overcoats on riverbeds in the East and Midwest, California enjoyed no such macabre epidemic. And for two years, Buggsy's branch office managed to maintain the status quo. Not a throat was cut. In fact, up to 1939, there had not been a bona fide gang slaying in Southern California in modern crime annals! It is too bad the record had to be broken on a strictly "lend-lease" job.

Because of its position in the underworld scheme, then, California's first big-time gang execution is detailed here from start to finish for probably the first time:

In New York, the opening of the Dewey rackets investigation

caused the mob magnates to bring into play their "bombproof technique," based on Lepke's philosophy that, "All investigations collapse when no witnesses are around." Various accomplices, accessories and associates were ordered to "lam." One such was Big Greenie, whose name was, variously, Harry Schacter, Harry Schober and Harry Greenberg.

For years, this large character had been an insider in dealings in the needle trades industry. Then Lepke decided to add that one to the rest of his industrial rackets. Naturally, Greenie did not like this. However, Lepke had too many guns, so Greenie wisely applied the old "if you can't lick 'em, jine 'em" theory. For some years, everything worked out well. He even became a member of the Bug & Meyer alumni association. Then came the Dewey probe, and Greenie hustled off to the mob hideout in Canada.

The lamster must shun all public spots. Only select contacts and hideaways may be used. These come high to the fugitive. To keep contacts loyal, he must pay more than the Law offers, for the informer works both ways. By early spring of 1939, Big Greenie was feeling the pinch. From his lair in Montreal, he wrote for additional funds. No doubt irked at being overlooked, he worded his request most unfortunately.

"I hope you guys are not forgetting me," it read, in effect. "You better not."

By this time, the investigation had put an awkward pressure on the boys. Lepke himself was in hiding, and a purge of potential witnesses was under way. Mendy Weiss was the acting general manager—and loving every minute of the authority it gave him. With the heat intense in Manhattan, he had moved headquarters over to Brooklyn. To Mendy, Big Greenie's note implied a threat.

"Make a meet tonight, by the big boathouse in Prospect Park," the hulking 200-pounder commanded the hoods. The peaceful patch of trees and lake, in the heart of residential Brooklyn, was never intended for the gangland kangaroo court it witnessed that night.

Like Mendy, the rest of them interpreted the letter as an ultimatum—"money—or else," meaning Big Greenie was reminding them he could talk. Jittery over the first investigative threat in almost a decade of virtually unmolested crime, the mobsters were quick to take umbrage at an associate even hinting additional troubles. The court decreed death penalty.

Allie was one of the dwindling number of staff killers still available. He was ordered to Montreal to do the job. Following the customary careful operations plan, the hotelkeeper's hoodlum son set up a watch across the street from Greenie's hideout. Not a sign of his target did he see, however, although he kept his vigil for a full day.

Now, Big Greenie was no door knob in the matter of brains. His knowledge of the gang had warned him that the silence since his letter meant he'd get something, all right—but not money. Even before Allie arrived, the bird had flown. In the next few weeks, a desperate race was on. The mob wanted Greenie. Any number of law-enforcement agencies wanted him. It was a Death Derby on a cross-country course, for high stakes. Greenie headed for Detroit, where he had friends, and holed up. The sensible thing, to him, was to make contact. The Purple Mob, holder of the local franchise in the Syndicate, gave him a cordial welcome. It was too cordial.

"They must have checked the New York office," thought Greenie, immediately apprehensive. They had—and the New York office replied:

"Keep him in tow until we get a couple of boys out there."

Once again, Big Greenie started West—this time, as far West as geography would permit, short of swimming. He was determined not to make the mistake again of exposing himself for contact. In California, nevertheless, his hideout in a Hollywood house was spotted. The word was relayed to headquarters. Firmly, the home office decided this was the end of the line. Lepke directed Mendy to "let Ben handle it." Buggsy was contacted.

"It's a contract," was all the Bug had to hear. He was especially pleased at this one. To him, this order direct from Lepke was both flattering recognition that he was head man in the West, and a tribute to his art in assassination.

In New York, two guns were stolen from a cargo waiting on a pier for shipment abroad, a stunt that was standard operating procedure. Foiled in Canada, Allie was given an opportunity to get in on the kill. Just before he boarded a plane at Newark airport, a ranking Jersey ganglord—still active, but now a self-styled "businessman"—sidled up and handed him a small black doctor's instrument bag. The guns were in it.

In California, meantime, Buggsy had turned over the fingering and casing to one of his imported staff specialists—Whitey Krakow, from New York's downtown. Frank Carbo, who was a Seattle fight promoter then—and controlling the world middle-weight championship—happened to be handy in Los Angeles. He was invited "in."

Next detail was the getaway car. And just about then, coincidentally, Buggsy received a visit from Sholem, the loner who worked so frequently with the mob in New York. Sholem was on one of his periodic vacations. Under mob law, however, when a contract comes up, a visiting trigger is on call to the local Syndicate director in whatever town he may be.

Buggsy was well aware of Sholem's specialized talent in acquiring transportation. "Clip a car," he directed the visitor. "Leave it on the parking lot down the street."

"Parking lot?" As a veteran of seventy-five to a hundred car thefts for mob jobs, Sholem was nonplussed. In his time-tested technique, a drop was required—a private garage, usually one of a row, and rented for an entire month. Buggsy, though, took advice from no one. And Sholem knew better than to argue with Buggsy's explosive egoism. In short order, a hot car was on the parking lot.

Just as Sholem had anticipated, the owner discovered the theft, and in practically no time at all, the police found the car on the lot and retrieved it. Thus, with the job approaching, there was an unexpected hitch. It was one, however, that could be easily ironed out. The Bug simply told Sholem to go get another car—and park it on the same parking lot. Tactfully, Sholem tried to suggest that, on this second go-round, the Brooklyn method be employed, beginning with the drop.

"Then, you get license plates off another car that you case to see the owner only uses it once in a while, like a Sunday driver," he detailed pleasantly. "By the time the guy finds out, you got the job done, and the cops are looking for him—why are his plates on a hot car. Then you . . ."

No out-of-town delegate was going to insinuate they did anything better anywhere else than Buggsy did it. "Who the hell are you, coming in and telling me how to do a job?" he ranted. "Out here, it goes my way. And don't forget it!"

Back in New York, although he worked smoothly on mob contracts, Sholem insisted on his individuality, and his status was respected. He felt he had a right to the same consideration here in the West, especially since he was breaking up his vacation for the contract. Sholem, annoyed, walked out. He got into his car and headed East. Buggsy had to assign a replacement to procure transportation. It was crystal clear that, while the Bug did not understand Sholem, Sholem did not understand Buggsy, either. The egomaniac moblord would never brook such defiance.

Meantime, the casing had disclosed that Big Greenie stayed very close to home base, in his quiet little hideout, out near suburban Bel Air. In fact, except for a brief nightly drive for the newspaper that kept him from "blowing his top" in his fear and loneliness, he never risked leaving his cover. On the evening of November 22, which was Thanksgiving Eve, Greenie, taking his usual precautions, opened the door of the house a crack and peered cautiously along the entire block. Satisfied at last, he slipped out and drove off for his newspaper. The trip took about fifteen minutes each way, and Big Greenie never dallied, going or coming. Within forty-five minutes, he was turning the corner of Yucca Street into his block once more.

Perhaps it was the balmy weather, or the neighborhood quiet. Anyway, Greenie's usual prudence was lulled. He should have paid more attention to the two cars parked near the corner. Of course, in the dark, they were simply two more automobiles, although no one would ever take Buggsy's showy Cadillac for just any jalopy. The other was the hot car which Sholem's substitute had obtained.

Earlier on that Thanksgiving Eve, Allie had picked up this vehicle from its waiting place and had driven Buggsy and Frank Carbo to Buggsy's Cadillac. The two-car caravan then proceeded to the suburban street where Greenie lived, arriving, as planned, while he was gone for his newspaper. Buggsy's car drove slowly the length of the block, to check the layout. Then, Allie told us later, Carbo took up a vigil in the shadows close to Greenie's house.

As the returning fugitive passed, the lights on the front vehicle blinked once, on and off, so quickly you wouldn't have been sure of it unless you were watching for the flash—like, for instance, the man standing in the shadows there. This was his cue. Before Greenie could get out from behind the wheel, the man walked over and pumped shot after shot into him. And Big Greenie, lamster, became Southern California's first important gang cadaver. The cycle of crime in the new territory was now complete: muscle to murder; extortion to extermination.

The gunman ran up the street to the hot car, which was the getaway machine. Buggsy's fancy Cadillac, with Allie driving, followed as the crash car. This carefully-studied touch is designed to obviate such items as a roving police car that may happen along, or a civic-minded motorist who might decide to pursue. With experienced wheelman, the crash car is simply maneuvered into the way, even to running the pursuer right onto the sidewalk, if necessary, to insure the flight of the getaway car. The driver can always claim that the excitement of it all got him. The crash car is always legitimate—legally registered and owned.

The two cars proceeded to an appointed spot, where a confederate was waiting with another automobile. Allie identified him as Champ Segal, a small-time hanger-on, hero-worshiper of mobsters and self-styled Hollywood barbershop impresario. He has sometimes managed prize fighters, many of whom have been noted for remarkable and peculiar performance. Allie, having fulfilled his assignment, was driven to San Francisco, where he took a plane back to New York.

Several months later and three thousand miles away, Kid Twist suddenly brought up Big Greenie's going away party. The Kid mentioned Allie, and Allie filled in the empty spots. Reles was unpleasantly boastful under any circumstances. On one development of the bizarre California murder chapter, his vanity became even more nauseating than usual.

Buggsy had been most indignant over Sholem's defiance in walking out on the Big Greenie job. The arrogant gangster was the sort who would rather not bother with stand-ins to do his shooting for him, a characteristic setting him apart from Lepke and Lucky and the other executives, once their authority was established. But the law was different now.

The structure of crime under the Syndicate forbade any assassination of a mob worker—even one of Sholem's purely associate member status—without the approval of the boss in the home territory of the accused. If the territorial ruler opposed, protocol required taking the dispute before the judiciary, the kangaroo court. Buggsy was so indignant he made a special trip east to demand the death penalty for Sholem.

"He ducked out on the contract," the Bug charged. "It was your contract, too."

But Sholem had friends in New York. Eastern bosses rated him one of the best "safe men" alive. Buggsy remained adamant, however. So persistent was he, that the kangaroo court was convened.

From the day it was set up, the Syndicate tribunal has granted to a "defendant" every constitutional safeguard a citizen enjoys in a court of General Sessions under American justice, even to representation by counsel (ordinarily another—but more articulate—mobster), presentation of testimony and introduction of evidence. About the only basic principle missing is the opportunity for a defendant to confront witnesses against him. Time, the ganglords felt, would only be wasted on extended cross-examination. The makeup of the court is a panel of five or seven or sometimes nine directors of the national ring. They are judge and jury—sitting in some hotel room, listening to evidence from both sides, and arriving at a verdict. And once they have spoken, there is no appeal.

Buggsy was so worked up that he prosecuted personally, and when he finished, there seemed no rebuttal against his deadly indictment. Walking out on a contract carried the death sentence.

Then up stepped Reles before the august gangster jurists as Sholem's counsel. The accused knew what we were to find out—that when it came to orating, the Kid was in a class by himself. The Kid called no witnesses. In fact, he admitted everything—that his client had left Los Angeles after receiving the order; had, if you wanted, run out. Nevertheless, the Kid was ready with his defense. He had put all his cunning into this. He pointed out, first, that Sholem had clipped the car on Buggsy's original order. So, why would he run out the second time around? No, said Reles, Sholem did not leave in deliberate defiance. There was something more involved here, something much bigger.

"The same day Ben gave him the contract," he pleaded with simple eloquence, "Sholem got word from New York that his mama is going to cash in. Sholem is a good boy," the Kid went on stirringly. "His mama is dying; he figures he should be there. You all know how a mama is. It makes it easier to go, if her boy is sitting there by the bed, saying nice things—he loves her and she is getting better and like that.

"So, Sholem does not even think of the contract. He don't think of nothing. He lams out of L. A. and hustles home to be with his mama when she checks out. He drives day and night. All he wants is to hold her hand. He is a good boy.

"And that, gentlemen," the Kid was laying it on thick now, "that is why Sholem left town. Not on account of he is ducking the contract. But on account his mama is kicking off."

The defense rested. There was, as they say, hardly a dry eye in the house. The judges did not even leave the bench to deliberate. The verdict was acquittal—unanimously. It was a marked personal triumph for Kid Twist, not only in the field of "law," but proved more precious to the ham actor, in the demonstration of his histrionic art.

By the time Reles and Allie finished talking about the Big Greenie job, there was a solid case. At the end of July, in 1940, I flew to California with it and turned over to Los Angeles authorities the informers' statements, plus details of motive and plot. It put the California officials in a position to take the matter before the grand jury. Early in August Reles and Allie, protected like a shipment of uranium, were loaded aboard a plane in utmost secrecy in New York and were flown across the continent. The Law, at last, was outgrowing its celluloid collar, and was taking advantage of modern methods that the criminal had adopted long before. As far as we were able to learn, that was the first time admitted killers were planed from one jurisdiction to another to testify. It was the antidote for the Syndicate system, in which one mob supplies another with killers.

All the time they were in California, Reles and Allie were referred to only as "Mr. X" and "Mr. Z." We had no way of protecting them there as we did at home. We had to take precautions that may seem melodramatic now, in retrospect. But, if the Syndicate could have found Messrs. X and Z—they would not have remained alive and well for long.

The Kid and Allie spoke their pieces to the Los Angeles grand jury. Five indictments charging murder were returned. From the coast set, were Buggsy, Frank Carbo and Champ Segal. From the Eastern chapter, were Lepke, in whose behalf Big Greenie was assassinated, and Mendy, who issued the execution order.

On the basis of the picture Reles and Allie had drawn, the hunt was on, too, for Whitey Krakow, who had cased Big Greenie. Whitey had left the coast for a visit to the old homestead on Manhattan's teeming East Side. The hunt was too late. Before August was out—and in spite of the burning heat of our investigation and prosecutions—the mob found him on Delancey Street, and silenced him for keeps.

There was one compensatory effect of the California indictments which we, in the East, felt quickly. Buggsy had been the comptroller of the "Defense and Lamming Fund" with which the Syndicate had been financing its harassed thugs and their families. But now his own enforced disappearance ebbed the flow of cash at once. The pinch became acute in Mobdom.

Eventually, Buggsy was dug out. The digging, actually, was up instead of down, for the Bug had picked a hideout in the attic of his palatial mansion. Carbo was tougher to locate. His disappearance, coincidentally, took place the day after I arrived in Los Angeles with information concerning the murder, and in spite of the fact that my arrival was supposedly unknown except to the innermost authorities in the investigation. Obviously, Carbo had his ear to the right sources. For a time, this Seattle character stayed in Pennsylvania—where so many lamming plug-uglies have found haven through the years. For a time, he was in Cuba. Chief Deputy District Attorney (of Los Angeles) Eugene Williams learned of a film actress who had been seen frequently with him before he vanished. If she knew where Carbo was vacationing, however, she did not let on. Eventually, both he and Buggsy were available. In the meantime, though, remarkable things had been going on in California justice.

Not many days after the grand jury reported, it was suddenly discovered that one of the local witnesses—neither Allie nor Reles, that is—had not told the whole truth. The indictment was thrown out. Notwithstanding the testimony that had been true, a new indictment was not sought until a full year later. Then, it developed that Buggsy, who had been charged with murder and for a connection with Lepke's flight to boot, was not in custody!

The Bug surrendered in October of 1941, and once more the case appeared ready for a trial. Delay followed delay again—until Reles was no longer among the living. Then it was too late to try Buggsy, for Reles was to have connected Lepke's command to the Bug's accomplishment on the Greenie contract. So, the indictment was dismissed—and this murderer was permitted to walk out, to build the most powerful crime empire California has ever known!

Carbo was put on trial eventually. Allie was sent across country once more to tell of his part in Southern California's first Syndicate murder. Walter M. Rheinschild, a lawyer who had lived across the street from Big Greenie's hideout, testified that he saw two men driving slowly by the house just before the slaying. He identified the pair as Carbo and Buggsy. Peggy Schwartz, a motion-picture research worker, related how she was walking along the street that night and heard five shots. "Like this," she said, and she clapped her palms in the macabre cadence of bullets plowing into Greenie. Immediately afterward, she went on, a man with a cigar in his teeth came running down the street.

"Is that man in the courtroom?" she was asked.

"That's the man!" she declared, pointing squarely at Carbo.

So, having heard the defendant twice identified, the jury deliberated fifty-three hours—and could reach no agreement. Carbo beat the rap on a "hung jury"! He was to have been retried a month later, but, in Brooklyn, O'Dwyer refused to let Allie go to Los Angeles again to testify, for some reason which I never did learn. As a result, the case was thrown out completely—and Carbo went his merry way, untouched!

For the record, Frank Carbo is the same gentleman often referred to today as an "undercover manager" of fistic stars—including some world champions. He has been investigated by the New York State Athletic Commission which adopts an attitude of marked resemblance to the ostrich, and holds that it can do nothing inasmuch as Carbo is not a "manager of record" for any fighters. His performers, or those he controls, continue to appear in major arenas, and their antics are truly astonishing, particularly when the betting odds are "right." In recent years, several peculiar "fights" have resulted, among them a notably odorous affair in New York's Madison Square Garden between Jake LaMotta, then middleweight champion, and Billy Fox, a Philadelphian whose ability lay, mostly, in his publicity releases. Carbo was prominently mentioned in that one. All of which indicates this man who got away with murder (if you believe the witnesses) has added to his repertoire without sweetening it any.

What with the Big Greenie business and the resultant Law's heat, it was late in 1941 before Buggsy was finally able to get back to his California crime expansion. By then, he was badly needed, for the Capone Mob had decided it was time to step up the war on the "wire service."

The "service" operates a transmission to bookmakers, over a nation-wide network, of all racing information that may have an effect on betting. This includes results, track conditions, changes in jockeys, scratches, and, as post time approaches for each race, up-to-the-minute rundown of betting odds. Sudden shifts in odds often are the tip-off of something unusual in connection with a particular horse.

Results are transmitted by the service immediately the horses cross the finish line. This transmission is, perforce, a violation, for a result may be sent legally from most tracks only after the race is declared official, which can, in the event of a claim of foul or a photo finish, involve a delay of many minutes. Service operators have devised many crafty schemes to get the order of finish from the track. The most popular is a series of well-disguised hand signals and relays from confederates at the finish line, to some spot outside the grounds, where an ally with high-powered glasses sits alongside a transmission wire, leased from a regular commercial telegraph company.

Speed is the service's reason for being. Sharp gamblers long ago learned that the bookmaker without the service, operating under the normal delay of legal transmission, is a prime target. A sharper sets up a quick relay of the result of a race to an accomplice who is, say, in a store next to such a bookie's shop. The confederate hurries to the bookie and places a bet on a horse which has already won. The bookmaker accepts the wager, because regular facilities have not yet informed him that the race has even started. This is known to the trade as "past-posting"—placing a bet after post time. Hence, no bookie dares run without the service.

Operators of the service have been able, through a monopolistic hold, to organize and control bookmakers who are not only willing, but anxious to pay extortion just to insure continued receipt of the rapid information. That, however, tells not even half the story. There are functional possibilities far more valuable.

Consider the unlimited potentialities in the control of a communications system with a branch office and staff in every town of any size in the country. The service is exactly that! James Ragan, who owned the far-flung Continental Service—and was murdered for it—always claimed the basic setup, in wrong hands, "can be used in the operation of prostitution and narcotics"—and that the Capone Mob knew this.

"The service," the California Crime Study Commission said, after a lengthy probe, "is a framework on which a whole series of criminal rackets can be organized and operated!"

Continental was the largest of the services, fanning out coast to coast. The Capone combination moved in through the West, with a rival network, labeled Trans America, concentrating on Arizona, Nevada and California. Tremendous pressure was applied. Buggsy was on the scene, and, by 1942, Trans America had won out in Arizona and Nevada, with California still holding out.

Before long, Buggsy's take was $25,000 a month in Las Vegas alone. He "acquired" interests in the Golden Nugget and the

Frontier Club, two of the busier joints. Then he came up with the dream of the Flamingo Hotel, a gaudy gambling trap that would have everything, except, perhaps, dice with neon lights. The constructing contractor for this plush palace of chance was Del Webb, who is also co-owner of baseball's largest single empire, the New York Yankees. The Flamingo cost $6,000,000 to put up, it is said. Not even Buggsy could churn up profits that fast. Long before it was finished, he hollered for help. The story is Frank Costello and some of the other financial tycoons bailed him out.

To this day, the flamboyant Virginia Hill remembers how Buggsy was always worrying about the place, as if it were an only child and he a doting father. She herself had a special reason for disliking it. The Flamingo is on the desert—and Virginia is allergic to cactus.

At any rate, from Buggsy's organizing talents, plus the fact that Nevada offers the only legalized gambling in America, Las Vegas suddenly acquired a lure for operatives of the Syndicate. By the end of the forties, delegates from the mobs all over—from Cleveland and New York, Detroit and Jersey, Texas and Chicago, and even Florida—suddenly found "business" in Vegas. They are still at it. In fact, Buggsy's heir in the Flamingo, Moe Sedway, is an old chum and gambling associate of the Bug's, with an ex-convict background.

Back in 1941, however, while Buggsy was concentrating on Nevada, his staff was carrying on in Los Angeles. The crime he had imported exploded in various directions about the premises. The California Crime Commission says that narcotics traffic became "an important activity" of some of Mickey Cohen's boys. Happy Meltzer was reported in charge of this department. The scope of this activity was publicly displayed in March of 1951 when, after an investigation extending halfway around the world, the federal grand jury in New York indicted twenty-one persons as part of a multimillion-dollar international dope-smuggling ring. And one was none other than Mickey's man, Happy Meltzer.

The ring procures raw opium in Turkey and Greece, ships it to Mexico, then smuggles it into the United States in private planes and in trucks with false-bottomed gasoline tanks. In secret laboratories, mostly in New York, it is cut and converted into the addicts' more popular heroin, then distributed across the country.

In June of 1951, Meltzer pleaded guilty in New York and was sentenced to five years in prison. This did not come as any particular surprise. The guilty plea has long been the mob's escape hatch to avoid having its secrets exposed from the witness stand.

An interesting sidelight, not brought out, lay in an incident that began a couple of years earlier, when Meltzer was picked up in California for carrying a pistol. He explained he had the gun only because he was deathly afraid since one Maxie Webber had charged him with cheating on a narcotics deal.

At first, Happy had whistled off the threat, because Webber was in hot water in Mexico over the murder of a narcotics agent. But then, Webber had somehow acquired a gun, shot two officers and escaped. Hence, Happy earnestly pointed out, he was a little nervous and was packing a pistol. His story must have sounded good. At any rate, the gun charge against him went out the window.

Now, in indicting the twenty-one dope smugglers in 1951, the grand jury in New York returned two bills. Only two men were named on both bills as members of the ring. One was Happy. The other was his deadly "enemy," Maxie Webber.

Meltzer landed in California after an interesting career in the East that hooked in precisely with Murder, Inc.'s, manipulations and manipulators in the ten years since our probe. A notable event in this biographical data was a dinner in a Hoboken, N. J., restaurant on the evening of July 16, 1948. Happy and two men were seated around a small table. One was Charlie Yanowsky, a Jersey City mobster and business agent for the Longshoremen's Union, with a background of water-front racketeering, gambling and general crime. In 1936, he was sent to Alcatraz for hijacking and bank robbery. Out again by 1938, he was linked to the machine-gun killing of James (Ding Dong) Bell, New York hoodlum. He had centered his racketeering around the New Jersey docks, after a futile effort to muscle into the West Side water front in Manhattan. Third man, with him and Happy, at that 1948 dinner in Hoboken, was Yanowsky's friend, Johnny DiBiasio, a Notre Dame alumnus from Elizabeth, N. J., a basketball referee and physical education instructor, who, it is feared, was not especially circumspect in his choice of companions.

Less than six hours afterward, Yanowsky's body, presumably chopped up by what was Murder, Inc.'s, favorite tool—an ice pick—was found in a field near a schoolhouse, not far from the restaurant. Twenty-five days later, a hail of bullets wiped out DiBiasio in front of his home. Oddly enough, Happy is the only one of that dinner party on whom the menu had no upsetting reaction.

Narcotics was only one of the varied interests occupying the West Coast branch office staff while Buggsy was busy putting Las Vegas into the paying column for the Syndicate in the early forties. Mickey, for instance, ran probably the only paint shop in history stocked with scratch sheets, racing forms and bookie impedimenta. One day, Max Shaman, a young bootlegging hoodlum, was killed in the place. Since Mickey was the only other person present at the time, there was some logic in the assumption he did it.

"I shot in self-defense, your honor," explained the little loud-mouth. And, with appropriate apology for any inconvenience, he went back to the oils and the enamels and the shellac—and the other things.

Peculiar things like that somehow just happen in Mickey's stores. Later, he operated a haberdashery on the Sunset Strip. One day, his bodyguard, Hooky Rothman, was blown apart among the socks and the fancy neckwear, just as Mickey stepped into another room to wash his hands, or something. The California Crime Study Commission, which is headed by retired Admiral William Blandy, believes it knows "one of the most probable reasons" for this one.

"Rothman was known to be so addicted to narcotics," the Commissioners reveal, "that his ability to withstand the rigor of underworld competition was impaired. . . . It was reported to police," they add, "that not long before, Mickey had Rothman severely beaten for disobeying orders."

Gambling, naturally, was the big thing in California then, just as it was (and is) everywhere else the Syndicate does business. Mickey, incidentally, can be indirectly thanked for a most revealing dissertation on the mob's outlook toward its chief source of income. This was gleaned from a conference held in Mickey's house. A transcript of what transpired rests in the Los Angeles police files. The California Crime Commission states that the accompanying report identifies the principal speaker as Mike Howard, one of Mickey's lieutenants. The remarks, as disclosed in the transcript, included:

"It ain't gambling if you play gin [rummy] and pick up pat hands, or if you roll the right dice. It's business. You must wind up a winner every night. Don't be a gambler—be a businessman. Get the dough, if you got to take it away from them, knock 'em down and put a gag in their mouth. You got to figure what is going on. You go to the ball game, and you come back with some money . . . don't make a damn who wins; you win anyway. For my dough, you can take those honest games and stick them. I go to the races and sit there for five races and drink ice tea, and bet on the last race, because it's fixed and I know it. That's not gambling; that's business. To hell with luck."

So, while Buggsy lined things up in Las Vegas in the early forties, his lieutenants were working, on that business policy, to secure all gambling in Los Angeles. The chief concentration was in rounding up local bookmakers under the banner of the Trans America service. For, while a bookie cannot run without the wire service—neither can a wire service run without bookmakers. For longer than the mob expected, Continental was able to hold off the attack. As a local boy, however, Buggsy's chief organizational aide, Jack Dragna, had many connections and neighborhood advantages that enabled him to convince bookmakers.

The end for Continental everywhere came in August, 1946— two thousand miles from Los Angeles. James Ragan, who had withstood the grab and the guns for six years, was finally liquidated in Chicago. Things cleared up speedily in Nevada and Arizona. But in California, Buggsy, amazingly, balked.

"Nothing doing," he defied the entire cartel. "I am gonna run the wire here—and it is all mine."

As much as any ganglord in the nation, the Bug knew that defiance of the Syndicate carries a mandatory death sentence. But Buggsy had a parental pride in his work in California; he felt it was his alone.

No one ever overawed him, regardless of reputation of ruthlessness. And now he was virtually daring the entire roster of the nation's ranking mob bosses to touch him. Not for nothing was he called Buggsy.

Until June, 1947, national headquarters was patient. Buggsy had always been a valuable man. He was, besides, unpredictable and dangerous; egoist enough to explode the entire security pact which had kept crime's top command immune to assassination for thirteen years. No ordinary chiseler, the Bug would have to be handled with kid gloves.

He had loyal lieutenants to back his play. Dragna stood firmly in his corner. Then, on June 7 or 8, two Chicago visitors reached Los Angeles. The California Crime Commission learned they talked to Dragna. Guessing, you'd say it went something like this:

"Look, Jack . . . the Bug is hotter than two stoves. Don't be a sucker . . . Move over and you won't be in the middle." Abruptly, Dragna was reported to have pulled out of the Trans America setup.

One evening, two weeks later, Buggsy was lolling on the richly upholstered living room couch in the lavish layout he had set up for Virginia Hill. In his bumptious egoism, he was sitting right in front of an uncovered window. That was really asking for it. Someone poked a gun in and blew Buggsy right out of this world.

Virginia wasn't there. For some time, she had been planning a trip to Europe, which was going to be one grand party. She hadn't bothered to tell the Bug, but some days previously, he had seen a letter a friend had written her about it, mentioning a particular companion she would see in her meandering. And he got just as jealous as the next fellow.

"He didn't like this boy I knew in France," Virginia explained afterward.

Buggsy put his foot down and said she couldn't go. As if that weren't enough, they ran up to the Flamingo for a few days about then, and Virginia did some drinking. One thing led to another, and right there in front of everybody, Virginia threw a large punch at another female guest. Buggsy wanted it understood he was running a strictly class trap.

"You are no lady," he flung at his love. Now, the Hill temper was every bit as touchy as Buggsy's. Virginia threw a night-gown —or maybe it was pajamas—into a bag, and off she hustled to Paris. She left, in fact, only four days before they shot Buggsy, which made it very timely, indeed.

In the sixteen years of the national Syndicate, Buggsy is the only member of the board of governors to draw the death sentence. An acceptable theory is the one you hear whispered here and there. (The insiders of Murder, Inc., do not usually go about making public pronouncements.) The theory goes like this:

Buggsy's continued defiance was affecting the mob's pocketbook. Naturally, this upset the directorate. But, because it was Buggsy, these ganglords, who made operational decisions, as a rule, with unhesitant certainty, suddenly were indecisive. They felt the need for the highest voice of authority.

"We got to get to Lucky to make a meet," the desperate directors agreed. Lucky Luciano was not the supreme boss of the cartel—there is none. But with Lepke gone by then, Lucky's was the most respected counsel extant. Lucky had been serving what amounted to a life sentence for prostitution extortion, but not long before, he had been paroled and exiled to Italy. To go to Luciano was out of the question. A gathering of gangland's leading society in the Imperiale in Rome or the Parco in Naples might be considered unusual, to say the least.

Lucky's exile, the year previously, had been as universally recorded as the German surrender. Yet, on the plea of the board of governors of the Syndicate, he somehow managed to elude the spotlight and cross the Atlantic to Cuba without being spotted. It is fantastic that the hood with the droopy eyelid was able to get there. But remember: the gates of Sing Sing opened for this man. Convicted during the Dewey investigation, he was pardoned and exiled on the ground that, from behind bars, he helped the American Army's Sicilian invasion during World War II. Just what this aid involved was not apparent to the GI's who walked into the fire of the beachhead at Gela.

At any rate, the most monstrous collection of gang rulers ever in one batch met on solemn business in Cuba in 1947. They assembled among the rhumba and the rum from all over this country. It was the Supreme Court of Crime—bent on ironing out a touchy problem. Many reasons have been advanced for Lucky's risky sneak trip to Cuba. The fact remains that no action had been taken on Buggsy's defiance up to then. And shortly after that Cuban conclave of the "justices" of gangland's kangaroo court, Buggsy was "hit."

At that, the Bug would probably be preening now, if he could still preen, over this contract. It is the only time it ever took the Supreme Court to call one.

Mickey Cohen thought he was just the man to fill Buggsy's shoes. His efforts appear to have been about as weighty as Mickey Mouse.

There have been some recent news-wire stories, attendant on attempts on his life, which sought to picture the undersized loudmouth as Buggsy's heir. The real power, though, appears to be Dragna—and no one knows it better than Mickey.

It is just that Mickey revels in getting his name in the papers; Dragna hides from a headline. For this, and for the stature of each man, you can take the word of the California Crime Commission, which has had a good long look at the goings on. (Lest there be any misunderstanding, the Crime Commission referred to is not to be confused with the Kefauver Senate Crime Committee.)

"Recently, when Cohen attempted to expand his bookmakers' association into areas Dragna regarded as his own, he met strong opposition, particularly from Sicilian groups over whom Dragna's influence is strong," the California Commission reports.

"Mickey has no appetite for a struggle with his rival . . . His organization has been badly shaken (by recent attacks). The immediate effect has been to strengthen the position of the Dragna group."

At this writing, however, a new power appears to be challenging both Dragna and Mickey. The California Commission identifies this latest entry as James Francis Utley, gambling trap operator, hockshop owner and apparently the big bingo game boss.

"He is not a gang leader in the ordinary sense," the Commission discloses. "He is associated with a group known as 'the Five' which is seeking to exert underworld control through political activity."

Utley's rise spells more trouble for Mickey. Some time ago, the noisy hoodlum and a strong-arm aide barged into Utley's restaurant to settle a difference of opinion. In his typically show-off style, Mickey picked a busy noon hour. They gave Utley a savage pistol-whipping, while some one hundred luncheon customers looked on.

It is just such flamboyancy that stamps Mickey as a plug-ugly who seeks to blow his importance up to the stature of a ranking boss of the Syndicate. It is notable that through the years, none of the big-shot mob moguls ever went around attracting attention in public, anywhere. They have, in fact, shunned all such antics. Lucky and Lepke and Frank Costello and Joey Adonis and the Fischettis and the rest—it is their very aversion to the public exhibitionism Mickey displays which has made them powerful.

More troubles have been piling up for Mickey here lately. His bodyguard, Frank Niccoli—who was also his partner-in-crime in his Cleveland days—was arrested for an assault. Mickey put up his $50,000 home, which he had protected by a ring of radar, as collateral for the bail bond. Niccoli "disappeared," and the courts ruled that Mickey had to make good the bond, even to sacrificing his house. Mickey's argument was that the mob rubbed out Niccoli somewhere.

"There just ain't no justice," the stumpy hood cried.

In the summer of 1951, the income-tax people aimed their guns at Mickey. This form of law enforcement was largely brand-new to the California mob set. Reawakened pressure was an obvious outgrowth of the California Crime Commission's charges in 1950 that "income-tax officials have purposely withheld tax prosecutions against the hoodlums." A possible method of co-operation was seen in enterprises of Patrick Mooney, who was simultaneously a chief field deputy of the Internal Revenue Bureau and organizer of the Mountain City Consolidated Copper Company. The California Commission hinted that purchases of stock in the company may have been the means by which tax evaders kept themselves out of hot water. This company, in fact, seems to have hit pay dirt without mining. It, the Commission points out, "never produced a ton of ore."

Mickey was placed on trial for cheating the government out of $156,123.48 on three years' taxes. He claimed, though, that the bookmaking business had been so bad he even had to "borrow" $260,000 from friends in the past four years just to get by. Some $35,000 of this came from the president of the Hollywood State Bank in 1948, without benefit of note or interest. (Or, rather, the ex-president of the bank now.) Mickey's trial, however, brought out that during those hard times, he was only able to buy four Cadillacs and had to get along with shoes at $50 a pair.

The jury convicted him, and he faced a possible twenty years in prison and $40,000 fine. He stood before Federal Judge Benjamin Harrison for sentencing.

"You're not as bad as you're pictured," the jurist said, as the eyes of newsmen and prosecutors popped. "Perhaps more of us would be gamblers if we'd been as lucky as you."

Judge Harrison's remarkable contention was that the fault lay in the fact Mickey had been "permitted to operate as a betting commissioner with what I think was virtual agreement of law enforcement . . . if they performed their duty, you would have been in some other business." This, mind you, of a hoodlum whose record goes back to 1934. It was all a bit confusing to U. S. Attorney Ernest Totlin.

"This apparently has become a society for the admiration of the good qualities of Mickey Cohen," he addressed the court. "Undoubtedly, Mickey has been good to his mother. But he is here for the bad things he did."

Judge Harrison sentenced Mickey to five years and $10,000 fine. This not only is but one-fourth of the punishment which might have been meted out, but actually leaves the noisy ex-pug eligible for parole in twenty-two months.

Meantime Jack Dragna goes on, virtually unscathed.

Since the Big Greenie contract broke the ice, gangland cadavers have been left in Southern California, the same as anywhere else. Most recent was the ambush of Sam Rummel, a noted attorney for gangland—including Mickey. One early morning in December,

1950, after a mysterious meeting in his Los Angeles office with two sheriff's officers, Rummel returned to his sumptuous Hollywood Hills home, garaged his car and started for the door. A shotgun blast, fired from a low cliff fifteen yards behind the house, caught him in the face.

The suspicious Sunday night meeting which preceded the slaying presumably was to discuss a forthcoming grand jury investigation into the Guarantee Finance Company. Ostensibly, this firm was a loan business. It turned out to be a multimillion-dollar bookmaking operation that seemed immune from the sheriff's office. In fact the sheriff's office was alleged to have told Los Angeles city police to "lay off."

At any rate, it would give Buggsy Siegel's king-size ego an amusing prod to see the boys he left behind squabbling over what he controlled all by himself, without argument or challenge. Until, that is, he got the idea he *was* California Crime, instead of just the guy who imported it for the Syndicate.

There is no doubt that he suffered more from gang justice than from California law, which did not take nearly the advantage it might have, of Murder, Inc.'s, informants on the Big Greenie killing. We continued to discover that the information was a prosecutor's dream. In fact, just a month after I turned the Buggsy Siegel data over to California authorities, I was able to go after the "Buggsy Siegel of Brownsville"—Pittsburgh Phil, himself.

11.　Mr. Arsenic gets his name
—and two more

The cremation of Puggy, who couldn't go straight—Anastasia and
Mangano, Unione big shots today, named in murder ten years ago
—the law on corroboration: a prosecutor's nightmare—Pittsburgh
Phil exits through the little green door—Vito Gurino goes to
church—the judge said a three-letter word—meet Mr. Arsenic.

IT IS lonely in Flatlands—quiet and sparsely settled, there in
southeast Brooklyn, just above Dead Horse Inlet. Through the
years, passing footsteps have worn a path in the grass where a
sidewalk should be along the corner lot at Fillmore and East Fifty-
second Street, two blocks from the shore.

Mrs. Louise Maurer, the night agent at the busy Canal Street
subway station in Manhattan, lived in the house next door to the
lot. She was always glad when she finished the lonesome three-
block midnight walk from the trolley after her night's work. She
would enter through the side door, light the gas under the coffee,
and, while waiting, she would go out into the back yard to feed
the cat.

On Labor Day night in 1939, Mrs. Maurer was in the yard just
after midnight—but tabby never got his meal. At that instant, a
blaze suddenly burst out of the darkness of the lot—"an unmerciful big blaze," she told her friends afterward. Mrs. Maurer
dropped the dish of scraps and rushed to fetch a pail of water.

Charley Cangeme and Mike Searson, two sixteen-year-olds of
the neighborhood, had just returned from a day at the beach and
were ambling along, when the fire flared up. At the same instant,
they saw a maroon sedan make a wide, sweeping turn and disappear around the corner on screaming tires. The boys reached
the blaze seconds before Mrs. Maurer. They were about to kick
at it, when a corner of it opened for just a moment—and there, in

the very center, was the flaming outline of—a human figure! Charley Cangeme will never forget it . . . "all curled up like a bundle and tied with ropes."

Mrs. Maurer came running up, and before the speechless boys could warn her, she had emptied her pail. The water split the sizzling pile, and Mrs. Maurer dropped the bucket as if it, too, had caught fire. She fell back screaming. A human head was framed in flame, and as the water struck, all the hair fell out and the face turned a bright copper.

"Run for the police," she shrieked. "There's a man burning there."

The fire was still going when Patrolman Joe Caunitz arrived, but its grim contents were etched clearly now. Minutes later, a prowl car screeched up. Patrolman John Fitzgerald yanked out the fire extinguisher and played it on the pyre. It took another full extinguisher, however, to do the trick.

What had once been a man was mostly scorched charcoal. The tongue protruded between gripped teeth, and the tip was burned black. Oddly enough, the brown-and-white sport shoes and the white socks were hardly damaged. There was not much to take back to the station house . . . a few scraps of rag, a ring, a wristwatch that had stopped at 12:15, and the shoes and socks.

A bit of paper in the left pocket had been spared, because the body had been lying on that side. This salvaged scrap provided a start toward identification. Before morning, Hyman Feinstein, a respected clerk in the law department of New York City, was summoned from his home in the Borough Park section of western Brooklyn. He was shown the blackened remains, the ring and the watch.

"That's my brother," he confirmed sadly. "That's Irv."

Irv was twenty-nine and was called Puggy, because of the trademark he took with him from a spell as an amateur boxer—a nose in the general shape of a mushroom. He never weighed more than 125 pounds in his life. Until recently, Puggy had been working in a doll factory. But at the time of his death, he was a minor-league gambler in Borough Park. He had tried very hard to go straight. Just how hard was related not long afterward in a letter received by Eddie Zeltner, who has done a column in the *New*

York Daily Mirror for years on that phenomenon known as Brooklyn life. The letter was from his friend, lawyer Sydney V. Levy. It said:

> Dear Ed:
>
> I desire to write a few words concerning Puggy Feinstein.
>
> Puggy and I played punchball together in the neighborhood. He was a small fellow, and wanted to be a big shot. So, we took different paths. But both paths are so closely entwined that we should understand those who take a path we just miss. He, too, had a fine background.
>
> Last year, Puggy enthusiastically told me how he was going straight . . . The cause of his return to his proper environment was that he was in love with a respectable Flatbush girl.
>
> But after he had bought the furniture and planned the wedding, a neighborhood boy went up to the girl's folks and told them of Puggy's past. This broke up the match and broke his heart.
>
> He reverted to type. And now I read that Puggy was a torch-murder victim.
>
> He was a swell punchball player.

After Puggy's charred corpse was identified, Dr. George W. Ruger, an assistant Medical Examiner, performed an autopsy. "The feet were free from burns," he noted. "A bloody froth clouded the larynx. The lungs were dark, bluish red. All signs pointed in one direction.

"I find that death was caused by strangulation," the doctor deduced. He added one more gruesome point. "The victim was burned with a volatile fluid. It smelled strongly like gasoline."

The next day, two young fellows walked into the Sixty-third Precinct station house and said they had heard about their poor friend Puggy, and they had something to report. They were Paul Perles, a caterer, and Lou Glaser, who had dabbled some in men's and ladies' millinery, but was more at home taking bets in a horseroom in a Union City, N. J., hotel and elsewhere.

About 8:30 the night before, they related, some of the boys were in front of the restaurant which was their favorite hanging around spot in Borough Park. Someone suggested, "Let's go for some girls," and Lou and Puggy and Paul started out in Puggy's brand-new blue sedan. They were driving along when Puggy suddenly swung eastward.

"I just remembered," he explained to his companions. "I gotta see a guy in Brownsville. I owe a shylock fifty bucks."

He parked a few yards from the Corner, and walked away. In a few moments, he was back. "Look . . . I gotta go find this guy," he said. "A guy here knows where he is. I'll be right back." And he was gone again.

They waited and they waited. They turned on the radio and listened to a disc jockey. Two girls passed, and they started up a conversation. "You know . . . kidding around," Lou explained. After almost two hours, they set out to seek Puggy. They looked in the poolroom and all the stores. They drove back to Borough Park and looked. They returned to Brownsville and hunted again. Then, this morning, they heard about his being set on fire in Flatlands—so here they were, telling the police everything.

They were not, however, as completely frank as they sought to indicate.

For one thing, they had omitted an incident that had occurred as they passed the Corner on that last swing through Brownsville. Lou had suddenly grasped Paul's arm. "That's Buggsy Goldstein there," he pointed. "Maybe he seen Puggy." Lou recognized the squat comic of the troop from his days in horse rooms.

"You don't know me," he began as he approached, "but I know you from seeing you around. I'm looking for a friend of mine . . . Puggy."

"Puggy?" asked Buggsy, puzzled. "Puggy who?"

"Puggy from Borough Park. He's a little fellow with a punched-in nose."

"No," replied Buggsy, turning away, "I don't know no Puggy."

"Okay . . . if you see him, tell him his friends went back." And Lou and Perles went home.

The reason Lou revealed none of this at the Precinct the next day was obvious. He knew nothing of the killing, but he did know that if he implicated any of these Brownsville guys, even by accident, he stood a very good chance of decorating a Flatlands pyre himself. He kept his mouth shut.

Through all that fall and winter, Puggy was one more unsolved murder. About the only conceivable deduction was that a shylock debt was involved. Then our investigation got under way, and Kid Twist started reciting—and Pittsburgh Phil and Buggsy were indicted for Puggy's murder. The Kid showed just how far wrong the deduction had been. Puggy was no slow-pay shylock "hit." Puggy was contract murder.

Pittsburgh Phil always said, "It's okay to do a murder—if I'm not caught." The suave blood-lusting killer had been arrested twenty-nine times in thirteen years, and was never convicted of so much as smoking on a subway platform. Now, with Reles singing, he knew he was caught. He could not make a deal. So —he decided to go crazy to beat the chair.

He put a vacant stare on his face. He pretended he didn't understand questions. He gave answers that were totally unconnected.

"You're going on trial for murder," his attorney said, and the handsome hoodlum replied, "They don't feed you nothing here."

He would scurry around his cell, and fight and kick. He would seize the bars and they had to pry him loose. He would scream and shriek. His hair grew long, unkempt and tangled. He let his beard grow, to prove he was crazy; the court said that proved only that he could grow a beard. You could hardly recognize the jumpy, disheveled character with the dirty whiskers as the Beau Brummell of the Brooklyn underworld. This gaunt bum used to spend an hour with his barber every morning. He had been the spic-and-span, six-foot-two fashion-plate who considered himself irresistible to women.

He was brought to court for arraignment, and Buggsy stared in astonishment at the baggy clothes, the beard, the snarled mop of hair that had been his resplendent partner.

"Geez," he curled his lip. "You make me sick to look at you."

When he went crazy, however, Pittsburgh Phil overlooked a couple of details. In asking for an interview only a month before, he had written us a perfectly coherent note. When he was brought in to talk, he had been entirely rational. The switch had set in powerfully fast—too fast. Three psychiatrists were summoned, and they asserted flatly that he was neither imbecile nor idiot. They reported, in effect, that he was "shamming and feigning."

Buggsy, meantime, suffered no such unbalancing effect. The irrepressible assassin had, in fact, only one complaint. He was locked up in the Richmond County (Staten Island) jail, in our effort to segregate the prisoners and witnesses as much as possible.

"Can't I go someplace else?" was his plaint. "The food here stinks." Looking at him no one would ever believe it. Prison had agreed as much with Buggsy as with his old pal Reles. He had put twenty pounds on his squat, round figure, and it gave off a general waddling effect now.

Buggsy had the peculiar character and disposition that kept him the most unruffled of the lot. He always got more laughs out of life than the rest of them. If you could call any of these thugs happy-go-lucky, then this moon-faced thirty-five-year-old was it—except, naturally, when he was on a job. He had come to know many police reporters and detectives by name, and greeted them with exuberant hellos. He had no awe at all in the face of authority, as he once demonstrated, in the headquarters line-up, before a hundred assembled detectives.

"The papers say I'm Public Enemy Number 6," he orated breezily. "I should get a better spot. I'm working hard on it."

He resembled Edward G. Robinson as a movie mobster. You couldn't convince anyone in the combination that Robinson hadn't based his film makeup on Buggsy's features. Buggs—which was the way his pals usually referred to him; "Buggs" or Marty—had been arrested thirty-four times, and had been nailed with only five very minor convictions. He had had a hand in some ten to fifteen killings, and Blue Jaw had revealed how he stooped so low as to strong-arm for a ring of contractors to force down the wages of their employees, so they could maintain a monopoly on city school painting contracts.

On September 9, 1940, this stumpy thug and his partner, Pittsburgh Phil, went to trial before Judge John J. Fitzgerald, a dour stickler for legal detail. The judge wore a hearing aid. One court attaché used to say, however, that, "The judge can hear a nickel drop into a bag of feathers—when he wants to." Once more, these hoods had the cream of criminal trial legal talent. For Buggsy, there was Leo Healy, a former New York City magistrate. Counsel for Pittsburgh Phil was Daniel H. Prior of Albany, a former judge, who, not too many years before, had won an acquittal for the notorious Legs Diamond, when no one believed he could. Both are top-flight trial lawyers to this day.

Before the case opened, we applied to the court to have Pittsburgh Phil shaved. He claimed his constitutional right to wear a beard. We did not dispute his legal contention, but this adornment was solely to thwart identification, the same as a man putting a sack over his head. The judge agreed. The Raymond Street jail barber—who serves an exclusive clientele—did the job. He used clippers only. No one was going to let a razor anywhere near Pittsburgh Phil. Not with his talents.

If the Whitey Rudnick case had been fireworks, the trial of Pittsburgh Phil and Buggsy for strangling and cremating flat-nosed Puggy was heavy artillery. The difference was obvious as soon as Reles climbed on the stand and opened up against the two best friends he ever had.

We were convinced that if the mob was going to spring anyone, it would be Pittsburgh Phil. So, when an explosion shook the room on the first day of the trial, more than one mind instinctively thought, "This is it." Nothing followed the blast, however. It took some time to discover that a practical joker had exploded a giant firecracker in the corridor immediately above the courtroom.

As usual, Reles reveled in the spotlight. He had become a father for the second time since his last appearance and he had some notion that it gave him added stature. He had, moreover, absolutely no compunctions about opening the door to the death house for the two who had been his buddies since Brooklyn was a whole goulash of gangs, and they were just punks. Buggsy had been winking and smiling at acquaintances in the press row. When he saw Kid Twist take the oath, he shook his head, as if trying to clear it from a stunning blow.

"When I see Reles on the stand and hear him talk on me," he had said time and again, "I'll be convinced. I'll be ready to quit then."

Well, here was Reles. For the next five hours, the Kid sat there and damned him. Buggsy's eyes burned into his old friend. Occasionally Buggsy's lips moved. He gave no other sign of life.

Early in August of 1939, the Kid began, he and Pittsburgh Phil were standing and talking at a crap game they ran in a fenced-in yard, some eight or ten blocks from the Corner.

"I was at Albert's house for supper," Pittsburgh Phil announced, not without a certain pride. "Albert give me a contract to take some guy."

"Yeah . . . what for?" Reles was always interested in mob doings.

"Albert says it is for Vince. This guy crosses Vince on something."

"Who is the guy?"

"I don't know . . . some small fellow . . . his name is Puggy . . . with a pug nose. You can't miss him. He comes from Borough Park."

Reles was eagerly ready for his big exposure:

Q—Who is Albert?
A—That is our boss. He was the boss.
Q—What is Albert's full name?
A—Albert Anastasia.

(This same Albert Anastasia spent several days waiting to be a witness before the Kefauver Senate Crime Investigating Committee at its public hearing in New York in March of 1951. His name was repeatedly brought into the testimony by half-questions, innuendoes and statements, asked of or drawn from other witnesses. Yet, although he was no further than an anteroom, Albert A. was not called—until after he became ill and was taken to a hospital, and thus was no longer available. More peculiar, he was never publicly asked the question whether he had ordered the

murder of Puggy Feinstein, as was sworn to eleven years before
—in testimony which was available to the Committee.)

"How long do you know Albert Anastasia?" I asked Reles
then.

"About twelve years."

"Had you business dealings with him?"

"During the last seven years."

The span would indicate formal "business dealings" coincided
with formation of the national Syndicate. What he did before that,
going back to 1929, Reles regarded as "favors" for the boss. The
Kid was not yet through with his sensations—not even after thus
identifying, for the first time in open court, "the Boss" of the
combination, commander of the Syndicate's execution squad.
There was still the individual for whom the boss directed a contract
as a favor.

Q—Who is Vince?
A—Vince Mangano.

Vince Mangano, who was important enough, even then, so that
an affront to him was an affront to the mob, is a water-front
character. Like so many in this seemingly immune organization,
he has always managed to slide through trouble. His recorded
career shows he enjoyed dismissal of assault and battery charges
as far back as 1919. He has been arrested in places as separated
as Cleveland, Ohio, and Jersey City, N. J. This geographical flitting about, plus word that has come along the grapevine for several years, lend credence to the often repeated allegations that
Vince Mangano *is,* in fact, among the national executives of
Unione Siciliano. Here, then, is testimony from the inside a decade ago, lifting the lid on identical top-level authority that continues to exist today. As far as I have ever heard, neither Albert
A. nor Vince Mangano has ever been asked a single question by
any law enforcement body concerning this testimony of an insider
naming them in a ruthless murder!

Going on, Reles explained that a week after their first conversation, Pittsburgh Phil brought up the Puggy contract again.
"We're looking for this guy, but we can't seem to locate him,"
the ambitious assassin admitted.

Reles had resented Pittsburgh Phil's pushing ways—the fact that his aspiring associate, and not himself, was having dinner at the boss' house, receiving contracts over the red wine and the scallopini.

"Unless you people are sleeping," he remarked acidly, "he ought to be easy to get."

More weeks passed with no developments. On the evening of Labor Day, Reles and his partners, Pittsburgh Phil and Buggsy, were on the Corner as usual, and as they idled there, a young fellow approached whom none of the trio recognized. The little fellow looked around uncertainly.

"Is Tiny around?" he inquired of the partners, after a bit.

"He's not around," Reles and Pittsburgh Phil chorused, practically in unison. "But if you got something for him, you can leave it over with us."·

This was not undue prying into Tiny's business. The 420-pound Tiny was their shylock representative at the biggest crap games. When it came to grabbing a dollar, it is a question which of the partners was quicker or more tenacious—although Pittsburgh Phil did have the longer reach. So, if someone wanted to leave any money for Tiny, they were not going to have his absence stand in the way.

"I got to see him personal," the stranger said, and he began to walk away.

"Who should I say was here?" Pittsburgh Phil called after him.

"Just tell him Puggy from Borough Park."

The little stranger had gone several paces before the light dawned in Big Harry's murderous mind. Here was what they had been hunting for weeks—here it was, like a special-delivery, parcel-post package. Mohamet had come to the mountain. Pittsburgh Phil nudged Reles.

"That's Puggy—that's the one I'm looking for, for Albert," he whispered. "You can see by the nose that it's Puggy."

Then Reles got it, too.

Q—What happened next?

A—So, Harry calls Puggy back and he says, "I'll take you to Tiny if it's important." Puggy says, "Okay. But I got a couple of friends of mine over in the car. I'll tell them to wait."

The brief interval while Puggy told his friends, Lou Glaser and Paul Perles, that he would be right back gave the plotting partners just the few moments they needed. The contract killers were adaptable to circumstances in murder. While they preferred not to, when necessity arose they could improvise without impairing their efficiency any.

"Me and Harry and Buggsy got into a consultation," Reles explained.

Q—What was said?
A—I says to Harry, "What are you going to do with him . . . burn the Corner up?" Harry says, "Take him to your house," meaning my house. "Why my house?" I says. And Harry says, "You're moving anyway." Then Buggsy says to me, "My wife is going over to meet your wife to go to the movies, so I don't think your wife is home." That settles it.

Harry says to Buggsy, "Ride him around about an hour. Make believe you're looking for Tiny. Then bring him there."

"Okay—I'll ride him," said Buggsy, always agreeable. Then he hesitated. "Hey—I ain't got no car," he remembered.

Q—Did Harry say anything to that?
A—With that, Harry spots Dukey Maffetore over at the newsstand there. He says, "Dukey will take you; don't tell him nothing."

Dukey and Pretty were Pittsburgh Phil's special "batboys." Reles and Buggsy distrusted use of such obvious weaklings on important business like contract work. But "the kids" played on Pittsburgh Phil's vanity, and he let them hang around and hero worship.

Meantime, Reles' mention of "burning up the Corner" had reminded Phil of the danger to the security of the mob's office if it became known later that this was the last place Puggy was seen alive.

"I'm going over to Albert's house and see if it's okay to take him off the Corner," he explained to Reles. "Give me the keys to your car so I can go. I'll meet you over at your house."

To Dukey, it was, as he testified later, all a big surprise. "I'm against the newsstand, reading a movieland book," he related. (He had exhausted the supply of comics.) "Buggsy comes over and he says, 'See that guy there.' He went with his head, pointing."

"Well," Buggsy went on, "try to get him in your car."

"For what?" The interruption to his literary interlude had annoyed Dukey. Buggsy gave him a look of disgust. Big Harry had emphasized that the punk was to be told nothing. So, Buggsy himself invited Puggy into Maffetore's car. With a sigh, Dukey laid aside his literature and got behind the wheel of his spanking new Pontiac sedan.

Q—What did Buggsy say?
A—He says, "Drive him to Tiny's house." Me and Buggsy sit in front, and this Puggy is in back.

Just as Buggsy anticipated, Tiny was not in at this hour—approaching 10 P.M. They continued to drive around, as Pittsburgh Phil had specified. Eventually, they pulled up at Reles' door. "I'll go in and see is Tiny in here," Buggsy offered. He climbed the steps to the porch and disappeared inside.

Reles, meantime, left carless on the Corner, had commandeered one of his bookmaking associates to drive him home. There, he testified, he ran into a minor hitch.

Q—What was that?
A—When I get inside, I see my wife there, and Buggs' wife, Betty, and the old lady . . . that's my wife's mother. I tell my wife, "Go to the movies with Betty."

"It's too late," Mrs. Reles complained. "We can't make the last show."

"Get dressed anyhow," urged the Kid. "Wait for me down on the Corner. Barney is outside. He'll ride you."

"So," Reles added, "her and Betty leave. The old lady goes to bed."

It was three-quarters of an hour before Big Harry returned from his mission. "Albert says it's okay—but do it 'clean,' " he relayed the boss' approval.

Q—What happened then?

A—He asks me have I got a rope and an ice pick. I walk into the kitchen and I start looking. Harry goes to the refrigerator to get himself a glass of milk.

Q—Did you find the rope and ice pick?

A—No. So, I go into the bedroom where the old lady is sleeping. I ask her, "Where's the rope we use up at the lake last summer for the washline." She says, "Down in the cellar in the valise." I go down and I get the rope. When I come up, I ask the old lady, "Where's the ice pick?" She says, "In the pantry." I go look in the pantry and I find it. Big Harry says to the old lady, friendly-like, "Why don't you go back to sleep?"

Pittsburgh Phil carried his glass of milk to the living room. "We got to figure out the best way how to grab the guy," he said.

He slid a deep easy chair to one side of the door, its back to the entrance, so that a person entering could not see anyone slumped in it. "I'll sit here with the rope and the pick," the avid assassin outlined. "You," he directed the Kid, "sit across there, so he'll walk that way and I can come up in back of him. Turn on the radio," he added a final touch. "Then he won't suspect nothing."

It was all neatly lined up when Buggsy entered fifteen minutes later. "I got him outside," he announced. "What do I do?"

"Bring him in," he was commanded. "You walk in first."

As Buggsy and Puggy started up the steps, Dukey joined them. This was in violation of Pittsburgh Phil's orders, but Dukey had followed uninvited. This, thought Buggsy, was neither the place nor the time to debate publicly the advisability of the punk remaining in the car. They entered the living room—Buggsy in front, Puggy a yard or two behind, Dukey the rear guard.

Q—When they walked in, what happened?

A—As soon as Puggy passes the chair, Harry jumps up and

puts his arm around him . . . mugs him . . . like this. (At-the peak of his story, Reles' eyes glinted. Rising from the witness chair, he gave the crowded, breathless courtroom a dramatic demonstration of the killer's art of curling an arm around a victim's throat from behind.) Puggy wiggles around and fights. So, Harry throws him on the couch. Puggy starts hollering, "Don't hit me; don't hit me. I got the money."

It was obvious that the little gambler was about to die without ever knowing why. He had the idea he was being "hit" over the tardy debt he had come to Brownsville to repay. The thought never struck him that this was a contract from Anastasia, the boss, as a favor to the boss' friend, Vince Mangano, merely because Puggy's small one-man gambling operation had encroached on Vince's territory.

Q—Tell us what went on in that living room, now that it started?

A—I put the radio on a little louder, because Puggy is making noise. I go for the rope. I go back over to the couch with it, and Harry is saying, "The bastard bit me in the hand." Harry is like laying over Puggy so he should not move. Buggsy is hitting him to make him quiet . . . pounding him.

I give Harry one end of the rope, and I hold the other end. Puggy is kicking and fighting. He is forcing his head down, so we can't get the rope under his throat. Buggsy holds his head up, so we can put the rope under. Then me and Harry exchange the ends . . . cross them, so we make a knot . . . a twist. Then we cross them once more. Then we rope around his throat again, to make two loops.

Buggsy gets Puggy by the feet, and me and Harry get him by the head. We put him down on the floor. He is kicking. Harry starts finishing tying him up. I am turning him like, and Harry gets his feet tied up with the back of his neck. He ties him up like a little ball. His head is pushed down on his chest. His knees are folded up against his chest. His hands are in between. The rope is around his neck and under his feet. If he moves, the rope will tighten up around his throat more.

The entire courtroom was one long-held breath of shocked horror. This was the first time Pittsburgh Phil's specialized art had been detailed for public enlightenment—this roping a man "like a little ball," so that any movement pulls the line a bit tighter, and eventually he strangles himself.

As Puggy lay there in his death throes, a bloody froth bubbled to his lips. The Kid's neat soul revolted.

"The guy is liable to dirty the rug," he pointed out. And, raising Puggy's head ever so slightly, he slid a newspaper under it. "There —that's better," he nodded.

Q—After the job was finished, was anything said?
A—Big Harry says, "We better burn this bum up so nobody will know him." He says to Buggsy, "Go get some gas."

Through the entire execution, Dukey had stood by, awestruck at the efficiency. The punk had never been treated to a front-row performance before. When Pittsburgh Phil had suddenly appeared from his hunched-down concealment in the chair, on Puggy's entrance, the slow-witted Dukey had jerked back in astonishment.

"I got scared," he testified later. "I don't know where he come from. I jumped back, out of the room, into the hall." This was too good to miss, though. He edged back inside and leaned against the door jamb. Mesmerized, he observed everything, right up to the finale, when Puggy lay there, still and white, and Pittsburgh Phil gave his roped-up corpse a violent kick.

"The son of a bitch give me some bite." He examined the hand into which the game little victim had sunk his teeth as he fought for life. A dreadful thought hit the master murderer. "Maybe I am getting lockjaw from being bit," he cried suddenly.

A tender picture indeed—the mobster who had done three dozen or more murders, on the verge of tears over a bit finger.

"Have you got mercurochrome in the house?" he whined, an urgency in his voice that Reles enjoyed. The Kid conducted him to the bathroom, and they applied the medication.

"All the time he is squawking, 'That bastard bit me,' " Reles remembered.

After some time, Buggsy reappeared and reported he had a can of gasoline in the car.

"Okay," approved Big Harry. "Take the bum down in the dumps—down on Flatlands Avenue and Ralph. Nobody will know the difference if you put a match on him there. The dumps are always burning."

Q—After he said that, what was done?
A—Me and Harry pick up Puggy and we take it out the side door and put it in Dukey's car. Buggsy and Dukey go out in the car. Me and Harry go in the house a minute. By the time we come out, they're gone. We go to the Corner to wait.

The spot Phil had designated for the cremation is at the head of Paedergat Basin, in deserted, untraveled municipal dumps. On the perpetually smoldering refuse heaps, one more blaze is never noticed. Puggy's ashes would settle into mountains of ancient residue, leaving nothing to show that murder had been done. But Buggsy did not know Flatlands as he knew Brownsville. His confused directions to Dukey, at the wheel, eventually landed them alongside a vacant lot, two miles from their target. Buggsy was lost. But one vacant lot was as good as another to Buggsy, Dukey testified later.

Q—What did he do?
A—Buggsy throws the body on the lot . . . rolls it out. He says, "Keep the motor running and stay on the wheel." He pours the can of gas on the fellow. Then he puts a match on it.

To Buggsy, pouring gasoline was just a matter of up-ending a can and letting the liquid fall anywhere. Not a drop touched Puggy's feet. That, then, was why the sport shoes and the white socks remained virtually undamaged in the cremation! As the match caught, the squat slayer jumped back into the car, remembering, of course, to bring the can with him.

"Step on it," he ordered. "Get out of here."

The bewildered Dukey, completely lost, made a sweeping turn.

The car squealed around the corner. It was their tail light which Charley Cangeme and Mike Searson saw blinking out of sight as they ran up to the blaze.

Eventually, the cremators found Brownsville again. Dukey made a turn to get to the Corner—and all but smashed into an approaching car. Buggsy immediately recognized his best friend, Blue Jaw Magoon.

"Hey, Cee," he shouted a greeting. He jumped out, and taking the gas can, he drove off with Magoon.

Dukey arrived at the Corner alone and reported to Pittsburgh Phil. The murder expert said, "Wait a minute, kid." From his pocket, he brought out thirty dollars. He put it in Dukey's hand, adding, "And keep your mouth shut if you know what's good for you." The warning was superfluous. "Wipe the car off," the fashion-plate felon reminded, "in case the bum's fingers touched anything." So, for driving the victim to his execution, transporting the corpse to its cremation and cleaning the car, Dukey received the grand sum of thirty dollars.

By the time Blue Jaw's car reached the Corner, Pittsburgh Phil's patience had run out, Reles recollected.

Q—What was said?

A—Big Harry says, "Where the hell was you?" So, Buggsy says, "What the hell are you hollering about? I pretty near got burned myself." He points to his eyelashes. They are burned.

The bickering ended abruptly as a car pulled up and two strangers emerged. Reles at once surmised they were Puggy's pals.

Q—Did you and the others do anything?

A—I says, "There's no use all of us being seen with them kids. Me and Big Harry walk away. They go up to Buggs. Harry says, "We should dump the two of them so there would be no heat on the Corner."

Q—What does dumping mean?

A—Killing them.

Definitely, then, Glaser and Perles knew what they were doing when they omitted mentioning their conversation with Buggsy on their visit to the police station the following day. On that murder night, though, Pittsburgh Phil did not press the "dumping" suggestion—perhaps because his dinner had been limited to the glass of milk he had taken in Reles' house. Temporarily, his appetite dominated his bloodlust. He and Reles and Buggsy and Blue Jaw all headed for Sheepshead Bay and a shore dinner.

Under cross-examination, the Kid casually admitted that never before the current investigation had he ever told the truth under oath.

"But those other times," he explained away all previous perjury, "I was a witness at my own trials. I had to try and get away with it."

In contrast to the half-dozen murders about which he had been asked at the first trial, this time the Kid was requested simply to list those in which he had a hand. He rattled off a string of ten of them.

> Q—Every time you committed a murder, you knew that you
>   were facing the electric chair, didn't you?
> A—If I was caught, I was.

As was expected, the most concentrated attack was leveled on trying to show Dukey as a participant in the murder, and thus destroy him as corroboration for Reles' hair-raising narrative on choking a man to death. On Reles' testimony, Dukey had no foreknowledge of murder when he drove Puggy to his execution. Nor did he have a hand in the actual slaying. Like Julie Catalano on the Rudnick job, the slow-witted punk's sole lawbreaking seemed to have been in driving a cadaver around the streets without a permit, which the Law holds is not a felonious offense.

Question after question was pounded at Reles—trick ones with hidden traps. He sailed through them serenely. Finally, counsel irritatedly exclaimed that Reles seemed to have a pretty thorough knowledge of what the word "accomplice" meant.

"I should." The Kid gave a shrug. "I was locked up enough times to know."

Reles' appearance, stunning to Buggsy in the courtroom, had a delayed effect on Pittsburgh Phil. The handsome homicide expert's insanity act included an attitude of paying no attention to the testimony. He did not fail, nevertheless, to gather its deadly import.

"Reles comes under my bed every night," he wailed in his cell that night. "But my brother comes and chases him away." And later he yelled, "Reles flies in here through the window; he tries to kill me."

Dukey repeated everything Reles had about the murder, including his own nonparticipating role, and he provided the added details of the cremation to complete the picture. When he finished, corroboration equally as devastating came from Reles' mother-in-law. Mrs. Rose Kirsch was a dignified, motherly woman who never raised her voice from an even, controlled pitch. She related how Reles had awakened her on that murder night, and had hunted up the clothesline and the ice pick, while Pittsburgh Phil sat at the kitchen table drinking milk. After they went back to the living room, she looked in briefly on Reles' son, sleeping in his crib. She was awakened again, entirely unaware of murder a few feet away, when Pittsburgh Phil and Reles walked into the bathroom.

"Harry was saying to my son-in-law that his finger is bitten, and he wanted mercurochrome," she recalled.

Q—Did you do any housework the next morning?
A—Yes . . . I cleaned up the living room. Things were very disturbed.

The clerk called Blue Jaw Magoon to the stand—and Buggsy fell apart. Up to that moment, the little killer had lived up to the reputation some detectives had pinned on him as the "nerviest of the lot."

When his old business partner, Kid Twist, had sworn him a long way toward the chair, he'd seemed to shrivel up. That was because he couldn't believe the previously uncrackable Reles would sing. But Blue Jaw was Buggsy's bosom buddy. Nobody could be any closer than Bugs and "Cee." Why, even when they had to lam over their strong-arming for the school-painting contractors, they lammed together; hid out for three months, and never a harsh word between them. And now, here was Cee's solid frame climbing onto the witness stand. That was the end of the world for Buggsy.

There hadn't been so much as a whisper, even, that Blue Jaw had joined the chorus. We had been very careful about that. The strong-arm specialist had been held in the Bronx for months in connection with the killing of Irving Penn, a prominent executive in the music publishing field. Until July 28, 1939, the mob had not even known that Irving Penn existed. That morning, a car was parked on a Bronx street in which were Dandy Jack Parisi, as deadly a killer as there is, Blue Jaw and Louis Capone. They had a contract from Lepke to hit one Philip Orlofsky, a clothing labor official who had been linked to Lepke in the garment industry once, but now, with investigations closing in, was considered too dangerous to stay alive. Orlofsky lived in the same apartment building as Penn, and they were the same general build and appearance. When the music publisher set out from home for his office that July morning, the waiting murderers thought he was the union man—and Penn became a case of mistaken identity that could not be rectified.

When Blue Jaw walked into court now, it was the first moment anyone outside of law enforcement knew that he was talking at all, about anything. It shattered Buggsy. The round-and-runty mobster broke down. Tears tumbled down his cheeks. He trembled all over. He lifted his arms in supplication.

"Tell the truth, Cee," he cried. "Tell them. My life depends on you, Cee!" He settled back again, like a collapsing tent.

All the blood drained from Blue Jaw's solid face. He looked like a man who has been hit by a .45 bullet. He stopped dead, one foot on the witness' dais. For the moment, I was not sure but that the mob muscleman would balk—would refuse to say a word. The very tough thug rubbed his eyes with the back of a hairy hand. He sat down and squirmed to one side in the chair, so he would not have to face his old friend. He could hear, though, and Buggsy was shaking with bitter sobs.

Then Blue Jaw pulled himself together. Coldly and methodically, he began to testify. About midnight on the previous Labor Day, he remembered, he was "just riding around" when this other car careened around a corner and all but crashed into him, head on. Buggsy exploded from the other car, a can in his hand.

"He jumped—sort of ran over to my car," said Blue Jaw. Obviously, Buggsy was glad to see his chum. He had singed his eyebrows in cremating Puggy, and he'd had to do all the thinking for the expedition. He wanted someone he could lean on.

Q—What did he say?
A—"The can stinks from gas," I says. He shoves it in the car, anyway. He gets in with me. I says, "What's the excitement; what's the rush?" He says, "Me and Dukey just burn a guy." I says, "Who?" "A guy named Puggy," he says. It didn't mean anything to me.

"Me and Pep and Reles," Buggsy went on, "have this Puggy in Reles' house. We strangle him. Then me and Dukey go out and burn him.

Q—What did you do?
A—He says, "Take me to the gas station; I got to pay the guy and give the can back." I says, "If you got to pay the guy, okay; but don't give him the can back. Maybe it got fingerprints," I tell him. Buggs says, "Geez, that's right."

At the gas station, Buggsy settled the bill, convincing the attendant that he had somehow lost the can. Then they drove off.

"Pick out a side street," he suggested, "and we'll throw the can." Blue Jaw stopped in a dark section, south of the Corner.

Q—What did he do?
A—We wipe the can off with a handkerchief. Buggs puts the can in the street and stamps on it and throws it up against a couple ash cans. Then we drive to the Corner.

They arrived only a few minutes before Puggy's mystified companions came up and spoke to Buggsy about his disappearance.

Q—After they left, did Buggsy say anything?
A—He says, "I would like to hit them both." I says, "Okay." It's none of my business.

They all repaired then to Sheepshead Bay for dinner. The snarling and the snapping over the seafood was something to hear, Blue Jaw attested. Evidently, Pittsburgh Phil's social pushing and hobnobbing with the boss still rankled Reles. He needled his partner for a "sloppy job" of strangling. Pittsburgh Phil came right back at him. It went on for several minutes.

Q—After that talk, what happened?
A—Then the lobsters came. We ate.

Mention of the cutthroats, coming from murder and sitting down to lobster covered with a blood-red sauce, brought Judge Fitzgerald to attention.

"That reminds me," he announced. "It's time for lunch. Recess."

Under cross-examination later, Blue Jaw's career in crime received a thorough going over. He admitted driving the cars on two murders, but did not recall if he stole those particular cars.

"I stoled any number of automobiles; I don't remember," he explained.

Q—You were the strong-arm man of the mob, weren't you?
A—I was not any stronger-armed than anybody else there.

Magoon was solid substantiation for Reles, Dukey and practically every other witness to the murder. He tied the ribbon to our case. The final seal to the package came from Benny Arent, a product of Sacred Heart School in Wilkes-Barre, Pa. Benny was the attendant at the gas station Buggsy patronized for the fuel to make Puggy burn more quickly. Benny remembered the incident well.

Q—Tell the jury how he came to the station that night.
A—He said, "Give me some gas in a tin can"; that he is stuck down the street. I filled up a two-gallon can. He turned around and was going out. I said, "Aren't you forgetting something? There's a deposit on it." He said, "I'm only down here a-ways. I'll be right back." And he left.

About an hour and half later, he came back. Somebody was with him. He told me the can is lost—he can't find it. He gave me a dollar bill. I put it in the cash register and gave him sixty-five cents change.

The defense was brief. Buggsy's attorney did not present a single witness—not even the excitable executioner himself to testify about his alibi that he "caught the late show at the movies" that night. Pittsburgh Phil played his hand out to the last card. Summoned as a witness, he kept up the same incongruous masquerade of madness that had marked his actions throughout. Three times the clerk administered the oath; three times Pittsburgh Phil remained mute.

"I don't know what is going on," the court ruled finally. "He listens and refuses to answer. Unless he is sworn, he cannot be a witness. Take him away."

Two psychiatrists who had studied the assassination specialist in his cell and during court sessions were called in his behalf. "There were no definite physical findings that were pathological," testified Dr. William McCarthy, concerning his examination. Dr. L. Vosburgh Lyons had performed a neurological study. "His reflexes were in good order," the psychiatrist reported. "There was nothing abnormal I could detect."

The closing summations convinced me more than ever that counsel were two of the most wily and shrewd criminal attorneys it has ever been my privilege to face. Both set out studiously to involve every one of the State's vital witnesses directly in the murder—even Reles' dignified mother-in-law. It was well calculated to confound and confuse.

"Would you convict a member of your family on this testimony?" one of them challenged the jury—not mentioning, of course, that no member of any juror's family was an associate of Pittsburgh Phil, Buggsy and Kid Twist.

They contended that Dukey was as much an accomplice as Kid Twist, and that Magoon "had a motive for his testimony," as a confessed murderer seeking leniency. Everyone was simply lumped in one package—Reles, Dukey, Magoon and Reles' mother-in-law.

"Every one of them had a part in Puggy's murder," insisted Pittsburgh Phil's counsel, with little regard for the facts. As for Mrs. Kirsch, he reflected, "I know if I woke my mother-in-law and asked her for an ice pick and a clothesline, she would want to know what I wanted them for." None of which, of course, took

Puggy's teethmarks out of Pittsburgh Phil's hand or the gasoline can and the match from Buggsy's pudgy fist.

In summing up for the State, I agreed entirely with counsel about the foul character of our songbird witnesses—but with one additional point:

"Would you expect the prosecution to go off to a seat of learning, like Harvard, and bring professors here to talk of these defendants?

"Don't you think the District Attorney would love to have Reles alongside his two partners? But could any law-enforcement agency ever break a case against these defendants from the outside? Break the case from the inside—get one to talk on the other; that is the way to break these cases. If we put Reles there with them, they would all escape. Is that logic?

"This is not a case of isolated murder. It is not a killing in the heat of passion. It is not a killing for greed or the possession of a woman or an article of value. It was not even a killing of a cornered rat on a holdup. It was planned, plotted, organized murder."

Buggsy's cockiness was back. At the midday recess, as he passed the press row, he stopped momentarily. Among the newsmen, he recognized one from a Brooklyn newspaper who had covered his police "appearances" for years. Before his guard could pull him along, Buggsy leaned over and said something in a low voice, which did not carry beyond the press section. Later, Harry Feeney, the *World-Telegram's* ace, told me what it was.

"That Turkus," said Buggsy, and he shook his head, "that Turkus—they oughta call him Mr. Arsenic. He's poison."

It was the nicest compliment the mob could pay me.

Point by point, the judge took up each facet of the law as he charged the jury.

He read the vital law on corroboration:

A conviction cannot be had upon the testimony of an accomplice, unless he be corroborated by such other evidence as tends to connect the defendant with the commission of the crime.

He read the law on accomplices:

A person concerned in the commission of a crime, whether he directly commits the act constituting the offense or aids and abets its commission, and whether present or absent, and a person who directly or indirectly counsels, commands, induces or procures another to commit a crime is a principal.

Then, one by one, he took up the status of the witnesses:

"Mere presence at the place where a crime is committed does not, of itself, constitute an accomplice. If Maffetore did what he did through fear, it would not constitute him an accomplice.

"There was no testimony that Mrs. Kirsch had any knowledge of the purposes for which these things [the rope and ice pick] were wanted. If you find she was not an accomplice, as a matter of fact, then her testimony directly connects the defendant [Pittsburgh Phil] sufficiently to justify the conclusion that he is guilty.

"Magoon, I charge you as a matter of law, is not an accomplice."

The jurors required just ninety-five minutes to deliberate. Then they filed back, to the traditional rote:

Clerk—Gentlemen of the jury, have you agreed upon a verdict?
Foreman of the Jury—We have.
Clerk—Rise, Mr. Foreman. How say you?

Walter H. Woodward, the stockbroker who had been the first juror selected, rose and read the verdict.

"Guilty of murder in the first degree as charged."

"Hearken to your verdict as the court records it," the clerk intoned. "You and each of you say you find the defendants guilty of murder in the first degree, as charged. And so say you all?"

"Yes, sir," concluded the foreman.

Near the rear of the courtroom, a man and a woman looked at each other and nodded. Then they slipped out. They were Mrs. Shirley Stimell and her brother, Hy, sister and brother of Puggy Feinstein—a little guy who tried to go straight until a girl turned him down.

A moment after the verdict was announced, Buggsy, without

warning, addressed the court. "Can I say something?" he begged. "Don't we deserve one little word?"

"No statement at this time," declared the judge.

That, of course, would not silence Buggsy. "We want to thank the jury for what they come in with," he spoke out unabashed. "With that kind of testimony, you had to come in with what you did." The irrepressible thug was still making friends—even with the jury that had doomed him!

A week later, he finally had his full say—a matter of routine when a convicted man is brought before the bar for sentence.

"I want to first thank the court for the charge he made that is sending us to our death," Buggsy began, not the least shy or nervous. "I only wish that the same applies to you and your family, Judge."

He had noted Judge Fitzgerald's hearing ailment. In his gutter thinking—with the judgment of death over him—the comedian of the combination decided on one more fling.

"Before I die," he proceeded, "there is only one thing I would like to do: I would like to 'pee' up your leg." A gasp swept the courtroom—except from the bench. Buggsy had spoken in a low monotone. The judge had not heard.

"Eh? What's that?" he leaned forward.

"I," Buggsy's voice remained in the same register, "would like to 'pee' up your leg."

Again the court was unable to hear the crude insult, and for the third time Buggsy repeated it. The judge still failed to get it. He turned to the court clerk:

"What's that he said?" he inquired. The clerk was embarrassed. He hesitated a moment, cleared his throat.

"He says he would like to urinate on your honor's trousers," was his parlorized version.

"Just one moment," the court cut Buggsy off. "One moment . . . "

Amiably, Buggsy changed the subject. "You cannot go to your death in a nice way," he went on, "you might as well go in a bad way."

And then, at last, Buggsy subsided. Only Pittsburgh Phil, in all that courtroom, hadn't been shocked at the indecency. He glanced down at his partner in murder, a completely detached glance.

The judge pronounced judgment:

"Having been tried and found guilty of murder in the first degree, the sentence is mandatory upon the court." He leveled his glance sternly on Buggsy. "The sentence of the court is that you be put to death . . . "

"In the electric chair," Buggsy broke in, mocking. The judge, taking no notice, continued:

" . . . in the manner and in the place provided by law, during the week beginning November 4, 1940."

"I will take it tomorrow, and I will be satisfied," Buggsy insisted on the last word.

The following morning, handcuffed together, Buggsy and Pittsburgh Phil made the last public appearance either would ever make. Buggsy put on quite a show, as he prepared to move to "the Big House Up the River."

"I would die happy," he told newspapermen, "if I could knock off Turkus and take care of Judge Fitzgerald."

He had one more request. "Just tell that rat Reles I'll be waiting for him." He turned serious. "Maybe it'll be in hell; I don't know. But I'll be waiting. And I bet I got a pitchfork."

Awaiting the car to take them to Grand Central Station, he suddenly began jumping up and down to thwart photographers. He accompanied the antics with a boisterous barking that gave him the general effect of a fat seal begging for a fish. The first smile in weeks crossed the face of Pittsburgh Phil as his buddy bounced.

"I'll give you all the pictures you want—when I come out in my wooden box," Buggsy promised. A thought struck him. "Too bad I can't hold Reles' hand when I sit in that chair. Reles in one hand and that dirty bastard Magoon in the other."

Noisy and uninhibited, although on the way to his doom, Buggsy continued sounding off throughout the trip—even after he became No. 98,649 in the huge penitentiary. Only at the entrance of the death house proper did his chatterbox cheer fade for a moment.

"I don't want to go in there," he moaned. "I never killed nobody."

Somehow, no one believed him.

While the trial of the Brownsville murder masters was still unfolding in September, 1940, there was a wailing and a blubbering late one night, at the door of the Shrine Church of the Sea on lower Tenth Avenue in Manhattan. A quavering, hysterical hulk burst into the rectory.

"Don't let them kill me," he begged the priest in a fit of trembling and terror. "They're waiting outside. Don't let them get me."

He was a sorry sight—a powerfully built gorilla reduced to a scared, stammering wreck in a white shirt that he must have been wearing a week and baggy gray pants that were total strangers to a tailor's iron. He blurted out the information that he was Vito Gurino—the staff executioner for whom we had hunted for seven months!

This hulk was no longer the bull-necked powerhouse, the efficient vicious Vito. All his nerve was gone. He babbled about hiding out on Long Island and in Jersey City, eluding the Law. Then as the War of Extermination assumed desperate purge proportions against all potential witnesses, Socko sensed he was one of those who knew too much—and was marked for assassination by the very ganglords his gun had served so well. He had tried to disappear—but they tracked him down. That very night three torpedoes had picked up his trail.

"So, I run into the church," he slobbered in panic. "For God's sake, keep them away from me."

No triggermen were to be seen outside. Nevertheless, Gurino was only too glad to remain under the wing of police. In forty-eight hours, we had this mental zombie indicted for the double murder of the plasterers, Siciliano and Lattaro—the slaughter he had performed with the dainty ladylike companion who turned out to be Happy Maione decked out like a streetwalker.

All told, he had been arrested twenty-six times—and had served only three very brief sentences. Yet, he was involved in eight murders, among them several out-of-state jobs. One was that of Al Silverman, friend of Frank Costello and Jersey Boss Longy Zwillman, who was found considerably cut up, hanging from a fence in Somers, Conn., in 1933, in a manner that also bespoke Pittsburgh Phil's talents. Another was the rub-out of Dave (Beano)

Breen, which has remained, through the years, one of Boston's outstanding gang executions. Interstate crime, indeed!

Gurino, originally sentenced to ninety days for vagrancy, had been released on bail pending appeal. Then the stoolpigeons named the 260-pound thug in both rape and murder. But when detectives went calling at his new home, it just happened the apelike plug-ugly was out driving with his red-haired bride. On their return, as they approached the house, Gurino spotted lights burning where he knew no lights would be unless he had unusual company.

"The cops," he grunted to his wife. "Keep going." They drove all the way to Ocean Hill. He dismounted and sent her home.

It was suspected that Mrs. Gurino knew a lot more about Vito and his vicarious undertakings than she told us. We told her of his doings—not excluding how her husband and three friends had kidnaped and raped an innocent seventeen-year-old, then tossed the child's mother $500 to keep her silent, under threat of death. We assumed that would cool off Mrs. Gurino's loyalty. It didn't.

"She really must love the big slob," declared one detective, giving up disgustedly.

When Gurino finally fled to sanctuary in the church whose precepts he had so long ignored, he confirmed Reles' disclosures that originally Albert Anastasia had assigned him as triggerman for Happy in the Ocean Hill branch of the combination. That was how he became a partner in the interstate handbook and other of Happy's enterprises.

Eventually, I took Socko into court. In deathly terror of the mob, he willingly pleaded guilty to second-degree murder.

"You have," said Judge Louis Goldstein, "a very distinguished record in crime. The court will deal with you in a proper and fitting manner."

Socko is now doing sixty years to life for slaying Lattaro and Siciliano. If he makes that, another twenty-to-life still awaits, for killing John Bagdonowitz, the Jersey hood who wanted to go straight. It is reasonable to assume that this trigger-happy gorilla will cause society no further trouble.

When the New Year arrived, we had quite a box score to look back on for 1940:

Four staff assassins in the death house; a fifth behind bars for the rest of his life, and Bug Workman on the way to a life sentence.

The Syndicate's nation-wide tentacles exposed for the first time.

The Brooklyn branch of the cartel closed—for extensive repairs at least, if not bankrupt altogether.

And then on the first day of the New Year, with no warning, the wall we had been building with such pains around this foulest mob in history was torn open at the very spot we had started to build it. The Court of Appeals handed down its decision on the first of the cases—and it reversed the convictions of Happy and the Dasher. And the reason for the reversal was one three-letter word!

Just as anxious and zealous as we were to wipe out these killers, Judge Taylor, in his charge to the jury, had listed fifteen points of testimony which, he said, could "be accepted as corroboration" of Reles. Among them were:

"The manner in which photographs showed the body was placed in the car."

"The misspelling of the word 'freind' in the note" found in Whitey's hip pocket.

"The character of the note as a warning" to stoolpigeons.

"The body being found in a stolen car with false license plates."

"If you find . . . *any* of those points to be duly established," the judge charged, "then it is for you to say whether such are corroboration tending to connect the defendants with the crime."

That little *"any"* was the tiny—and gigantic—accident. There is no doubt that Kid Twist's testimony on those points had been borne out by other evidence. However, those points were merely physical or circumstantial facts; none of them connected Happy and the Dasher with the crime. In advising the jury otherwise, Judge Taylor had committed a reversible error.

"Evidence which merely shows the crime was committed as described by an accomplice is not corroboration as required by law," concluded the majority opinion of the higher court. It was by the barest of margins—a four-to-three split among the justices of the Appeals bench. That was small solace for society, however, for Happy and Dasher, convicted of murder half a year before, stood convicted no longer. It was a heartbreaker.

The months of chasing clues, of investigation and preparation, of apprehending Scaffo, the lily-fingered laborer, in perjury, of uncoving undertaker Blanda to wreck the alibi—everything wiped out. And by one three-letter word!

Of course, we would have another chance at the thugs, but a retrial always favors a defendant. We had exposed our entire case. The defense was forewarned. Besides, the confidence of our witnesses might suffer, affecting their co-operation.

So, ten months after the first trial of Murder, Inc., began, the whole thing started all over again, against the same pair of killers. Once more, Happy and the Dasher faced Judge Taylor and a Blue Ribbon jury. Mostly, it was a duplicate spin on the merry-go-round—except that there was a substitute perjurer! There was a remarkable lack of originality in the substitution, though. The trickery centered on the very same spot—the card party in the Sinclair station, from which Julie and Joe the Baker saw the goings on around the Sunrise Garage, the night skinny Whitey was chopped up.

Both Julie and the Baker had sworn that the third player had been Frank Trucchio, the night attendant at the gas station. At the time of the first trial, Trucchio was in Comstock Prison for a garage holdup. We had not bothered with him. He could add nothing to our case. And the aroma attaching to him certainly would not improve the perfume of a Reles. When Happy and Dasher made their pleas to the Court of Appeals, however, they had attached an amazing affidavit, sworn to by Trucchio in prison. It said, in part:

> At no time during that (murder)morning or night was there any card game in progress on any part of the premises.
>
> Deponent (Trucchio) definitely states that he never in his lifetime played cards with Catalano, and . . . did not engage in any card game with Catalano, Liberto or anybody else during (that) night.
>
> Deponent read newspaper accounts of the trial of these two

defendants, in which it was stated that Catalano maintained he played cards with deponent.

Therefore, deponent wrote a letter to Alfred Rosner (counsel for Abbandando).

When Scaffo had been dropped in our laps, the first trial was already under way. For this one, we had time to look around beforehand. Trucchio was promptly brought down from Comstock. He repeated his assertions to us and to the grand jury. He vowed that the reason he was so positive he hadn't played cards that night was because he never played cards in his whole life until he went to prison, a year after Whitey was assassinated!

"The other guys in Comstock showed me how," he related. "I shot crap and played pool for money, but I never played cards before."

Trucchio was a bedraggled little man in a black overcoat that was, perhaps, four sizes too large. When he was called to testify at the trial, he wanted to be anywhere else in the world. His Adam's apple bobbed up and down and he quaked and squirmed.

"I don't want to swear to nothing," he all but wept, as soon as he took the stand. "I don't want to be implicated."

To any number of questions, he had no answers at all. "I forget," he fretted. "I lost my mind a little bit doing time, I guess."

Under cross-examination, I drew from the rabbity convict the information that his wife, Lilly, visited him in prison about two weeks before he signed the affidavit. She told him she had come up from Brooklyn with Carl Maione, Happy's brother—the same brother who had induced Scaffo to perjure himself!

Still Trucchio stood by his affidavit. The general feeling was that his appearance had been a bad break for the State. We, however, were not finished with him yet. We wanted first, to hear other testimony. The trembling Trucchio was told he could step down for now—but that we'd be seeing him. It was five days before we were ready. Trucchio was brought back, and his Adam's apple was bobbing double time, as he tried to swallow his nervousness.

He said his wife never left him more than a dollar or two on her visits to him in Comstock. By this time, though, I had obtained the prison Pay Record Book, in which all money received by an inmate is recorded. The shaky gas-station attendant was confronted with his page. It showed that up to August, 1940, in a two-year stretch, his wife had left him a grand total of six dollars. But in the next four months, after he wrote the letter to defense counsel, she left him ten dollars on each of two visits and five dollars on two more occasions. Trucchio realized he was trapped. He broke down. He had been bribed to lie in the affidavit, he confessed.

Q—And the affidavit was untrue, wasn't it?
A—Yes, sir.
Q—Wasn't that all part of the deal by which you signed the affidavit?
A—Yes, sir.

It came out then why he was so uncomfortable on the stand. He had been assured that the affidavit was to be used only in the appeal, and not in a courtroom trial. He never expected he would have to take the witness stand and publicly swear to the details. That scared him.

He had written one letter to his wife, saying, "I'm going through with it. If anybody talks to you, keep your mouth shut."

In a few days, he wrote again:

"The candy tasted fine on someone else's dough. I would not get sore if he wants to be Santa Claus again, sending you up here. All you have to do, Lilly, is keep your mouth shut and just yes them to death."

The letter was on prison stationery. Next came the letter he had written stating he wanted to give an affidavit.

Q—That letter was part of the money deal you made, wasn't it?
A—Yes, sir.
Q—Now, didn't you play cards with Liberto at least ten times over in that gas station?
A—Maybe more. Maybe a hundred times.
Q—When you were on the stand before, you were in fear— worried about the safety of your wife and [three] children?
A—Yes, sir.

That was another revelation the killers hadn't been expecting. The thugs simply could not leave well enough alone. They had their affidavit for the appeal; now they wanted to make sure he would not go back on it. They had to try strong-arming for "insurance." Late one evening—after the trial had started, but before Trucchio was called to testify—four men forced their way into the Trucchio home, a block or two from the hub corner of the Ocean Hill hooligans. Two of them stayed on guard at the front door. The others invaded the living room. The children clung fearfully to their mother's skirt. One of the hoods patted a tot on the head.

"You love your kids, don't you?" he said to Mrs. Trucchio. "Well, if your husband don't testify for Maione and Dasher, somebody is gonna get killed."

The terrified mother came to the Law then—and brought her husband's letters with her. A detective guard was placed near her home.

Even that did not stop the combination. It was known that Sam Mazzi was a friend of Trucchio. They had once been involved in the same holdup. On a cold icy night, three hoods swept Mazzi into a car, drove to a lonely area, stripped off his clothes, and threw him into a snowbank. He climbed out, blue with cold. They demanded that he go to Mrs. Trucchio. Since he was a friend of her husband, his visit would arouse no suspicion in the nearby guard. He would prevail upon her to get her husband to "stand up" —or he would get worse than a dip in a snowpile. Mazzi did as directed—and Mrs. Trucchio called the detectives. For the second time, perjury about a card game had failed Happy and the Dasher.

Kid Twist loved every minute of his stay on the stand in the retrial. Counsel concentrated on badgering him into trading wisecracks, and it gave the Kid full stage for his hamming. It also led to the most memorable incident of the trial.

With sharp barbs, the attorney had been accusing Reles of doing the Rudnick job himself. "Didn't you expect to take Rudnick to your home and strangle him?" he inquired.

The Kid thought for a moment. Happy was sitting there sneering at him.

"Not to my house; maybe to Maione's," Reles taunted.

Happy's savage temper went off like a rocket at that. Before a guard could move, he was on his feet, screaming.

"You dirty bastard," he shrieked. "In my house! You was never in my house, you bastard."

Ablaze with fury, he grabbed up the closest article. It happened to be the glass of water on the table before him. He reared back and fired it at the Kid's round smirking face. Judge Taylor disappeared beneath the bench. I ducked as far down as I could. The glass just grazed the head of my trial aide, Louis Josephs, as it whistled past. It was fortunate Louis's hair was getting a little thin on top. The tumbler landed with a resounding crash and splash against the edge of the witness box, mere inches from Reles' chest.

The Kid just sat there, immobile as a wooden Indian. He never even blinked. When the commotion subsided, after several dozen more of Happy's choicest invective had sulphured the atmosphere, Reles kept right on reciting, as if he were taking a curtain call.

It was duly noted and recorded that Happy had fired his "fast ball" with his left hand. Julie had sworn that he knew Happy from school days, and that Happy had always been left-handed. Happy had denied it. By that one pitch, Happy had placed, in his own fist, the meat cleaver which had been driven into Whitey's skull!

In the end, the result was the same as in the first trial. "Guilty as charged," the jury found. This time the verdict stood.

The retrial, however, gave Buggsy and Pittsburgh Phil the distinction of being first of the mob to pay for the years of lawlessness—of strong-arming, of extortions, of rackets, and, most of all, of murder. On June 12, 1941, the blood-lusting Pittsburgh Phil and his squat sidekick in manslaughter went to their doom. The swagger of their sunny gun-toting days on the Corner was gone. In its place was a coolness, a hardness that chilled the fifty newspapermen and prison personnel who were the official witnesses.

Buggsy fretted a bit at the wait through the last long evening, in the pre-execution cell. "What's the use my sitting here?" he howled once. "Why don't you put me in the chair and get it over with?" His father, his brother and his wife came up for a final good-by. He would not see them. "Send them away," he directed.

Pittsburgh Phil finally gave up his insanity game, and got himself a smooth shave for his farewell party. Not long before it was over, Evelyn Mittleman was permitted in under a special court pass, to bid him farewell. They talked for a while. Then the "Kiss of Death" girl left—and Big Harry, specialist at slaughter, was alone.

At 11:03 P.M., Buggsy walked silently through what the fiction writers have long liked to dramatize as "the little green door." It is not green, and it is about the same size as any other door. Buggsy went quickly, and, only moments later, his foppish friend sat in the chair. Pittsburgh Phil stared at the witnesses, a half-sneer on his face, until the black mask was lowered over his head. At 11:06, Dr. Charles Sweet, the prison physician, pronounced him dead. The Syndicate had lost the first two enforcers in its history to the Law.

With appeals and legal moves, Happy and the Dasher were able to stretch out their period of grace to February 19, 1942. Then, the Ocean Hill hoodlums, too, ran out of time.

The Dasher's body was returned to Brooklyn for burial. As his brother, Rocco, emerged from the services in the Church of Our Lady of Loretto, he spied a newspaper photographer assigned to cover the funeral. The cameraman was weighted with his equipment and heavy kit bag. For no reason, Rocco charged him and pummeled and kicked him until he was pulled away.

Even in death, violence trailed the thugs.

12.

Sociology's stillbirth: the king of the rackets

Lepke sells Lucky a bill of goods, and wins the clothing industry —more on the purge of Mafia—Longy Zwillman, and interstate crime the Senators overlooked—industrial extortion made easy— Winchell, J. Edgar Hoover and the deal that wasn't—a mob operation with Sidney Hillman?

GOING all the way back to the beginning, you wonder how Louis Buchalter ever wound up that way.

His parents were decent, honest people who worked night and day for their brood. One son turned to the pulpit, and today is one of the leading clergymen in the Rocky Mountain area. Another became a pharmacist and is highly respected in his Midwestern community. A third is a successful, admired dentist. The only daughter took to teaching and, when last heard from, was head of the English department of her school.

And then there was Louis.

He was born to these respectable, industrious people on Lincoln's Birthday, in 1897. With the heritage of the Great Emancipator's name and the environment of decent family life—what did Lepke become?

"The most dangerous criminal in the United States," said FBI chief J. Edgar Hoover in 1939; and:

"The worst industrial racketeer in America," declared District Attorney Thomas E. Dewey.

Nor did the incongruity stop there. The family called him Lepke, an endearing diminutive of his name. Lepke grew up to be a devoted husband and family man; rarely drank or gambled. Yet, he ordered the murders of seventy or more men in his infamous career, contracting for killings with the efficiency of a management

331

company assigning the installation work on a new building.

Where other criminals tore their plunder from the gambler, the alcoholic and the dope addict, this unimpressive-looking crime king preyed on the ordinary needs of the ordinary citizen. He cut in on the clothes people wore, the bread they ate, the motion-picture theaters they patronized. In fact, on the very work they did. The pay envelopes they earned. In the prosaic fields of labor and industry, it has been officially estimated that he extorted from $5,000,000 to $10,000,000 a year for a decade. And not only in New York, either.

Statistics show that more than sixty per cent of the clothing worn in the United States comes from the New York region. And Lepke virtually "owned" the clothing industry in the Metropolitan area. After paying off his organization, his connections, his protection—his take-home pay on this one racket alone still was a fantastic one million dollars annually.

He didn't even look like a hoodlum, and he acted like one even less. Barely five feet seven, he had an almost apologetic manner, a dimple in his left cheek, and soft collie-dog eyes that hid the piracy and the homicide lurking behind them. His reputation through gangland was that he never lost his temper or became excited. The men who worked for him did not let that fool them. Sholem summed it up for all when he said:

"I don't ask questions; I just obey. It would be more healthier."

This was Lepke: Louis Buchalter, sociological enigma. Heredity, environment, upbringing . . . everything said Lepke should turn out law-abiding. But he became, in many ways, the most powerful crime king of all. Little publicized until 1939, few ranked him with the Lucianos, the Costellos, the Capones, the Adonises or the Zwillmans. Few, that is, except these underworld czars, themselves. They knew his talents. When the national Syndicate of crime was formed in 1934, his was one of the most respected counsels on the board of governors.

When Lepke was thirteen, his father, a small hardware merchant, died. His mother tried to keep things going, but the fight was a losing one, though. In a year or two, she was forced to seek charity with relatives in the West. Louis, she directed, was to stay with his older sister. She would care for him and see that he grew up a good boy. But, the sister related later, she never saw Louis any more after Mother Buchalter left.

In the fall of 1915, in a space of a few weeks, Lepke was picked up twice for burglary. He beat both raps, but, to permit things to cool off, he trekked to Bridgeport, Conn., to the home of an uncle. Only days after his arrival, he was caught stealing a salesman's sample case, and was put in Cheshire Reformatory. In two months, he won a parole. Instead of reporting to the parole officer at specified intervals, the nineteen-year-old delinquent went back to New York, where he knew his way around.

This was not the Lepke, by any means, of the political fix, the easy money for bondsmen, the killers under contract, the vast organized setup for extortion. He began by chiseling on pushcart peddlers and stealing packages. He had nothing "going for him" yet, as they say. In 1917, a loft burglary backfired. Lepke did a year in Sing Sing. He was out only a year when another loft job failed. That time, he served almost two years.

Now, the mob type of underworld group was just then coming into its own. Lepke was quick to appreciate that the loner had none of the protection and opportunity afforded those who run with a pack. Even as early as that, Lepke demonstrated the cold analytical capabilities that drew special notation nearly two decades later. In the underworld, in fact, just as Frank Costello is known as "the Prime Minister" and Lucky Luciano as "the Boss," Lepke was "the judge." In inner circle conversation, it was always "Judge Louis."

From the time he left Sing Sing in 1922 until he ran into his final series of legal headaches in 1939 and 1940, he always moved with a gang. He was arrested eleven times in that stretch, for everything from assault to homicide—and never saw the inside of a jail.

It was at about that time, too, that Lepke picked up with Gurrah, a youthful sneak thief then. They were a sharp contrast, the outwardly undistinguished Lepke with the bucolic brown eyes, shunning the spotlight, and his loud, hulking, heavy-handed, slow-thinking, strong-arm Russian-born partner. Early in their association they won the label of the Gorilla Boys. As felony brought fortune, this was polished up to the Gold Dust Twins. At their peak, the Gold Dust Twins were big business. There was hardly anything anyone could use, eat or wear that their claws did not try to grab.

Contrary to the general belief that Prohibition spawned the underworld gang on the American scene, the criminal mob actually sprang from the wars between labor and management, just before and subsequent to World War I.

Prohibition, of course, became a mighty contributing factor to the development. But in labor wars lay the birth of mobdom. Labor unions were not yet the powerful, rich, well-organized institutions they have become. In industrial disputes, they were on their own. Management, on the other hand, recognized—and could afford—the effective method of combatting the workers. The employers simply hired one or another of the early-day hoodlum gangs to "handle" strikers, pickets or any others they regarded as fomenting unrest—especially in the billion-dollar garment industry.

Lepke and Gurrah were soon working with such an enforcement gang. Another member of the same troop was Waxey Gordon, who was to become one of the very biggest of bootlegging figures—as well as an early income-tax evasion casualty among mob moguls. In fact, Waxey's tax woes had a lot to do with generating the shuddering respect the underworld has held for this prosecution weapon ever since—when, of course, it is in the hands of a vigorous and honest prosecutor. Today, most gang bosses advise their henchmen that the mob is behind them all the way—up to and including murder—but that if they get themselves tangled up in tax troubles, they must untangle themselves alone. (Waxey sank lower and lower on the mob social ladder. In the late summer of 1951, after his name had been missing from the police blotter for several years, he was arrested while sitting in a car—with a package of heroin in his hand. Authorities announced he was the powerful leader of a huge narcotics ring. That didn't quite add up, though. No one ever heard of a ringleader being caught actually holding a batch of the "powder" in his hands. Such risks are usually for the pushers, the peddlers.)

Before the twenties were very old, Lepke and Gurrah stepped up into an exclusive crew headed by Li'l Augie Orgen, whose forte was strikebreaking strategy, and Curly Holtz, who was skilled at labor-union organization. Li'l Augie Orgen is not to be confused with L'il Augie Pisano (or Hooko, as he is more familiarly known in Brooklyn's Gowanus Canal district), who skyrocketed to power with Joey Adonis on the strength of political connections.

As time went along, hard-headed realists began to rise from the union ranks. "If the bosses hire mobsters," they reasoned, "why not the unions, too?" And the gang system of crime went into the upper brackets. By 1921 some unions already had gang gunmen on their payrolls, and were developing huge funds for the conflict. With the market thus widened, Orgen frequently rented his crew out to both sides in the same dispute, or would contract to supply both with guns, bullets and blackjacks.

With profits high, intermob competition, naturally, became fierce. The gang of Kid Dropper, a vicious, ruthless downtown torpedo, was at the throat of Li'l Augie's crew. Until, that is, Lou Cohen, one of Holtz's men, shot Dropper's head off as he sat in a taxicab with Police Captain Cornelius Willemse in front of a Manhattan courthouse. Cohen got off with a prison term. (In 1939, he was to be assassinated by his friend Lepke's triggers.)

The mobs waxed fat; so did the unions. The bitter, historic International Tailoring Company Strike and similar labor explosions brought violent civil war to the garment industry. Paul Berger, a stalwart Lepke strong-arm and collector for a dozen years or more, turned State's evidence in our investigation years later and lifted the lid on the mess.

"We had a hundred sluggers and a brigade that threw acid on merchandise of companies fighting the union," he recalled. "The union had spies working inside who tipped off who should be slugged."

A dress manufacturer was thrown from a tenth-floor window. A picket was killed. Seven men followed a worker into a trolley at 6 A.M. and slashed his face to keep him from work. It was reported the unions spent three million dollars on the struggle. The upheaval was inspired as much by Communist prodding as anything else. A reminder that perhaps some things have not changed overmuch since those days of 1926 was contained in testimony of J. Edgar Hoover before a Senate Committee in March,

1951. The Director of the Federal Bureau of Investigation alleged that Communists are infiltrated into unions generally today to incite violence and foment trouble. The end result back in the twenties, however, was not quite what the left-wingers had in mind. The moblords glimpsed the opportunities, and when the smoke cleared, the gangsters—far more fascist than Communist-minded—were moving in.

Li'l Augie, taking sole credit for the mob's progress, considered himself an astute businessman now. While Curly Holtz continued as boss in labor matters, Augie branched out—to narcotics and other things. Neither Lepke nor Curly liked his new stock in trade. In labor and industry, the economic base of the nation, they could play it safe.

Toward the end of 1927, a labor dispute developed in the painting trade. The boss painters' association offered Augie $50,000 in cash to "prevail" on the union to end the strike. Orgen accepted without consulting his board of strategy. He issued orders to the union to cease the walkout forthwith. One union official, however, was a friend of Jack Holtz, Curly's brother. Jack asked Curly to keep the mob out of this one. Orgen was aghast when, shortly afterward, he displayed $50,000 to his boys and they demanded that he return it.

But $50,000 is a lot of money. Orgen sought out the notorious Legs Diamond and agreed to split the fee in return for help in the painters' strike. Legs was alcohol and dope and even holdups. He was a stranger to the fine points of labor racketeering. Lepke and Curly regarded him as nothing more than a low-class crook. They took umbrage at Orgen.

At 8:30 P.M., on October 15, 1927, Li'l Augie and his new associate were walking along a lower Manhattan street. A black sedan picked its way through the pushcarts. Behind the wheel was Lepke. Next to him, pistol in hand, sat Gurrah. The lumbering Gurrah was about to plunge out and start shooting, in his typical muscle-headed manner.

"Only Augie," warned Lepke sharply, aware, even then, that indiscriminate, unnecessary killing led to trouble.

So, Gurrah hit the sidewalk yelling, "Move over, Diamond!" Legs fell back instinctively against the building. Li'l Augie, transfixed, was killed. Diamond got a bullet through his shoulder—for butting in. If he hadn't drawn his gun, he would not have been touched.

Lepke and Gurrah went into hiding until "lines" could be laid. Then they ambled in and blandly said to the authorities, "We understand you want to see us." All the witnesses, it developed, had suffered a sudden loss of memory. Not even Diamond himself was "able" to identify them. Li'l Augie's friends, though, had announced reprisal intentions. When the partners left court, as a result, they were accompanied by fifty detectives and policemen. To those aware of the recent strike operations of the two thugs, the photographs in the next morning's papers had but one message: the two were strolling out from a murder charge, with a protective cover that would have done justice to the President. Obviously, they could get away with murder—with a police escort! After that, their power was assured.

With Augie gone, the partners took over. Smart and ambitious, Lepke saw that their ambidextrous affiliations with unions as well as employers offered far greener fields than just hiring out as strong-arms. There was nothing to stop them from controlling whole industries. The "gimmick" was captive labor unions and captive trade associations.

"That way," figured Lepke, "you got both management and labor in your pocket." Such was Lepke's recipe for organization.

As gang wars continued to eliminate other mob leaders, he and Gurrah hand-picked the best of the suddenly detached torpedoes and built a powerhouse force of 250 triggers. They fomented or broke strikes for fancy fees. They moved and muscled and manipulated until they had their fingers—up to the armpits—in most of the rackets of metropolitan New York. In industry after industry, controlled organization was the goal; violence the means to achieve it. Lepke had a gift for both.

"Send a sixty-watter to so-and-so," he would command one or another of his enforcement agents. Soon a vial of acid, a tear-gas bomb or a stench bomb, of the general dimensions of a 60-watt electric bulb, was deposited in the business establishment of an owner who could not see paying a fancy figure to halt a strike or to belong to a protective association. How could an investigator, listening in, say, on a tapped telephone, connect violence with the mere mention of a light bulb? That was the point of the jargon. The same cautious operational double talk also produced such mob-ese as "contract" for an order to kill and "hit" for a murder target, so popular with the Brooklyn branch of the cartel.

The strikes of 1925 and 1926 showed Lepke where he wanted to specialize in his chosen profession. No matter how or with whom he and Gurrah worked on other rackets as the years passed, they kept the clothing industry as their first love.

The Amalgamated Clothing Workers is a giant parent body of many labor unions, which turn out perhaps three-fourths of the country's ready-to-wear men's clothing. For many years, its leader was the respected Sidney Hillman, who sat high in the councils of the nation during World War II.

The making of men's suits requires many crafts . . . spongers, cutters, fitters, long and short pants workers, buttonhole makers, etc., and truckmen for transportation. As Lepke found it, each group had its own local in Amalgamated. This giant numbers some 375,000 workers now. Even then, a quarter of a century ago, it was an army of 25,000 to 50,000. (The truckers, incidentally, have since switched affiliation to the teamsters' union.)

It was about 1927 when Lepke first cast a covetous eye in this direction—and envisioned a gold mine in a suit of clothes. Obviously, the parent group was too large to attack frontally. Lepke, however, made a remarkable discovery. The hub, the heart of this sprawling collection was the cutter, who cut out the sections of the garments from patterns, and, next to him, the trucker. They were a key that could lock the industry up tight, if they stopped work. What's more, the cutters' union numbered only 1,800 members, and the truckers' about 80. Thus, on a base of less than 1,900 workers, rested the continued operation of an entire industry of, perhaps, 50,000.

Lepke moved in on the cutters. The manner of the invasion was comparatively simple. Max Rubin, one of Lepke's staunchest organizational arms, revealed the details during our murder investigation. Lepke had early spotted Rubin as an expert on labor manipulations. He used him on many grabs.

Lepke, Rubin related, convinced certain of the cutters' leaders that it would be to their advantage if his entire crew were taken on to replace Terry Burns and Ab Slabow, who were then the local's staff musclemen. Rubin said they had been on Amalgamated's payroll since 1923.

"So, Lepke and Gurrah and Curly Holtz became connected with the union," Rubin recalled. "They took the place of Burns and Slabow."

At about the same time, Philip Orlofsky, who had been a business agent, suddenly was made manager of the cutters' local. Paul Berger, the professional strong-arm, told us that he "became a slugger for the union when Orlofsky became manager."

A year or two later, Amalgamated was rocked by what seemed to be spontaneous internal rivalry between the Hillman group, heading the parent organization, and the Orlofsky faction in the key cutters' union. Orlofsky launched a rebel parent organization, challenging Amalgamated's supremacy. Not until 1931, with battle lines drawn for the showdown, did the curtain go up and expose the "spontaneity." Lepke was quickly revealed then as the real boss—the power—of the comparatively tiny cutters' unit that could tie up the industry. He was moving in now to wrest control of the whole works. In fact, Rubin already had begun operations in his behalf in the truckers' union.

The bitter run of this civil war in the clothing industry has been detailed to some extent earlier. It was here that to counter the menace of Lepke's troops, the forces of Salvatore Marrizano, or Maranzano, leader of the remnants of Mafia, entered into the intramural war. He assured Lucky Luciano that he would "make no trouble" for Lucky's friend, Lepke. There was shooting, however, and Lepke persuaded Lucky that Marrizano actually was waging war on Lucky's newly powerful Unione. The chances are, of course, that Luciano would eventually have done something, anyway, about removing the survivors of the "Mustache Pete" oldsters in the Italian Society. Lepke's persuasiveness, nevertheless, was the convincer. Lucky fell for it, and the purge of Mafia followed. Lucky's trades were numbers and narcotics. He is never mentioned in clothing industry extortions, except in Rubin's testimony during the murder trials.

In the dispute between the Hillman and the Lepke-backed Orlofsky factions, a key man was Bruno Belea, who was Amalgamated's general organizer, and, through all disturbances, Sidney Hillman's efficient expediter. With Marrizano removed by the purge, Lepke applied his fine conniving touch toward control of the entire industry. He suggested to his friend Lucky that Belea had been as responsible as anyone for introducing Marrizano to the dispute. And he proposed that Lucky add Belea to his other victims! He was moving in for the kill now.

One day, at the height of the interfactional battle, Lepke came to see Rubin.

"I just had a meet with Charley Lucky and Belea," he announced. "We made a deal."

"What was it, Louis?" Rubin inquired.

"The deal is for Orlofsky to give up his union. He is out; him and the others with him. We'll see they get a year's pay after the union breaks."

Some of the minute details of how he worked it will forever remain clouded in racket connivance. Certainly, the threat on Belea's life was a key move. If Lucky was on the Amalgamated organizer, Lepke would be in a good "dealing" position. A man marked for death will hardly quibble about details if a way out is offered. The treachery involved in dumping Orlofsky was just as easy for Lepke's persuasive skills. He simply sold the mob on the sound economics that "Hillman is a sucker; Orlofsky is a sucker . . . we'll stay with the sucker who has the most dough."

"Tell you what I want," he continued with Rubin now. "Get a hotel room where we can meet. Then get hold of Orlofsky and get him up there."

Rubin complied. At the conference, he related, Lepke came right to the point.

"I just left Charley Lucky and Belea," the ganglord informed Orlofsky. "You have to break up your organization."

That's all there was to it. In short order, Orlofsky's rebel organization, which Lepke had backed, was wiped out at Lepke's order. It had served its purpose. Orlofsky simply was thrown out. Lepke was now at the throat of the industry.

As part of the reorganization, Rubin was called to Belea's room on Eleventh Street, just off the clothing district. There, he recalled, he found Lepke with Belea. By this time nothing surprised him. Hillman's organizer told him, Rubin related, that Danny Fields, a tough torpedo, and Paul Berger were to be the "intermediaries" between the union and Lepke, because Lepke wanted to remain "out of the picture." It was not to be a permanent post for Fields. He, too, was murdered on Lepke's command in the late thirties, because he knew too much.

Berger supplied additional astonishing details of Lepke's assumption of power, and of just how high that power reached. The strong-arm said that he accompanied Mendy, Lepke's operations aide, to a certain office on one occasion to get a victim to "come across with the money." Evidently, the victim was not entirely convinced of the mobsters' position, and Mendy wanted to impress him with their influence.

"Mendy forced me to tell him about everything that was going on in the union office . . . tell him about the bonus he [Mendy] got from Hillman for $25,000 for Lepke, after the strike," Berger testified. (The strike referred to a work stoppage in the early thirties, during which Lepke's might was confirmed to all, including management.)

It was startling. Here was a sworn charge in open court, by a man on the inside, linking the highly placed Hillman, either directly or through aides, with top-level lords of organized crime while he was head of Amalgamated! And most startling of all, at the very time this was alleged, Hillman was co-director of the Office of Production Management in the United States' World War II effort, considered in many quarters to be as close to the White House as any man in the nation!

When Lepke took over, a number of tailoring contractors were moving to small towns in Pennsylvania and New Jersey, where they could run non-union shops and escape the periodic violence in the industry. New York workers were complaining of this loss of income, particularly at that dismal stage of the business depression.

In the summer of 1932, Lepke summoned his boys and reported that there was to be a "stoppage." Although he had no formal connection with Amalgamated, here he was giving the orders. Rubin testified that, as far as he knew, Hillman called the "stoppage."

"When union officials are not sure of getting people out for a strike," Rubin explained the form, "they call a stoppage. If it falls down, or there's a double cross, nothing is said. If it picks up force and people respond, then you call it a strike."

Lepke took an early hand in its direction. "The stoppage got to be called in the truckers," he pressed, "to keep the work from going out of town." To his own set, he privately added, "Whenever a manufacturer goes out of town, there is no chance for us to make a dime."

"You're the business agent for the truckers," he turned to Rubin. "No truck rolls on the street . . . see!"

Rubin anticipated difficulty with only three companies: the big Garfield Express of Passaic, N. J., owned by Louis Cooper, who was often called the "czar of the New Jersey clothing industry"; Branch Stores, another successful New Jersey outfit; and New York & New Jersey Truckers, which did considerable hauling to plants around Wilkes Barre, Pa.

"They'll be tough," Rubin forecast.

"If you have any trouble, see me," Lepke directed.

Rubin had trouble. He saw Lepke, and the boss adjusted it. And in the adjustment, Lepke personally wound up owning a considerable portion of each of the three firms without paying a penny! Rubin testified to the conference on the stoppage between Lepke and Louis Cooper of Garfield Express:

"The hell with you," declared Cooper, flatly rejecting it. "I been double-crossed by Amalgamated before."

"You got nothing to worry about this time," replied Lepke. "I am Amalgamated now."

Cooper's outlook on the stoppage changed suddenly at that.

"If you'll come with me . . . be my partner . . . I'll stop," the truck executive invited, evidently quick to appreciate the situation. So, Lepke "accepted" a half-interest in Cooper's thriving firm as a gift, all legal, with official partnership papers. Then he snatched for "his" company the better accounts of New York & New Jersey, which he forced out of business. And finally, he emerged from the "adjusting" with a block of stock in Branch Stores.

During the entire run of the stoppage, Berger and the other sluggers reported to Lepke nightly for instructions. "We stopped trucks and slugged drivers . . . things along those lines," the strong-arm said.

With labor now practically in the palm of his hand, Lepke aimed at management. Under threat of strikes or sabotage—threat and actual practice—the Gold Dust Twins extorted anywhere from $5,000 to $50,000 from individual manufacturers or boss truckers, who paid solely so that they might carry on their legitimate business. From 1934 to 1937, Rubin admitted, he "participated in shakedowns from $400 to $700 a week . . . some weeks more." And he was just one of an entire company of collection men. The state charged afterward that reputable garment trucking firms alone yielded Lepke a million dollars a year for ten years!

In several cases, the twins demanded—and took—a piece of a perfectly legal firm or they usurped an entire business. Maufacturers and truck operators were frankly afraid to seek the Law's help against two racketeers who had walked out on a murder charge with a police escort. In some cases special subsidiaries were formed by large companies through which to handle the financial pay-offs.

When Lepke went "on the lam" in the late thirties, he continued to receive hundreds of dollars each week, for the entire time he was in hiding, from his interest in clothing firms into which he had muscled. In fact, as late as 1944, after he had been in prison for five years, he was still collecting sums running into many thousands annually.

(Long before the stench of Lepke was finally lifted from the industry, both management and labor came to their senses and moved to clean up. Today, the clothing industry may be cited as an example of labor and management functioning individually, as well as together.)

Even while Lepke was clinching control of the garment trade, he set his sights on his second target: the hundred-million-dollar rabbit fur industry. A needle trades industrial group, representing a considerable portion of labor, was on the way to forcing the furriers to negotiate with it exclusively—until an organizer was blown apart in Chatham, N. J., by a bomb placed under the hood of his car. Just by coincidence, of course, Lepke popped up with three small fur workers' unions precisely at that time, and gained control of everything.

His organization collected dues, fixed prices, placed a tariff on furs, supposedly to develop a union "expansion fund." Furriers were ordered to join a "protective" at a fee as high as $100,000. One recalcitrant had his place bombed and acid smeared on his face. Another had his head bashed in. There were bombings, beatings of furriers and their families—and the resistance ended.

Early in his manipulations in trade and economics, Lepke discovered what amounted to the atomic secret of labor-industry racketeering: Stop transportation and you stop an industry; control the truckers and you control the work. The methods he employed were most effective—burning merchandise, beatings, overturned trucks or trucks with machinery wrecked by sand dumped in their transmissions.

The discovery was a priceless formula when he turned to the baking industry.

Everyone ate bread. In a city of 7,000,000, reasoned Lepke, that added up to a lot of loaves—and money. Trucking is an integral part of this industry. The flour brought into New York each year is not too far from a billion barrels. Bread, when baked, must be delivered, too.

Applying his specialized persuasions, Lepke won the bakery truckmen's local. Through it, he took charge of both management and labor. Incredible as it sounds, he exacted his "slice" from almost every loaf of bread bought by New York's millions. He even caused the price to be raised for the consumer!

Hundreds of thousands of dollars were extorted from many of the most successful baking firms. Max Rubin, Lepke's official trouble-shooter in every new venture, demanded up to $20,000 from each of various concerns on threat of sabotage and strikes. He told us of a $15,000 extortion paid by the Gottfried Baking Company, one of the largest in New York. This pay-off, he revealed, was made in the office of the Tammany District Leader for lower Harlem—and, he added, the politician got 10 per cent as a "commission." The widely advertised Mrs. Wagner's Pies, said Rubin, was a victim of a $1,500 bite on at least one occasion.

Controlling both sides of the industry, Lepke applied high-handed systems in either direction. Thus, in 1939, the drivers were notified of a wage cut. The truckers defied their "agreeable" union officers and voted to strike instead. Lepke had put William Snyder in as the union president, and Snyder, surprisingly, backed up the truckers.

"If I didn't," he pointed out, "I couldn't control them any more." To Lepke, though, failure was never explainable.

Arbitration was suggested, and one evening, fourteen delegates met around a table in a downtown restaurant. In came an inane-looking individual with receding chin and blinking eyes. He walked up behind Snyder, who had his back to the door. As the other thirteen "arbitrators" ducked—that, they said later, is what they did—the mousy man fired two bullets into the union president and killed him. The abrupt abdication advanced Vice-President Wolfie Goldis to the presidency—at least nominally. The strike never came off.

Two witnesses told detectives they heard the dying Snyder name Wolfie Goldis' brother, Morris, as his assassin. The killer's car turned out to be a rented vehicle. One Sam Tratner insisted that he had hired it for Wolfie's brother. Two waiters at the restaurant identified the brother's photograph. The "custom" of the District Attorney's office was not to take witnesses before the grand jury, to get their statements under oath, until a suspect was apprehended. It was seven weeks before this was accomplished. By then, Tratner asserted it wasn't Morris, but some stranger who had paid him to rent the car; the waiters could not identify the suspect—and the witnesses to Snyder's dying statement were never called. A man who had committed murder in front of thirteen witnesses—got away with it!

By 1932 and 1933, Lepke ruled as absolutely and autocratically as any czar over a feudal state. His power magnified in many directions, not the least of which was the protection he enjoyed. He reached into high places politically—and not necessarily on a cash pay-off basis. A force of 250 sluggers and gunmen, who could strong-arm voters at election time or vote several times each themselves—with proper prearrangement as to addresses on vacant lots or in cemeteries, for instance—was a handy item for any political machine. The commander of such an army was an asset to be fawned upon—and forgiven minor transgressions like murder and extortion.

Local 306, Motion Picture Operators Union, was wealthy and powerful. It controlled all operators' jobs in the city. It had set high minimum wages, and required every theater to maintain two operators, on salary, in each projection booth. To buck an organization as powerful as this constituted a challenge to Lepke—as well as a profit.

He started a rival union, backed by strong political tie-ups. Members were supplied on recommendation of various Tammany leaders. He offered special inducements to theaters. Before long, some movie houses were deserting Local 306. Eventually, after spending over a million dollars in the fight, Local 306 bought out its rival. And almost at once, another new union appeared—run by the same insidious "Judge Louis"! Pitched battles blazed. Then, the first rival reappeared. The struggle continued until 1936, when Local 306 was able, at last, to emerge alone—and then only because the closing-in investigations were keeping Lepke busy hanging on to more remunerative extortions.

Long before then, though, the cow-eyed plunderer had annexed vast territory to his empire. He had a "grab" in the leather workers, the milliners, the handbag makers, the shoe trade. He was providing gorillas for cabarets in a partnership with the Bug & Myer Mob. He ran the taxicab racket, was a partner in the poultry-market racket, seized the restaurant racket from Dutch Schultz, and, with Lucky Luciano, operated the cleaning and dyeing industry piracy.

After the formation of the Syndicate, in which he was a prime mover, he spread ever wider. When slot machines were hard hit in New York, he financed and organized setups in Florida, in Havana and New Orleans. Perhaps it was pure coincidence that his New Orleans' interests corresponded to Frank Costello's transfer of his establishment to the Louisiana metropolis.

He was high up in the mob in Florida and Saratoga gambling. He was active in sending Buggsy Siegel out to open the California territory.

About then, too, he departed further from what he regarded as the sound industrial-labor rackets, and dipped into narcotics. Dipped? He leaped in! Government officials later said it was the most important dope-smuggling operation in the history of federal enforcement. The repeal of Prohibition had a helping hand in this.

In the early thirties, Lucky Luciano had gone into the formation of an Atlantic Seaboard bootleg monopoly group. Connected to it, in one way or another, were such characters as Joey Adonis and the abdicated Chicago ganglord, Johnny Torrio; Longy Zwillman from Jersey, Cy Nathanson of Atlantic City, the Danny Walsh outfit in Providence, R. I., King Solomon of Boston and Nig Rosen in Philadelphia. A valued workman in this outfit was Yasha Katzenburg, who was frequently called "King of the Smugglers." Police of various world capitals conceded Yasha was one of the biggest American buyers ever to appear in the international markets. When repeal broke up the liquor group, he was too good a man to be out of work. So, he was brought into a newly organized dope-importing ring.

Lepke, as the financial backer, was in for one-third of the profit. He was too shrewd to set up this operation as a continuing business; the odds were against that. The ring wanted just "one good shot," as the boys put it. By bribing a customs man, a hole was opened through which, for a short period, any amount of narcotics might be smuggled, if the mob worked fast. They went at it so fast, they were practically supersonic. They smuggled in ten million dollars' worth of morphine and heroin from China in exactly six shipments!

There were simultaneous plans for a similar haul from Europe. Curly Holtz, Lepke's old co-worker in the Li'l Augie mob, went over on the buying trip. Astonishingly, federal men seized the dope he bought. Not long afterward, Curly was missing from his usual haunts. Reles told us what happened. Curly, it seems, bought only a portion of "the stuff" he was supposed to, and pocketed the balance of the cash. To keep the mob from learning of his double cross, he tipped off the Federals about the amount he had purchased. Lepke, however, had ways of finding out things. Curly has not been seen since.

Once success arrived, Lepke and Gurrah lifted themselves off the firing line and into the front office. Then the little hood who had taken to the streets at fourteen found out how the other half lives.

He had a swank apartment in Manhattan's midtown. He wintered in California, in Florida, or took the baths at Hot Springs, Ark. One of the more stylish groups patronizing the Arlington Hotel at the Spa consisted of Lepke, Lucky, Joey A., Meyer Lansky, Jimmy Hines, the New York political boss, and the local "Arkansan," Owney Madden, who had migrated from his New York alcohol addresses not long before.

Lepke summered at the shore, or, later, made annual migrations to Carlsbad, for the German baths. The businessmen of such industries as clothing, furs and baking—and, in turn, the public—footed the bill as the rackets ruler romped, de luxe style. He married Mrs. Betty Wasserman, daughter of a London (England) barber, and legally adopted her son. The killer who sucked at the veins of the honest workingman was so devoted that the stepson later said, "Louis was better to me than my own father could have been."

In November of 1933, a federal grand jury indicted 158 persons for violating anti-trust laws through "interference with interstate commerce." Actually, it was for the fur-industry racketeering, and marked the first time the anti-trust act ever was invoked on the rackets. Two of the 158 were Lepke and Gurrah. In 1935, they were convicted. Each was sentenced to two years in prison and fined $10,000.

"It is just a slap on the wrist," mourned Federal Judge John C. Knox, sentencing them. "But that's the maximum for these violations."

The judge refused to permit bail pending appeal. But two weeks later, Judge Martin T. Manton, senior member of the U. S. Circuit Court of Appeals, mysteriously and remarkably opened the doors —permitting them to post bail and walk out. And then the Circuit

Court—Judge Manton presiding—reversed the conviction of Lepke!

It was, though, no more than you might have expected of Judge Manton. He was the tenth-ranking jurist in the United States— yet, as far back as 1927, he was writing decisions that made racketeers happy. In that year, Big Bill Dwyer appealed his sentence for running one of Prohibition's most gigantic bootleg rings. Judge Manton's opinion vigorously maintained the bootleg baron should get a new trial. One of those indicted with Dwyer, incidentally, was Frank Costello—the same imposing Frank C. of today's national Syndicate. Judge Manton made so many weird decisions, in fact, that eventually, a few years after the Lepke stunner, his days of playing angel to the underworld came to an end after too long. He was ignominiously removed under charges that his decisions were frequently influenced by something more than legal merits.

Lepke was free under $3,000 bail. When he was called, he did not answer. Three months later, he walked in, all tanned up. He explained that he'd been in Carlsbad taking the baths, as he was every year, and, he claimed, the call hadn't quite reached to Germany until it was too late. He asked for his bail back—and he got it, too!

At first, the soft-eyed extortionist was inclined to scoff at the rackets investigation in 1935, and the selection of Dewey as the special prosecutor. Potential witnesses who might be sought were sent out of town. Lepke continued to direct his hoodlums, even though he was under constant surveillance.

"I sneak away from the cops . . . I lose them . . . mostly in the subway," he explained to Paul Berger. Then he would meet one or another of his mob on a subway platform, in the lobby of the Flatiron Building or in Madison Square Park. His office was watched; his phones were tapped. He himself would answer only when a caller asked for "Murphy." A dictaphone was spirited into his office. He foiled that by installing a portable radio and turning it up full strength whenever he had a conversation. And all the time, he was collecting thousands in extortion and was overseeing rackets and beatings—and murder!

Eventually, though, the boss had to follow his fugitive employees.

It was no pell-mell flight. Calmly, in midsummer, 1937, he told Berger, "Things are getting too hot here; I'll have to lam. Be careful." Until that moment, said Berger, Lepke was "on the payroll of the Amalgamated Clothing Workers."

Even from his hideaway, Lepke continued to direct the outfit. Mendy was left in charge of payrolls and finance. When there was a contract, however, consultation was ordered. Reles explained afterward that he and Pittsburgh Phil frequently sat in with Mendy and the astute Albert Anastasia on such occasions.

As the heat grew, more drastic steps became necessary. Lepke decreed his War of Extermination to silence any singing before a wrong note could be trilled. When all the canaries—real or potential—were out of the way, he was convinced he could walk into headquarters—and walk right out. What followed was a blood bath. That was when he was officially labeled "America's most dangerous criminal."

Lepke gave orders to the Brooklyn troop, through the years, for more than thirty contracts that our stoolpigeons knew about. The "hits" by his own staff and assigned gunmen, other than the Brooklyn torpedoes, doubled that figure, and then some. As the chief opponent of indiscriminate killing, he felt every one of these murders was necessary.

As the investigations crowded closer, however, Lepke really went kill-crazy. By 1939, the evil boss was desperately ordering one murder on top of another. Sometimes he had two firing squads on the road at once. At least a dozen contracts were performed by Brooklyn, Inc., in that single year alone.

The Law steamed up to a fever pitch as the terror spread. A nation-wide hunt was begun for a reported underground, harboring wanted criminals. The whisper was that doddering Al Capone, serving time for income-tax evasion and trying to look good with his keepers, had hinted of this. A special federal grand jury in Newark, N. J., subpoenaed Longy Zwillman to ask if he knew anything about where Lepke was holed up.

"I know Lepke a long time," Zwillman admitted, "but I haven't seen him in three-four years. So far as I know, he was a pleasant fellow . . . and clean morally."

His avowal of not having seen Lepke did not jibe with what Reles told us afterward. The Kid said that only a few months before this incident, a meeting was held at the home of Tony Romeo, alias Spring, and that among those present were both Longy and Lepke. Reles drove Lep over from his hideout, and sat in on the session. Among the leading citizens on hand, he recalled, were Albert Anastasia, Willie Moore, the New Jersey gambling man, and Jerry Rullo, better known as Jerry Catena, a Jerseyite who is chummy enough with Frank Costello to have visited with him in New Orleans and Cuba. And then there was Three-finger Brown, from Harlem. Brown claims he is a manufacturer of ladies' coats. However, the Federal Narcotics Bureau has a report in its New York office on the very active "107th Street Mob" of dope hustlers, and, as of midsummer, 1951, the report states, the head man of this crew is Tommy Luchese—who is called Three-finger Brown, because of a couple of missing digits from one of his hands.

The meeting at Tony Romeo's house that night, Reles explained, was called because Three-finger Brown had his eyes on a portion of the garment district. With the almost parental feeling Lepke had for the clothing industry, he, naturally, was opposed. Anastasia and Reles were aligned with him against the others.

"Nobody moved in on me while I was on the outside—and nobody's gonna do it just because I'm on the lam," Lepke laid down the law. "There's no argument. . . . The clothing thing is mine."

Reles said that when Lepke showed them he felt that way about it, that's all there was, and the meeting adjourned.

Zwillman's grand-jury testimony of an apparently somewhat casual friendship with Lepke did not quite fit another of Reles' sworn revelations. This one concerned the only time in his life Kid Twist was in real terror. He had been subpoenaed by the New York federal grand jury investigating Lepke's disappearance. He was about to grasp the knob of the door to enter the juryroom, when two men sidled up. They advised him, he said, to testify that he didn't know where Lepke was; better still, that he didn't even know Lepke. And, he said, they further cautioned that if he so much as whispered anything different, he knew what would happen to him. In real dread—for he knew these men—the Kid went in and perjured himself up to the eyes.

"Who were those two men who threatened you at the door to that grand jury room?" I asked him.

"They were Longy Zwillman and Willie Moore," he swore.

Now, for two New Jersey bosses to have come to New York to protect a director of the national Syndicate, who had his fingers in rackets and murder from California to New York to Florida, smacks mightily of interstate crime—and here a remarkable peculiarity appears. Interstate crime is what the Kefauver Senate Crime Committee was set up to investigate. Yet, when Longy and Willie appeared before the Committee in 1951, neither was asked a single question concerning this incident involving interstate crime. This disclosure, sworn to in open court, might, under proper interrogation, have uncovered some highly interesting information as to the scope of a national organization whose members are so devoted to each other. The Committee's questioning of Moore centered, rather, on how he bets the horses when he goes to the race track. Much of Longy's appearance was taken up with his vending machines, plus an interrogation by Senator Charles Tobey, an avowedly pious New Hampshire politician, as to whether Zwillman is known as "the Al Capone of New Jersey." Longy's answer was "no,"—enlightening, indeed, to a study of interstate crime.

Lepke on the lam was the white-hot center of one of the most intense, concentrated manhunts that crime-fighting has ever undertaken.

For the first time in history, New York police set up a special squad to track down a single fugitive. Twenty detectives were assigned to the picked detail. FBI agents ranged halfway across the world on the hunt. The City raised its reward offer to $25,000. The federal government announced it would match that. One million "wanted" circulars were distributed all over the nation. By contrast, only 20,000 were sent out for the Lindbergh baby kidnaping.

There were rumors that Lepke was in Havana, in South America, off the coast of Mexico on a yacht, in Poland setting up a kidnap enterprise. All were checked. And all the time—for the entire two years he was hunted with a $50,000 price on his head—

Lepke never left Brooklyn! Part of the time, he was within a mile of police headquarters. On dozens of nice afternoons, Kid Twist took him for a drive on the public highways, or he went walking alone on the streets.

In his walks, he happened one day upon a public garage, in front of which was a long wooden bench, where hangers-on gathered on pleasant afternoons. Lepke felt secure behind his brand-new mustache and dark glasses. Anyway, who would expect a man, sought the world over, to be sitting on the bank of the Gowanus Canal? So, on several sunny days afterward, Lepke dropped by and lolled among the neighbors. Occasionally, he even invested two dollars on a horse with the gentleman who obliged the bench-warmers.

He was sitting there one afternoon when a sedan slammed to a stop in front of the bench. Before anyone could move, four menacing men got out and flashed shields. Lepke cast a glance this way and that, but there was no way out.

"Line up," commanded the plainclothesmen. Their tone indicated this was a mission of utmost importance. They pushed the idlers into an uneven rank—including Lepke. There were seventeen of them, and the detectives set about methodically searching every one, not omitting the sweatbands of their hats and the inside of their shoes. Lepke got the same. They never batted an eye at him; he never batted an eye at them. Finally, the officers said "ah." They yanked one fellow out of line, and bustled him triumphantly into the car, as if he must have tried to blow up Brooklyn Bridge, at least.

"The rest of you bums—beat it, or you'll all go in," the detectives threatened. The rest of the bums beat it—including Lepke, the man who was being sought all over the world with a $50,000 price on his head. The one they kept, alas, had a few horse-bet slips in his pocket.

His friends, Albert Anastasia and Kid Twist Reles, were careful administrators of Lepke's hideout spots. Right from the start, they demonstrated they were scientists at this sort of thing. For, while the hunt went on across the earth, they hid Lepke in a dance hall! This was the Oriental Palace, a trap in Coney Island once owned by Louis Capone. Later, Reles listed the visitors who came while "the Judge" stayed there. There were Mendy and Albert A. and Moey Dimples, Lepke's agent in the Florida-New York gambling mob, and a character who went under the weighty tag of "Fat Sidney." He had two claims to fame: he weighed 350 pounds and he was married to a movie star.

The Oriental, however, was too prominent. People were always coming in and out. After a while, Mendy had the alternative. A modern six-story apartment had only recently been completed in the Flatbush section. Mendy had personally laid out the plan for one of the suites, as part of a contemplated narcotics enterprise to be operated from a fashionable apartment in a respectable section. The flat was designed so no one could notice a thing. Mendy's interior decorating featured secret panels and storage nooks and special bolts and one thing and another. Pending the cooling off of the current investigations, however, the operation was held in abeyance. Mrs. Dorothy Walker had been ensconced in the place. She was the widow of Fatty Walker, who had wound up second best in a gun fight in New York's notorious Hotsy Totsy Club. Lepke was spirited out of the Oriental and moved in with the mobster's widow.

Lest there be scandalous implication attributed to this idyllic arrangement, be assured that the relationship of the widow and the moblord remained pure and platonic. On this subject, the Law stipulates there must be three coincident factors: opportunity, capacity and, most important, inclination. Passing lightly over the first two, it can be said that the inclination of even a myopic gentleman would be reluctant to discern, in the Widow Walker, charms to arouse the baser emotions. And Lepke's eyesight was perfect; his tastes discriminating.

Lepke's sojourn there, however, did include virtually every other diversion. His contemporaries paid their respects, and they came laden with gifts. The expected penitentiary existence of the hunted fugitive was entirely absent. Instead, it was one continuing round of lavish living, sparkling with vintage wines, finest cigars and viands to titillate the appetite of a maharajah. And Lepke presided over the entire gay company. From this bizarre spot in the next several months, a number of contracts were dictated. It seemed, from every angle, the perfect hideout.

But a man with a $50,000 price on his head is very hot. Such a cash prize might give anyone ideas. Eventually, too, Mendy was forced to flee from narcotics charges. Available triggers and aides were dwindling. The hideout arrangers, Anastasia and Reles, decided a new place was necessary—one that could be kept top secret from all but the closest of Lepke's co-workers.

Then Anastasia remembered. About two years before, one Eugene Salvese had come around and said he hailed from Albert's home town in Calabria, in Italy, and Albert had given him some odd-job work. One day, Salvese needed a certain paintbrush which was back at his living quarters. Anastasia offered to pick it up for him, and there had met Maria Nostro, who was also Calabrese. She had the basement-first-floor quarters in this shabby house, and Salvese lived with her. Albert and Maria got to talking about the old country. Pretty soon Albert asked if a friend of his might use Maria's first floor once in a while. Maria readily acceded. So, occasionally, Lepke had gone there to meet his wife, who was brought to the rendezvous by Louis Capone.

That first-floor of Maria's quarters was just the thing, Albert recalled now, in midsummer of 1939. The entrance was through the basement, an excellent security arrangement. Maria willingly let them take the first floor for three dollars a week. (The mob would have paid probably a hundred times that, if necessary.) In the dead of that same night, Lepke slipped from the Widow Walker's modern rooms into Reles' car, and was transferred to Maria's threadbare "duplex." Lepke had grown his thick black moustache —the Groucho Marx variety—and he had put on fifteen or twenty pounds. To Maria, he was never anyone but "Charley."

Lepke was now, after two years, more secure than ever. Law enforcement was, if anything, farther from finding him on August 1, 1939, than on August 1, 1937. All he had to do was stay put, and he probably could hide out until the ink on the warrants faded into illegibility.

And then Lepke surrendered!

A most interesting story has been handed down as to just why the fugitive moblord, apparently safe for as long as he wanted, voluntarily gave up. The story goes like this:

The FBI felt it had to beat state authorities to Lepke in order to "save face," after two years of futility. So, J. Edgar Hoover sent a flat fiat to Joey Adonis and Frank Costello, the ranking "brass" of Unione Siciliano: Unless Lepke came out of his hole and gave up *to the* FBI, every Italian mobster in the country would be picked up. Mr. A. and Frank C. could not afford to let this happen. They sent an ultimatum to their old pal, "Sorry, chum—surrender to the Feds or we'll have to deliver you personally."

Lepke recognized an edict when he heard one. He set out to do the best he could for himself. The federal government had a narcotics rap against him, good for a maximum of ten to fifteen years in prison. Dewey already had announced that he had sufficient evidence for the State to put him away for five hundred years.

Lepke made a deal with the Federals. He would give up and take his narcotics sentence—provided he remained in federal custody. And on that basis, he surrendered—with the avowed assurance of the federal government that it would protect him from the state.

That is the accepted story—but the evidence says that is not what happened. Beyond the evidence, moreover, is the contention in this accepted version that J. Edgar Hoover was making deals for guarantees he knew were impossible to keep. And in the name of the federal government, at that. Besides, as a director of the Syndicate, Lepke would hardly have acceded to any edict that did not come from the full board of governors. In research for this book, the authors have come upon just about conclusive information that something altogether different lay behind Lepke's capitulation.

A manhunt, remember, was going full blast. The heat was on the underworld as it has been applied but rarely, blistering the ranking racketeers from coast to coast. Much of the country-wide extortion enterprises were singed. What's more, the "industry" would remain locked up until this Lepke thing was settled—not only in New York, but any place the mob did business, which was all over the United States. The pocketbook of the cartel was affected.

Naturally, a tremendous amount of advice began to pour in on Lepke from his close associates among the Syndicate's top magnates. As the rackets were hurt more and more, sentiment veered in one direction—Lepke should surrender before operations were ruined across the country. After all, they pointed out, the temptation of that fat reward, plus the pressure the Law was increasing day by day, created a greater and greater risk that he not only would be uncovered, but would stop a bullet in the process. The smart thing to do, then, was to turn himself in.

Lepke was suspicious of their motives. "Those bastards are more interested in their own take than they are in my hide," he growled to Reles on several occasions.

Nevertheless, even as imperturbable a man as Lepke could not fail to feel the tense urgency. And Lepke was as imperturbable as a square yard of hard concrete. Months of being cooped up alone produced in him none of the mental depressant—the "stir-crazy" effect—that it did in most lammisters.

"He's the toughest kind," insisted Major Garland Williams of the Federal Narcotics staff, after a study of Lepke's known characteristics for a possible clue to where he might be. "Give him some books and magazines, and he's content to hole up in one room for six months."

But now Lepke's own friends and business associates were putting the heat on. The unshakable moblord became fretful. Then the thought of a new danger crept in. "Judge Louis" knew the credo of the cartel—that no one man matters against the well-being of the organization as a whole. The suspicion seeped into his mind that the ever-increasing counsel to give up was really only a lightly disguised decree; that if he did not move voluntarily, the board of governors was going to call a kangaroo court on him, much as they all respected and admired him. Lepke had handed out dozens of death assignments; had sat in on scores of murder meetings. As a result, the more he pondered these suspicions, the more uncertain he became. He was in so strange a state, for the unexcitable Lepke, that for three nights the only sleep he would risk was on a couch in a room with one small window—and then only while Reles stood guard, pistol in hand.

Now, aside from the Kid, about the only others Lepke felt he could still rely on—about the only others, in fact, who came to see him any more—were Albert A. and Moey Dimples, Lepke's long-time lieutenant. As the Florida-New York-Saratoga gambling delegate, Moey was feeling the pinch more than most. He only had the gambling going for him—and even Saratoga was hot from the Law that August.

Dimples, naturally, thought often of the situation. To him, it seemed that all the Federals were after was to get their hands on Lep, to give him a "reasonable" jail term. The recognizable danger lay in the possibility that the boss would be turned over to the state, where Dewey had five hundred years waiting for him.

One day, Dimples walked into the hideout fairly bubbling, and he dropped a blockbuster into the indecision and uncertainty.

"A deal is in with the Feds," he announced. "The guys told me to tip you off."

Lepke listened avidly as his henchman explained. He had been delegated to bring the word, said Dimples, because not many visitors were permitted at the hideout any more. The deal had been approved by J. Edgar Hoover and the Department of Justice, Dimples went on. Lepke was to surrender to the FBI and answer only for the narcotics violations. It was guaranteed that he would not be turned over to the state for prosecution. Later, Reles corroborated it for us.

"The understanding was that he would get ten to twelve years, and would not be turned over to Dewey," the Kid recalled when he sang.

To Lepke, hammered at from all sides, the word that the government would guarantee him against the risk of a life sentence was a rope to a drowning man. One lone voice, however, dissented. As a matter of fact, through all the controversy, all the urgency, one man consistently counseled against surrender. That was Albert Anastasia. To each new proposal to give up, the curly-haired boss of the troop had one invariable word in rebuttal: "Why?" Now he was still opposed.

For two years, Albert had kept Lepke hidden, and Lepke was

as secure now as the day he'd gone into hiding. More, in fact. Few, even, of the mob, were aware of the hideaway in Maria's mean quarters. Reward or no reward, Albert insisted he could harbor Lepke for years more in spots he knew. Moreover, the underworld is fully cognizant that nothing hurts a prosecution's case more than delay. Witnesses—particularly stoolpigeons—are not easy to keep overlong in a co-operative frame of mind. Public clamor cools off in time. Determined, aggressive prosecutors move on to other offices.

"So, what's the hurry?" Anastasia countered Dimples' report of the deal. "You can always walk in. But while they ain't got you, they can't hurt you."

Here again is convincing proof against any ultimatum from Adonis and Costello, dictated on command of the FBI or otherwise. Anastasia was, and is, an Adonis man. Had an edict been issued by Joey A., Albert never would have been against it—and vociferously against, at that. In fact, Albert stayed with Lepke to the very end, assumedly ready to protect him from gunmen or law enforcement.

Lepke respected Albert. Through these months, the commander of the killers had proved that Lepke could trust him with his life; even with his clothing industry racket. On the other hand, this deal Dimples detailed removed all risk of falling into the hands of the state. That changed the picture; the odds were now going for him. Besides, highly as he regarded Anastasia's opinion, Albert was but one against every voice in the Syndicate. In the end, Dimples' report swung the balance.

On the night of August 24, 1939, a car pulled away from No. 101 Third Street, Brooklyn. A swarthy, hard-faced man was at the wheel. In the rear, sat a meek-looking little fellow in dark glasses, with a red-headed woman and a baby. Just looking at them, you'd guess that a generous car owner was agreeably taking a neighbor's small family for a ride on a hot evening.

The automobile drove across the bridge and proceeded among the dark and towering offices and warehouses of Manhattan's east Twenties. It continued until the driver sighted a parked car, for which he evidently was searching. He stopped. The quiet little man got out and joined a man in the parked car. From some yards away, where he had been waiting, a sturdy heavy-set man walked over and entered the car. That is how Walter Winchell, who was the man in the automobile, and J. Edgar Hoover, waiting close by, "captured" the most wanted man alive, shortly after 10 P.M. on a hot August night.

The hard-faced driver from Brooklyn was Albert Anastasia. The mild individual in the back seat had been Lepke. Louis Capone's sister-in-law, pressed into service, was the redhead, and the baby she carried had been borrowed from a friend. The masquerade was deemed necessary to prevent recognition while the party was navigating the streets of the metropolis. Albert A. had lined up all the details. Through himself and agents to whom he delegated some of the arrangements, he made the necessary contacts, including the one with Walter Winchell, the syndicated columnist of the *New York Daily Mirror*. And he did it while wishing, all the time, that Lepke would change his mind about giving up.

Hoover spoke to Lepke when he entered the car—and almost with the first sentence, a ton of rock landed on the extortion executive. Anyway, he told a friend long afterward, that is what it felt like. For, from the FBI chief's very first words, Lepke realized there was no deal; there had been no deal; not Hoover nor Winchell nor the Department of Justice nor anyone else had been a party to any deal! And then it hit him: Dimples had double-crossed him. Dimples, who used to say, "I'm with you a million per cent, Louis" . . . Dimples had sold him a bill of goods!

"I wanted to get out of that car again as soon as I heard," Lepke revealed to the same friend. "Only I couldn't."

There was one brief final touch to the story of the hired hand who double-crossed the boss so he could never get out of it. In 1943, one evening, a shooting match shattered the decorum of a midtown restaurant in Manhattan. When the smoke cleared, a man lay there dead. He was identified as one Wolinsky, alias Moey Dimples.

Lepke was in prison by then, with little chance of ever getting out. A friend brought him the news—a friend who shall remain nameless here, and who incidentally was not aware of the "deal" that wasn't.

"You know," reported the friend on his return, "when Louis heard that Dimples got it . . . I never saw him look happier. I always thought Dimples was his pal."

Considerable feeling developed between state and federal law enforcement after the surrender. Justice Department officials refused to permit Dewey even to question Lepke. New York police were no end riled. They revealed that during the manhunt, the FBI had made an agreement: anything the police learned about Lepke anywhere in the country outside of New York, they would turn over to the G-men; anything the FBI found out about him, involving New York City, they promised to give to the police. Police authorities charged now that the Federals had broken their word—had not let them know that Lepke had established contact, or was even in New York.

This conjured up a shuddering picture. Suppose a New York policeman, unaware of what was in the wind, had seen that tiny group and that suspicious business of switching cars. And suppose the officer had recognized Lepke and started shooting. Whose responsibility would it have been had the Director of the Federal Bureau of Investigation and one of the most widely known columnists been killed in the gunplay?

The federal government convicted Lepke for his narcotics smuggling at the end of 1939 and sentenced him to fourteen years. Only then was Dewey permitted a crack at him—and promptly convicted him for his nefarious bakery operations. For this, "Judge Louis" drew thirty years to life.

The government took him back then, put him in Leavenworth and said the rackets czar would have to serve out his narcotics "rap" before anything else. Thus, he would do fourteen years for the Federals and then start thirty-to-life for the State. The irony of it was that, for years to come—as many as he lived, probably— the public would still be paying the freight for Lepke. He would be fed and housed and live off the same taxpayers on whom he'd been living by extortion all his adult life.

His hands ran with blood—all law enforcement in America was

positive of that. But all were just as positive that the Law had done as much as it could to him. Lep had covered up too well to be caught in murder.

Then, two months later, we stepped up and announced we had the murder to pin on him; and we had an indictment to show we meant business. We had opened up on the national Syndicate some time before, but what with the Brownsville and Ocean Hill torpedoes to be nabbed in our own front yard, Lepke's name had not previously been mentioned.

That was in the spring of 1940. For the next year, I was deep in convicting Pittsburgh Phil and Buggsy, in the trial and retrial of Happy and the Dasher, in running out to California to supply data in the murder case against Buggsy Siegel and Frankie Carbo, and in furnishing information to New Jersey to put Bug Workman away for the Dutch Schultz slaughter. In all that time, I was almost unaware of the Lepke case. Various others in the District Attorney's office handled it, and apparently, in that year, it was not put together for trial. What happened, I don't know. The first I really knew about it was, one day, after the second conviction had put Happy and the Dasher away for keeps, the file on the Lepke case was dropped on my desk.

To get Lepke from federal authorities for trial, I went to Washington and saw James V. Bennett, the Federal Director of Prisons.

"If you have a murder case, and can prove it, he's yours," agreed Bennett. He made one stipulation: unless we could convict Lepke of murder in the first degree and make it stick, we would have to give him back to serve out his narcotics sentence. So, Lepke came to Brooklyn on lend-lease for murder.

13.

They all make one mistake

Ten bullet holes a hat could cover—Kansas City, hide-out haven for lammisters—fugitives are off to Salt Lake City and Saratoga ... and Frank Costello in New Orleans—Lepke loses his temper—a one-in-a-million miss—the obliging sheriff of Jackson County, Mo.—Johnny Torrio's in real estate now—the czar is guilty of murder one.

Louis Stamler, the tailor, awoke at 6:45, as usual, on Sunday morning, September 13, 1936, to get his son up for his job in the neighborhood delicatessen.

The Sabbath morning quiet was on Brownsville. But as he leaned over the boy, a series of loud reports echoed in quick staccato, like a string of Chinese firecrackers. The tailor reached the window barely in time to see a black sedan, carrying four men, surge away from the front of the little candy store across the street. Leaning out, he was able to catch the license number just before the car swung around the next corner.

His eye returned to the candy store, and on the floor, just inside the door, he made out the figure of a man, still and ominous. Tailor Stamler threw on pants and shoes and charged down the stairs and out onto Sutter Avenue, silent and deserted. A block away, though, was the welcome blue of a police uniform. Stamler stood there in the middle of the street and began to yell just as loudly as he could.

Patrolman Guglielmo Cappadora was turning on the avenue's traffic lights for the day when this shrieking shattered the calm. "Help! Murder! Police!" it went, and the patrolman came running. The tailor could only point and say, "In the candy store . . . a man is laying there."

The store was just a cubbyhole, and the man was flat on his back, arms outstretched. He was drenched with blood. A stream of crimson, trickling across the floor, had puddled against the counter. Newspapers were all around him, as if he had just opened for the day and lifted them inside.

The dead man was Joseph Rosen, forty-six. He had taken over this tiny sweetshop only four or five months before, and he and his wife eked out a living in it. Rosen had seventeen bullet holes in his body. Ten bullets had made them—most going clear through and coming out on the other side. An ordinary man's hat could have covered all ten of the original holes. Four bullets were directly beneath the body, buried in the floor, a point which nettled the quickly gathering investigators. It was hardly likely the victim would have been lying on the floor when the murderers came. And if he was, why weren't all the bullets in the floor, instead of just four?

The alarm went out for the black sedan with the license the tailor had memorized. Four hours later, it was found, abandoned, thirteen blocks away, close to the corner where the IRT and BMT subway lines bisect, and a stairway leads to a bridge over the tracks, exiting on the next street. Hirsch Merlis, who operated the news stand at the stairway entrance, remembered this car coming around the corner and stopping suddenly at about seven o'clock, while he was sorting out the bulky Sunday editions.

"It was going pretty fast," he told the detectives. "Four men got out and walked past me, up the stairs."

More than a mile to the west, Samuel Pearl, an embroidery manufacturer, was taking a Sunday stroll. As he passed an empty lot, a reflected gleam attracted his eye. Curious, he reached into the weeds. The object was a gun. At first, he thought it was a child's toy. "But then, I realized it is too heavy; it is the real kind," the embroidery maker explained breathlessly to the policeman directing traffic at the next corner, to whom he virtually fled so that he might get rid of the weapon.

An expert gunsmith had worked on this pistol. The police ballistics bureau's strongest acid tests failed to reproduce even the faintest glimmer of an identifying numeral on the metal.

"The obliteration is too thorough," reported Sergeant Henry

Butts, commander of the bureau. And if the sergeant gave up, that was final, for he was an authority, consulted by police from coast to coast. It was Sergeant Butts who adapted the technique of comparing the rifling on a test bullet from a suspect weapon against a bullet from a murder—a process which is standard the country over today.

A thorough investigator, the sergeant made that test now on weapons in the bureau, and before long, he discovered that four of the bullets which had blasted Joe Rosen had been fired from the .38 police action special the embroidery man picked up two miles from the murder and a mile from the abandoned car. The car itself had been stolen from another section altogether, and the theft reported twenty-four hours before.

The plates were not those registered to it, and had not been reported missing. Detective Simon Ambraz checked to find out why. The owner was surprised to discover the lock on his garage had been broken; even more surprised that the licenses were gone from the car inside. It seems he was mostly a "Sunday driver" and hadn't looked at his car for several days.

Brooklyn was aroused. This was not another of the gangster murders that too often shattered the peace of the borough. Joe Rosen was a legitimate decent citizen, with a wife, a son, a daughter. The press hammered embarrassingly at authorities as the weeks passed. Occasionally, law enforcement caught a glimpse of what might lie behind the killing, but no more. At one point, assistant District Attorney William McCarthy progressed sufficiently to voice confidence behind the closed door of the D. A.'s office.

"I think we're on the way to one of the greatest pinches we've ever made," Bill told his associates.

Mysteriously, Bill McCarthy was abruptly taken off the case. In fact, three different assistant prosecutors were assigned and were called off, one after another. The months stretched into years, and the Joe Rosen murder became one more unsolved homicide gathering dust in the police files. By 1940, the newspapers were still bringing it up embarrassingly, but not nearly so frequently any more.

Then Reles started to talk about national rackets. He mentioned a Joe Rosen contract. As he promised on that Good Friday night when he offered to sing, he knew where corroboration could be found. Eventually, we were able to obtain an indictment naming six men in the slaying of the candy-store keeper that had been the bane of law enforcement in Brooklyn for four years, and one of the six was Lepke, the czar of the rackets, whom law enforcement was convinced it could never get for murder.

Not all would be available for trial for the wanton killing. Pittsburgh Phil, for instance, was already doomed for roping and cremating Puggy Feinstein. Dizzy Jimmy Feraco had apparently been taken care of by the mob. He was never heard from again. But Lepke and Mendy and the suave Louis Capone and Little Farvel, Lepke's close chum—there was nothing to prevent them from standing trial. If, that is, we could get our hands on all of them. We had Capone, the dignified restaurateur who was Albert Anastasia's front and liaison with the troop. We had nabbed him early as a material witness. Lepke was in federal custody. But Little Farvel and Mendy were missing when the grand jury handed up the indictment.

Oddly enough, Mendy had been brought in only a few weeks before. But the investigation had just gotten under way then, and the pick-up had been premature. We had nothing on Mendy yet. We questioned him a while, and we let him go. Police Captain Frank Bals, who was the District Attorney's chief investigator, was to put a tail on him. In some manner never explained, he eluded the tail and disappeared.

For a year, federal as well as state authorities hunted the hulking killer almost as relentlessly as they had searched for his boss, Lepke, in all forty-eight states and several foreign countries. New Jersey wanted him for four murders, after we had advised authorities there of the circumstances of the Dutch Schultz shooting match. We had him down for four slayings, too. As a result of our information, California was after him for ordering Big Greenie's execution in Hollywood. The federal government had indictments in Texas and New York, having to do with his business in "cutting" morphine and distributing it from New York to Chicago to Dallas.

In the spring of 1941, Mendy's trail was picked up at last in

Kansas City. On the night of April 6, Agent Albert Aman of the Federal Bureau of Narcotics spotted the new car Mendy was reported driving. Two ladies were with him. Even with the newly added weight and the reddish mustache covering his upper lip and the eyeglasses, Aman recognized his man. Aman's party closed in. One of the ladies was the girl friend of a prominent Missouri gambling man. The other was Mendy's wife.

"I am James W. Bell," Mendy insisted. "What's the idea?"

"Cut the kidding, Mendy," broke in Joseph Bell, district Narcotics Bureau supervisor. "We know you." He pointed to the "wanted" circular on the wall of the local bureau, advertising Mendy's meaty countenance. The outsized outlaw realized there was no use carrying the argument further.

Mendy obviously was prepared for a long haul. He had a brand-new car. He had $1,000 in a local bank. He was carrying $2,713 in cash, although he had then been on the lam for over a year. On his finger, sparkled a diamond ring that had very nearly the illuminating power of a headlight. And supporting the strap around his solid middle was an expensive gold buckle with a star outlined in diamonds.

Mendy had holed up between Colorado and Missouri for fourteen months, and everywhere he had acquired background as James William Bell. His wife had even joined the wartime Bundles for Britain as "Mrs. Bell."

"Did you do that to give the color of legitimacy to the name?" I asked her afterward.

"Oh, no," she exclaimed. "I was interested in the work."

Mendy had all sorts of credentials showing he was James William Bell of 204 South Seventh Street, Rocky Ford, Colorado, and 420 West 46th Street Terrace, Kansas City. His neat business cards identified James W. Bell as Vice-President of the Chihuahua Tungsten Mining and Development Company of Black Hawk, Col. That bewildered Agent Aman.

"Is the mine doing business?" he inquired.

"Who knows?" Mendy shrugged. "I stuck $500 in this thing and was made vice-president. You know how it is when you're on the lam. You got to have something to cover yourself up."

In Kansas City, during the six months before he was nabbed,

he had been able to gather, under the name of Bell, a social security card—and a draft registration! The social security card was easy. "Anybody can get one of these things," he said. The Selective Service registration for James W. Bell presented more of a mystery. Ostensibly an officially signed bona fide draft card from the 18th precinct of Kansas City's Seventh Ward, it described Mendy's physical characteristics minutely, even to the "six-inch scar, lower right leg." However, the name of James W. Bell was not listed in the draft board files. Mendy was touchy about discussing this valuable bit of paper. "I just got it," was all he would say.

Most fanciful of all, though, was the fact that while his picture decorated the wall of virtually every station house in the country, Mendy was picked up fifteen times by Kansas City police for traffic violations—and was let go every time! "I just talked my way out," he grinned. From my observation, the thick-lipped bruiser was not that good a talker. Indeed, Kansas City had been a most convenient hideout. Just the spot where a Charley Binaggio could build up a politico-underworld business, as he did. Until, that is, he couldn't deliver on a contract for the Syndicate. Then the underworld itself left him on the floor of a political club, all full of holes, in the spring of 1950.

One item in Mendy's collection was a card for Martin's Indoor Poultry Farm, a beroofed establishment specializing in fryers, broilers, hens and eggs, just outside Kansas City.

"I buy chickens there," Mendy disclosed. "Sometimes I call up and they deliver."

For Agent Aman, owner Louis Martin pointed out an apartment on West Forty-eighth Street, Kansas City, where he had delivered Mendy's birds. It was a considerable distance from where the mobster had said he lived. Through this was uncovered the fact that others of the mob had been hiding out in the Missouri metropolis—just as comfortably and unbothered by the Law as Mendy was for over a year. For Murder, Inc., Kansas City was practically a second home.

In all mob history, no one had ever put a murder case together and made it stick against a ranking gang executive. Against the hired hands, the stooges—yes, occasionally. Against a top man—never. Not too many, therefore, took us seriously when we showed we were not fooling about putting Lepke on trial.

The mob, though, was taking no chances. If the case were never tried, the boys reasoned, so much the better. They attempted all the legal moves and loopholes. The delays stretched out. Not until September 15, 1941, sixteen months after he was indicted, did Lepke finally go to trial. It was just five years and two days after Joe Rosen was left lying in his own blood in his little candy store.

On trial with the soft-eyed rackets overlord were the suave Louis Capone and the hulking Mendy. That accounted for all those indicted except Lepke's old and trusted friend, Little Farvel. He had been caught, all right. A short time before, a girl friend had donated a key to Farvel's hideout. Silently, while he slept, detectives surrounded his bed, and Farvel woke up—with the muzzle of a police pistol squarely in his mouth. We severed him from the others in the Joe Rosen murder, because, frankly, we did not have the required corroboration on him.

Farvel's forthcoming time was, at any rate, well assigned. He spent the next eight years in prison for narcotics operations. When he came out, in 1949, things were different. He kept his eyes open, and his observations led him to conclude that illegal characters, if preyed upon, could not run to the Law. So, Farvel organized a protection extortion against bookmakers. Whether the bookies decided to take drastic steps about this shakedown, or whether some other part of his past caught up with him, has never been learned. Nevertheless, in the early morning of September 16, 1949, Farvel was dumped on a suburban road in Valley Stream, Long Island, with six bullets in his head.

We were not too disappointed in not being able to try Farvel with the others for the Joe Rosen murder. Lepke, Capone and Mendy were the big game, high in interstate crime—Lepke with his rackets across the country; Mendy, who ordered murder on a coast-to-coast basis, and Capone, with shylock connections from Brooklyn to Detroit, and a director of the extermination squad that killed anywhere it was summoned. Capone, incidentally, did not like the idea of being tried with the others, because, he wailed, they were so notorious. He could not understand when it was pointed out that a man who messes with garbage cannot expect to come out smelling like Chanel No. 5.

For me, this was the big one. It meant cutting into the very heart of this evil ring we had uncovered, after chopping away at its tentacles. It meant getting Lepke, a king of the rackets. It would be the end, if convicted, of a ranking commander—a chief of staff of the Syndicate. It would show, for the first time, that the men who pulled the strings on lawlessness were no longer "sacred."

The cartel, generally, doubted our chances, but it did realize the possibilities. The SOS was broadcast. We heard of the arrival of three ace sharpshooters from distant points. Very likely, there were others. They were told to get the songbirds, even in the courtroom if necessary. Double guards were posted outside the courthouse as well as inside, and United States marshals, responsible for Lepke's custody, augmented fifty police and detectives. Every officer had his pistol out of its holster and in his coat pocket, his fist clenched around the stock, ready for firing.

And the legal talent! You would have to look in many a courtroom to find as brilliant a staff of attorneys as the battery of nine, assembled to defend the big shots of mobdom. A former judge of General Sessions court was among them, along with two former assistant Federal Attorneys, a pair of one-time assistant District Attorneys, and a famed criminal lawyer who was winning important cases while I was still in P. S. 130. The reports were that the fee for this banner line-up was $250,000. Incredible? Well, in preparing for Lepke's rackets trials, some of the "boys" had sought out Sam Leibowitz, the noted criminal attorney who had defended Albert Anastasia frequently and successfully through the years—as well as countless others. The boys lifted a briefcase and upended it. A cascade of packaged green piled high on the desk.

"There's two hundred and fifty G's, counselor," they proffered. "It's all yours—win, lose or draw—to take the case." Leibowitz refused; he was already thinking of other fields. A short time later, he was elected to the post of county judge.

That was for Lepke's rackets defense. This was for murder—

for Lepke's life. A quarter of a million, then, did not seem out of line for the defense legal lights. Heading Lepke's staff—retained especially as trial counsel—was Hyman Barshay, former assistant District Attorney, a master to this day at the technique of lulling a witness with the velvet glove, then tearing him apart with the mailed fist underneath. Capone's chief counsel was the veteran Sidney Rosenthal, looked on by the profession as one of New York's outstanding trial lawyers. For Mendy, the defense was in charge of former Judge Alfred J. Talley, brilliant, caustic as poison, especially at prodding a witness into an emotional outburst—which, of course, can always lead to a remark that might cause a mistrial.

When selection of the jury finally was begun, the battle really warmed up. It took eight days to seat the first juror; twenty-two days to get half the jury picked. An entire panel of 250 talesmen was exhausted and a new panel called, and still we were at it. All told, it was five weeks before the twelve men and two alternates were seated. In the course of this long-drawn-out questioning and rejecting and challenging, Lepke's counsel complained about our referring to him as Lepke.

"You have not proved that he is known by the name of Lepke," the attorney maintained.

I was willing to bet that he was known to more people by that than by his legal label. Before the trial was over, the dispute had been completely forgotten. Even his own attorneys were calling him Lepke.

Max Rubin was an ace operative at labor racketeering—but you would have taken him more for a college professor.

The silver-thatched union organizer was remarkably erudite. His strictly un-ganglike manner of expression, against the dese-dem-and-dose of his hoodlum pals, was as incongruous as ice cream served on french-fried potatoes would be. He had had such divergent callings as longshoreman and analytical chemist. He had been a draft-dodger in World War I, and a soapbox orator on Marxist economy in downtown Manhattan's tempestuous Union Square.

"I have never been a Communist, though," he avowed. Then he

explained that shortly after the end of World War I, he went to Germany (on a forged passport) and "engaged in the transmission of money to the Soviet Government."

Through his vociferous espousing of Socialism, he met an official of Amalgamated Clothing Workers, and was brought into the cutters' union. By 1921, he was a union official. His advance was rapid. Through Lepke's reign, Rubin was an intimate and trusted aide, collection man in the clothing truckers' union, flour union, expressmen's association and from various manufacturers, bakery concerns and truck fleet operators, from whom tribute was exacted.

They'd been close once—Rubin and Lepke. But as he sat on the stand now, the organizer hated his old boss and was happy to testify against him. Before Rubin, sixteen preliminary witnesses had been required to lay the framework for this intricate case, for, through the years, Lepke had been too dexterous ever to leave an open road of proof to himself. He was as infamous for his cunning as for his crime.

Rubin had come to know Joe Rosen from "around the clothing district." For all of his adult life, Joe had been in clothing trucking—trying to hit the jackpot, said Rubin. And, in 1932, he appeared to be on the way, at last. He had developed a number of tailoring-contract customers around Wilkes-Barre, Pa., who were solid accounts. With them as assets, he had been given a partnership in the New York & New Jersey Truck Company.

Then, with no warning, Rubin, as the union business agent, came in near the end of July and announced a work stoppage. That was bad enough. But Rubin also said that all hauling to Pennsylvania, where many houses were nonunion shops, was permanently banned.

"That's the only thing I got in this business," Rosen pleaded. "I was made a partner only by bringing in this Pennsylvania work."

Joe was summoned to a meeting with Lepke and Gurrah. He had been noticing that these tough guys from downtown were having more and more to say in Amalgamated. They demanded his books. As they came to each client in the accounts receivable ledger, Gurrah growled, "You can't go to this house," or, "You can't truck clothes to this place. . . . Or this one. . . . Or this."

"Why not?" Rosen finally demanded. "I got a legitimate business. If the manufacturers are willing to give me the work, I'm going to take it."

Rubin knew these men. "Don't hit your head up against a stone wall, Joe," he said. "If they tell you do something, do it."

"But if I lose the Pennsylvania business, I lose everything I have in the company," the truckman argued. He stormed and he broke into bitter tears. "I been in the clothing business all my life, and now I'm being pushed out of it," he cried.

"Don't worry," soothed Lepke, apparently more impatient to end the session than from any feeling of pity. "If you have any trouble in the company, we'll do something for you."

The stoppage was eminently successful from Lepke's point of view. He wound up with a 50 per cent interest in Garfield Express.

"Garfield got all of the New York and New Jersey business—all except knee pants, which is the smallest part of the clothing business," Rubin testified now.

Q—What happened to Rosen?
A—He was out of his concern.

Rosen's daughter testified the firm lasted only a few months after the stoppage, and then "there was no more business left." A few months later, shorn of his livelihood as he had feared, Joe sought out Rubin in the clothing district.

"Lepke and you promised I would be taken care of," he prodded. "Everybody is back to work, and I'm still on the street."

At Rubin's suggestion, Lepke got Rosen a job with his new partner, Louis Cooper, in Garfield Express. But Cooper fired him after eight months, and for eighteen months he was out of work. Rubin had to depend on Lepke—and Lepke did nothing. When the rackets investigation began in Manhattan in 1935, Rubin saw the danger ahead.

"This is bad," he told Lepke. "Joe is around complaining he's got a family, and he doesn't have anything to eat. We got a desperate man on our hands."

Finally, a job as driver was obtained for Rosen. Before long, however, his heart began acting up, and he was forced to quit. On borrowed funds, he opened a little candy store in Brownsville in the spring of 1936. Rubin did not have time to pay much attention, because the investigation was warming up. Then one day, Lepke brought up Joe Rosen's name.

Q—When was that?

A—In June, 1936. He told me, "Rosen is going around Brownsville shooting off his mouth. He is saying that he's going down to Dewey's office."

Q—What did you say to him?

A—I told him, "The fellow is harmless, Louis. He must need a couple of dollars." I said I would have the union members go to the candy store and do some shopping there.

Through Rubin's urging, a number of union truckers journeyed to Brownsville to patronize Joe's shop.

Q—Did you have another talk with Lepke about Joe Rosen later?

A—Some time around July, he told me again, "Rosen is going around saying he's going down to Dewey's office and speak about Lepke." I again said there is no harm in the man. Lepke said, "I want him quiet."

The way he said it made Rubin apprehensive. He suggested that he visit the candy store himself.

Q—What was Lepke's answer?

A—I had about $500 of Lepke's money. He said, "Take two bills and give it to him, and tell the son of a bitch to get out of town until I tell him to come back."

Q—How much is two bills?

A—Two hundred dollars.

Q—That $500 you had—was that from some financial transaction for Lepke?

A—Yes—with the Flour Truckmen and Expressmen's Association.

Q—Did you go to see Joe Rosen?

A—I went to the candy store. I said, "Here's $200. Lepke wants you to go away until he tells you to come back. You better do what he says." Joe said he would go to his son's place in Reading, Pennsylvania.

Three days after Joe left, however, he phoned Brooklyn and his wife told him she was quite ill. Within a week, he was back.

Q—When was the next time Lepke spoke to you about him?

A—On September 11, 1936, in his office at 200 Fifth Avenue. I remember that date vividly.

One reason the occasion was etched on Rubin's memory was that Lepke lost his temper.

"I no more than walk in," the witness recalled, "when he was yelling. His face was flushed."

"I stood enough of this crap," Lepke roared. Rubin had never heard him raise his voice before. "That son of a bitch Rosen, that bastard—he's around again, and shooting off his mouth about seeing Dewey. He and nobody else is going any place and do any talking. I'll take care of him."

Rubin was thoroughly frightened. "Don't be foolish and do something that will get us in trouble, Louis," he pleaded.

"Enough is enough," Lepke was obdurate.

Rubin begged some more. He was sure the union officials could do something to quiet the ex-truckman they knew. "Give it a chance," he entreated. Grudgingly, Lepke agreed.

Rubin, however, could get no co-operation at union headquarters. "Rosen is too tough to handle," they said, and they changed the subject to talk of the Local's annual baseball game the next day at Vineland, N. J.

A disappointed Rubin returned. He was relieved to see that Lepke's temper had cooled off. "All I got was an invitation to a ball game," he was forced to report.

"That sounds like a good idea," the soft-voiced boss was almost jovial. "Go ahead to the game. But do something for me now—get me Paul Berger. Send him up right away."

At union headquarters, Rubin found Berger, who was Lepke's intermediary with the cutters' union, and delivered the message. The next morning, Rubin and his family drove to Jersey, to remain overnight.

On receipt of Rubin's message, Berger went to Lepke's office. A strong-arm with a hard jaw and thinning hair, Berger had always assumed an air of respectability—and had been in labor racketeering since the early twenties. As a boy, he had changed his name from Hamberger, because the other kids called him meatball. Foreign-born, he had been in the American Army during World War I. Yet, he never realized until late in 1941—when another world war was on the horizon—that he was not an American citizen. He caught on then because authorities checked to see if he had registered as an alien.

"You know that Joe Rosen?" Lepke asked him when he arrived at the office that September afternoon in 1936. Berger did. "Well, I want you to point him out to somebody. Let's go."

Q—When you got downstairs what did you do?
A—There was a taxicab line outside the building, but Lepke walked a block and hailed one cruising. (For all Lepke knew, a detective might be planted in a cab at the entrance to his building.)

They drove downtown and met Mendy on a corner. It was near the store which was the Manhattan boys' hangout—right next door to a police station. Lepke whispered to his oversized aide for several minutes.

"You go with Mendy and point out Joe Rosen to him," he directed Berger finally, and he left. The two drove to Brooklyn. Mendy stopped briefly to talk to Louis Capone on a Brownsville corner. Then he parked on a side street, just off Sutter Avenue. They sauntered onto the avenue, and when they were opposite the candy store, Berger nudged his companion.

"That's him . . . Rosen," he nodded. "By the store there, fixing the papers on the stand." Mendy crossed the street for a closer look. "Can't miss now," he said, when they were back in the car.

Q—When you fingered Rosen, did you know he was going to be killed?

A—No. I thought it was going to be a schlammin."

"But," added Berger, "I know what would happen to me if I was not willing to agree, anyway."

The mob worked fast. Mendy had already set the wheels in motion in his brief talk with Louis Capone. Later that same Friday, Sholem and Pittsburgh Phil were sitting in Sholem's car, across from the coffee pot where some of the shylocks lazed. As they chatted, Sholem related when he took the stand, Louis Capone, Mendy and Farvel strolled up.

"Hey, Pep," they called to Pittsburgh Phil. "Come out here."

The homicide specialist walked away with the trio. After three-quarters of an hour, all four returned. Sholem was still sitting there.

Q—What was said.

A—Pep said to me, "Go and clip a car and get a drop."

Sholem was an old hand at this. The dreamy-eyed loner cruised around until he noticed a string of small private garages. After a bit of haggling with the woman superintendent, he paid a month's rent on one. That evening, he sought out his friend Muggsy.

"Muggsy is a car thief and radio crook," he testified. "The best in the business."

After midnight, they drove out of Brownsville. "I wanted Muggsy with me," Sholem explained, "because I knew he would take the radio from the car. So, if the car is found, it would look like it was stolen for stripping—just a little job." He had no idea what Pittsburgh Phil wanted a car for, but he knew it was not for joy-riding.

In the East Flatbush section, they spotted an automobile that met their fancy—a two-door sedan.

Q—Describe to the jury the manner in which the car was stolen.

A—First Muggsy broke the window. He reached in and opened the door. Then he picked up the (engine) hood. He had a jump box with him. Then he started it with the jump box.

Q—The jury does not know what a jump box is.

A—That is to start a car up . . . a hot box . . . when you don't have a key.

The stolen car was taken to the drop, and Muggsy promptly ripped his night's pay out of it—the radio.

Q—What was the next thing you did?
A—I took the door handle off. I went to a locksmith and he made up a key. The door key fits the ignition, you know.

At four o'clock that afternoon, which was Saturday, Sholem met Pittsburgh Phil. Louis Capone was there, too. Capone's brow darkened when he heard Sholem had procured a two-door car. "What the hell is the matter with you?" he accused. "You should know you got to have a four-door."

Sholem realized then that the car was to be a getaway vehicle. A two-door car on a getaway is like a subway turnstile at 5 P.M. It is likely to create a bottleneck for those who want to get through in a hurry. And a getaway is no place for a bottleneck.

Without concealing his disgust for Sholem's stupidity, Louis said, "Come on with me." He drove to Linton Park, a tiny patch of green with a fence around it, a block from Sutter Avenue.

"Now watch good," he cautioned. "This is going to be your job . . . what route to drive." It was the first Sholem had heard that he was slated to steer on a getaway.

Turning into Sutter Avenue, Capone nodded toward a small candy store. "That is where somebody is going to get killed," he said. From there he navigated a zigzag route, emphasizing each turn with a "watch this" or "make sure."

"This is the place where you dump the car," he said when they reached the corner of Livonia Avenue, where two subway lines bisect.

Q—Then what did Capone do?
A—He showed me the route again . . . and again. . . . Seven or eight times, we went over it. I learned it by heart.

Capone had a final assignment for Sholem. "Go and steal plates," he ordered. "Take them where they won't be missed right away. Put them on the hot car and bring it over about half-past ten tonight."

That evening, armed with screwdriver, pliers and precautionary gloves, Sholem trekked out of Brownsville to a quiet residential neighborhood in which residents were likely to be mostly once-a-week drivers. He broke the lock on one of a long row of garages and removed the plates from the car inside. Returning to the drop, he took the plates from the hot car and replaced them with the licenses he had procured.

"Then I broke up the old plates and threw them in some sewer or ash can," he testified.

He drove the hot car to the rendezvous. With Pittsburgh Phil and Capone, were Mendy and Farvel and Jimmy Feraco, the torpedo.

Q—What happened after that?
A—Somebody brings a package over to Pep. He give it to me and says, "Put it in the glove compartment of the hot car."

At Mendy's order, Sholem drove to the little park off Sutter Avenue, around the corner from Rosen's candy store.

Q—What did they do?
A—Mendy tells me get the package from the car. I give it to him. Mendy opens it up and he puts the pills in.
Q—What do you mean by pills?
A—Bullets. It was guns in the package, and he fills the guns with pills. He gives one to Pep and one to Jimmy and he takes one for himself with extra pills.
Q—Did he say anything?
A—Mendy says he is going over to take a look at the store and see if it looks good. He says to Pep, "Come on; see how you like it," and both of them walk away.

When Mendy and Pittsburgh Phil returned, some fifteen minutes later, the latter had an objection. The scheme was to murder Joe Rosen that very night. But, across the street from the candy store, Pittsburgh Phil had recognized an ice-cream parlor which was a hangout for shylocks.

"That ice-cream place," he said, showing what was, for him, rare hesitation. "Somebody is liable to make me there."

Q—What does "to make" someone mean?
A—Recognize. If you are identified, that is being made.

"Well, I'll tell you what we do then," Mendy conceded after a moment's thought. "We'll hit him in the morning when he opens up the store. The ice-cream store will be shut then." He gathered up the guns and turned them back to Sholem for storing in the hot car. Sholem returned the car to the drop, and then proceeded to an address Mendy had given him. It was Farvel's apartment.

Q—What happened?
A—I went into the living room and slept on the rug.
Q—Who woke you?
A—Mendy got me out at five o'clock in the morning. He told me go and get the car and meet them in the little park.

Feraco, Mendy and Pittsburgh Phil were waiting there. Mendy distributed the pistols again.

"Come on," he ordered. He led the party, afoot, across Sutter Avenue, to an apartment house. "From over here," he pointed out when they had slipped into the vestibule, "we can see when that rat comes out of his house to go to his store. His house is right across the street there."

For an hour, they waited. It was far too early on Sunday morning for any resident to be stirring and notice them. Mendy, near the door, peered continuously at a row of small houses opposite.

Q—After that hour, what took place?
A—Mendy said, "That rat just come out." He says to me, "Go over and get the car and stop in front of the candy store. Be sure the motor is running."
Q—Tell the jury what you did.
A—I took the car from by the park and drove it around the corner. I saw Mendy and Pep and Jimmy Feraco walking toward the store. I pulled up in front of the store, like he told me. I kept the motor running.
Q—What did you see them do?

A—Mendy and Pep walked into the store. Jimmy Feraco stood outside . . . the lookout. I heard a lot of shots. Then Mendy and Pep come running out of the store. I got the car door open and I got the front seat picked up to make it easy to get in, because it is a two-door car. They run into the car, with Jimmy Feraco. I start on the route Lou Capone told me.

At the "dumping" spot, he pulled up. The four of them walked unhurriedly past the newsstand, climbed the stairs to the bridge over the tracks, and descended on to the next street. There Sholem found out why Capone and Favel had not been in the murder party.

Q—What did you see there?

A—Lou Capone is waiting in my car. Farvel is in his car. Mendy give me his gun and says, "Break it up and get rid of it." Lou Capone and Mendy and Pep went in Farvel's car and take off.

Sholem dropped Feraco at a subway station. Suddenly he had an alarming thought. When he had "clipped" the sedan, he hadn't known it was to be used on a killing. He'd had no objection to Muggsy ripping the radio out. But radios have serial numbers.

Q—What did you do?

A—I went looking for Muggsy in his house. I got the radio. I took it to Canarsie and broke it up and threw it in the bay.

"Now that there is a murder, I didn't want any trouble," Sholem explained.

In the cellar of the garage where he stored his car, Sholem attended to Mendy's gun. "I broke it up with a sledge hammer into little pieces," he related, "and threw the pieces into sewers."

Q—When did you learn the identity of the murder victim?

A—When I picked up the paper that night. I seen a picture of the killing, and the name. I didn't know the man.

In that same Sunday night edition, Max Rubin, returning from his overnight sojourn, also discovered, to his horror, that his old trucker friend had been slain. From the same paper, too, Berger learned the fingering he had done was for a murder, not a schlam-min. Berger, a muscleman used to violence, took the news as a matter of regular business. Rubin, though, was no strong-arm. Panic-stricken, he rushed to Lepke.

"Don't worry," the ganglord reassured him. "As far as the law in Brooklyn goes, we got nothing to worry about."

But a week or two later, a news story mentioned a "union official" who had been seen handing Joe Rosen money in July. "It does everything but give my name," wailed the frantic Rubin.

Again Lepke calmed him. "What are you worrying about?" he said. "Are they asking for you?"

Rubin quieted down. "I was very secure in the magical powers of Mr. Buchalter," he testified, with a slight shudder. In the following weeks, though, the papers prodded the District Attorney pointedly.

"There's an assistant D. A. over there named McCarthy who is going around saying he's going to make one of the greatest pinches ever—he's going to pinch Lepke and Gurrah," said Lepke, show-ing a remarkable knowledge of what went on behind closed doors in Brooklyn law enforcement. "So," he suggested to Rubin, "you should go away for a while."

Matter-of-factly, he proposed a trip upstate, to Saratoga, where Gurrah and the strong-arm, Danny Fields, were already in hiding. "Before you go, though," he requested, "fill Paul Berger in on what you are doing with the unions, and let him meet the people to go to for the dough."

Rubin stayed away only five days. He'd been lonesome, he com-plained. Fields had his girl friend in hiding with him. "He's never around, and I'm on my own," he said plaintively. Clearly, cops and robbers was not Rubin's game.

Lepke was being tried then for anti-trust violations. On bail during trial, he held daily conferences with his henchmen across the street from the courthouse, in the office of Willie Alberts, a bail bondsman who was a sponge for picking up information. That was how he got the idea for what to do next about Rubin.

"Willie Alberts has a relation in Salt Lake City," he proposed. "You go up there for a while."

Rubin tried to talk him out of it. He even had Lepke see the union's attorney, Edward Maguire—without mentioning the murder, of course.

"What I said to Rubin," the attorney told the racketeer, "was that flight is a suspicion of guilt. Let Rubin face whatever he has to face now."

Lepke countered by reciting the philosophy he so often repeated to his workers. "All I know," he shrugged, "when a witness ain't around, there can't be a case."

"I didn't want to say it in front of the mouthpiece," he confided later to Rubin, "but that case in Brooklyn is going out the window in a little while. That McCarthy is being taken off, and another assistant D. A. is getting it. Then he'll be pushed off to something else, and it will die. All you gotta do is stay out of sight a while more."

Rubin went to Salt Lake City, where Willie Albert's relative ran a florist shop on Broadway. But after three weeks, he was so lonely, he came back again without notice. Lepke was suspicious now.

"Have you got something in the back of your head?" he asked.

"Look, Louis," Rubin pledged his loyalty. "I got no notions. It's just that I'm a lonesome man when I can't see my family."

He had been home a week this time, when Lepke called him. "I got just the spot for you," said the boss invitingly. "You'll be occupied and you'll make some money besides."

Q—Where was that?

A—In New Orleans. Lepke said, "Frank Costello is up there and he's running the machines—all kinds of slot machines." He said, "You go around and help with the machines, and you'll be occupied. You'll have money from New York, money from me, money from there. You'll be okay."

"Call and tell Berger where you are," Lepke advised. "Then I'll get in touch with Costello to look you up."

Rubin phoned, and told Berger he was registered in the Hotel New Orleans, as William Harris. The next day, a mystified Lepke accosted Berger.

"Those people in New Orleans called, and the son of a bitch

is not in the hotel," he related. "Call up and find out what's wrong."

Berger waited until 9 P.M. to phone. ("The rates are lower then," he testified.) The fretful exile had checked out. The next day, Rubin notified the strong-arm that he was home in the Bronx again. That night, Berger drove Lepke to the Bronx. Lepke warned the muscleman to check against "being tailed," Berger recalled on the witness stand.

Q—What did you do?

A—I drove the wrong way through a one-way street to make sure I am not being followed.

Lepke left the car at a street corner, and Berger went alone to Rubin's house. The returned traveler was ready for bed. He dressed at once when told Lepke wanted to see him.

"When the king directs, you go," he testified.

Lepke was waiting under an awning, out of a torrential downpour. Frequent jagged lightning gave an eerie effect to the street. Rubin ducked under the awning. He was not afraid. His chief was always cordial to him. As a matter of fact, Lepke liked Rubin— erudite, non-violent and practically everything else he himself would have liked to have been.

"Max," he chided softly, "you came back again without permission."

"But, Louis," Rubin was sure his benign boss would understand, "I couldn't take it any more, Louis. I had to see my wife and child. You know how it is, Louis."

"But Max, you came back without permission." Lepke's tone never varied; his eyes were still soft. Yet, there was something in the repetition that upset Rubin. He even dropped the pal-to-pal "Louis" he always used.

"Don't get ideas, Lep," he pleaded. "No one knows I'm in town. I didn't talk to anybody."

For a moment there was no answer. Lepke seemed to be pondering.

"By the way, Max," he suddenly inquired, entirely disarmingly, "how old are you?"

The switch was startling. "I'm forty-eight, Lep. Exactly."

"That's a ripe age, Max, isn't it?"

And, on that ambiguous note, Lepke ended the interview. He didn't explain it, and Rubin didn't ask. He was just glad the session was over. They rejoined Berger. The boss issued orders. He never raised his voice, but it had the impact of thunder.

"You are going out of town," he commanded. "And this time you're doing it my way."

Rubin couldn't come home from this one. Lepke sent him out on the road with a man who traveled by car—and kept moving. They toured the Atlantic Seaboard for two months. Rubin let his hair grow long, donned glasses and acquired the conventional mustache disguise of the mob. And he fretted.

By the end of February, 1937, he was practically crying to go home. They were in Washington in a hotel—and suddenly Lepke walked into the room. Apparently, he had been summoned.

"You can't come back; that's all," was his greeting. Rubin begged. He implored. Lepke put up an argument which he thought would surely change Rubin's mind.

"If you come back and get into any trouble," he stipulated, "you can't come to me crying. If you need a lawyer or money or something, I'm out of it. I'll foot no bills."

Rubin was desperate, though. "Okay—I'll stay on my own," he accepted the terms. Thus, he was allowed to come home, after being on the run for half a year, because of a murder to which he was not a party—which, in fact, he had tried desperately to prevent.

Why, then, had Rubin fled? Because, he swore in cross-examination, he was deathly afraid Joe Rosen's assassination would be pinned on him! He knew the power Lepke had in Brooklyn in those days.

"You know," he testified, "there are honest D. A.'s and there are dishonest D. A.'s."

"You mean to say," counsel was incredulous, "that some District Attorney was going to frame you?"

"Positively!" Rubin almost shouted it. "Yes . . . positively!"

For three or four months after returning, he worried. Then he went to Lawyer Maguire. He didn't mention the Rosen murder; wild horses couldn't have dragged that out of him. He mentioned rackets. The lawyer gave him sound counsel. "See Dewey," he suggested. Rubin visited the prosecutor and began to expose some of Lepke's manipulations.

He resumed his post as business agent of Local 240, Clothing Drivers and Helpers, as though nothing had happened. Frequently he met Berger for an early lunch, without even hinting at his negotiations with law enforcement, of course. He was an ostrich, though, to think it would long remain a secret to this insidious Syndicate.

Late in September, Mendy sought out Berger. "We got information that Rubin is singing," he revealed. "He has got to be hit. You finger him to Shloime." (Shloime was one of the minor torpedoes.)

Mendy could not have timed it better. Berger had a lunch date with Rubin that very day. "Be in the Childs on Fourteenth Street before 11:30," he instructed Shloime. "The guy with me will be the one." Thus, even while breaking bread with him, Berger was fingering his old friend for death.

"But I know what will happen to me if I don't agree," he repeated in explanation. And he did pick up the luncheon check.

On October 1, Rubin appeared before the Manhattan grand jury and tied Lepke thoroughly to the flour and bakery racket. When he entered the subway to start for home, the tailing Shloime phoned his mobmate, Cuppie, who was waiting in the Bronx for the word of Rubin's approach. Leaving the subway, Rubin turned into Gun Hill Road. He was just opposite the hospital there, when he heard a shot, he testified.

Q—What happened to you?
A—I was stunned—and then I fell down.

It was a miracle, in fact, that he was here now to talk about it. A torpedo had stepped up behind him, had virtually pressed the muzzle of his gun into the base of Rubin's skull, and fired one shot. The bullet entered the back of his neck, went clear through his head and came out between the bridge of his nose and his eye. The odds are about one in a million, after such a shot, that the victim lives long enough even to realize he has been hit. The gunman was obviously so sure, he didn't even bother to fire a second time. The nerves of Rubin's neck were severed, the muscles shattered, and his head was left permanently crooked. But he lived. He was the one-millionth.

For thirty-eight days, he lay between life and death in a hospital. And as he lay there, it finally came to him just what Lepke had meant that night in the rain. When Lepke said, "Forty-eight is a ripe age, isn't it?"—this was what he had in mind, Rubin realized.

Q—After you left the hospital, were you given a police guard?
A—Yes. At first it was three men. After several months, it was cut down to one twenty-four-hour guard.

Even with their target surrounded by Law, the mob did not give up. "Look at that lucky son of a bitch," sneered Mendy to Berger. "He gets hit in the head and he's still alive." And a short time later, as Rubin stood on a street, his bodyguard at his side, Berger fingered him a second time—to Blue Jaw Magoon and Cuppie. Rubin held no animosity for Berger, though; no yearning for revenge. As much as anyone living, he understood that even if Berger had revolted, he would have been fingered anyway, by someone else. And Berger would then have ended up no better than he.

Despite a constant watch for an opportunity, the mob never got another shot at Rubin without his police escort. "We don't want to hit a cop, too," Mendy explained querulously to Berger one day. So, Rubin remained alive.

Nothing worse than this one-in-a-million "miss" could possibly have happened to Lepke. For, while Rubin's neck was permanently paralyzed, Rubin's tongue was loosened—and vengeful.

In spite of his loosened tongue where the rackets were concerned, however, not even his brush with death could unlock his lips about the Joe Rosen murder. In December, 1937, assistant prosecutor Bill McCarthy, who had caused Lepke concern previously—until he was taken off the case—came to Manhattan to get a statement from Rubin. That statement, the labor expert testified now, was deliberately and thoroughly false. Before he could answer a question as to why he had purposely perjured himself, the judge sent the jury from the courtroom.

It was a wise move. Rubin had teetered on the edge of the grave; he knew it was Lepke who had put him there. And still, he

had not been able to drive himself to talk about the murder that
Lepke had ordered, and in which he himself was not involved.
That was the immensity of his terror of Lepke's power. As a
matter of fact, just getting him to take the stand and face Lepke
had required more persuasion than it ever took to convince the
proverbial horse to drink. Or a whole herd of horses, for that
matter. Only after five or six weeks of every argument we
could offer would he even accept the fact that we were serious
about trying the deadly rackets czar at all. Police Inspector Mike
McDermott and I proved to him that we were on the level, and
still he was no more than half-convinced. An assistant D. A. might
offer him immunity from prosecution—but not from Lepke. That
is how much Max Rubin dreaded.

"Who are you?" he challenged me. "They'll break your back,
and you'll be out of here."

The one thing above any other that finally changed his mind,
I feel, was the awful weight of that secret he had been carrying
for so long. Back from the grave, he was now, at last, unburden-
ing himself of this thing that had been gnawing and burning at
him for half a decade. And a more co-operative witness never
took the stand. His stay stretched out to four full days and a good
portion of three more. Under that strain, he had every right to be
emotional.

Counsel set out to explode those emotions. These were the
cleverest of attorneys. Here was as damning a witness as they would
face. They ripped at him, and blasted. Bluntly, they tried to make
him out a murderer. Everything was calculated to blow Rubin into
an outburst. If those emotions should explode with sufficient force,
he could very well say something that would necessitate a mistrial.
For Rubin, goaded into a rage, was all but uncontrollable. He
brushed aside the court's "please" or "stop" with the same dis-
regard as for an attorney's objection.

It was an astute move on Judge Taylor's part, then, to send
the jury out, so there could be a preliminary dry run of Rubin's
reply as to why he had perjured himself three years before, about
this murder. Rubin took excellent advantage of the opportunity.
Weeping in rage, his face a red blotch under the silver hair, he

charged that Lepke even had pipelines into the grand jury room in the Dewey investigation.

"I went to the grand jury where nobody knew where I was, and I was shot in the head!" He pounded the bench in his agitation. "Do you mean to tell me I would give that man [McCarthy] or any other man a true statement? Like hell I would! It was like giving it directly to that man. It would be as much as death to myself and my family." He pointed a quavering finger at Lepke. "That man had an 'in' there, and he knows it. And I know it, because he told me. And if I had fifty cops around me, I would still have been killed with rifle shots from two blocks away." He was on his feet, firing an imaginary rifle—and he seemed to be aiming squarely at Lepke's head. The gang king's face remained a blank mask, but Mendy drew back, and growled unintelligibly.

That reply, naturally, was forbidden the jury. Rubin was permitted to say only that he lied through fear. Later, Attorney Talley persisted in returning to Rubin's allegations concerning the Brooklyn prosecutor's office in 1936. Each time, the attorney tossed in gratuitous slurs at Rubin. Once he described him as "a polluted source"; again, as "a cowardly killer," which, of course, lacked something in accuracy. Judge Taylor called Talley finally.

"Do you expect this witness, after what he has gone through, to be without emotion and be insulted . . ." He got no further.

"He is a fakir and an actor," Talley interrupted the court. As a former judge himself, he certainly knew better.

Rubin boiled over. He leaped to his feet, his blood-red face rage-swollen. He stabbed a shaking finger at Talley.

"You are a front," he cried. "You are getting paid because you're a great big front . . . because you were a judge, and not for what you can do." You couldn't have shut him up with a gag of concrete. "I'm fifty-two years old," he went on. "Until I met that man, Lepke, I never did anything wrong. And only to do him a favor, I got into trouble. I never was a murderer. You filthy swine, to call me such names. I'm not involved in this thing. I came here voluntarily."

This time, the jury had heard. The courtroom gasped. Before the expected motion for a mistrial could be made, however, Judge Taylor leveled a sharply accusing glance squarely on Talley. "The unwarranted insult was for the purpose of causing this outbreak," he charged. "The whole thing is disgraceful, and a discredit upon the one who caused it." The trial went on.

Up to that point, the combined stories of Lepke's former lieutenants, graphic as they were, could not convict. Sholem and Berger, as wheelman and finger, would have to be corroborated. Rubin was not an accomplice, but he could tell none of the assassination details beyond the moment when Lepke's smooth calm forsook him and he threatened to "take care of" Rosen. Capone had not been linked as production director of the contract, aside from Sholem's unsubstantiated story. Mendy's role as triggerman, pictured by Sholem, was not corroborated. And Lepke, the biggest of the big shots—the only thing on him was that he was angry and asked Berger to point out Joe Rosen to Mendy. It would take a whole lot more to change their seats at the defendants' table for the squat oaken chair in the death house.

As crime bosses go, Lepke was up with the best. "A directional genius at lawlessness," one court had candidly characterized him. Even after his rackets had caught up with him, no one in or out of law enforcement (including the man himself) believed any one of the seventy or more murders he perpetrated or contracted would ever snap back on him. That was part of his genius—that remarkable talent at covering himself.

But Lepke, like the best of them, made one mistake. And he apparently never realized he'd made it!

That was the drama of the situation for me as we sprang it now —that suspenseful expectancy when the clerk called "Allie Tannenbaum," and the hotelkeeper's son who looked more like a mousy musician than a triggerman, ambled to the stand.

Counsel did not suspect what was coming. That had been evident when Berger, several days earlier, referred to a meeting with Mendy after our investigation started. Mendy had said, "It looks like Allie is talking, and I'll have to duck." Counsel had objected vehemently to any reference to Allie's activities in the spring of 1940, three and a half years after the murder, since he had not been shown to have any connection with or knowledge of the killing. Even the court was mystified.

"How do you connect Allie with that?" the judge asked.

"We will unfold it," I promised, volunteering no other information except, "We will have Allie here in court."

"Let it stand then," the judge allowed, still not completely convinced. "I could not recall where Allie had been shown to have any knowledge of the Rosen murder."

Aside from that brief reference, and a casual allusion to Allie by Rubin, the tall torpedo had not entered the case up to the moment he was called to testify. And he was the only man in the world through whom the Law could cash in on Lepke's lone mistake in murder!

Allie proceeded to tell how, as Lepke's "specific assignment" man, he reported only to the boss. His orders did not come directly from Lepke. That was to be expected. "Judge Louis" was far too shifty to leave himself open through a hired trigger.

"They come from Gurrah or Mendy," Allie explained. "Lep told me do what they say."

Allie, though, made his reports to Lepke, personally, at Lepke's private office on lower Fifth Avenue, in the suite of the Raleigh Manufacturing Company. This was a Baltimore Clothing Firm to which Lepke became "attached" during his invasion of the industry. Allie got to know the place well, and as time went along, he dropped in frequently, even without a report to make, just to kill an hour or two.

Now, in the late summer of 1936, he was vacationing in the Catskills when Mendy sent an order to "hit" Irv Ashkenaz, the Lithuanian-American taxicab operator who was to tell of the cab racket in New York.

"I did the shooting in that one," Allie testified.

It was incumbent upon Allie to make his usual report on a mission accomplished. Several days later, he was back in the city and on the way to Lepke's office.

Q—Merely to fix the time, have you heard of the death of one Joe Rosen?

A—Yes, sir.

Q—On the Friday before his death, where were you?

A—That was the day I went up to the office to report to Lepke.

Allie had handled the contract neatly, he thought. Lepke would be pleased. Lepke, he mused, was a good boss—never got steamed up over anything. That is why Allie was so startled when he walked into the private office that day. This wasn't the same Lepke at all.

Q—Who was there?
A—Lepke was there. He was with Max Rubin.
Q—Did you observe Lepke's face, his demeanor?

Everyone in the courtroom got it then. Rubin had said that Friday was when Lepke blew up for the first time that he could remember; had hit the ceiling over Joe Rosen's persistent threats to "go downtown to see Dewey about Lepke." Objections came like hail from the defense table—and were promptly melted by the court.

"Lepke's face was flushed; he was angry," vowed Allie. That was what had startled him so—seeing Lepke angry.

Q—Was that a usual occurrence—Lepke with his face flushed?
A—No, sir.
Q—What was Lepke doing, when his face was flushed?
A—He was yelling at Max. (More objections; more motions to strike out the testimony. And more denials by the court.)
Q—Does Lepke usually talk in undertones?
A—Not undertones . . . soft.

And, with frequent and desperate defense interruptions, Allie corroborated Rubin's every word:

"Lepke was yelling that he gave this Joe Rosen money to go away, and then he sneaks back into a candy store, after he tells him to stay away. Lepke was hollering. He says, 'There is one son of a bitch that will never go down to talk to Dewey about me.' Max was trying to calm him down. He was saying, 'Take it easy; take it easy, Louis. I'll handle Joe Rosen; he's all right.' "

Q—What did Lepke say to that?
A—He says, "You told me that before." He says, "This is the end of it. I'm fed up with that son of a bitch," he says, "and I'll take care of him."

And Allie substantiated how Rubin begged Lepke to let him get the truck union officials to "straighten Rosen out." Then Rubin left, and Allie reported on his "special assignment."

Q—What did Lepke say about your report?
A—He says, "All right; that's good; go ahead," meaning I should go.

Allie did not know Joe Rosen from John Doe. What had Allie so agog was this display by Lepke—this blow-up by the boss who never exploded. Two nights after seeing Lepke fly off the handle, for the only time in all the years he worked for the self-contained executive of crime, Allie picked up the bulldog edition of the morning paper and read that a fellow named Joe Rosen was "hit" in his candy store in Brownsville. The name clicked. Lepke had said he was going to "take care of" a Joe Rosen.

Q—Did you think the Rosen Lepke mentioned was the same one?
A—It occurred to me it might be.

"The papers said Dewey was looking for this Rosen," added Allie. That had clinched the connection in his mind.

Between engagements, Allie dropped into Lepke's office the day after reading of the slaying. He was just sitting there, doing nothing, when Mendy entered. The meaty murderer strode right up to the desk, behind which Lepke was ensconced. He didn't even notice Allie in the corner.

Q—What was said?
A—Lepke says, "Was everything all right?"
Q—Did Mendy reply?
A—He says, "Everything is okay. Only," he says, "that son of a bitch Pep." He says, "I give him strict orders not to do any shooting, but after I shoot Rosen, and he is laying there on the floor, Pep starts shooting him."
Q—Did Lepke say anything to that?
A—Lepke says, "All right; what's the difference?" He says, "As long as everybody is clean and you got away all right." And he pats Mendy on the back.

For perhaps half a dozen seconds, you could have heard a beetle blink its eyes in that courtroom. Allie, corroborating Rubin on Lepke, corroborating Sholem on Mendy—and not even remotely involved or connected with the Rosen job himself—had all but unlocked the door to the death house for his long-time business associates. Then an excited buzz breezed through the silence, as the realization dawned that in Allie's testimony, too, was a simple explanation for a point that had nettled investigators ever since the murder was done.

It had been deduced that the four slugs buried in the floor directly beneath Joe Rosen's body could mean only that one of the pistols was fired after the victim was already down. But such sadism, such sheer viciousness just didn't happen. It made sense now. Reles and the rest had conclusively established that killing people was sheer voodooism to Pittsburgh Phil. Now Allie had authenticated it. Even after Mendy specifically directed, "Let me do the shooting," and had blasted the candy-store keeper with the entire magazine of his pistol, Pittsburgh Phil had to get into the act. Deliberately, he had pumped four shots into—and through—the body *after* Joe Rosen's lifeless form had hit the floor. Only the ecstatic executioner, the bloodthirsty thug . . . only Pittsburgh Phil would be lustful enough for that.

But more than anything else, Allie had pointed up, like an Empire State Building in a row of Neissen huts, that even Lepke —even the cool, calculating king—could make one mistake. Almost never did Lepke himself give out a contract directly to the gunmen of the mob. That is why he told Allie to take his orders from Gurrah and Mendy. Only on the rarest occasions did he mention a job where more than one person could hear him, and then only when, perhaps, a Reles and an Anastasia, or two such trusted workmen, were simultaneously present. Always he had thought out these murder patterns with reasoned controlled cunning. And through some fifteen years the Law had not even been able to indict him for a single slaying.

What's more, neither the toughest mobster of the early days nor the sharpest investigators ever could get enough of a rise out of Lepke to make him raise his voice. Then, along had come a little man in a little candy store in Brownsville, who kept saying, "I'm going down and see Dewey." The chances are Joe Rosen had no intention of informing. Very likely, he repeated his defiance only because he knew Lepke would get to hear it, and that, since Lepke had put him in his desperate economic plight, the ganglord would take care of him—financially. He pressed that, "I'm going down and talk on Lepke," until it got to be the relentless dripping of a faucet, and after a while, the dripping was a waterfall. And finally, Lepke blew up. For the only time in his reign as czar of the rackets, he spoke out of turn.

He had been so enraged that the little man in the little candy store would dare defy him—him, the mighty Lepke, with his connections and his torpedoes—that afterward he did not even recall Allie in the room at the time. Did not recall it, in fact, until this moment, when mild abstracted Allie spilled it on the stand. If his rage hadn't blinded him into forgetfulness, Allie, for having overheard, undoubtedly would have joined Joe Rosen—and not too much later.

"The witness," I nodded to the defense, "is offered for cross-examination."

That was about the last thing the defense wanted just then. There still remained nearly an hour until the usual adjournment time, but counsel earnestly requested an overnight delay before starting cross-examination. So that "we can get our notes together," was the plea.

Allie had been an earthquake. He had made a two-seater out of the electric chair, so that Mendy, the kingpin's chief lieutenant, could stay right with his chief all the way.

(Allie faded from sight not long afterward, and for a decade, no one heard of him. In 1950, some of the boys bumped into him in Florida, where he was visiting. It seems Allie has completely rehabilitated himself and is now peddling lampshades in Georgia.)

Capone's counsel was unperturbed. As far as Allie's testimony was concerned, Louis could just as well have put on his hat and coat and walked right out of the courtroom. About the only thing with which the thug with the restaurateur's front could be charged, in 2,400 pages of testimony up to then, was that he did not associate with the right people.

Berger had related how Mendy stopped for moment to talk to Capone on a street corner. You could guess it was to have Capone begin preparation on the Rosen job. But guesses are not proof. Without corroboration, Sholem's story of Capone drilling him on the getaway route and of picking up the killers after the getaway car was dumped, did not carry the weight of the paper it was printed on in the record. We had, however, no intention of slighting Louis.

Actually, Louis had made the same mistake as Lepke. And, like the boss, he did not remember a thing about it! Unlike Lepke, however, he had not been enraged or irked or upset. He was having a quiet conversation in his parlor, three and a half years after Joe Rosen was shot down—and he had put his foot in it. We had been saving Blue Jaw Magoon to show exactly how. The same Blue Jaw who, a year previously, had been such a stunner to his best friend, Buggsy, and Pittsburgh Phil.

Blue Jaw started out on how well he knew Louis Capone. Well enough, he said . . . "I was to his wedding and parties at his house."

Q—In April, 1939, did Capone speak to you in reference to a man named Friedman?
A—Yes.
Q—Were you told to do something with reference to this man?
A—Yes.

Of course, I could not bring out that what Louis wanted Blue Jaw to do "with reference to" Whitey Friedman was to help Pittsburgh Phil shoot Whitey dead, right on the street. After receiving his orders, Blue Jaw had gone out to look over the lay-out. He did not like what he saw, he testified now, and a few days after the first conversation, he paid Capone a return visit.

Q—Where did you go?
A—I went over to his house. We were in the parlor.
Q—What did you say?
A—I asked Capone if it was advisable for me to work on the Friedman thing, because I hung out only about a block

away, right off Sutter Avenue there, and I might be recognized.

Q—Did Capone answer you?

Even before all of the question was out, the storm broke. Virtually the entire battery of defense attorneys were on their feet, making motions. Counsel were not disturbed so much over Blue Jaw's anxiety at being recognized on "the Friedman thing," as over Capone's reply about that anxiety.

We had realized early that getting Capone's damning words on the record would present some complications. Here he was, having a talk in his parlor with Blue Jaw about a murder that had nothing to do with the one at hand. And during that conversation, he had tossed in a remark putting himself precisely in the center of the Rosen slaying. He had, however, said it in such a way that, by itself, his admission made no sense. It had to be heard in its entirety, with the allusion to the killing of Whitey. That was the rub.

When a man is on trial for one crime, any reference to another he may have committed is usually a walking-on-eggs process, loaded with mistrial potentialities. A trial may be blown right out of existence by such a reference. There are a few exceptions. An independent crime may be established, for instance, if, in so doing, it proves "spoliation" or destruction of evidence. Thus, Berger's disclosures of how Lepke's torpedoes "hit" Rubin was admissible. Rubin's testimony was evidence; killing him would definitely have "spoliated" it. A jury may accept spoliation as implied admission by a defendant of his guilt of the charge for which he is being tried.

There is another equally well-settled—although less-used—rule. The layman knows it by the familiar expression (particularly overworked in mystery fiction of all shapes and sizes), "Anything you say may be used against you." In legal parlance, any declaration "against interest" by a defendant may be introduced against him, no matter how he said it or to whom. However, where the admission "against interest" is coupled with that of another crime, the court puts up a red flag, and compels separation of the two—if possible. Otherwise, where there is a paucity of evidence, a jury might say, "Well, he was guilty of another crime; so we'll convict him of this one." If, however, the admissions are so inextricably linked that severance would render the pertinent one meaningless, then it is just too bad for the defendant. In that case, the whole conversation goes in. For, the rule holds that *anything* you say may be used against you.

In this case now, the defense definitely did not want application of this simple rule, apropos as it was. The row that was stirred up was the hottest of the trial over a point of testimony. To thresh it out, Judge Taylor dismissed not only the jury, but the witness, too, from the courtroom. The defense was going to make every effort for a mistrial, or, at least, to get something on the record which could be raised as reversible error on appeal. To admit into evidence Capone's statement, counsel contended, was improperly charging another crime to Capone, thereby violating every safeguard surrounding a defendant. The trial must be thrown out, they claimed, if the jury heard a word of it. When it was all over, though, Blue Jaw was permitted to pick up from where he had left off and carry on. The question was repeated:

Q—Did Capone answer (concerning Blue Jaw's hesitation about working on the Friedman job near Sutter Avenue for fear he might be recognized)?
A—Capone says, "What are you worried about?" I said, "I'm not worried, Louie; I'm just asking for advice." And Capone says, "Why, I worked on the Rosen thing, and it was right on Sutter Avenue, and I wasn't recognized."

It was obvious at once that this was every bit the shocker Allie had been earlier. Capone himself maintained the mute poker face he had worn through the trial. His attorney, however, made no secret of the devastating effect.

"I, of course, had no knowledge until this man took the stand . . ." he began, somewhat shocked. Then: "This witness and his testimony are an absolute surprise to me."

He pleaded for early adjournment so that he might interview Capone before cross-examining Blue Jaw—"in order to bring before the jury whatever defense there may be," he explained.

Capone, though, had no answers. So surprised was counsel, in fact, that he spent considerable time in cross-examining Blue Jaw about a single car theft thirteen years before, although the tough hoodlum already had admitted stealing fifty automobiles . . . "fifty or better," he had said.

Capone had completely forgotten that snatch of conversation, three years after the Rosen murder and more than two years before this trial. That single sentence—"I worked on the Rosen thing"—had come back to haunt him. Magoon, involved in any number and degree of crimes—but connected in no way with the wanton shooting of Joe Rosen—was corroboration of all Berger and Sholem had said about Capone.

It just about completed the State's case. Rubin, Berger and Sholem had laid the foundation and built the walls; Allie and Blue Jaw had put the roof on. Now the defense could try to knock it apart.

Lepke, the pilot, led off for the "team." He did not take the stand. He offered no alibi. But he brought in seven witnesses to speak for him, and the gist of what they said was:

Why should the great Lepke have been annoyed by a little truck driver like Joe Rosen? And as far as his own temperamental blowup was concerned . . . nonsense! Neither Rubin nor Allie, who testified to it, were in his office that Friday.

Of all people in the world, Lepke produced as a witness one of Joe Rosen's partners in the New York & New Jersey Truck Company. Nat Sobler was a small, quick-tempered individual, and he was there to show how bad the company's business was in 1932, when Lepke was accused of ruining it. I was already acquainted with Mr. S., however. About two months before the trial, it had come to our attention that he had been seen with a relative of Lepke. We had Sobler into the D. A.'s office for a chat, which had been transcribed to paper. We asked him to read it and sign it under oath. Sobler said he didn't have his glasses with him. He asked if he could borrow a pair from a detective. What an easy out that would have been, if the affidavit ever snapped back at him. We had sent him home with it—and a detective. He read it with his own bifocals and signed.

Sobler was confronted with the affidavit on cross-examination now, and he changed his mind about several things he had testified to on direct. He admitted the affidavit's declaration that "there was a good living" for Rosen and his trucking partners from their firm. And he conceded that after the work stoppage of 1932, the cream of the company's lucrative accounts were taken away and went to Garfield Express, in which Lepke had become a partner. Early in cross-examination, I referred him to a most unusual alliance of which at least one member of his family might boast.

Q—Your brother-in-law was in business with Dutch Schultz, wasn't he?
A—He might have been.

Somewhat later, this same association was alluded to again:
"Did you not see your brother-in-law and Dutch Schultz about this matter of the work stoppage?"
The effect on the balding old trucker was startling. "You insult me," he shouted. He put up his right hand like a traffic policeman. "I'm going to get off this stand," he proclaimed. And get off he did. Witness Sobler was going to walk out.
He took several determined steps. Then a husky bailiff, towering over him, gently nudged him back to the stand. Sobler mumbled and grumbled, and he kept popping up and down like a yo-yo.
"Who do you think you are, telling me that?" he was working himself into an explosion. "Are you bringing me in with gangsters? You have no business to call me Dutch Schultz. The hell with this. I'm getting out of here!"
For the second time, he undertook to walk out. This time, to avoid the attendant, he tried to climb over the side rail of the witness box. It was the histrionical high of the trial. Not even Max Rubin's emotional best topped this.
To throw the lie to the testimony concerning Lepke's enraged outburst, the defense summoned Carl Shapiro. His appearance was a complete surprise to us. He was a brother of Gurrah, Lepke's loud partner, and he was treasurer of the Raleigh Manufacturing Company, in whose quarters Lepke had his private office. Ironically enough, Raleigh had the distinction of being the largest non-

union clothing plant in the East . . . and with two such staunch advocates of labor organization as Lepke and Gurrah so close, too!

"Neither of them [Allie or Rubin] was in that office that day or any other day," maintained Shapiro, in his testimony. And besides, Lepke just did not yell. "I don't believe I ever heard Mr. Buchalter raise his voice," he went on. "He had very little to say at all times."

Although he alternated between Raleigh's Baltimore and New York establishments, Gurrah's brother knew "absolutely" that he had been in the New York plant that entire day. The reason for his certainty lay in a batch of the company's checks of that date. He had signed every one of them, and they were definitely checks of the New York office, because the Baltimore office used a different color. Under cross-examination, though, it developed there was nothing at all to stop him from (a) having New York checks with him in Baltimore, signing them there and mailing them to New York, or (b) signing postdated or blank checks on any day.

That disposed of Lepke's defense; abruptly it seemed. It had been well "advertised" that Gurrah had been brought up from the Atlanta Penitentiary, where he was spending time for racketeering, and that he would be a surprise witness to pull his old partner, Lepke, out of a very tough spot. But the heavy-handed hoodlum was never called.

Gurrah did, however, get a message through to Lepke. It referred all the way back to 1935, when Gurrah sided with Dutch Schultz against the entire board of governors of the Syndicate, and voted for the assassination of Thomas E. Dewey. The message, excluding its sulphurous preliminary, was brief.

"I told you so," it said.

Mendy's defense was next, and since he had been put at the scene of the crime, a smoking pistol in hand, he brought an alibi with him in the form of his brother, Sidney. It was well tinged with family devotion and ties that bind.

On Saturday night, September 12, 1936, Mendy's brother testified, Mendy could not possibly have cased Joe Rosen's candy store in Brownsville, as Sholem had said. The reason, said Mendy's brother, was because it was a very special night. It was the eve of Sidney's twenty-sixth birthday, and Mendy had arranged a party.

There were the two brothers, their mother, Mendy's wife and her girl friend, Dottie. They all drove uptown, had dinner, went to the theater, had a late snack, and generally made a large night of it. Mendy drove his brother and his mother home, and then headed for his own place with his wife and her girl friend. It was about 4 A.M.

It was such a pretty picture. It was practically a shame to put the light on it under cross-examination. It was almost as if, 'way back there the night before the murder, Mendy had already set up his alibi, making sure to include an "outsider"—Mrs. Mendy's girl friend, Dottie—so all the support would not come from his family. It was recalled, too, that the murder originally had been scheduled for that night—the night of the birthday party—until Pittsburgh Phil's hesitancy about being "made" caused an overnight postponement to the following morning. Nor was that all.

Q—Of all the birthdays in your life, this twenty-sixth birthday was the only one you celebrated?
A—That is right.

That seemed to take care of Mendy's alibi. Dottie told much the same story. Although married, she had been along unescorted. Hubby, it seems, was just then doing a bit for picking pockets.

Cross-examination of Mendy's brother brought out any number of other interesting points. While Mendy was hiding out in Kansas City, for example, his brother had made three trips there—but only after first telephoning Ben Portman, who is not altogether unknown in certain circles in the Missouri metropolis, such as gambling. The trips, the witness wanted it understood, had nothing to do with the purchase of narcotics. Then, in August of 1941, after Mendy was nabbed there, Sidney telephoned Kansas City one night to ask Walter Rainey, a character of some influence in gambling and politics thereabout, how things were going.

"Didn't Rainey say to you, 'You guys got us into a helluva lot of trouble; everything here is red hot?' " I asked Sidney. He just couldn't recollect the conversation. He undoubtedly suspected by this time, though, that someone had been listening in.

In the ten years since the trial, incidentally, Walter Rainey has grown no less influential in Missouri gambling—or political—

affairs, particularly in Jackson County, in which Kansas City is located. He is credited today with being able to swing a large number of votes through the county, a factor which would not be likely to detract from the benevolence that County Sheriff Purdome seems to feel toward him. In fact, it has been pointed out that when Rainey's gambling enterprises ran into trouble in Kansas City in the late forties, he merely shifted his base of operations to the portion of Jackson County outside of the city. This move, naturally, took him from the jurisdiction of the annoying city police and placed him under the wing of the benevolent sheriff. It is said, incidentally, that the benevolent sheriff's office has been cozy enough with slot-machine distributors so that the distributors have even presented small gifts, like money, to some of the deputies.

With Mendy's defense completed, it was Capone's turn. Before the trial, it had been announced that Louis would claim he was living the life of a gentleman farmer with his family up on the tomato farm at Milton, N. Y., when Rosen was shot down. Blue Jaw had buried that alibi before it saw the light of day when he testified that this bucolic retreat had been one of the mob's handiest hideouts. Anastasia, Dandy Jack Parisi and various others had holed up on it from time to time when they were hot.

In spite of Blue Jaw, courtroom "experts" had felt that Capone stood a good chance, if he would take the stand in his own defense and gamble on getting through cross-examination with a whole skin. We expected he would. Our case was not nearly as powerful against him as against the others. But now, suddenly and dramatically, Capone's counsel rested without offering a word of defense, not even his own! Sitting there and watching defense witnesses falter, one after another, evidently had decided Louis against trying it himself. Capone, it is feared, was no gambler.

The defense attorneys took three days to sum up. Lepke's counsel sounded the keynote for all with the usual cry of "frame-up." There was neither rhyme nor reason, he added, for a big-shot racketeer—a role he conceded for Lepke—to have killed a little "peanut" like Joe Rosen. All counsel, however, skirted the chief point emphasized through the weeks, which was that Joe Rosen had been shot ten times and this vicious threesome was squareley in the middle of it, on the testimony. The state's summation had to bear down on that.

"Here we have the boss who has been described by his own lawyer as the czar of the industrial rackets," I pointed to Lepke. He never batted an eye. "Here we have the man behind the scene, the lieutenant who planned and directed the murder." Capone remained straight-faced. "And here, the triggerman who fired the actual shot." Mendy, already slouched, tried to hunch down even lower.

In the early morning hours of that same day, detectives picked up a dapper little man on a street corner. He was Johnny Torrio, the one-time boss of Chicago—the genius of gangdom honored by the underworld for giving the embattled moblords of the early thirties the idea for syndication. And in the courtroom at that moment, on trial for his life, was one of the very top magnates who had adapted and perfected that "gimmick" in a coast-to-coast cartel.

The coincidence was so marked that Johnny's appearance quickly gave credence to reports that some of Chicago's picked torpedoes had joined the rest of the imported gunmen in town. With the case going so badly against Lepke, the whisper ran, those carefully chosen killers were planning one final all-out pitch at liberation. The half a hundred local and federal officers in the guard were speedily reinforced and alerted—a warning they hardly needed.

It was a large comedown for Torrio, that arrest. Only two weeks out of Leavenworth, where he had paid for evading income taxes, he was booked as a common vagrant. He had less than fifty dollars on him. Johnny said that didn't mean a thing. He was in real estate, he explained, and he owned property in Honolulu, Florida, Maryland and Brooklyn. Nevertheless, he was put away overnight to "cool off," and then was told to get out of town— but fast. (Johnny's interest in real estate has continued, incidentally. As recently as 1950, there was a disclosure of one remarkable transaction between himself and Sheriff Hugh Culbreath of Hillsborough County [Tampa], Florida.)

Charging the jury, Judge Taylor finally and completely crushed the customary defense argument concerning the character of our witnesses.

"When rogues fall out, it is a wise man's delight," he stated. In ten words, he thus put what I had spent a half-hour trying to explain in summation.

At 10:15 P.M., on Saturday night, November 30, 1941, the fate of the commander, his lieutenant and his gunman was placed in the hands of the twelve men. They would decide whether this trio with nation-wide crime connections had murdered a little man in a little candy store in Brownsville. To reach this hour, fifty-two witnesses had appeared. They had given some 4,000 pages of testimony. The trial had started in September's Indian summer, had struggled through the entire fall and was in the overcoated days of early winter now.

By midnight, a quick verdict seemed doubtful. By 2:30 in the morning, Judge Taylor was debating whether to lock the jurors up for the night. As he was about to give the order, the word came, "They are ready." The jury had been out four hours and a half. Late as it was, the crowd of spectators practically bulged the walls when the twelve men filed back in. Charles E. Stevens, the envelope company sales manager who was the foreman, rose.

"We find the defendants, and each of them, guilty of murder in the first degree, as charged," he announced slowly.

The foreman might have been a hot-dog peddler, hawking his wares at a ball game, for all the emotional reaction on Lepke's controlled features. But a thin dew of perspiration oozed out and glistened at the edge of his thinning hair, and he mopped it away very slowly, with a dirty handkerchief.

Word of the conviction quickly penetrated the courtroom's closed doors. There was a scream from the corridor. "It's Lepke's wife," someone whispered. For a moment, I was reminded of a letter she had written to him in Leavenworth six months before.

"I was in a restaurant last night and I saw Turkus and Judge Leibowitz," she had penned. "The latter nodded to me, but didn't speak. The former is a typical jerk. It is only a pity that innocent men have to fall into the hands of a man like that. *He* [the underline was hers] should be behind bars—not the men whom he knows are innocent of the crimes they are convicted of."

The letter, like any dangerous criminals' mail, had been screened before it was handed to him in his cell. I had remembered having dinner with Sam Leibowitz in a midtown restaurant, but I could not remember him nodding to any particular female. Of course, I didn't know the lady then, and Sam has a large acquaintance. When he dines out, he is nodding almost as often as he is chewing.

On Monday morning, the three prisoners were back in the courtroom for the last time, to hear their doom. There was no secret about it. The penalty, by law, had to be death.

Lepke walked steadily to the bench, but he put his hands on the guard rail, as if to brace himself. The raised bar of justice dwarfed the rackets king. Judge Taylor fastened a stern glance on "Judge Louis," and began:

"Louis Buchalter, alias Lepke, for the murder of Joseph Rosen, whereof he is convicted, is hereby sentenced to the punishment of death." Each word came to life and stabbed at the prisoner. "Within ten days from this date, subject to any legal impediments, the Sheriff of Kings County shall deliver the said Louis Buchalter to the Warden of Sing Sing Prison, where he shall be kept in solitary confinement until the week beginning with Sunday, January 4, 1942, and upon some day within the week so appointed, the Warden of Sing Sing Prison shall do execution upon him, the said Louis Buchalter, alias Lepke, in the mode and manner prescribed by Law."

Only the whiteness of Lepke's knuckles, as he gripped the rail, showed that he had heard—and understood. His doom was one month away.

Mendy came next, red-faced, his gargoyle leer gone. His arms remained folded across his chest as the judge passed sentence. Capone's jaw jutted defiantly through the same grim pronouncement—the words which, unless higher courts changed them, meant the keeper of the pasticceria would do no more "fronting" for Anastasia.

To consign all three to the chair took just nine minutes. Everything after the first three minutes—after Lepke's doom had been confirmed—was anticlimactic, however. His was the first death sentence ever imposed on a top-level executive of the national Syndicate. They had heard prison terms invoked before . . . for rackets operations, for tax evasion, for one thing or another. But, never before Lepke—back to the founding of the cartel—had a ruler of crime been condemned to pay with his life for one of the countless murders by which they had welded their criminal empire together.

It was a day I should remember. It was my thirty-eighth birthday.

14.

The man who might have been president

The federal government's peculiar anxiety about a killer—Lepke's death house song of politicians—the 1944 presidential election might have been different—king of the rackets gets the chair—the Kefauver Committee misses a point, or six—the Ambassador and his underworld chums.

"Subject to any legal impediments," the court had stipulated, Lepke was to be taken to Sing Sing within ten days and locked up in the death house. Judge Taylor was, of course, thinking of possible complications over Lepke's status as a federal prisoner. But calling them just plain "legal impediments" turned out, in the light of what happened, to be the understatement of the year.

No such conditions stood in the way as far as Mendy and Capone were concerned. In forty-eight hours, they were headed for the forbidding pile inside the thick armed walls at Ossining, thirty-five miles upriver.

Even before the gangster trio was sentenced, speculation already was buzzing over the disposition of Lepke, because of the prior fourteen-year federal term for narcotics standing against him. There was, however, precedent and procedure which we felt definitely applied to getting his transfer to state jurisdiction. This went back to 1922, when America's most infamous mail robber, Gerald Chapman, was sentenced to twenty-five years for America's most notorious mail robbery—the historic $2,400,000 Leonard Street holdup in New York.

Placed in Atlanta Federal Penitentiary, the million-dollar bandit escaped, was recaptured, escaped again. More than a year later, Policeman Jim Skelly was killed during a robbery in New Britain, Conn. The crime pointed directly to the fugitive. In January, 1925, he was nabbed at Muncie, Ind. Connecticut convicted him and sentenced him to death.

Desperately, Chapman raised intricate points of law. He contended that the government had had no right to turn him over to the state. To iron this out, President Coolidge commuted his twenty-five-year sentence to the time already served, thus relinquishing federal claims. Chapman countered with the argument that a commutation was really a pardon, and a prisoner constitutionally does not have to accept a pardon. He carried the case to the Supreme Court.

"A pardon," the high tribunal ruled, in effect, "is a gift, and any gift, of course, may be declined. A commutation, on the other hand, is not a gift but the withdrawal of restraining powers and claims. Therefore, Chapman must accept it."

On April 26, 1926—thirteen months after he was sentenced—Connecticut hanged Gerald Chapman, mail robber and holdup-killer.

That was the parallel we felt would govern Lepke's case. There was added basic support, too, in a decision by President Taft when he was Chief Justice. He held that the penitentiary is no "sanctuary" and may not be used as "immunity from capital law." Before anything could be done, though, all hands had to wait until the State Court of Appeals ruled on the convictions of Lepke and his two henchmen. In New York, it is mandatory for the highest appeals court to review every conviction carrying the death sentence. The only time on record it was omitted was in the case of one Leon Czolgosz, in 1901, and on that occasion, no one cared a bit. Czolgosz was the anarchist who assassinated President McKinley.

It was ten months before the Appeals Court decided. Then it upheld the conviction of all three.

"Guilt was clearly established," said the majority opinion.

It was now up to the federal government to turn Lepke over for execution, and thus save the taxpayers his room and board. What followed was probably the longest and certainly the most bizarre and needless controversy ever waged between national and state authorities over one man. Before it wound up, it involved government officials right up to the President. It stands as a monumental example of the guarantees of individual rights in American justice. But the developments were so weird they left any number of observers with the distinct impression that persons in very high places were most meticulous about keeping this underworld king, with seventy murders on his tally sheet, from the electric chair he so justly deserved. In fact, in the course of the interjurisdictional strife, President Roosevelt was charged with "protecting" Lepke. And the *New York Times* alleged: "Knowledge Lepke has of an old murder involving labor leaders said to be close to the present national administration . . . is said to be one of the factors [in] the long involved negotiations."

The extent of this drawn-out tangle is perhaps best depicted by a straight chronological account, from the time the State Court of Appeals upheld the conviction on October 30, 1942:

Nov. 9, 1942—Brooklyn District Attorney's office wrote Pardon Division of Dept. of Justice, requesting a "conditional" federal pardon for Lepke.

Jan. 1, 1943—U. S. Supreme Court affirmed Lepke's conviction.

Jan. 8, 1943—Dept. of Justice insisted Lepke case was "not a proper case" for pardon. (Here, after waiting two months to reply, was the first of the government's remarkable contentions—which were so appreciated by Lepke.)

June 1, 1943—U. S. Supreme Court, by unanimous decision, again upheld the conviction. The second appeal was based on what Lepke said was the "poisoned atmosphere" at the time of the trial.

July 8, 1943—District Attorney's office made personal appeal to Attorney General Francis Biddle for release of Lepke to the state.

July 10, 1943—Justice Dept. officials refused to advise Lepke's release for resentencing and execution.

July 17, 1943—Justice Dept. said it would produce Lepke for resentencing, which added immensely to the absurdity.

July 20, 1943—Lepke, Mendy and Capone resentenced to death; date set for week of Sept. 13.

Sept. 2, 1943—Gov. Dewey demanded that President Roosevelt pardon Lepke to permit his execution; new execution date set for Oct. 18.

Oct. 7, 1943—District Attorney's office again appealed to Attorney General Biddle. (No answer was ever received to request of July 8.)

Oct. 14, 1943—New execution date set for Nov. 29. Gov. Dewey cited President Roosevelt's failure to release Lepke; declared he will not order the execution of the lesser Mendy and Capone, while the boss remains alive.

Oct. 18, 1943—Federal District Attorney (for New York) suggested to Brooklyn District Attorney that governor hold clemency hearing, and that if governor refused clemency, federal government would turn Lepke over. State pointed out a clemency hearing was incongruous without custody of the prisoner. Besides, no announcement is ever made when clemency is refused; governor simply remains silent, and the execution takes place.

Oct. 20, 1943—Attorney General's office, in letter to District Attorney, referred to "the understanding"; District Attorney pointed out there had been no "understanding" —that the New York Federal Attorney had merely made a "suggestion," and it had been rejected.

Nov. 20, 1943—Gov. Dewey charged Lepke "was protected from punishment by failure of the President of the United States to grant the customary unconditional pardon." Execution date set back for fourth time—to Jan. 3, 1944.

Nov. 30, 1943—Attorney General Biddle refused to make a formal request to President Roosevelt for commutation of Lepke's sentence. (Second anniversary of Lepke's conviction.)

Jan. 1, 1944—Governor Dewey postponed execution date to Feb. 6.

Jan. 17, 1944—Attorney General Biddle offered a compromise: state would be given "full authority" over Lepke for a clemency hearing; if clemency is refused, government would then pardon Lepke so the state could execute him. Said the newspapers: "The federal administration offered the concession because the case is too hot to handle in a presidential election year."

Lepke, who had spent the entire time in the Federal House of Detention in New York, was moved at last to Sing Sing. The transfer was made in a bulletproof sedan, with the rackets czar handcuffed to Corrections Officer John McAvoy, and so surrounded by guns that the car looked like an army tank on rubber tires. He was placed in the house-at-the-foot-of-the-hill—which so few ever leave alive.

Up to then, Lepke had been sitting tight while the federal government did his fighting for him. The unexpected change of attitude, in the election year, was followed by a burst of activity. In Kings County Court, where the death sentence had been imposed more than two years before, he asked for a new trial, claiming the judge had been "prejudicial." The timing was excellent, for Judge Taylor was in Florida on vacation. The judge heard of it, flew back . . . and denied the new trial. Claim after claim was made by the long-condemned trio. Mendy produced the best one.

"I have never even met Lepke," he insisted, with a straight face.

On February 3, the governor held the clemency hearing. The desperate threesome asked for a special commission to investigate the facts. This, mind you, after their conviction had twice been upheld in the United States Supreme Court!

The executioner was ordered to report for work on March 2. Almost without exception, Sing Sing holds its executions at eleven o'clock on Thursday nights. That would make March 2—Thursday of the week of February 28—the date on which Lepke and his aides would pay up for murder.

Lepke's attorney, still trying desperately to stay his doom, sought a habeas corpus writ, claiming the ganglord's transfer by the government to the state was illegal. It was the old cry of Gerald Chapman, the mail robber. Federal District Court refused the writ. On March 2, the Circuit Court of Appeals affirmed the refusal.

Only hours were left. The condemned killers were shaved,

bathed and dressed in the conventional white socks, carpet slippers, and the black trousers with the slit in one leg—so the electrode can be laid on bare skin.

They were placed in the pre-execution cell, a mere twenty-five feet from the chair itself. Here, the last mile begins—the mile that is twenty-five feet long. It is so laid out and partitioned, this pre-execution chamber, that the prisoners cannot see each other, but can talk back and forth. The underworld calls it the Dance Hall. They were given the traditional choice of menu for their last day on earth. Lepke put in an order for steak, french-fried potatoes, salad and pie for lunch; roast chicken, shoestring potatoes, salad for dinner. "I'll take the same," echoed Mendy, and Capone repeated. Even at the door to the next world, they were still following the boss.

But Lepke never lost his confidence. "Something can happen yet," he called out to his partners in the Dance Hall. "I can feel it."

At 9:40—an hour and twenty minutes before he would walk that twenty-five-foot mile—Lepke's wife said her last goodbyes. She drove all the way back to New York with her grief—and when she got there, she read in the newspapers that Lepke's "something" had happened! The governor had directed a forty-eight-hour stay of execution. His announced reason was that the Supreme Court had granted a last-ditch review of the habeas corpus proceeding, but could not squeeze it into the court calendar until Saturday. Later, other factors, which seemed considerably more pertinent, came to light.

Warden William E. Snyder designated Rev. Bernard Martin, one of Sing Sing's chaplains, to carry word of the last-hour reprieve to the pre-execution cell. Mendy just kept saying, "Fine, fine, fine," over and over. Capone could do no more than gurgle. Lepke was neither surprised nor excited. "He seemed to be sure that this was going to happen," Father Martin related.

Saturday—the last day of the stay—came. The Dance Hall became so crowded that visitors were shuttled in and out in relays. Once more, the trio ordered their final meals. Mendy seemed to have been infected by a bit of his boss' confidence. He grinned a thick-lipped grin at the guard and said, "Well, at least we get good eats again."

Even in the early afternoon, when the radio blared out that the Supreme Court had denied the final appeal, Lepke still acted as if he expected a last-minute miracle. Only late that evening, with the final minutes of his life ticking away, did he slowly begin to realize that maybe he had relied on the wrong miracle-maker.

From the Executive Mansion in Albany, a telephone line was held open through the night to the Warden's office in Sing Sing. At 10:55 P.M., the Warden made a last check. "No change," was the word. Society was done with Lepke Buchalter.

For the first time in twenty-seven years, Sing Sing was to have a Saturday night execution. The thirty-six newsmen and the other witnesses filled the four rows of benches off to one side of the chair. Thomas Kelley, principal keeper of the penitentiary, made up his mind on the order of "appearance," based on the mental condition of the three men as they faced the final seconds. Newsmen, waiting through the dragging hours, had drawn a "pool" on the order he would choose. Capone would lead off, Keeper Kelley designated. Louis had a heart condition; the strain might break him at the end.

At 11:02, big and solid, the murdering restaurateur strode into the harsh light. He said nothing. He just sat down and died. At 11:05, it was all over for Albert Anastasia's hand-picked representative with the murder troop. His body had barely been wheeled out when Mendy, bull-shouldered and working on a wad of chewing gum, entered. So, Lepke was to be the boss to the end, the one least likely to crack. Already seated in the chair, Mendy turned to Warden Snyder.

"Can I say something?" he asked. The Warden nodded. Attendants, already moving forward, stepped back. "All I want to say is I'm innocent." It had been Mendy's refrain since the day he was sentenced. "I'm here on a framed-up case. Give my love to my family and everything."

Three minutes after he entered, Mendy was gone. That wound up what is often cited as the longest occupancy in the history of Sing Sing's death house, although official records are not kept on this matter. Mendy and Capone had been in the house-at-the-foot-of-the-hill exactly two years and three months—while the fight for Lepke went on.

The collie-dog softness was no longer in Lepke's eyes as he strode into the harsh chamber that reminded one newsman of a chapel. The witnesses' benches are the pews, this correspondent had written; the chair, the pulpit; the wheeled stretcher behind it, an altar table. Lepke's eyes were hard as the muzzles of the pistols his assassins had used so often at his bidding. Hard—as if he had been expecting something and it had not materialized. His step was brisk, almost defiant, like a man with something unpleasant that has to be done. He walked across the chamber and almost threw himself into the squat seat.

For two years and three months he had stood this moment off. Had stood it off so successfully, in fact, that many were willing to bet it would never happen. But now, there was Lepke in the chair. His strange steel-bright eyes swept to the right, to the newspapermen and witnesses. He seemed to pick out one or two he recognized.

The attendants tightened the eight restraining belts, fastened the electrodes—made sure the one electrode was attached to his bare bony leg through the slit in his trousers. As the head electrode was lowered into place, Lepke's eyes glanced up at it. That was the last thing he saw.

Warden Snyder dropped his hand. Unseen, Joseph Francel, the official executioner, pulled the switch. There was a whir of motors. Twenty-two hundred volts slammed into Lepke's body. The impact hurled his 165 pounds against the straps. The whirring stopped. The attendants bared his chest, matted with hair. Dr. Charles Sweet, the prison physician, applied the stethoscope.

"I pronounce this man legally dead," he intoned. The body was loaded onto the hospital stretcher and rolled into the autopsy room.

"You look at the face . . . you cannot tear your eyes away," wrote Frank Coniff in the *New York Journal American* the next day. Frank is more accustomed to the noise and the pleasures of Manhattan's plush night spots. "Sweat beads his forehead," he wrote. "Saliva drools from the corner of his lips. The face is discolored. It is not a pretty sight."

A kingpin of national crime was gone, a czar of the rackets. The Syndicate that rules the underworld and has connections in the highest political places had lost its first major figure to the Law.

Ironically, for all his power and his killings, it was the murder of a little man that caught up with Lepke, and ended him. Justice proved she plays no favorites; she works for the man who pulls the strings as well as the one who pulls the trigger. Before then, no executive of organized crime ever sat in the chair. Since Lepke, there has been no other.

Not much news was sensational enough to take an eight-column headline away from the biggest war in history in the early forties. But Lepke could. The revelations and chain-exposures of the soft-eyed ganglord's fabulous empire and his equally fantastic skill at staying out of the electric chair for so long flooded the courts and the news from 1940, when he was locked up in Leavenworth, to 1944, when he was carried out of Sing Sing in a wooden box.

There were, through those four years, persistent recurring reports of information Lepke had, involving men in high places. They popped up continually, these reports, and they stated variously that Lepke had "talked" to save his life, that he had offered to talk to save his life and that he had talked—but not enough to save his life. From people in and out of law enforcement, emanated fact and rumor and a combination of both, which contended that if Lepke did open up, he would "blow the roof off the country"; that among other things, he could "deliver":

A nationally prominent labor leader on a murder charge.

A noted public official of New York City on a conspiracy charge.

A close relative of a very high public officeholder as a "front" for at least two of the ganglords who are credited with controlling crime in the United States.

"If I would talk," Lepke himself said, "a lot of big people would get hurt. When I say big, I mean big. The names would surprise you."

He finally did talk some, near the end; that is certain. Manhattan's District Attorney Frank S. Hogan spent an hour and a half with Lepke in the death cell—at Lepke's request—two days before he was executed. More than seven years have passed, but the prosecutor has never disclosed what they spoke about. Two newspapers insisted that Lepke also forwarded a statement to

Governor Dewey, on which the governor has never commented.

Lepke did release his version to the press in a dramatic gesture on the very day he died. During that afternoon, word came from the prison warning newsmen to gather in Ossining's Depot Square Hotel, half a mile from Sing Sing, or they would miss a good story. They had no sooner crowded into the combination bar and eating place than Lepke's wife, wearing dark glasses, appeared, her Persian lamb over her shoulders. From her purse, she brought a sheet of lined yellow paper covered with penciled writing.

"My husband just dictated this statement in his death cell," she said. "I wrote it down, word for word."

She began to read from the creased sheet, slowly, enunciating each syllable so the reporters could get every word Lepke had spoken:

"I am anxious to have it clearly understood that I did not offer to talk and give information in exchange for any promise of commutation of my death sentence. I did not ask for that!" (The exclamation point was Lepke's.)

There was more. And it concluded:

"The one and only thing I have asked for is to have a commission appointed to examine the facts. If that examination does not show that I am not guilty, I am willing to go to the chair, regardless of what information I have given or can give."

Thus, Lepke himself publicly stated that he had talked some, and he would talk some more—if he stayed alive. He had not, he clearly declared, "asked for" any promise for "information I *have given*"; whatever he had spilled had no strings attached. It sounded very much as if he had provided data he felt would titillate the appetite of the governor into keeping him alive to hear more.

By releasing the statement through his wife, Lepke also was, I am convinced, giving an unmistakable signal to the mob. He was broadcasting to his Syndicate associates that he had not and would not talk of them or of the national cartel. About politicians and political connections and the like—yes; the crime magnates would seek no reprisal for that. But not about the top bosses of crime. It was pure and simple life insurance. No member of his family would be safe if the crime chiefs believed he had opened up on the organization itself.

Of all the matters that Lepke could or did talk about, none had such far-flung significance as the murder of Guido Ferrari. As a matter of fact, to this day, nationally prominent names are linked to it.

Guido Ferrari was associated with his brother, John, as contracting tailors on children's coats, with a shop on Carroll Street near Fourth Avenue, in Brooklyn, which is virtually next door to where Joey Adonis' automobile agency used to be.

The accepted version is that Ferrari was slain as the result of a row over unionization. From what we were able to learn during our investigation, however, Guido's assassination was actually accidental. The slayers really were after his brother when they shot Guido down in the driveway of his home on July 31, 1931. Nevertheless, the murder was tied up with clothing labor strife, with Lepke and Lucky—and with the end of Mafia!

Although it happened two decades ago, the Ferrari murder has stubbornly reared its head down the years.

At the time, the hoodlums were neck-deep in the war for power in Amalgamated Clothing Workers between the factions of Sidney Hillman and Philip Orlofsky. As previously detailed, the bitter feud ultimately found Lepke's trigger company and the mob of Salvatore Marrizano, or Maranzano, as rival enforcement squads in the war.

One summer day, some of Marrizano's sluggers threw rocks at the window of a clothing district shop in Manhattan. By coincidence, John Ferrari was in the place. He led a contingent outside and gave determined battle to the rock-throwers. Gurrah went gunning for revenge on the Hillman faction hoods, and shot an Amalgamated business agent in the leg. Marrizano was ordered to get even for this affront. Since John Ferrari had been so active in touching off the series of unpleasantness, Marrizano directed his men to take care of Ferrari. Only, they "hit" Guido by mistake.

This was the incident, actually, which set off the Purge of Mafia. It was on this killing that Lepke convinced Lucky that Marrizano was, in reality, making war on Unione in an effort to win back Mafia's faded power.

The murder of Guido, the wrong Ferrari, was enjoying a particularly publicized revival in the early forties, especially in 1941, when William O'Dwyer and the incumbent Fiorello LaGuardia were locked in a dirty mud-throwing duel for the New York mayoralty.

"He [LaGuardia]," proclaimed O'Dwyer at one point, "knows that when Amen [then conducting a special investigation of corruption] gets through with the Ferrari murder case, I will step in. He knows that Sidney Hillman was in that case. He [LaGuardia] was a lawyer. Vincent Sweeney was a detective. The first thing LaGuardia did when he became mayor was to appoint Sweeney a magistrate."

As far as O'Dwyer's threat to "step in" went, nothing ever happened—a failing he has, which several people have recognized, and of which the Kefauver Senate Committee took special cognizance. But, after O'Dwyer tossed in the names of LaGuardia and Hillman, the affair Ferrari was repeatedly, and even more emphatically, referred to whenever the possibility arose that Lepke was singing.

Things reached a head on March 2, 1944—the Thursday Lepke was to have been executed. That morning, the *New York Daily News,* in a copyright story, asserted that Lepke had sent a signed statement to Governor Dewey, which charged "one New York political faction with seeking, through him, to fasten high crime upon another and better entrenched faction." Referring to a "visitor from Brooklyn" who went to see Lepke in Leavenworth in 1940, the *News* said the crux of the visit was:

"If Lepke would make a statement to the visitor which would involve three men, all highly placed in public life, in the murder of a contractor in New York in 1931, the visitor would see that the Rosen murder indictment was quashed."

The governor would not comment. But on that same Thursday, late in the afternoon, District Attorney Hogan in Manhattan received a phone call from Warden William Snyder at Sing Sing. Come at once, he was informed; Lepke wanted to talk to him. Lepke had been convicted in Brooklyn, and here he was calling for the Manhattan prosecutor, a situation the newspapers were careful to point out. We, in fact, heard not a word of this development until it was over.

District Attorney Hogan rushed to Sing Sing with two assistants

—Sol Gelb and Joseph A. Sarafite. The prosecutor was ushered into Lepke's cell, and he stayed with the rackets boss for ninety minutes. As soon as he returned to New York that evening, Hogan communicated with Governor Dewey, for whom, incidentally, he had been an outstanding assistant when the governor was prosecutor. And at 9:50 P.M., Dewey suddenly ordered a forty-eight-hour stay of execution.

The reprieve came several hours after Lepke's counsel had advised the chief executive that the Supreme Court had agreed to hear his final appeal. It was, however, only an hour or so after Hogan had informed Dewey of details of his visit to Lepke's cell. Evidently, it was more than mere coincidence that Lepke had maintained, throughout that Thursday, his remarkable confidence that "something can happen," in the face of hopelessness expressed by just about everyone around him.

Speculation was a roaring fire. Lepke had reportedly made a statement to the governor; Hogan had interviewed Lepke; Hogan had contacted the governor; the governor had ordered a two-day reprieve immediately afterward. The stay gave Dewey forty-eight hours to ponder whatever information Lepke had provided. The rackets czar knew how to play his cards to get the most out of a hand. His persuasiveness in convincing Lucky Luciano to do his fighting for him, when he was reaching out to grab the clothing industry, was ample demonstration of that.

This was March of 1944; Dewey already was a candidate for the Presidency of the United States. Obviously, then, Lepke's information must have had, at least in his own conviction, a powerful and significant relationship to Dewey's aspirations. The facts and the deductions all pointed unerringly in one direction:

Lepke's talk consisted of an offer he was convinced Dewey could not resist—an offer of information on politics which he felt was so national a sensation that, if publicly disclosed during a close presidential campaign, could put Dewey in the White House!

Naturally, the metropolitan New York newspapers printed sensational story after story during the two days the reprieve lasted. Some were speculative; many were flat statements offered as fact (see Appendix 2). Not until Lepke died, however, did the import strike home. Then the *New York Mirror* reported:

"It is said Lepke offered material to Governor Dewey that would make him an unbeatable presidential candidate."

Whether Lepke's revelations would have altered the course of history will, of course, never be known. However, to aspire to the Presidency and be handed information of such national implication that it might swing the tide was undoubtedly as great a temptation as a man ever had. Few, if any, ever were offered it; or, if offered, rejected it. To the credit of Dewey, he did resist and he did reject. He would not do business with Lepke, even with the greatest prize on earth at stake—the Presidency of the United States!

It is ironical that when Lepke finally wanted to talk, no one would listen; but once, when he could have had listeners, Lepke would not talk. Not on their "terms," anyway.

Those earlier negotiations began while he was still in Leavenworth. On October 22, 1940, O'Dwyer and Captain Frank Bals left on a six-day trip to Kansas City. Twice they covered the thirty-five miles from Kansas City to Leavenworth to visit Lepke and try to get him to open up. Harry Feeney, the *World-Telegram's* reporter, who was close to O'Dwyer then, wrote that Brooklyn officials "offered to suspend prosecution if Lepke gave information involving persons of importance." When Lepke was transferred to Brooklyn to face murder charges, O'Dwyer told Feeney that negotiations were reopened. Whatever the "terms," Lepke spurned O'Dwyer's proposition.

Since neither the governor nor the Manhattan District Attorney have publicly spoken (see Appendix 3), and since Lepke clearly wanted no part of me at his conference with Hogan, a verbatim report of what he said may never appear. But this much is certain: when Dewey permitted the cow-eyed kingpin of the underworld to go to his death in that presidential election year, a goodly number of persons in places high and low breathed easier. And the Guido Ferrari murder remained exactly where it was—loaded with reports of politico-gangland goings-on, with implications hot enough to influence a presidential election.

As this is written, the final report of the Senate Crime Investigating Committee under the chairmanship of Senator Kefauver has recently been presented to the United States Senate. Its 195 pages are well sprinkled with error, and in its references to Murder, Inc., the misconceptions fall like rain.

Consider a choice example:

"None of the top six (of Murder, Inc.) were prosecuted" (p. 126).

Lepke? The report kisses him lightly off as "a narcotics king and killer." Lepke—the topmost czar of labor-industry racketeering the underworld ever saw, in a dozen businesses in many states, a ranking director of national organized crime; Lepke just a dope-and-gun man? No one can slight "Judge Louis" like that. As a matter of fact, the record establishes that in his entire career of two decades, Lepke tried narcotics-importing exactly once—and that time he was caught. And nowhere was there any evidence that he, personally, ever pulled a trigger.

Of the end of Lepke's narcotics venture, the Committee's report states:

"He received prison sentences totaling 12 years. This blow shook the Buchalter empire" (p. 167).

Aside from the fact that the prison sentences were for fourteen years, the following indicates his shaken empire:

He was collecting extortions running into thousands annually, more than four years after being convicted for narcotics.

When he went on trial for murder, almost two years later, his shaken "empire" was firm enough to come up with a quarter of a million dollars to pay for his defense.

After he was sentenced to death, his empire was still functioning to such an extent that he was able to stay out of the chair for two years and three months more—and that was almost five years after his narcotics conviction.

I have no doubt the Senators tried to do a thorough job on their probe. By pointing up much that has been forgotten, although long since revealed, the investigation shocked the public into a new consciousness of the politico-crime danger. However, no purported investigation of organized crime in the United States should have so casual a misconception of the national cartel. For, in the transcripts of Lepke's murder trial and the others we prosecuted are references galore that hold good in the organized underworld today, both personnel and rackets—from Frank Costello to Lucky Luciano, from gambling in Florida to murder in California and industrial racketeering in New York. As a matter of fact, up to now, the very blueprint of Murder, Inc., has been regarded as required reading by every investigator of organized crime since. Even a casual look would surely have avoided such inaccuracies as the following from the Committee report:

> (Concerning the start of the Murder, Inc., investigation):
> "The [District Attorney's] office had managed to indict a number of young gangsters for stealing cars which were later used in the commission of murders. . . . One of these gangters was Abe Reles, who was induced to turn State's evidence" (p. 125).
> (Concerning the results of the investigation):
> "Between 1940 and 1942 . . . neither he [the District Attorney] nor his appointees took any effective action against the top echelon of the . . . murder rackets" (p. 144).

It would take a great deal of research to find two paragraphs more completely erroneous. The facts are: the probe of Murder, Inc., most definitely did not start with indictments for stealing cars; it started with indictments for murder in the first degree in the killing of Red Alpert. It did not start with "young gangsters" being indicted; it started with Reles and his pals, Buggsy, and Dukey Maffetore, and Reles and Buggsy were veterans of some fifteen years in killing and extortion. By no conception of the imagination was Reles "induced to turn State's evidence"; he made up his mind all by himself in his jail cell. If any "inducing" was done, in fact, Reles had to do it. He had to "induce" a prosecutor to let him sing, and break open, for all to see, the very criminal organization which the Kefauver Committee discovered only after a year of investigating a decade later.

The Senators' personal allegations against O'Dwyer, who was the District Attorney then and the U. S. Ambassador to Mexico now, are between them and him. That argument is not mine. As for the contention that no appointee in that office "took any effective action" against the top murder mobsters—not even members of the most exclusive debating society in the world could possibly find support for so utterly false a claim. The record shows that. I was an appointee in that office—a strictly nonpolitical appointee, but, nevertheless, an appointee. I prosecuted seven killers of the national Syndicate who had done perhaps two hundred murders across the country, and every one of the seven paid the death penalty. An eighth, who committed eight more murders, will never see the outside again. A ninth, with perhaps twenty slayings to his credit, is doing life in New Jersey on information I supplied.

To convict Lepke, czar of the rackets—especially the murder racket—took eleven weeks in a trial court against the pick of New York's criminal lawyers. And Lepke sat in the electric chair. Evidently no one of the large staff the Committee employed pointed out to the Senators, J. Edgar Hoover's statement that Lepke was "the most dangerous criminal in the United States," or the fact that federal and state governments had a $50,000 price on his head. That puts any racketeer in the "top echelon"!

The Committee's investigation, remember, was made in the name of the United States Senate. As such, the report automatically bears the stamp of authenticity of the federal legislature. Local law enforcement and crime-fighting agencies undoubtedly use a paper from the United States Senate as a guidebook. A misconception that is unfortunately harmful.

From courtroom testimony and sworn statements we obtained a decade ago from gangsters who were on the inside—and who were giving information voluntarily and freely—the evidence clearly showed the modern underworld organization in this country to be one huge Syndicate, one single powerful Syndicate of many gangs. The Committee report, on the other hand, pins the classification of "syndicate" on almost any local mob at all, as loosely as Hollywood bestows "glamour." The report mentions a Chicago "syndicate," a New York "syndicate," a New Orleans "syndicate," one each for Cleveland, Miami Beach and Michigan, plus the "Guarantee Finance Syndicate" of Southern California (which, incidentally, the California Crime Study Commission, in its exhaustive and productive probe, was content to call by its operating label of Guarantee Finance Company). Time and again, the report refers to the national setup as "two major crime syndicates" (New York and Chicago) plus any number of "syndicates and gangs throughout the country," all "loosely knit" together through "personal, financial and social relationships." The Committee offers no source as a basis for such a theory. During our probe, it was the mobsters on the inside who insisted that the single national Syndicate is bound by a government of its own, just as tightly as General Motors or the National Baseball League, and that this government has absolute power.

"Outside gangs coming into an area," the Committee report says, "will often use local hoodlums and local gangs."

Under the Syndicate, as the mob informers, who knew, pictured it for us, this is not nearly the friendly gesture the Committee implies. In reality, one ganglord enters another's territory only with his consent and approval. And when such a move is made, the invading mogul must use local thugs, unless specifically permitted otherwise. That has been inviolate mob law since the cartel began.

Actually, in the Committee report itself is unmistakeable evidence to indicate that the "one Syndicate" system is still in operation nationally, just as the "insiders" depicted. This is found in details of the manner in which the thugs from gangs in various cities suddenly show up working together in the same enterprises (see Appendix 4). New York-Detroit-Cleveland get together in running a Florida hotel; Detroit-Cleveland-Chicago operate a gambling spot; New York-Chicago-Kansas City have a numbers business, or narcotics. These are, perforce, Syndicate operations. The coincidence is too strong to be otherwise. Surely, the Committee does not suggest that these hoodlums are hooked up in such enterprises on any basis so pure as a "personal" or "social" relationship.

Such joint intercity mob business has been going on, too, ever since the Syndicate was put together, back about 1934. A great deal of the personnel, in fact, remains the same. In Lepke's trial, in 1941, Sholem testified that Mendy got him a job in 1937, in the Frolics Club, which he identified as a gambling trap just off the causeway in Miami. "I was a spotter—stopping people so they shouldn't cheat," Sholem explained.

Q—Who was running the Frolics Club at that time?
A—Game Boy, Moey Dimples and Tommy Cutty.
Q—Was a man named Lefty Clark connected with it?
A—Yes, sir.

Game Boy is, of course, Sam (Game Boy) Miller, who remains the chief field representative for gambling of the Cleveland mob, in Nevada as well as Florida. In one of his recent enterprises, he has been identified with the Island Club, in the Miami neighborhood. Cutty was a New York operative. Dimples was Lepke's general manager for gambling. And Lefty Clark is otherwise William Bischoff of the Detroit mob. Obviously, Lefty, too, still functions as usual. Recently, he has been connected with the Greenacres Club in Broward County, Fla., along with Joey A., the Lanskys and Mert Wertheimer, the Detroit executive. Lefty also has had business in recent years in the Arrowhead, one of Saratoga's leading palaces of pleasure and chance, in which Adonis, too, has had more than just a passing interest.

The report also details co-operative effort in traps in Las Vegas, Nevada, in New Orleans—even in parts of northern Kentucky—in which the New York, Chicago, Detroit, Cleveland and Kansas City hoodlum crews are represented. It is most surprising, then, that the Committee persists in its organizational picture of many groups, loosely-knit.

The California Crime Study Commission, in its Third Progress Report, went into the source of mobsters in the Far West branch. "They find their origins in Cleveland, Detroit, Chicago, New York and Miami," the California body states. These were, of course, the various regional contributions to the buildup of Buggsy Siegel's staff, when he opened the West for the Syndicate.

Turning to another phase of modern underworld organization, the Senators report:

"There is a sinister criminal organization known as the Mafia operating throughout the country. . . . The Mafia has also been known as The Black Hand and the Unione Siciliano. The membership of the Mafia today is not confined to persons of Sicilian origin. The Mafia is a loose-knit organization. . . . The Mafia is a binder which ties together the two major criminal syndicates, as well as numerous other criminal groups" (p. 2). And "The Mafia is a secret conspiracy" (p. 146).

We have gone fully into the fall of Mafia earlier. Suffice it to say that Mafia and Unione never were synonymous, and that Police Lieutenant Joe Petrosino proved forty years ago that no central Black Hand organization even existed. There never was the day when a non-Sicilian could get into Mafia; Unione is no such stickler concerning the spawning grounds of its thugs. Mafia was a closed corporation, demanding the scratched wrist-to-wrist blood-brother initiation and the dread code of Omerta. In fact, it seems any organization would have to be contortionist, indeed, to fit the Committee's contention that it is both "loose knit" and a "secret conspiracy" at one and the same time.

Perhaps the most pertinent evidence against the existence of Mafia in modern-day crime is found in the Committee's own confession that after an investigation which lasted one year, traveled to fourteen cities from coast to coast, heard more than six hundred witnesses and cost $250,000, it was unable to uncover one single member of Mafia, or anyone, for that matter, who even admitted he knew a member. The report describes Phil D'Andrea, of the Midwest set, as a "notable exception," because he said Mafia "was freely discussed in his home when he was a child." There is nothing unusual in that. In almost any Italian home, in which are old folks from the old country, they are likely to talk of Mafia, much as an American-born parent might bring up the bogeyman or goblins. To older generations of southern Italy and Sicily, Mafia and Neapolitan Camorra were names to whisper.

Finally, on this subject, the Committee noted:

"One notable concrete piece of evidence is a photograph of 23 alleged Mafia leaders from all over the United States, arrested in a Cleveland hotel in 1928" (p. 149).

As "evidence" bearing on the Italian society as constituted in 1951, this is now twenty-three years old. What's more, it occurred three years before Lucky's purge of Mafia.

Almost one-half of the Committee report is devoted to a section entitled "The City Stories," which are the Senators' ideas of the underworld situation in individual communities and areas. We point out certain additional factors here, solely to fill out the picture of organized crime.

Under the thirteen-page subhead, "The West Coast," there is much on Mickey Cohen, the loudmouth gambler. But not once in the section on California is the name of Jack Dragna so much as mentioned.

Here, however, is how the thoroughgoing California Crime Study Commission places the Far Western bosses on the executive level:

"Dragna was, during [Buggsy] Siegel's lifetime, more important than Cohen. . . .

"In spite of Dragna's relative obscurity, he was an important underworld figure when Mickey Cohen was nothing more than a minor prize fighter and petty gambler. . . .

"Although he [Dragna] was and still is successful in avoiding the fanfare of publicity which Cohen seeks and enjoys, his importance was not underestimated by [James] Ragan [operator of the racing wire service], who, shortly before his death, described Dragna as 'the Capone of Los Angeles.'. . .

"During the latter part of 1949, when his [Mickey's] gang was under mysterious attacks, he suffered from the defection of a number of his group who joined forces with the Dragna gang."

Coming eastward, the Committee report devotes half a dozen pages to the situation in Detroit—but does not mention the Purple Mob; and five more pages to Cleveland, with no reference to the Mayfield Road Gang. Both have been franchise holders since the national Syndicate was "incorporated." In the New York section, the report does a lengthy survey of Frank Costello—his business, honest and otherwise, his fortune and his political perambulations. Concerning his rumrunning days, the report states:

"Costello was indicted for bootlegging together with Bill Dwyer, the bootlegger king, and 61 others in December of

1925, but this indictment was dismissed against Costello after many others were tried and convicted" (p. 115).

Simply to keep the record straight on this puffed up bum, we detail the actual history of those incidents: The original indictment was dismissed *before* any others were tried, so that the government could concentrate on Dwyer, who was the top man in alcohol then. A new indictment, however, was returned, naming Frank Costello, his brother Ed and thirty-one others—including thirteen bribed coastguardsmen. Costello *was* tried early in 1927. The jury disagreed, and he walked out. His brother was cleared on a directed verdict by the judge. The case had any number of sensational aftermaths. Costello was never retried. And, in 1933, when someone thought to look for the file on him, it had "disappeared" from the Federal Attorney's office!

The Committee report's picture of Costello, up to his slicked-down hair in New York politics, shocked blasé New Yorkers into a renewed realization of the sinister situation in their city government, which has so frequently been pointed out to them in the past.

As a matter of fact, there has not been a New York political campaign since the early thirties in which the name of Frank C. or one of his close associates wasn't heard almost as often as the candidates'. Fiorello LaGuardia linked him to O'Dwyer in the mayoralty battle of 1941. In 1945, Judge Jonah Goldstein, campaigning against O'Dwyer, shouted to the skies not only of Costello-O'Dwyer connections, but also of Irving Sherman, a comparative man of mystery who is called a "good friend" by both the gang boss and the former mayor. Good enough, in fact, so that, according to sworn testimony, he arranged for a wire-tap expert to protect the phones of both O'Dwyer and Costello. And O'Dwyer admits Sherman "helped" his 1945 mayoralty campaign. Sherman has been flitting about the local scene for years. At the moment, he is a dress manufacturer—and a big bettor. During the war, he was a shirt manufacturer, doing business with the Navy—and a handy man on government contracts, although no one can say if he worked on a five per cent basis in this respect. In 1945, O'Dwyer told a grand jury he wouldn't be surprised to learn that his good friend Sherman had close relationships with Lepke, Cos-

tello and Joey Adonis. Long-distance telephoning from all over
has gone on between O'Dwyer and this choice character for half
a dozen or more years, but notably during the war, when
O'Dwyer's army job had to do with straightening out suspicious
military contract operations.

Half a dozen years ago, the fact was exposed that Costello
"entertained" O'Dwyer and assorted Tammany politicians with
a cozy cocktail party at his apartment in 1942. Costello was reported as a $25,000 cash contributor to a candidate seeking
"high office" in New York in 1941, as the newspapers put it. In
fact, it is safe to say there is not an election district captain in the
metropolis who is ignorant of Costello's pitch at politics—and that
goes for any political party.

If anything, Joey Adonis has ranked even more powerful than
Costello—and in spite of a temporary setback in the mid-thirties.
Mr. A. has been revealed as contributing $25,000 to LaGuardia's
mayoralty campaign in 1933. Four years later, with LaGuardia
again a candidate, Adonis switched horses. LaGuardia, who hadn't
said a word against him in 1933, took the stump in 1937 to label
Joey A. "a gangster and the leader of the underworld."

The influence of Costello and his henchmen is hardly confined
to the local level. These mob moguls fully appreciate the value of
national as well as state and city "contacts." As far back as 1937,
a wonderful gathering at the 1932 Democratic National Convention in Chicago was thoroughly publicized. At that conclave, the
New York delegation was split, with Jimmy Hines, the top Tammany boss, leading the faction committed to Franklin D. Roosevelt, and Albert Marinelli, then a rising challenge to Hines,
pledged to Alfred E. Smith. Jimmy Hines' roommate in a suite in
the Drake Hotel was none other than Frank Costello. And Marinelli shared quarters with Lucky Luciano! The boys evidently
were intent on being on the right side, no matter which side was
"right."

Nor are allegations concerning O'Dwyer's performance—or lack
of it—as District Attorney and mayor brand new. Some have been
far more blunt than the Committee's declaration that rackets boys
seem to benefit no matter whether O'Dwyer's "motivation is
action or inaction." There was an exhaustive grand jury probe of

O'Dwyer as far back as 1945 that flatly charged his administration with "negligence, incompetence and flagrant irresponsibility." Yet, in 1950, the United States Senate confirmed O'Dwyer as Ambassador to Mexico *after* these charges were pointedly called to its attention!

In recent investigations, an incongruity has developed in the seemingly popular pastime of "playing down" Joey Adonis as a sort of court jester for Costello. Senator Kefauver's *Saturday Evening Post* article of April 28, 1951, was entitled "I Meet the KING of the Underworld," with reference to Costello. As we have sought to emphasize continually, no single person wears the purple toga of gangland. This is a Syndicate in every sense of the word, with directors doing the directing. Costello does not outrank Luciano or Adonis or the Fischettis or anyone else on the board of governors. Not even in his political influence can Frank C. boast alone. Long before "the Prime Minister" was consorting with politicians and public officials, Joey A. had contacts that caused the underworld to adopt the reverent tone hoodlums always employ whenever they mention "Mr. A."

No one can find fault with any investigative group for linking up gangsters and politicians at any time for the public to look at. The practice of exposing these "betrothals" should become periodic. A horrible deed like the Scottoriggio murder, for example, should never be overlooked. This is the one politico-gang crime on which New Yorkers would have appreciated some light, more than on any other felony in the books. And New Yorkers still wonder why not a single question dealing with it was brought up at the Kefauver Committee's New York hearings, which developed into a television circus. Although no more revolting evidence of the modern-day hookup of crime and politics could possibly be found, it is not mentioned in the Committee's report by so much as a syllable.

It was in 1946, as mentioned earlier, that Joseph Scottoriggio, an honest Republican election captain, who had worked against former Congressman Vito Marcantonio, was beaten to death on a street corner on election morning, as he left his home for the polls in East Harlem. Trigger Mike Coppola and Joey Rao were held as material witnesses in that slaying, as a result of a mysterious meeting in Trigger Mike's flat the night before. Joey Rao's position both in mobdom and politics in New York has been taken up previously. Trigger Mike is regarded even more highly— once was considered first lieutenant to Luciano, himself. In the late thirties, it was reported that when Lucky took the lush artichoke racket from Vito Terranova, who was known at the "Artichoke King" during Joe the Boss's heyday, he gave it to Trigger Mike to handle. Certainly, with both Trigger Mike and Rao assumedly available, the Committee should not have been at all reticent about summoning one or both for some pointed questions on this shameful slaying that reeks of politics-mob tie-up.

A subtle touch that must have been appreciated all the way from Missouri to Washington is found in the section of the Committee report dealing with Kansas City, which includes a subsection on "Crime and Politics." There is frequent reference to the murdered mobster, Charley Binaggio. But the only time the report even concedes the existence of the notorious Pendergast Machine, which sat at the throat of the state for so long, is thus:

> At the time of the Democratic primary for Governor in 1948, Binaggio had gained considerable influence at the expense of the Pendergast element which opposed [Forrest] Smith in the primary (p. 40).

Thus, for having opposed the gangster Binaggio in this particular case, the Pendergast "element" or machine or mob, or what have you, may be inferred, from the report, as violently against gangsters and mobism. The fact that it took a position opposite to Binaggio in a single instance is hardly a purifier.

Occasionally, in the 195 pages of the report, an item appears that is entirely puzzling. Such a one is:

> "When criminal gangs and syndicates . . . peddle narcotics . . . they are guilty of violating state laws, and it is upon state and local prosecuting agencies, police and courts that the major responsibility for the detection and punishment of offenders rests" (p. 5).

(The Federal Bureau of Narcotics will no doubt be surprised to ascertain that it has been fighting against violators of "state laws" all the time.)

Frequently, there appears to be an aura of amazement, a naïveté, if you will, over the "discovery" that mobsters infiltrate legitimate labor unions and industry, and that business concerns hire hoods in labor strife. Time after time, the Committee claims it "has learned" or "has found" the existence of such nefarious goings on—which have been going on, actually, since before World War I, and exposed as such through the years. The prosecution, as recently as 1943, of several Chicago hoodlums who were shaking down the motion pictures through labor, the report states, "marked a milestone" in coping with "union infiltration by gangsters." Yet, more than half a dozen years earlier, the government already had convicted Lepke for his labor-industry extortions which ran high in the millions, and had successfully prosecuted the fish market racketeers who used labor organization to work their shakedowns. Then there were also state prosecutions through 1941 which thoroughly exposed the active presence of organized mob control in the clothing industry, the bakery industry, in furs and trucking and motion-picture theaters and several more—all by union infiltration.

The report continues:

> In some areas of legitimate activities, the Committee has found evidence of the use by gangsters of the same methods of intimidation and violence as are used to secure monopolies in criminal enterprises . . .
>
> In some instances, legitimate businessmen have aided the interests of the underworld by awarding lucrative contracts to gangsters and mobsters in return for help in handling employes, defeating attempts at organization and in breaking strikes. And the Committee has had testimony showing that unions are used in the aid of racketeers and gangsters, particularly on the New York water front (p. 5).
>
> The Committee found leading industrial concerns admittedly co-operating with notorious hoodlums for the purpose of suppressing labor difficulties. . . . Where business uses racketeers, there is a tendency for labor unions to use tactics of violence, and vice versa (p. 172).

Any casual study of mob history, any skimming research of newspaper files would have found that as long ago as World War I, a party named "Dopey Benny" Fein was getting "contracts" from businessmen to break up labor organizations and beat down strikes. When Dopey Benny retired, Li'l Augie Orgen's outfit and Kid Dropper's Mob carried on, and both management and labor employed them. When they were "dethroned," Lepke and Gurrah moved in, and, as early as 1926, were using labor unions to exploit legitimate business. During our investigation, Blue Jaw Magoon swore that painting contractors used him and his partners before 1935 to suppress labor forcibly, in order to keep wages down so they could obtain contracts for painting New York City's schools by submitting low bids.

The decried labor situation on New York's water front goes back even farther. Before Prohibition, a notoriously tough character named Paul Kelly—born Paolo Vaccarelli—commanded a crack crew which included Johnny Torrio. Kelly ran much of the dock district by organizing various harbor and water front labor, beginning with the garbage scow trimmers. And Paul Kelly was a vice-president of the International Longshoremen's Association! Eventually, in the thirties, Joey Adonis and Albert Anastasia moved in.

In fact, all but a small portion of the entire picture which so shocks the Senators now actually was thoroughly exposed in the investigations, both Dewey's and ours, that removed Lepke from the scene ten years ago. Beyond any doubt, the technique by which the insidious "Judge Louis" put together his multimillion-dollar empire is the very same pattern from which current mob activity is cut. Today's national organization is as the boys would say, a dead ringer for it.

15.

The canary sang— but couldn't fly

Reles goes out the window, with guards all around—investigations galore, and facts that never came out—was he pushed or did he fall?—the who and the how of Kid Twist's mysterious end—it could be anything; it looks like murder.

THE morning of the day Allie damned Lepke with his own words, Harry Feeney telephoned me at home, before I left for court. He was all excited.

"Hey, Burt," he blurted out breathlessly, "Reles just went out the window."

Now, anyone who has anything to do with a courtroom—or the underworld—knows what "out the window" means. Ask the police reporter, the lawyer, even some judges, or any hoodlum, "What happened with that rap on Joe Blow?" If the charge was disposed of so that Joe Blow was cleared without trial, the answer, ninety-nine times out of a hundred, will be "out the window."

But Harry was saying it was Reles who went out the window, and I knew Reles was not slated to make any courtroom appearance; at least not for another three days. And then, he would appear as one more in the parade of songbirds singing Lepke, Mendy and Capone to their doom. Besides, Reles was under lock and key in the Half Moon Hotel in Coney Island with three more of the stool-pigeons, all supposedly guarded like the gold pile at Fort Knox.

"No, no . . . you don't get it," Feeney persisted. "Reles really went out the window . . . out of his sixth-floor window at the hotel. He's deader than a mackerel!"

The most important cog in the entire investigation dead! The insider who had broken open the national Syndicate—and was still picking out important pieces—gone! I had the general feeling of being kicked in the stomach, that morning of November 12, 1941. Not that Reles was absolutely vital to convict Lepke and his murdering mates, although extra corroboration never hurts. But without him, how far could the investigation go beyond Lepke? The Kid, after all, was the mainspring. Moreover, here was an indication of how peculiar things had become in the District Attorney's office by then. The key witness plunges to his death right in the middle of the biggest of all Murder, Inc., trials (there could be none bigger, certainly) and the trial prosecutor has to learn of it from an outsider. It was not, by a considerable margin, the only peculiarity which had developed.

Harry had only scant details. The police had reported that some time shortly after 6:45 A.M., Reles had twisted two bedsheets together, tied a length of wire to them, and wrapped the wire around a radiator pipe. He had flipped his homemade rope out—according to the police—had slid down it, and was trying to get into the window of the room below his own when the wire came loose. The Kid crashed forty-two feet to the roof of a kitchen extension of the hotel. And all with a cordon of detectives supposed to be protecting his every move!

Naturally, Reles' demise was a sensation. The songbird who had exposed national crime had been headlined from coast to coast. Now, he had plummeted to his death from the center of a guard that would have made the crown jewels safe in Jesse James' parlor. The hows and the whys of his death dive were a major mystery—and have remained just that to this day, a decade later. In fact, the investigation was reopened by the present District Attorney in the spring of 1951, and, in September, as this was written, it was being taken before a grand jury.

Much of both fact and fiction has been recited through the years concerning the fantastic finish of this fantastic informer. This much is established:

For over a year, Reles, Sholem, Allie and Mikey Syckoff, who was called the "shylock's shylock" by the mob, had been guarded in the Half Moon Hotel, a tall brick hostelry on the Coney Island oceanfront, which has since become an old folks' home. The witnesses and their guards occupied the entire east wing of the sixth floor. Physically, this was designed to be an impregnable fortress. At the entrance, where the main corridor turned off into this ell, a steel door had been erected from wall to wall, sealing off the entire section. Back of the door was a short hall with rooms on each side, ending in a double parlor. The four outside rooms looked out on Twenty-eighth Street; those opposite fronted on a court. The room just back of the steel door, on the outer side, was used by the detectives guarding the entrance at all times. All the rest on both sides of the hall, and back to the double parlor, were bedrooms for witnesses.

Reles occupied the outside room, next to the parlor—third from the guard room. (Considerable eyebrow-raising was occasioned during the Kefauver hearings in 1951, when committee counsel Rudolph Halley, questioning O'Dwyer, declared, "Reles had a room at the end of a corridor, away from the post where the police were stationed." Sworn statements flatly refute this. Allie, on the witness stand at the Lepke trial, testified:

(Q—How close to Reles' room was yours?
(A—A few feet . . . right across the hall.)

On the evening of November 11, 1941 (Tuesday), Reles' wife visited him. The witnesses said she left about eleven o'clock. Before her departure, they had a heated quarrel, details of which no one gathered, except that one policeman reported it was "quite a fight." Allie saw the Kid a few minutes after his wife left. Not long afterward, the informers retired.

At about 6:45 the following morning, the assistant manager of the hotel, Al Litzberg (sometimes Lisberg), heard a thud from the direction of the extension roof. He paid no attention to it. Detective James Boyle, a veteran officer, said he made a check of Reles' room at 6:45—a regular periodic check, he explained —and saw the Kid in bed. Sometime between seven o'clock and 7:10, Detective Victor Robbins looked in on another routine check—according to his testimony. And there was no Reles! Rushing to the open window, Robbins saw, six floors below on the extension, a sprawled body. He got down as fast as he could, and indentified the remains of Kid Twist.

The corpse lay more than twenty feet out from the wall of the building; some reports say twenty-seven feet. Reles was fully clothed. Some investigators disclosed that he had on a gray sweater which, mysteriously, had not been in his wardrobe up to the day before. In his pocket was a cap, which also was something new. Two bedsheets fluttered about the lifeless form.

The entire scene, as described by investigative authorities, created the impression that Reles had slid down his bedsheet rope, which was only long enough to reach to the window below his own, and that the makeshift line had given way. Whether that is what he did or did not do—that, nevertheless, was what appearances indicated.

For more than half an hour, the death was officially reported only as that of "an unidentified man." Then, at a time he estimated to have been 7:46—more than half an hour after the police said they discovered the corpse—William Nicholson, secretary of the Coney Island draft board, happened to look out of his office window and saw a body. He called Litzberg. The hotel's assistant manager was reminded of the thump he had heard earlier. He phoned the police guard on the sixth-floor. Not until almost 8 A.M.—and not until an outsider happened to see the body—was it announced that the cadaver on the roof was Kid Twist.

"He was all right late last night," Mrs. Reles wept when told of it. "What have they done to him?" And then, over and over, "Who did it? who did it?" Up in the Bronx jail, Reles' friend Blue Jaw Magoon, also rejected as fact the impression created by the death scene.

"There must be something in back of it," he insisted. And when he was brought over to testify at the Lepke trial, he told reporters, "I haven't been able to sleep since it happened."

The autopsy report of Dr. Gregory Robillard, the assistant Medical Examiner, was sent to the District Attorney's office. There, it was announced that the report said the Kid had suffered a fractured spine, as the result of a fall. Reles apparently had landed in a sitting position. No other injury was mentioned in the announcement. Dr. Robillard sent Reles' internal organs to Dr. Alex Gettler, the City toxicologist, for laboratory examination. The District Attorney's office, announcing Dr. Gettler's report also, said there was "no trace of poison or drugs."

The death was officially listed as accidental. Investigations galore were started. Charges of neglect of duty were filed against five officers on duty in the suite that morning. The hard-to-believe story was that all of them had fallen asleep at the same time. Police Captain Frank Bals, who headed O'Dwyer's staff of investigators, had set up the guard. He had assigned eighteen men to handle the detail around the clock—presumably six on each shift.

Those are the facts as publicized at the time. I was, perforce, in court, working to put Lepke into the electric chair. And it is elementary physics that the same body cannot be in two places at the same time.

O'Dwyer assigned assistant District Attorney Edward A. Heffernan to investigate. Later that day, Heffernan issued a statement to newspapers, in which the following points were brought out (the capitalized words are ours, merely to emphasize factors which became pertinent to the mystery):

There are FIVE DETECTIVES WORKING IN EIGHT-HOUR SHIFTS keeping a strict supervision over the material witnesses.

After the witnesses go to bed, the doors to the rooms are opened. Reles was sleeping alone in room 623. HIS DOOR WAS OPEN.

The rooms in which these material witnesses are kept are visited at FIFTEEN MINUTE INTERVALS.

Sometime between 7 A.M. and 7:10 A.M. Detective Victor Robbins went to Reles' room. He discovered Reles was missing, although the SLACKS USUALLY WORN BY HIM HUNG ACROSS A CHAIR. Robbins looked out and saw the body of a man on the extension. He rushed downstairs.

It was discovered that two bedsheets were knotted together, one end of which was attached to about four feet of insulated wire, the end of the wire being wound around the piping of the radiator. The wire was brought to the room by the hotel engineer to fix a radio SEVERAL MONTHS AGO.

At the time, the RADIO WAS PLAYING, and Reles probably left it on all night.

It is the belief of the District Attorney's office that Reles tried to swing into the room below, Room 523, RECENTLY VA-CATED, in order to MAKE HIS ESCAPE. The sheets were only long enough for him to REACH THE FLOOR BELOW. We found the window of Room 523 raised about five inches, and the screen pulled from the top. The investigators discovered that both his shoes were scraped, which perhaps occurred when he stood on the window ledge and tried to open the window. He probably made a misstep and his weight (160 pounds) UNWOUND THE WIRE from the radiator, and he fell.

The three other material witnesses were ASLEEP in their rooms at the time.

Twenty-four hours later, Reles was buried. Less than three dozen mourners paid respect to the boss of Brownsville. As the simple pine casket was lowered, a small animal ran across the mound of earth.

"That's a gopher . . . the rat's in the grave," remarked one of the mourners. The widow's screams grew louder—and the services concluded.

The five police officers accused of neglect of duty were given a departmental trial. And O'Dwyer testified in behalf of these men, whose ostensible negligence had cost him the most valuable witness a prosecutor ever got his hands on! All five were sent back to pounding a beat. They were Detectives Boyle, Robbins and John E. Moran; Patrolmen Franceso Tempone and Harvey F. X. McLaughlin. Boyle and Moran have since retired. No charges were preferred against their commander, Captain Bals, or Sergeant Elwood Divvers, Bals' designee as second in command of the guard.

Inextricably wound up in the mystery are questions that remain now, ten years later, if not unanswered, at least unsettled. A natural curiosity exists over why the death was listed as that of "an unidentified man" for more than half an hour. There are sharp differences, too, that popped up before the first day was out . . . popped up, actually, on the witness stand in the courtroom where I had Lepke and his co-killers on trial.

O'Dwyer and Bals had announced—and Heffernan's report had stated—that no officers stayed in the informers' bedrooms at night; that they made spot checks from time to time. The department trial brought out from the guards that they "looked in on each informer at frequent intervals." But Allie, who lived in the suite, swore under cross-examination, on the day Reles died, that it wasn't that way at all.

Q—You were under guard constantly?
A—Yes, sir . . . twenty-four hours a day.
Q—When you went to sleep, where did the guards stay?
A—There is a chair there; they used to sit down.
Q—At the door?
A—No; inside the room.
Q—Did the same thing apply to Reles' room?
A—Yes, sir.

And two weeks before, identical testimony had come from Sholem on the same point:

Q—Who sleeps in the room with you?
A—Nobody but the detectives guarding me.
Q—You and the detectives sleep there?
A—They don't sleep. They guard me . . . they stay up . . . they sit next to me.
Q—They sit next to your bed while you are sleeping; is that it?
A—Yes, sir.

Obviously, some liberty has been and is being taken with the truth here, by someone. Certainly, there is a vast difference between an overnight vigil maintained inside each witness' room, which the witnesses themselves swore was the method employed, and the occasional spot-check system announced by authorities. The two can hardly be confused. And if detectives sat alongside Sholem's bed and Allie's bed, on guard through the night, they surely would have devoted no less attention to Reles, who was the star of the show.

The second clash of facts concerned the number of officers on duty in the suite that morning. The police, O'Dwyer, Bals and Heffernan all announced it was five. Five were given departmental hearings. On the other hand, with Allie under oath in open court, the testimony was:

Q—How many policemen were guarding you at a time?

A—At a time . . . six.

During the Kefauver hearings, O'Dwyer and Bals, who had been in charge of all arrangements, both held to six under oath.

And finally, in Harry Feeney's reporter's notebook, under date of November 12, 1941—a notebook I have only seen since Harry's death late in 1950—is this cryptic memo:

"Six guards and not five, as police say."

To me, this means nothing more than what it says. In those days, Feeney was especially close to O'Dwyer. Later, the ardor of the friendship cooled considerably.

Now, if there *were* only five guards on duty that morning, then why weren't there six? The assigned detail consisted of eighteen men splitting three shifts, which would make six per shift. It is a discrepancy which, as far as I know, has never been publicly pointed out, much less cleared up.

Reopening the investigation in 1951, Chief Assistant District Attorney Edward Silver revealed that he had discovered several remarkable factors. "I was more impressed with what the investigators did not do [in the original investigation] than with what they did," he stated.

In a talk with one of the authors of this book, he disclosed, for instance, that the Medical Examiner's report had mentioned "other injuries" in addition to the fractured spine which alone was announced by the prosecutor's office in 1941.

"What they are," Silver added, "I am not at liberty to say until after the grand jury receives all the evidence."

"One of the most important things that has to be cleared up is the time element," he added, in reply to a question about the listing of the body as "an unidentified man" for over thirty minutes. Another question in his mind—a question, in fact, that has existed in everyone's mind since the Kid became a corpse—concerned the bedsheets, which had ostensibly been used by Reles as a rope.

"I don't know whether they were used to climb out on, or whether they were used as 'props,'" Silver confessed.

During the renewed probe, an allegation was frequently heard that the toxicologist's report had revealed a quantity of alcohol in

Reles' stomach when he died. For ten 'years, the only disclosure had been that there was no poison or drug. If alcohol was found, the question raised, of course, is whether there was enough to have made Reles drunk—and helpless. The Kid was not a drinking man. He would take a drink, certainly. But all the mob said he had an extremely light touch on the bottle at all times. How much would he have had to drink, then, to pass out? There is, besides, the matter of when he did the drinking—and was he alone? His wife was there until eleven o'clock, or later, the night before. Allie saw him after she left. And Allie, like all the rest in the suite, insisted he heard nothing during the night.

Mrs. Reles was questioned at length during the renewed investigation. She had married a year after the Kid hit the extension roof. Various others with an "interest" of one sort or another in Kid Twist were interrogated . . . Tiny (the Blimp) Benson, Reles' 420-pound crap-game shylock; Captain Bals; Police Sergeant Divvers, assistant District Attorney Heffernan, and O'Dwyer himself. The District Attorney also spoke to James J. Moran, a huge man who was chief clerk in the prosecutor's office under O'Dwyer.

There were and there are four theories as to why and how Kid Twist, the most priceless figure in the Law's first exposure of national crime, managed to get himself killed with detectives all around him. They are:

Accident while attempting to escape.

Accident while attempting to play a prank.

Suicide (which is rarely mentioned).

Murder.

There is some fact to support each hypothesis. But only in murder is there more "for" than "against."

The escape idea was the official diagnosis. Reles, however, told me, time after time, there was no place on the face of the earth he could stay alive, except under guard in that fortified hotel ell.

"You don't know those bastards like I do," he declared, shuddering. "Anywhere in the world, they'd find me, if I was on the outside. Anywhere in the world. And they'd knock me off!"

Why, then, would he want to get out? And when did he change

his mind? The newspapers quoted a "tip" dropped by an unidentified someone in the District Attorney's office that Reles had been offered a large sum of money to try it—and Reles loved money. The story was that "powerful West Coast interests" had somehow contrived to slip word in that he could have $50,000 if he fled before the murder trial of Buggsy Siegel and Frank Carbo in California, then only a few weeks off. One newspaper reported: "One official said, 'A well-known West Coast racketeer was sent here a month ago with orders to see that Reles escaped or was killed.' " Supporting this story was the appearance in Brooklyn, along about then of Meyer Lansky, Buggsy's partner in the old Bug & Meyer Mob.

This entire supposition is untenable in its most basic element— which is: just who would trust whom to fulfill his end of the bargain first? Would the dollar-hungry Reles, who trusted no one, be willing to wait for the $50,000 until after he got out of the hotel? Would the mob, already so painfully faced with his treachery in singing, pay him in advance? And above all Reles simply was not fool enough to believe the ganglords would let him live, no matter what they promised. No one could conceivably have "conned" the realistic Kid Twist with any $50,000 bait, much as he adored a dollar bill.

Some tried to attribute the escape motive to reports that, for some inexplicable reason, Reles was in fear of having to testify against Lepke at his trial. I don't believe that. Through the months he talked to me, he never once indicated any such terror. In fact, I got the distinct impression that he was looking forward to this appearance, just so that he could publicly display his past intimacy with the mighty Lepke.

In 1951, one newspaper came up with a brand-new reason for the escape idea. Reles had been custodian of a $75,000 "sinking fund" belonging to himself, Buggsy and Pittsburgh Phil, this story went; so he had set out to flee the hotel, in order to dig this cache up and turn it over to his wife. The reporter delving into this one suddenly recalled a snatch of conversation ten years before, on the train taking Buggsy to Sing Sing with his pal, Pittsburgh Phil. The irrepressible little assassin had moaned because the entire slush fund would fall to Reles—who had put his partners in the chair.

However, as far back as May 15, 1940—two months after he turned state's evidence and half a year before Buggsy's plaintive wail—newspapers already had published the story that Reles had told his wife where he had buried between $50,000 and $75,-000. He even bragged about not having it in a bank.

"The government finds out about banks," he pointed out knowingly. "Then they hit you with that income tax. Look what happened to Al Capone."

So, his Captain Kidd treasure was no deep ten-year secret. Nor was there any reason for him to gamble with his life to spade it up personally. His wife could have recovered it just as well, leaving him in one piece—and protected.

The strongest argument against the escape idea, though, is that this entire effort just did not add up to Kid Twist. The Reles stamp was not there. Here was a veteran murder specialist who had laid out the tricky details of many foolproof assassination plots. Certainly, he was not going to stake his own precious skin on a plan that, even for an amateur, would not have been especially good. Reles was handier with a rope than a gaucho of the pampas or a deckhand on a four-master. He had done the knotwork on strangling contracts; he'd packaged bag jobs. His artistry may not have been quite as classic as that of Pittsburgh Phil in this respect, but there never had been any complaints against the Kid's work, either. Yet, the impression created by the death scene would have you believe that, risking his own neck, Reles, tied a knot which came undone almost as soon as his weight pulled against it. Or that, after all the successful getaways he had blueprinted, he prepared no better for his own flight than that flimsy one-story-long bedsheet rope, which came apart on the first try. Not Reles!

How could the Kid know that the room on the fifth floor, just under his, was empty? It was only recently vacated. And if he had managed to pry open a window and get into that room without arousing anyone, where was he going then? He would have to creep, unseen, down five stories. The lobby of that hotel and the area generally were supposedly crawling with police. Any number of eager-eyed hotel employees would start hollering "cop!" as soon as he hove into view. They couldn't possibly miss him. For more than a year, his picture had decorated the newspapers more often than Miss America's. At that hour—about 7 A.M.—the downstairs of a resort hotel would not be so teeming with humanity that he could have lost himself in a crowd.

But say he made it, somehow, to the street outside. With Kid Twist's background in getaway planning, he would definitely not have started this without some means for taking off as soon as he got out of the hotel. He would have arranged for the getaway car and the wheelman, at least. Likely, the crash car, too. At that particular stage of his informing, though, the only person living in whom he had the slightest faith—in fact, the only one he could trust—was his wife. And the dark-eyed consort of the bad man of Brownsville was hardly the type to be steering on a getaway.

More than anything else was the fact that no one knew better than Reles himself that he was a clay pigeon for the Syndicate's torpedoes anywhere except in back of that steel door on the sixth floor of the Half Moon. The way his eyes would dart this way and that around a courtroom, searching out each spectator present, would convince even the most skeptic that he appreciated full well the mob's talent for digging out fugitives anywhere on earth. There simply was no incentive strong enough to induce him to leave, voluntarily, the only sanctuary in the world open to him.

When the police discovered Reles' body on the extension roof, the first man they summoned was their boss, then-captain Bals. In his ensuing diagnoses, the captain covered the field. In police department records, he is quoted as saying, at first, that "while it doesn't look like suicide to me, if we gave any other opinion, we'd just be guessing." Several months later, in a report to the District Attorney's office, he contended Reles "attempted to escape." And at the Kefauver Committee hearings in 1951, he testified he believed the Kid was trying to get into the fifth floor so that he could come right back upstairs and thumb his nose at the detectives— just a fun-lover's prank. Bals was hammered hard on this, particularly in some horribly distorted attempts at humor by Senator Tobey, whose comic talents evidently do not lie in the spoken word.

Nevertheless, Walter Laurie, a realistic, highly respected first-grade detective, firmly believes to this day that Reles' attempt to play a prank is exactly what happened. Laurie retired from the force a year or so ago. He was on the squad of eighteen forming the hotel guard, but he was not on duty the morning Reles plunged out. The basis for Walter's conviction is twofold: that Reles had been threatening this gag for months, and that his perverted sense of humor was made to order to try it.

"There never was a bum with a crookeder idea of fun," Laurie relates. "All he wanted to do was play practical jokes—at other people's expense."

The Kid would wad up a handful of toilet tissue, soak it under the cold-water tap and fling it into the face of an unwary detective. If a guard sat in a chair near a radiator, Reles would sneak up and tie his shoelace to the pipe so that, on rising, the officer would fall on his face. He gave out the "hotfoot" willy-nilly; he would spoon pepper into the food of anyone who wasn't looking; he would do anything contemptible and nasty—and roar with derision.

Once a detective, on duty for twenty-four hours, went home at midnight, dog-tired. At 4:30 A.M., the telephone roused him. "Detective so-and-so?" Reles announced officiously, giving no name. "We are making a check. Just look out your window and see if the street light is lit, will you?"

Laurie remembered a phone call he received, but did not appreciate. He had set the date for his wedding in 1941, and was given twenty-four hours for a honeymoon. At about 2 A.M.—long after the newlyweds had retired—the phone in their hotel room sounded sharply. Walter was almost afraid to pick up the receiver for fear it was a call to return to duty.

"Detective Laurie?" a lazy voice said.

"Who is this?" Walter was thinking guns-and-knives.

"This is your friend, Kid; I just want to know how you are?"

For many minutes, the caller kept up the conversation. Walter does not like to offend a friend; he couldn't guess who it was. Impatiently, he inquired, time and again, "Kid who?"

"You know." The caller finally relented. "Kid Reles. I just wanted to see how you're enjoying your honeymoon."

That was how the twisted mind of this beetle-browed plug-ugly operated. And the orders to the detectives were not to rile him—to keep him in a pleasant frame of mind so that he would continue supplying information. He milked the opportunity for all he could get out of it.

For a year or so, he had been telling his guards that they did not know their job; that he could escape from right under their noses.

"You guys are tin-badge cops," he sneered repeatedly. "I can get outa this sardine can any time I want."

So, Laurie believes, it was perfectly possible that, on that November morning, Reles set about making good his boast. He would have broken into that fifth-floor room, come back upstairs and taunted the guards with "I told you so's" in his inimitably obnoxious way.

Here again, though, the physical facts are against it, just as they virtually rule out the escape concept. First and foremost are the knot that was tied by an expert and didn't hold and the flimsy contraption he used as a rope. Why, too, would he pull this prank at 6:45 A.M.? Not even Reles would feel particularly humorous at that hour. And finally, the same old question: how could he know that fifth-floor room was empty?

The very few who hold to suicide as the motivating force behind the death dive maintain that illness suddenly snapped the Kid's mind. In spite of his prodigious strength, Reles had a great deal wrong with him. He'd been ulcerous for years. There was more than a slight suspicion that he was suffering a rectal cancer. On top of everything else, he had developed a form of paresis, which, while not particularly noticeable, seemed to give him delusions of respectability.

"I'm gonna get a spot as a warden at some little jail upstate," he confided once to some of the others in the hotel. "I know how to treat prisoners . . . I could reform 'em." Another time, he said, "I'm gonna get me a farm and grow Plymouth Rocks and Leghorns." A creditable ambition—but probably not even his wife could picture the strong-arm murderer of the Syndicate as a bucolic chicken farmer.

The suicide idea, however, is not reasonable at all. To begin with, a madman with a sudden suicide fixation would hardly have stopped to dress before plunging out the window. And he certainly would never have put together that bedsheet rope for a prop first.

Thus, by any and every logical analysis, the facts simply do not add up to escape, prank or suicide. That leaves but one theory— foul play. And when murder is considered, the first question is: "Who?" There were, of course, ample reasons why.

A far greater number of people wanted to see Reles dead than wished for his continued well-being. Indeed, aside from his family and some in the District Attorney's office, perhaps, there were very few cheering for this miserable murderer in any way.

The closest pals he had ever had would have relished nothing more than to see Kid Twist in a coffin. Hadn't Buggsy lamented that his only objection to the electric chair was that he couldn't hold Reles' hand when he sat in it? And Happy had even tried to kill him at the door to the courtroom.

When Pittsburgh Phil offered to sing in May of 1940 and was brought into the District Attorney's office, he mentioned bits about various killings. He must have known they were murders of which Reles already would have told us.

"Let me talk to the Kid," he suggested then. "Put me in with Reles, and more things will come back to me."

He seemed just a bit too anxious. That proposal failing, he made the impossible offer to "open up" if he could "walk out clean," presumably aware that it would never be accepted Eventually, it became obvious he never had any intention of singing a note. All he wanted was a moment alone with Reles. Long months later —just before he sat in the electric chair, in fact—he told an attorney how anxious he had been to get into the same room with his former partner.

"I just wanted to sink my tooth into his jugular vein," the blood-lusting assassin confided. "I didn't worry about the chair, if I could just tear his throat out first."

Nor were the former friends the Kid had shoved toward the death house the only thugs who fervently hoped for ill to befall the swaggering boss of the Corner. The very witnesses he lived with despised him. Only three weeks before the fatal plunge, Sholem's young wife had visited her husband one night. The Kid made an insulting remark. From somewhere, Sholem produced a knife and lunged for him. If the detectives had not been quick, it is unlikely

Kid Twist would even have been available to go out the window. Frequently and fervidly, Sholem expressed the wish that the Kid would die of his ailments.

When the Reles case suddenly heated up again in the spring of 1951, Walter Winchell led off his column (April 3) with several paragraphs concerning an extortion letter sent by "an underworld figure who allegedly was in the room" with Reles. The letter said:

> Why don't you get wise? Do you know what I can do to you? I guess again you are saying you are too smart. Don't kid yourself. They are only waiting for me to break and talk. Like I told you before, I'm standing up and will stand up if you are going to be alright with me. I'm in a tough spot, my wife hasn't got a quarter. I have everything in hock . . . I would have never mixed up with them guys if not for your brother [name deleted by Winchell]. I was obligated, if you know what I mean. . . .
>
> I'm going to give you EXACTLY ONE WEEK to give my wife $200 dollars and five dollars every week. If you don't I'm sorry. I'm going to put you in with me.

There was a P. S.: "tell Mr. Joe B. that goes the same way." Winchell omitted the signature, and ended the item by asking:

"Mr. District Attorney, isn't it true that the writer of the extortion letter slept in the same room with Reles that night? Doesn't that lend weight to the underworld theory that he killed Reles in return for protection for the rest of his life? And isn't all this plausible in view of the underworld talk that many police figures were 'partners' in Murder, Inc.?"

This evidently had to do with one of the sensations that developed while Sholem was under cross-examination in the Lepke trial, although both Sholem and Allie swore Reles slept in a separate room in the Half Moon. Sholem, on the stand, was questioned about writing threatening letters. He admitted sending "four or five from the hotel. The attorney pressed one into his hand:

Q—I ask you if that is in your handwriting?
A—Yes, sir.

It was addressed to Ben Glass. "That is Cherry's brother—Al Glass', my partner's, brother," Sholem explained, and, later:

Q—Does anyone owe you money?
A—I had a partner; he ran away.

Of other associations, he recalled a trip to California on which he was accompanied by one Joe Bernstein. This Joe B., he said, was no relation . . . "he worked for the mob."

Q—Do you remember going out to California to kill anybody?
A—No, sir. Joe Bernstein went alone, about a year after.

He identified as his, photostatic copies of several letters. The texts were not allowed in evidence, however. Under the rules of evidence, a copy is allowable only if the absence of an original can be accounted for as unproducible. The questioning continued.

Q—Look at this letter. You wrote that while you were in custody in the Half Moon?
A—Yes, sir. With a detective beside me. He seen it, sir.

While obviously threats to outsiders, the letters, however, could not be pointed to as indicating that Sholem had anything to do with Reles' going out the window, much as he hated the Kid and undoubtedly enjoyed his finish when it came. Besides Sholem, Allie, whose Brownsville days went back to the Shapiro Brothers, never lost any love for Kid Twist. And certainly, Albert Anastasia, Reles' boss, wanted him out of the way. Reles alive constituted a permanent threat to him. Joey Adonis, too, must have considered him a menace.

O'Dwyer announced, during our investigation, that in his singing, Reles had involved Adonis in one of the troop's contracts. During the Kefauver Committee hearings, O'Dwyer testified he could not recall which case this was, except he believed "a man and a woman were killed." This is a reminder for both O'Dwyer and the Committee, then, that Reles named the victims as "Matty Brown and his wife," who disappeared one day in the mid-thirties, never to be heard from again. The Kid said the case involved the taxicab racket, into which Dewey was just then probing. One of

the interrogators, who questioned Reles about it during our inquiry, prepared this abstract of the Kid's information:

"An investigation was being conducted by the District Attorney
of New York County (Dewey) into the taxicab business in which
one Joe Biunde was involved. Biunde also conducts a Ford agency
in Brooklyn. Both Brown and his alleged wife were alleged to be
in possession of valuable information which, if they disclosed it
to the said District Attorney, would involve Adonis and be very
damaging against him and others."

"Joey Adonis made a personal contact with Albert A. about
these people," Reles added, explaining that he first heard the
matter mentioned on a visit he made with Louis Capone to Adonis'
home. Later, he said, Pittsburgh Phil also mentioned it.

"Pep tells me," he disclosed, "that Albert tells him he got two
people to take care of, and it is important because Dewey knows
these people are hot. He says Joey A. is interested in this."

Reles also had a reasonably good idea of the technique involved
in doing away with such cases as the man and his alleged wife.

"The method used in disposing of these persons," said the interrogator's abstract of the Kid's information, "would be for somebody close to them to give them false information which would
involve themselves, and thus persuade them to leave town."

"When people are some other place away from home, they
could be nailed easier," the Kid said afterward in a general discussion of homicide.

As a matter of fact, every one Kid Twist ever knew in the mob
—even those he had never met—hated him and blamed him for
the troubles he had brought. Julie Catalano had even hung a new
nickname on him, which was adopted unanimously. It was: "Ras-
putin."

The guards in the hotel, who stood his insults and lopsided
jokes for so long, abhorred him. He never stopped making demands on them. Once, he caught a cold and awoke, sniffling, at
4 A.M.

"Get me my medicine on the bureau," he ordered one of the detectives, pointing a few feet away.

"Look, Reles," snapped the officer, "I'm here to stop a bullet for you. But be a nursemaid . . . not me! If you died of natural causes five minutes from now, my eyes couldn't get up one tear."

Some authorities had an even more realistic reason for hating him. John Harlan Amen, then conducting a special investigation of corruption, had requested a "loan" of Reles from O'Dwyer on several occasions, to go into the subject of protection. The fact that peculiar things had gone on in certain sectors of Brooklyn law enforcement in the thirties had been dramatically brought out in Max Rubin's outbursts on the witness stand, concerning Lepke's widespread power. O'Dwyer's recalcitrance about "loaning" the Kid out, however, was so marked that it was the point of an address by Justice Matthew F. Troy of Special Sessions Court only ten days before Reles went out the window.

"I charge that District Attorney O'Dwyer has failed to prosecute politicians and political fixers," Justice Troy charged. "Reles and the other informers can name the politicians and political fixers and can give the necessary evidence to put them in jail. These politicians and political fixers are just as immune under the administration of O'Dwyer [as before]."

The Justice's attack on the District Attorney was bitter. "O'Dwyer has taken all the credit for Murder, Inc.," he concluded. "Yet the record proves that a young assistant District Attorney —Burton Turkus—who is not a member of the Democratic machine organization, has prosecuted all the murderers. O'Dwyer has only appeared in the courtroom for the cameras."

With pressure being applied, any official whom Reles had "taken care of" undoubtedly felt that eventually he would be turned over to Amen for the probe of corruption. Such officials certainly would not cherish Kid Twist.

Obviously, then, if Reles was murdered, any listing of the "who" involved could include everyone in gangland from Buggsy Siegel and Frank Carbo in California to Lepke in New York— plus any number of persons outside of mobdom. To narrow it down to the most likely brings up the logical question of "How?" How was this most valuable of witnesses, supposedly guarded by picked police every minute of every day, with three other witnesses in adjoining or close-by rooms, thrown out of a window on a quiet morning? How was it done with no one hearing a sound or seeing a person or movement, although the Kid was a physically power-ful thug who would surely have put up a noisy fight for his life?

If everyone in that fortress suite—five (or six) officers and three other witnesses—were involved, there would almost posi-tively have had to be a leak in the ten years since the Kid went out the window. No secret so explosive, shared by eight per-sons or more—for there is the definite possibility that a "stranger" may have been present—could have been kept by all of them for that long a stretch. Human nature is not built that way. It can be assumed, then, that not all of the eight were in on it. This does not, however, preclude the fact that there was ample time for one man to have done it, whether a witness, a guard or anyone else.

This individual could, in some manner, have taken Reles by surprise and shoved him out. Or, perhaps the lone killer was someone Reles knew, of whom he would not be suspicious. When the man said, "Look here . . . look what's out on the sidewalk," or some such thing, the Kid would have stepped to the open window to comply. Then—a strong push, and it would be all over. It would have to be a big man, though, to have done this alone . . . huge and powerful, and as nervy a killer as any in Murder, Inc.

On the other hand, it might have been two men. They could have cradled Reles in their arms and flung him out so that he landed in a seated position, as the Medical Examiner's report in-dicated—according to the District Attorney's office.

But which one or two could it have been then, in the light of the testimony by Allie and Sholem that detectives sat guard through the night inside the witnesses' rooms? Well, the story is that all of the guards fell asleep at the same time that morning. Then, of course, one of the other witnesses might have slipped into the Kid's room and done it. But neither Allie nor Sholem nor Mikey fits the picture of the large, powerful man who was requisite if Reles was conscious when killed. The Kid very likely could have handled any one of them. He was remarkably strong, and experienced in all alley-fighting niceties. He was well aware, too, that he would win no popularity contests with any of them. Even if he were so-cializing with one or another at 6:45 A.M., he would certainly have his guard up, especially when standing near an open sixth-floor window. Still they cannot be ruled out altogether, if for no other reasons than their hatred and their presence in that suite.

It could, of course have been one of the police guards. Suppose, for instance, not all of those five, or six, officers did fall asleep that morning. Suppose one who says he slept, stayed awake. The four or five sleeping policemen would not know who he was, naturally. He could have done it.

Or suppose this guard who did not sleep opened the door for an outsider that morning—a stranger never mentioned, either then or in all the recurring revivals of the Reles scandal in the past ten years. Such an outsider would have had to be someone with considerable authority—authority enough to gain admittance and to keep his presence quiet afterward. If one of the witnesses, say, had awakened and spied him, he would have needed such authority that he could have sealed the witness' lips by a threat of a prison term, perhaps, or a murder prosecution, or death. And finally, his authority would have had to be such that Reles would have accepted his entry into the bedroom.

With Reles disposed of—what, then, of the bedsheet rope? Rigged, of course. Perhaps the murderer or murderers put the wire and the linen together and sent it fluttering after the Kid's plummeting body, to "make it look good." Maybe he or they even had foreknowledge of the vacant room downstairs. One could have gone down, opened the screen and made a few scratchy marks on the sill, thereby completing what, after ten years, remains a perfect crime.

There is the hypothesis, on the other hand, that the killer or killers, having finished with throwing Reles to his death, did not bother with creating an impression of accident or escape. However, one or two of the guards, discovering their prized responsibility unaccountably dead, could have done the rigging to "cover up." The sheets and wire could have been tied together and thrown out in order to hide their own dereliction. According to the District Attorney's office at the time, the wire used on the bedsheet rope had been in that suite for several months, left there by the hotel engineer. Is it reasonable that a stout piece of radio lead-in wire escaped the attention of the guards for that length of time, and, at a convenient moment, suddenly was available to use in rigging up a prop?

Aside from the "surprise" element, Reles would have had to be unconscious, induced either by alcohol or some other means not mentioned in the District Attorney's announcements of the Toxicologist's and Medical Examiner's reports. Otherwise, the Kid would never have gone through that window without such a struggle that it would have awakened half of Coney Island. This even rules out the surprise idea to a large extent. For, even if caught off guard and pitched or pushed out, Reles had plenty of time in a drop of forty-two feet to have let out at least one substantial scream that, at 6:45 A.M., would have attracted the attention of more than just the seagulls fluttering about the parapets of the hotel. It certainly was not done in his sleep, for how, in that case, would he have remained somnolent while he was being dressed and lifted from his bed to the window?

Unconsciousness can, of course, be induced by external means. According to the District Attorney's announcement, however, there were no head injuries, no drug or poison. Alcohol? No one admits that, up to now. But suppose the oft-repeated statement is true. Then those living in the suite would surely have heard something, if only the clink of glasses. Drinking is normally accompanied by conversation; the more drinking, the more conversation. If Reles' door was open and Allie's door was open, and all the doors, as was pointed out in the announcement on the original D. A.'s investigation, then, surely, any sustained carousing must be overheard. Especially with Reles' radio probably playing through the night, as that same announcement pointedly explains.

It may be presumed Reles was not just suddenly converted from a mild one-or-two-drink-man to a "loner" nipping at the bottle in solitude, until he got himself so besotten he was helpless. But if he was, and he did, then how, where and from whom did he get the liquor? Ten men were living in close confinement—six guards and four witnesses. Their eyes presumably were on one another frequently. The police officers were trained in observation. The others were thugs, in a business where it pays not to miss any tricks if one wants to stay alive. It is hardly likely, therefore, that any one of them could have obtained a bottle of whisky without several of his companions having noticed.

Visitors to that suite were carefully scrutinized. The visitor would have had to be slick, indeed, to have imported a jug past a sentry at the door. If he did manage it, the visitor would have had to be someone the sentry knew, perhaps, again, someone with sufficient authority to say to whoever saw him that not only his presence, but his package as well, had best be forgotten.

There is, too, the fact that Reles was fully clothed—but, according to the statement of the District Attorney's office, not in the clothes he was accustomed to wear. He had no intention of making any outside calls that day, so it is not logical that he was up and dressed before 7 A.M. But if he were, why would he change, on that particular day and at that hour, from his regular costume, especially since it was so conveniently folded across a chair close by his bed?

Assume, now, that someone or ones gained admission to Reles' room that early morning, got him drunk, or rendered him otherwise pliable, then dressed his unconscious form and heaved him out. Unless it were done by two men cradling him in their arms, it is not plausible that he would have landed in a sitting position, as has been contended—and unchallenged, up to the current investigation, anyway. A conscious man dropped out of a window—particularly one fighting to save himself—is more likely to try to land feet first than any other way. The figure of an unconscious man simply pitched out, like a shoveful of coal heaved into a furnace, would certainly turn in mid-air, and would be unlikely to land other than sprawled out or feet down. For ten years, a fractured spine has, supposedly, been the only injury Reles suffered. That would necessitate his having landed seated. However, assistant District Attorney Silver now says there were "other injuries." It is possible they may shed some additional light on the mess, especially if the "other injuries" should turn out to include a knife or bullet wound, hitherto undisclosed—even unwhispered.

The fact that Reles' body was found more than twenty feet out from the wall of the building almost definitely leads to the conclusion that he exited with some force. Even a strong wind would hardly have carried his 160 pounds that distance in a forty-two-foot drop, if he had been hanging close in on his bedsheet-rope when he fell, as the death scene sought so pointedly to portray.

The conclusion, then, is that murder by one or two men is the likeliest of all the theories advanced for Reles' startling and mysterious end. The others simply do not add up to the facts. At any rate, one point is incontrovertible: if all the sighs of relief which went up when Kid Twist hit that extension roof were laid end to end, the breath expended would, no doubt, have come close to filling one of the Navy's larger lighter-than-air ships, And, from coast to coast, none breathed a more lusty sigh at the Kid's finale than Albert Anastasia, his boss.

16.

The one that got away

Albert Anastasia, the killers' boss—thirty years, thirty murders; no convictions—extortion on the water front; it never stops— O'Dwyer's "perfect murder case," and what he did, and didn't, do with it—Please, Mr. Senator, help the local law man.

ALBERT ANASTASIA has been getting away with murder for thirty years now, and a lot of people have been helping him. Since 1920 —three years after he jumped ship and smuggled his way into the United States—this hard-mouthed, curly-haired hoodlum has been close to some thirty assassinations with gun and ice pick and strangling rope, either in person or by direction. And that includes only those of which we heard details. The killings claimed by the torpedoes of the troop he commanded ran well into three figures.

The Law knows the who, what and why of, and his link to, perhaps twenty slayings. Yet, Albert Anastasia's only jail penalty has been a practically overnight trip for carrying a gun, twenty-eight years ago! For five murders, he was arrested. For two, he was tried. For one, he even went to the death house, and there languished more than a year before help arrived. His "boys" left bodies all over America—and, remember, after the formation of the Syndicate, underworld law decreed they could not kill without his approval. Truly, the commander in chief of Murder, Inc.'s, enforcement squad gets away with murder.

Reles recited chapter and verse of twenty or more of Albert's escapades in homicide. Some he told of under oath in open court. Blue Jaw Magoon said "if you cross him, you cross the national Combination." Brooklyn police said he had "high political connections." O'Dwyer, who has been charged with letting Anastasia

459

escape punishment, said no mob murder "was committed in Brooklyn without Anastasia's permission and approval."

He has been linked with beatings and extortion, robbery and labor piracy and harboring of criminals, and much else that is violent. His social set includes considerable of the cream of hoodlum society. His particular friend is Joey Adonis. When Lucky Luciano was exiled to Italy in 1946, Narcotics Agent George White has testified, Albert A. was at the shipboard bon voyage party. Anastasia insists, however, that he does not know Frank Costello from a hill of beans. Assuming he is telling the truth, it just goes to show that a boss mobster can get along very well, indeed, without having to be a buddy of the man many try to crown "king" of the underworld—which has no king.

Primarily, Albert A. has been the water front czar for nearly two decades—and that does not mean only the docks and dock labor. He feels, evidently, that any man who rules the water front should also have considerable to say over all business, trade and life along it.

In fact, there are two notable characteristics about the Anastasias—or Anastasios, to give them the family name before alterations set in. One is a general tendency to get tangled up with the Law. The other is what seems an irresistible fascination the water front has for them—at financial profit, of course. There is a third remarkable similarity in this crew. To a man, they entered the United States illegally. All told, there are eight Anastasia brothers of Calabria. The two oldest still work on the Italian railroad. Another lives in Australia. The other five are in the United States. They arrived at various times, from twenty to thirty-five years ago. And all did it by jumping ship and smuggling themselves ashore. Four wound up on the water front, in one capacity or another—and all four have collided with the Law, for one thing or another.

Guiseppe (or Joseph), who works on the Manhattan piers, beat a murder rap as far back as 1925. Gerardo, immigration authorities say, has three bookmaking arrests. With that qualification—and without citizenship until 1951—he still managed to become an official delegate for the longshoremen's union.

Anthony calls himself a stevedore contractor. It is feared, he may have borrowed Albert's shoes on occasion. Recently, authorities have described him as a water front racketeer and labor strike-breaker. In fact, both he and Albert were involved in a bitter, and at times bloody, eight-month strike at the huge Phelps-Dodge copper plant at Elizabeth, N. J., in 1946, in which one striker was shot to death. Strike leaders accused Anthony of supplying the strike-breakers. Anthony, it was alleged, boasted of receiving "heavy sugar"—$1,000 daily—from the company. Anthony has denied all. All he did, he claimed, was furnish labor to take copper from Yonkers, N. Y., to New York City. For such service, he gets ten percent of the gross payroll of whatever amount he supplies.

Albert, of course, is an old hand at water front affairs. He has enjoyed an unchallenged reign in Brooklyn for years. With his residence in New Jersey in 1947 (where he once more became a neighbor of Joey Adonis) he appears to have taken some of his business there, as well. In fact, Assistant New Jersey Attorney General Nelson Stamler said in 1951 that he would not be at all surprised if Albert's labor activities had expanded far beyond the docks. He might even, the prosecutor said, be the labor "enforcer" in general strike-breaking activities in New Jersey.

"Several strikes here have been settled very suddenly," Stamler explained. "It bears some looking into."

The water front has been Albert's apple almost since the day he slipped into the United States in 1917. Since 1948, though, he claims, he has been part owner of the Modern Dress Company of Hazleton, Pa., making pretties for the ladies—which is quite a switch from stevedoring. His partner in Modern Dress, incidentally, is one Harry Strauss. When this was heard in Brooklyn, it occasioned no end of lifted eyebrows. Many of the boys recalled another Harry Strauss with whom Anastasia was once associated —the one they used to call Pittsburgh Phil, the most eager murderer of them all.

There is a vague recollection of the underslung Mussolini jowl in Albert's hard features, although, like all successful mob bosses, Anastasia is not nearly as noisy as Il Duce used to be, screaming from his balcony on Palazzo Venezia. Obviously, though, after what he's done, Albert must have had help along the way to have kept a whole skin. No one could stand off all that alone.

Take the Joe Turino murder, now. That was 'way back in 1920. Joe Turino, a longshoreman, stood in the way of young Anastasia's ambitions. Joe Turino was killed. Anastasia and a friend of his, one Jimmy Florino, were convicted and doomed to the chair. After a year and a half, however, a new trial was granted. Albert stayed in the death house eighteen months before he returned for his second chance. And then the case went "out the window." The delay had been just long enough so that four of the State's witnesses, whose testimony had convicted him in the first trial, had been murdered!

That "near miss" is remarkable evidence of what the proper help can do. There was another time, in 1933, when he and his gunman, Tony Romeo, were hauled in for assassinating Joe Santora, who had objected to the "muscle" in the laundry racket then being practiced in the water front sector. By then, Albert even had engaged, as his attorney, Sam Leibowitz—when Sam was one of the most brilliant of criminal lawyers. Romeo was discharged. Albert went to court—and was quickly acquitted. And the reason this time was that one of the State's principal witnesses perjured himself!

For most of the other jobs over the years, Albert hasn't had to go to that much trouble. In fact, just four months after he was rid of the Turino rap, he was back in for murder again, and was discharged in Magistrate's Court. A year later, again—for shooting a man to death; discharged. In 1928, once more—this time murder with an ice pick; discharged. In 1932, the police thought they had some especially good information on him. John Bazzanno, a Pittsburgh tough guy, believed he was tough enough to crack the Manhattan "business." They found Bazzanno stabbed and strangled and cut up into pieces of assorted size, and stuffed into a burlap bag. The investigators swiftly swept up sixteen persons in the dragnet. What happened to the other fifteen, I never had occasion to learn. Anastasia "won" a quick dismissal in Magistrate's Court.

Through his connections with Joey Adonis, Anastasia was an

early part of Unione. Early enough, as a matter of fact, so that the police credit him with a hand in eliminating Joe the Boss Masseria in Scarpato's excellent restaurant, the night Lucky Luciano went to wash his hands, and missed all the shooting. To be perfectly fair, though, the police records do not state that Albert put the ace of diamonds in Joe the Boss' hand that night.

In the late twenties Albert became acquainted with the tough kids of Brownsville and Ocean Hill, who were every bit as ambitious as he, although lacking some of his cunning executive thinking. The acquaintance was planted and flowered in Louis Capone's pasticceria. Along with the rich viands that Capone fed Kid Twist and Happy and Pittsburgh Phil and the Dasher, Louis and Albert A. served them the idea of working as a team, an army, to handle Brooklyn mob enforcement.

Albert became their boss, their commander. He kept in close touch by having Capone as liaison with the Brownsville boys and Vito Gurino as a torpedo with Happy's platoon. His personal handy men handled everyday water front problems, since Brownsville and Ocean Hill are clear across the borough from the docks. Among these were Jimmy Florino, one of the very few marksmen with a rifle of which gangland has boasted, and Albert's death house mate in the Turino murder when both were young; Dandy Jack Parisi, as deadly a killer as mobdom has spawned, and Jimmy Feraco, whose value lay not only in his trigger talent, but also for property in which he was interested in Lyndhurst, N. J., that served the mob as a "graveyard."

When syndication came, about 1934, Albert's friendship with Joey Adonis, plus the exceptional ability of his enforcement squad, brought the entire Brooklyn combination into the cartel. As the informers pictured it for us, the contracts would come to Albert, and he would relay them by Capone, Reles, Pittsburgh Phil or Happy. Like Lepke and Lucky and all the executives, he appreciated that the more he himself stayed out of the picture, the fewer trails could ever lead in his direction. Only once did he leave the tracks uncovered. But with his connections and his customary cunning, it stood to reason Albert A. would get away with that one. It did keep him hustling for a spell, though.

Of the dozen or more contracts Albert's boys handled for Lepke during his War of Extermination in 1939, the cold-blooded assassination of old Morris Diamond, a labor delegate who did not like racketeers, was a model of the planning and technique these experts put in their work. It is the heritage they left to their organized heirs of today.

That spring, the Dewey investigation turned to the trucking rackets, particularly that branch by which the mobsters had a stranglehold on the clothing industry through control of transportation. Morris Diamond was the business agent for Teamsters Local No. 138. He went to Dewey's office to tell of the manipulations, and the mob found out.

Lepke decreed the death sentence. At a planning conference at Anastasia's house, Mendy was delegated to the "casing" and fingering, so that the necessary personnel would recognize Diamond when the time came. Mendy recruited Allie to arrange the identification. Anastasia introduced him to a dapper character with a scarred face, Dandy Jack Parisi. Allie knew Dandy Jack by reputation. Next, Mendy had Allie meet an individual who had once been connected with Local 138, and thus knew the prospective victim by sight. Allie made a date with him in Manhattan, and brought Dandy Jack along. The former union man led them to a spot opposite the Forty-second Street building in which Diamond had his office. With an almost imperceptible motion, he pointed out a man in the emerging throng.

"That's him," he muttered. "That's your guy." Parisi took a careful look. He would now recognize Diamond, in the event they should ever meet—on a street-corner, say.

Meanwhile, Albert was becoming impatient. Reles, unaware of and not working on this contract, said he dropped in at Anastasia's house about May 10, and found Mendy and Charlie the Bug Workman there.

"I come over to talk to Albert about our bookmaking business," he explained, "and these two guys are sitting there." He was, naturally, not particularly startled to discover their conference concerned murder. "They are discussing a Mersh Diamond matter," he related in his recital to us. And Albert was chiding Mendy for the delay, the Kid reported.

"Everything is ready, and you still didn't tell us where the bum lives," Albert accused Lepke's staff executioner.

"I'm working on it, Albert," Mendy assured him. "As soon as I can get it, I'll give it to you."

"When I get it, we will take care of him," Anastasia promised.

Reles said he had nothing to do with this one. He would not have been informed, therefore, that Mendy's reconnaisance eventually reported that Diamond lived, conveniently, in Brooklyn—on Sixty-eighth Street, not far from the intersection of Eighteenth Avenue, far across town from Brownsville.

On the evening of May twenty-third, Julie Catalano was in a coffee pot, having a snack and reading the pictures in the tabloids, when an impatient automobile horn interrupted him. Through the window, Happy was waving him outside.

"Come on," his bookmaking employer directed as Julie emerged. "I got a piece of work for you. You're going to work with a very good man . . . Jackie . . . one of Albert's men."

Happy and his employee drove to a spot near Albert's hangout, the City Democratic Club. In five minutes, Julie recalled, Anastasia himself came along, and the three of them talked about the task ahead, in which Julie's role, as usual, entailed his driving skill.

"The job is tomorrow morning," Julie received his orders. "Be there at 5:30."

A dapper individual joined them, and was presented to Julie as "Jackie." There was a brief but complete conversation on plans. Albert now suggested a ride to the scene, so that Julie might familiarize himself with the layout. On Sixty-eighth Street, just off Eighteenth Avenue, they halted.

"Now, tomorrow morning, park right here," were the boss' instructions. "Jackie will be there, on the northwest corner, like he's waiting for the bus. When he sees Diamond, he'll begin walking across. You start up the car, slow. When he hits Diamond, be right there on the crossing so he can jump in. Then take off . . . whether the light is green or not."

The casing of Diamond, as finally reported by Mendy, had suggested this carefully-timed operation—on a busy street corner during the morning rush hour! The labor leader was known to set out from home for his office at about the same moment each morning. He passed the southeast corner of the intersection on his way to the subway station. Standing at the corner diagonally opposite, glancing through the morning paper while apparently awaiting transportation, Jackie would attract not the slightest suspicion. When he saw Diamond approach the southeast corner, he would cross and arrive at the moment his target did. In that way, he would not have to wait at the spot of the slaying, where a witness might recall him later.

Julie was given two full trial runs over the getaway route, until he was absolutely certain of every inch. Each run was begun with a pantomime dress rehearsal of the entire operation. Only the victim was missing. And the gun. The route was laid out to pass a certain building construction, in front of which was a huge sandpile. Julie was to slow down there long enough for the death weapon to be buried in the sand. It would not be found for days . . . might never be uncovered at all, as a cement or concrete mixer took huge gulps from the pile. This was double-barreled precaution, for the gun could not have been traced, anyway, even if found. It had been doctored beyond checking.

"Now," said Anastasia to Happy, finally satisfied, "be sure you have him here by half past five in the morning."

"He'll be here," the sour thug assured his chief.

Julie went to bed early. He set the alarm for 4:30, before turning out the light. When the alarm went off, though, the ex-cabdriver reached out a lazy arm, turned off the buzzer—and slept blissfully on for an hour more. At half past five, he awoke. As he rubbed sleepy eyes and yawned widely, memory returned. Throwing on his clothes, he rushed to the meeting place. Happy was there, fretting and impatient. He had worked late the night before. After leaving Julie, he had stolen a set of license plates, and had put them on the hot car, which had been acquired earlier by Blue Jaw Magoon and stored in the mob drop on Pennsylvania Avenue.

With Happy following closely, Julie drove rapidly across Brooklyn. Jackie was pacing the corner. "It's too late," he advised, matter of factly. "The bum already went down in the subway."

Late that afternoon, Happy came looking for Julie. "I saw

Albert," he informed his hired hand. "Everything will be ready for tomorrow morning. Now, be on time."

Julie slept fitfully that night. The urgency not to be late again for mob business was on his mind. He responded to the first tinkle of the alarm. When they met, Happy did not lead the way to the drop. The appearance of the car in the vicinity the morning before had dictated a precautionary transfer to the garage below Happy's house. Julie started for the murder site from there.

"A block from the corner," he said afterward, "I see Albert A. parked in his car. I holler 'hello' and he waves back to me."

Julie drew up half a block from the corner. Jackie was already at his station. In black trousers, grey, high-necked sweater and slouch hat, the torpedo was simply a workman waiting for a bus. As Julie watched, Jackie folded his newspaper and stepped from the curb. The wheelman let him get about halfway across before putting the car in gear. Slowly, he rolled toward the intersection.

The timing all around was perfect. Jackie reached the opposite sidewalk precisely as a man arrived from the other direction. Any number of persons were only yards away. The newspaper was held so it concealed the gun in the triggerman's hand. From hardly more than inches away, he fired the entire clip of cartridges into his victim. Julie's driving skill had the barely-crawling car exactly at the corner as the sixth shot sounded. Jackie had only to run a dozen steps, jump in—and they were gone before a single startled pedestrian realized what had happened. Only one witness really saw any part of it. Bennie Siegel, a teen-age neighborhood youth, was just opening his father's store for the day when he heard the shots and rushed outside.

"Mr. Diamond was struggling toward a cellar door," he reported to detectives afterward. "A man ran past me. He got into the car, and the car drove away, fast."

Such was the contract work performed by the troop Albert led. This one happened to be in Brooklyn. The next, as likely as not, would be Jacksonville or Minneapolis or San Francisco. From a point of view of national crime, this Syndicate service was their big function and made them infamous. Albert, though, did not wax fat on the cross-country murder business solely. His interests and major operations centered on the Brooklyn water front.

"In Brooklyn," Reles said very early in his exposure, "we are all together with the mob on the docks."

It was no secret to us that the "mob on the docks" had an iron grip on five miles of the Brooklyn water front—one of the busiest shipping centers in the world. But no one had even the vaguest idea that it was "all together" with the Brownsville combination.

"And it takes in from two to five blocks in from the water, too," the Kid staked out the complete area. "It has a lot going for it."

What Reles meant was that just about every soul in a region five miles long by two to five blocks deep—everyone from candy store proprietor to ship line operator—had to pay tribute to the mob. Virtually every man who worked for a day's pay had to "kick back" a portion of his earnings, simply to be allowed to work at his trade, regardless of its legitimacy or his personal honesty. On the docks, not every person called it a kickback, though. The mob's front men in the longshoremen's union, who did the collecting, had a neater way of putting it.

"We got to go to the boss' house tonight to buy wine," they would remind each other periodically. The "purchase" of the nectar of the grape was their symbol for handing the extorted funds to the top man.

Control of operations in this region included everything—the gambling and the bread housewives bought, the shylocking and the protection, and the workers' pay envelopes. All of these were, of course, in addition to the grabs on the piers themselves.

"Albert A., who is our boss, is the head guy on the docks," said the Kid in confirmation. "He is the law."

The District Attorney's office began an immediate investigation. Officers and delegates of all locals of the Longshoremen's Association were rounded up, and their books and records demanded. In some cases, the investigators were too late; the thugs burned the books the moment they heard of the probe. In some of the locals, no books at all were kept. In others, records were inadequate or falsified. There were indications that at least three, and very likely more, of the seven locals were in the hands of gangster officers, risen to power through phony elections. Tony Romeo and Dandy Jack Parisi controlled locals. Dock labor was caught in a vise that kept up a perpetual squeeze. And over all, it developed, Anastasia just about owned the entire water front.

Chief Assistant District Attorney Joseph Hanley, who checked this angle, revealed that the mob's direct kickback amounted to as much as ten dollars a week from each man. Then there were indirect demands: each worker was compelled to patronize a certain barber to the extent of $2.50 a month; each man had to buy his wine and his shirts at specified shops—at specified prices, which were, by no means, bargain rates. The only conclusion possible was that the mobsters were stealing hundreds of thousands of dollars from the union and its honest workingmen. It went far beyond labor, too. Thefts in cash or merchandise, running into six figures, were perpetrated against steamship lines, truck outfits and stevedoring firms. Extortions for loading and unloading were demanded. As boss of the dockworkers, Albert had more to say about the movement of freight than the shipowners.

One union executive explained that when expenses were paid—officers' salaries, rent, dues to the International, etc.—there was $400 to $500 a month left in each local.

"This is turned over each month to a notorious gangster," Hanley asserted. "That notorious gangster is Albert Anastasia."

Oddly enough, just as the District Attorney's investigation of this far-flung water front racketeering was hitting its peak, it was suddenly stopped. Five years later—in 1945—a grand jury censured O'Dwyer severely for this peculiarity.

(The lawlessness rampant on the water front then is not peculiar to any single era since Albert A. slipped into the United States. The racketeering goes on today, through the same terrorizing methods. In 1948, for instance, an unaccountable, mysterious picket line was suddenly set up at a dock where a ship from Canada was about to unload newsprint for the *New York Daily News*. The pickets demanded $100,000 to end their interference. That failing, they proposed tribute of one dollar a ton. Since *The News* uses 300,000 tons of newsprint yearly, such piracy, once started, could run into important money. The ship was taken to

Philadelphia, unloaded there, and its cargo sent to New York by freight—at a cost of $25,000. "It smacked of a racket," insisted Philip Stevens, *The News*' business manager, and added, "One of the names I heard in connection with this was that of Anthony Anastasia."

(Since the dock worker's occupation is seasonal, shylocking is especially active on the water front. In 1950, Lawrence Rice, a stevedore, borrowed one hundred dollars during his off-season. The shylocks, as is their custom, demanded his pay card as security. The dock worker must present his pay card in order to collect his wages. When Rice started work again, the loan-sharks picked up his pay with his identification card, and took out ten dollars each week. After thirty-six weeks, at ten dollars weekly, Rice inquired how he stood on his original one hundred dollar loan.

("You," he was advised, "have only paid the interest up to now. You still owe the hundred." And Lawrence Rice's case could be multiplied by hundreds.)

The picture of Anastasia and his water front control, which was uncovered for public view back in 1940, pointed up very sharply the fact that any time there had been a threat to his reign and to the mob's firm grip on dock labor, the threat had usually wound up very dead. That brought up Peter Panto.

In mid-summer, 1939, Peter Panto was waging a determined war against gangster rule on the water front. For months, he had been whipping up the longshoremen to shake off the mobster grip. Panto was only twenty-eight, but he already had become a leader of rank-and-file dock labor.

"We are strong," he urged the union men. "All we have to do is stand up and fight."

Little by little, he was winning them over. The mob fought him with everything—including propaganda. "He's a Red," they spread the whisper. "He's a radical. He'll get you and the union in trouble."

On July 8, Panto called a rank-and-file meeting of Local 929, International Longshoremen's Association, and 1,250 men attended. Every one was a bona fide dock worker.

"The elections are coming; insist on honest elections," the earnest young leader exhorted them. "Make sure the delegates you vote for get in."

He was cheered at that—and the cheering did it. The applause was a sign to the hoods that their control of a very lucrative racket was menaced.

On the night of July 14, Panto was visiting Alice Maffia. They were planning to be married in October. It was still early—only ten o'clock—when he put on his hat that Friday night.

"I've got to meet two men and go to a union committee meeting," he explained. "It won't take long. I'll be back in an hour and help you with the sandwiches, so we can get an early start for the beach tomorrow."

Peter Panto was not back in an hour. Or two. Or ever. For half a year and more, not a clue was uncovered. Then Reles talked.

"Panto met two guys that night, all right," the Kid related. "I don't know their names, but they were brothers. They talked to him, and then took him to see certain people. One brother got ninety bucks for the job; the other guy got eighty-five."

The "certain people" offered Panto a sum of money to call off his crusade. He scorned their reflection on his sincerity. The "certain people" bundled him into a car. Mendy, who was just visiting from Manhattan, was in the car. Reles said he heard that Albert's men, Florino the rifle expert and Dirty-face Jimmy Feraco and Tony Romeo, were mixed up in it somewhere, too. Florino was a particularly slippery operator. Once he was brought in for having a gun, but he produced a legal permit, bona fide, right down to the signature. It stumped Walter Hart, a State Supreme Court Justice now, but a member of the District Attorney's staff then. Although the permit seemed perfectly valid, Hart decided to check on the number, anyway. It had been issued all right, he discovered—but to another party altogether, a jeweler who needed a pistol for protection. Whoever had made up Florino's "permit" so neatly, had accidentally picked out a number currently in use.

In the car, that July night, no one had to tell Peter Panto he was being taken for a ride. He gave them a terrific battle. Mendy was a 200-pounder, built like an ox. The labor crusader was a slim one hundred and sixty-three. He struggled with the desperation of a man fighting for his life. Somehow, he managed to get his teeth around one of Mendy's stumpy fingers. He clamped down hard, and came so close to chewing the digit clear off that the mobster had to see a doctor about it later. Brave as he was, though, Panto was no match for a gang.

"Mendy strangled him as a favor for Albert," Reles revealed the outcome. The hulking hoodlum was not particularly proud of that one, though.

"Gee, I hated to take that kid," he confessed to Reles and a couple of the others later. "But I had to do it for Albert, because Albert has been good to me."

With Panto dead in the car, routine procedure called for dumping the body out in the gutter or a vacant lot somewhere. But these racketeers were businessmen and organizers. It was well known that Panto had no enemies except the mobsters. The corpus delicti, discovered in some gutter, would make a martyr of him among the longshoremen. It would complicate the gang's control; undoubtedly incite an upheaval in the union. Thus, it would be best if the corpse never turned up.

"So," related Reles, "they take him and dump him in the grave-yard over in Jersey. It's in a chicken yard near Dirty-face Jimmy's brother-in-law's place—across the street from Jimmy's house . . . in a place called Lyndhurst. I think there is six or eight stiffs planted there."

For weeks, a steam shovel chewed at the spot, vainly seeking the graves. They were, naturally, unmarked. One day, a relative of Feraco suggested moving the excavation work about a hundred yards closer to the placid Passaic. On the sixth thrust into the new site, the steam shovel hit what it was after.

One huge six-hundred-pound lump of earth, clay, rock—and quicklime—was brought to Brooklyn. The entire pile was much too fragile to disseminate, with any expectation of pulling anything in one piece out of the searing lime. X-rays were taken of the frozen mass. They revealed what was left of one body and part of another. We believed the skeleton was Panto's. However, identification would not have been vital for justice in this case. The law of New York provides the death penalty for kidnapers, unless the victim is returned alive before the abductors' trial begins. No corpus delicti is necessary.

Reles supplied one final typical touch. He and Pittsburgh Phil were standing idly on the Corner, talking of this and that, a short time before Panto was murdered.

"Albert mentions to me a couple of days ago that something will have to be done about a guy named Panto," Pittsburgh Phil remarked, with the crowing air he always adopted to throw his importance up to Reles. "This guy is making trouble in the dock union."

The Kid did not give his partner the satisfaction of a reply. Several days later, they were once more standing in front of the all-night candy store. By now, Reles had been apprised of developments.

"What happened with that Panto contract?" he brought the subject up, almost maliciously.

"Oh, that one," sighed Pittsburgh Phil. "I run into bad luck on that. I see Albert yesterday, and I ask him what's new on it. He says, 'It's all finished, and everything's all right.' It's too bad. I wanted to lend a hand with it."

The gangland grapevine never sent a message faster than it clicked out the news that Kid Twist was singing. Even before he actually had agreed to talk that Good Friday night—while he was still trying to make a deal—the word flashed through mobdom: "The Kid is ratting."

Detectives were out before dawn—and found the cages open and the birds flown, one after another. Dandy Jack was gone. Dirty-face Jimmy—gone; Tony Romeo, too, and Vito Gurino. And Albert Anastasia, the boss! A country-wide alarm was broadcast for the commander.

"He is very dangerous," the police alert cautioned all authorities—a most modest word of advice, indeed. Week after week, as the hunt failed to find the head man and his picked torpedoes, we waited, jittery over the safety of our witnesses, with these sharpshooters on the loose.

As Reles continued his recital, and Allie and Julie joined the chorus, however, impatience equaled and even surpassed anxiety. For now—for the first time—the District Attorney claimed a case against Anastasia. Up to then, there had been eye-witness statements galore about him and murder; but never a case that would stand up in court. In killing after killing, he'd covered the trail of corroboration with the cunning of a sleight-of-hand artist. But now, at last, in the murder of old Morris Diamond, he had left a single track.

Allie could tell of Albert helping in the fingering. Julie would tell of getting his instructions from the chief and of his presence at the scene, overseeing the operational smoothness. But Julie and Allie were accomplices. Neither of them was corroboration. There was, though, one person alive who was not involved in the plot himself, but who could put the commander of the killers right in the middle of it.

It was irony at its peak that, of all the thugs, Reles should be the non-accomplice to furnish substantiation against the head enforcer. Up to then, he'd been a full-time performer in almost every throat-cutting about which he had testified. In this one, however, he had simply visited Anastasia's home, and he had heard Albert and Mendy talk about killing old Diamond. And Albert had said, "As soon as you give me his address, we will take care of him." That was the corroboration to damn the boss with his own words. That was what made O'Dwyer call this one "the perfect murder case" against Anastasia!

The manhunt for Albert A. ranged far and wide. The chase led to Cuba and even to Italy. It was almost certain, however, that Anastasia would never go very far from home base. He had been able to hide Lepke in Brooklyn for two years, when Lepke was the most hunted man in the world; surely Albert could take care of himself as well. Informers who came in later offered bits of gossip or information. One said, "I think Anastasia is hanging around the water front in old clothes, most likely staying in a basement." Gurino, when he broke babbling into church in mortal terror of mob guns, said that, for a while, Albert had been holed up at the tomato farm hideout at Milton, N. Y.

Wherever he was, he was not dug up through 1940 and 1941. Then, Reles went out the window in November, 1941—and Anastasia did not have a thing in the world to fear. The D. A.'s bright and "perfect" case against the chief of the worst set of killers crime has ever seen hit that extension roof with the Kid—and died with him. And left behind so peculiar, astonishing, remarkable, weird and mystifying a set of circumstances, that they haven't been unraveled yet—and probably never will be!

They begin, actually, with the very start of Reles' song. The Kid had quickly brought his boss into his aria. Between that night and the morning he plunged to his death were nineteen months. Yet, in that nineteen months, and in spite of what he himself jubilantly called "the perfect case," O'Dwyer did not obtain a murder indictment against the head killer. He did not direct anyone else to get an indictment. In fact, he was dead set against getting one at all, he calmly confessed, although he was fully aware Anastasia had to approve every murder done in organized crime in Brooklyn.

Anastasia and Parisi, the triggerman in the Diamond murder, were fugitives anyway, so what was the use, O'Dwyer maintained. His reason for not putting his witnesses under oath before a grand jury, the now-Ambassador to Mexico explained, was because of "a small boy who was reported to me as delicate."

"He was apparently sitting on a stoop very early in the morning when old Mr. Diamond was going to work and Parisi shot him," O'Dwyer testified before the Kefauver Committee in 1951. "It was all right to take grown-ups and throw them in as material witnesses. They would have to protect themselves. In the case of this little boy, if we were to take him in . . . first of all he was delicate; secondly, the danger of these gangsters threatening his father and mother . . ."

The "little boy" obviously referred to Benny Siegel, who, as a matter of fact, was opening his father's vegetable store for the day a few paces from where Diamond was murdered, and saw the killer make his getaway. This "delicate little boy" happened to be sixteen years old at the time, and, like a dutiful son, was sturdily handling his father's business establishment all by himself. Here, too, is another mystifying touch. The boy could not give one word of testimony about Anastasia, simply because he hadn't even seen Anastasia. What he had to say concerned Dandy Jack. Catalano was the only witness who could put Albert at the scene—a full block from where the boy was working. Moreover, detectives were competently and securely guarding the families of Reles and Dukey and Pretty and others who were important as witnesses. Surely the boy and his family could have been just as capably and competently protected, at home or in a hotel, as all the other witnesses and their kin.

In the spring of 1942, O'Dwyer took a leave of absence to enter the Army. He left the office on June 1. Several weeks before—in March—he requested me to prepare a review of the status of the murder investigation against Anastasia. Now, asking me for this made little sense. I had not had a thing to do with the Anastasia matter. The investigation had been carried on entirely by others while I was either preparing cases, or was in court trying them. It has since been explained that O'Dwyer and assistant District Attorney Heffernan and Captain Bals and the office's chief clerk, James Moran, were in charge of the Anastasia case. I explained to O'Dwyer that I could not possibly give any competent appraisal on Anastasia unless I had a full and detailed report in writing from the chief of his investigation, Captain Bals. On April 8, such a report was furnished to me, along with a supplemental memo on the Diamond case, specifically.

Based entirely on Bals' report and memo, I compiled a "confidential memorandum." It was labeled just that—"Confidential Memorandum"—in spite of various references to it as a report, a review, a record and what-not-all, not only by O'Dwyer, but by the Kefauver Committee and its counsel, Rudolph Halley. During the Committee hearings, the Ambassador, the counsel and the senators made public references to this memorandum, by various cryptic and confusing allusions. But, strangely, not once was mention made of the Bals' report which was the basis for it. It is about time, therefore, that these documents are set out now, for the first time. First is the major and pertinent portion of Captain Bals' report (the number is that of the Criminal Bureau file on the subject):

REPORT RE: ALBERT ANASTASIO (B-57,939.)
On March 22, 1940, Abe Reles was brought to the office of the District Attorney of Kings County, and expressed a

desire to reveal all his knowledge and activities in reference to the underworld and the killings for which they were responsible. Reles at the time gave information that about seven or eight years ago, there came into operation among the gangs an unwritten law, that there could be no killings by any mobsters without first getting permission from the "boss," who was designated (in Brooklyn) as Albert Anastasio. Besides having sole power to grant or deny such permission, Anastasio, in many instances, participated in mapping out plans for the execution and designating the killers.

Reles further states that the following killings were committed by Anastasio, either in person or by direction.

(There followed here a list of sixteen murders, most of which have been reviewed and mentioned heretofore. Bals then detailed how Pittsburgh Phil also offered to "talk" in May 1940.)

The report continues:

Both Reles and Strauss had personally contacted and dealt with Anastasio as their "boss."

Louis Capone and Mendy Weiss, who are now in the death house on the Rosen killing, also dealt personally with Anastasio. Lepke . . . is in federal custody, awaiting the outcome of the appeal from his conviction. The last three named mobsters contacted and dealt with Anastasio . . .

(Captain Bals then devoted several paragraphs to individual assassinations and Anastasia's part therein, such as those of Diamond, Panto and Puggy Feinstein.)

The report continues:

The actual killer in the murder of Irving Penn in July 1939, in Bronx County, was Jack Parise (Parisi), who was described by Reles as being the "ace triggerman" for Anastasio, and a mobster whose services could only be had by and with the knowledge and consent of Anastasio . . .

It must be remembered that the activities of this murder mob were not confined to the Borough of Brooklyn; that . . .

their activities took them to Sullivan County, New York, and out of the state to New Jersey, as exposed in the Panto and Dutch Schultz cases, as well as across the country to California . . .

In the case of Anastasio, legal corroboration is missing . . . On November 12, 1941, Abe Reles, who was under police guard in the Half Moon Hotel, Brooklyn, attempted to escape and fell five (Ed. note: five was the figure Bals used.) stories, being instantly killed. This not only seriously hampered the investigation, but deprived the State of his testimony and information.

At the present time, the only testimony adducible against Anastasio is that of accomplices.

Accompanying Capt. Bals' report was this:

MEMORANDUM IN RE KILLING
of
MOISH DIAMOND

Abe Reles stated that one evening about two weeks before the shooting and killing of Moish Diamond, he went to the home of Albert Anastasia on Ocean Parkway near Avenue H, Brooklyn . . . That when he arrived there, Albert Anastasia was home with Mendy Weiss and Charles Workman. He remained there with them about an hour and a half. That Anastasia and Weiss talked about the shooting and killing of Moish Diamond. That Anastasia stated to Weiss that all plans were ready and that the only thing that he was waiting for was Diamond's address, and that Weiss stated that as soon as he got it, he would give it to him (meaning Albert Anastasia). Anastasia replied, "When I get it, I will take care of him". . .

> FRANK C. BALS,
> Chief Investigator

Dated: April 8, 1942.

> SPECIAL INVESTIGATION SQUAD,
> District Attorney's office,
> Kings County.

From those two documents, I reported the following:

CONFIDENTIAL MEMORANDUM

re

ALBERT ANASTASIA

To: Hon. William O'Dwyer, District Attorney.

From: Burton Turkus, assistant District Attorney.

The annexed four-page report of Chief Investigator Frank C. Bals, dealing with the status of the investigation as to Albert Anastasia, sets forth that the investigation to date has failed to adduce a scintilla of available competent evidence, aside from or in corroboration of the testimony of accomplices. The corroboration supplied by Reles, as set forth in the supplemental report of the Chief Investigator, likewise attached hereto, expired with Reles. Thus, as the investigation now stands, no successful prosecution of Anastasia may be had. This, despite the fact that under the set-up of the criminal organization or "Combination" of which he was "The Boss," not a single murder . . . was perpetrated by "The Combination" without Anastasia's permission and approval. His was the exclusive right to grant or deny such permission. In many instances, Anastasia not only gave the order for the murder, but also mapped out the plan of its execution and designated the killers to perform the murder. In the Diamond case, Anastasia was actually present at the scene of the murder for the purpose of making certain that the murder was carried out precisely in accordance with his plan and order.

Based upon the known facts as disclosed by the investigation, should Anastasia frustrate justice, it would be a calamity to society. Somewhere, somehow, corroborative evidence must be available.

Investigation focussed upon the matter of corroborative evidence should proceed with redoubled effort and every lead in such direction should be followed through exhaustively.

Dated: April 8, 1942.

BBT:jjc.

In the face of these documents, it is mystifying, to say the least, to come upon such statements as the following in the record of the Kefauver Committee (the italics are the author's):

> O'Dwyer: Why, I had Turkus make a *study* of the Anastasia case, of *all* cases that we might have had against him in *May,* just before I went into the Army, and he gave me a written *report.*
>
> Committee Counsel Halley: It was in April that Turkus said the Anastasia case *was a good case* which *should be prosecuted.*

It is even more confusing to read this in the Committee's final report under Senator Kefauver:

> "Before he left (for the Army), O'Dwyer stated he had Burton Turkus, the *indictment* lawyer, prepare a *review* of the case, and his report, on the file, *indicated* that while there was no case against Anastasia at that time, the man's record was such that the investigation should be carried on."

Aside from a trivial confusion between April and May, O'Dwyer knew, of course, that I made no "study" prepared no "review," and gave him no "report" on the Anastasia case. I simply submitted a memo based on Captain Bals' report. Even more weird is the remarkable mental process by which Mr. Halley can take from that memo the statement that "no successful prosecution of Anastasia may be had," and seriously glean from it the meaning "the Anastasia case was a good one." Hence, we will pass lightly over the fact that I was not "the indictment lawyer" and did not "indicate" there was no case against Anastasia. I stated it flatly and unequivocally—five months after Reles died.

At any rate, it was on April 8, 1942, that the District Attorney's office had a memo urging redoubled efforts to land the most eminent murderer of them all. And exactly twenty-six days later, the "wanted" card on Anastasia was removed from the files of the Police Investigation Bureau! Not only his—but also those of Dandy Jack Parisi, the toughest of the torpedoes, and Tony Romeo, Albert A.'s ace rackets specialist.

These cards are the police department's notification that a man is wanted and should be picked up. Removal of a "wanted" notice has the effect, virtually, of a formal announcement to the police that the District Attorney no longer is seeking that particular man. And were these cards on Anastasia and his assassins removed by the District Attorney? Or an assistant D. A.? Or even a competent investigator? They were not. These cards, a grand jury determined, were removed from the file on order of the chief clerk in the District Attorney's office! And why?

"I knew there was no reason to keep a wanted card in there; there was no case against Anastasia," explained chief clerk James Moran when the question came up, much later. He explained, too, that special assistant Attorney General John Harlan Amen had "called Thomas Craddock Hughes, the acting District Attorney, and asked him if he wanted Anastasia, and Hughes said he didn't." The odd point in this, however, was that Hughes did not become Acting District Attorney until O'Dwyer left for the Army, which was June 1. The cards were removed on May 4.

"The removal of the card," Moran shrugged, "was purely a clerical move."

Later, O'Dwyer was questioned about the fact that Anastasia was no longer listed as a fugitive for twenty-seven days while he was still in active command. His reply was that he didn't hear of the removal of the cards until the fall of 1945, when a grand jury became interested in the matter!

The order to lift the "wanted" label from the chief of the killers was given to Police Sergeant Elwood Divvers—the same sergeant who was second in command of the guards who slept so soundly the morning Reles jumped, fell or was thrown from the Half Moon Hotel. In 1945, a grand jury, after hearing testimony on the case, had this to say of the incident:

> Police Sergeant Elwood Divvers, in command of the Detective squad assigned to the Brooklyn District Attorney's office, testified that on May 4, 1942, he issued the written request . . . for the removal of the wanted notices . . . on the direct order of chief clerk James J. Moran . . . Referring to Moran, the (Divvers') quotation is 'it was usual for me to go to him on police matters.' The general feeling in the (District

Attorney's) office among the police was that Moran was practically the spokesman for the District Attorney.

Of all the odd developments in the Prosecutor's office since the investigation began, perhaps none was so fantastic as the position of this James Moran, chief clerk. He is a giant of a man, well over six feet and two-hundred pounds, powerful, with a yen for dancing and handball. When O'Dwyer became a magistrate in 1929, Moran was an obscure court clerk. As O'Dwyer climbed the political ladder, he brought Moran with him. When O'Dwyer became Mayor, he appointed his large friend First Deputy Fire Commissioner at a $10,000 salary. In 1950, just before he resigned the mayoralty to become Ambassador to Mexico, O'Dwyer gave Moran the remunerative post of City Water Supply Commissioner—at $15,000 a year for life. It did not last that long. In June 1951, Moran was convicted of perjuring himself over the frequency of his association with Louis Webber, a numbers operator and convict. He was forced to resign.

While he was close to O'Dwyer, Moran assumed remarkable importance in New York political life. During those years, the *New York Herald Tribune* said, "Virtually every major political problem had to be cleared through Jim Moran." And District Attorney Miles McDonald of Brooklyn testified in 1951 that he heard Moran had "demanded cash contributions" for O'Dwyer's 1948 mayoralty campaign from many gamblers in the city. His authority under O'Dwyer, in a District Attorney's office staffed by competent lawyers and investigators, was nothing short of incredible. And with O'Dwyer's sanction, to boot!

The investigating grand jury of 1945 declared:

> It was testified that . . . during the years 1940 and 1941, James J. Moran, chief clerk of the District Attorney's office, who was not . . . even a member of the bar, authorized the institution of proceedings before the grand jury.

Of this, the *New York Times* reported:

> Moran testified . . . that before a case could be presented to the grand jury, approval in writing by someone in authority

had to be obtained, and that those authorized to grant this approval were O'Dwyer, the chief assistant and himself.

The grand jury referred to a complaining letter addressed to O'Dwyer from Peter Masi, former associate of and successor to the murdered Peter Panto as leader of the rank-and-file dock labor.

"This complaint," the jury said, "charged that the Brooklyn water front rackets were still in existence. . . . On the face of the letter, there is written the name 'Moran' underlined. The complaint of Masi," the jury concluded, "was never interrogated, nor was any action ever taken with regard thereto."

At any rate, when Moran—this clerk with the remarkable authority—had the wanted card on Anastasia taken from the police files, Albert A. came out of his hole and waltzed back into town. Actually, he was not questioned on a single Murder, Inc., assassination or activity! His stay at home was brief. In mid-1942, the Army drafted Anastasia from—of all places—Utica, N. Y., which may or may not have been a tip-off as to where one of his hideouts, at least, was located in the year and a half he holed up until Reles went out the window so fortunately for him. He spent two years in uniform—even had his picture taken at New York sporting events. The newspapers published it, too—although Albert was hardly anxious for such publicity. Sometime during those two years, he obtained his American citizenship, a remarkable accomplishment, indeed, inasmuch as he had been bluntly turned down for naturalization in 1934, after District Immigration Director Byron Uhl learned of his five arrests for murder.

The removal of the "wanted" cards which, in effect, advised police there was no longer any reason to pick up Albert and his boys, had a tragic aftermath for Tony Romeo, one of his crack gunmen—as well as for law enforcement. It was at Tony's neat home, Reles had said, that Lepke and Longy Zwillman held their meeting over a garment district dispute while Lepke was on the lam. Tony had been an Anastasia man ever since he built up an early reputation as an election-day slugger along the water front. His criminal record sported several arrests for murder. He was picked up with Anastasia for the laundry racket killing of

Joe Santora in 1933, and he was questioned in Peter Panto's "disappearance." For years, he carried a card as a delegate in the International Longshoremen's Union, was Albert's bodyguard, and a general handy man in seeing that dock labor stayed in line and did not fall behind in tribute and kickbacks. When our probe started, Romeo fled with his chief. But when the "wanted" cards disappeared, he, like Albert, returned.

Now, once Reles was gone, if there remained any hope of ever nailing Anastasia, a good chance rested on eventually getting Romeo to open up. He knew a great deal about Albert and his machinations—and about the Peter Panto murder. It would be assumed, then, that the District Attorney would be eager to talk to him. Romeo was arrested on May 12, 1942—a day or two after he hit town, and nearly three weeks before O'Dwyer left for the Army. The police lieutenant who picked him up immediately notified the Bureau of Criminal Investigation. The Bureau informed him, however, that the "wanted" notice had been removed—and therefore Romeo was no longer wanted! Two weeks later, Romeo was released. At no time was he questioned by the District Attorney's office, although he was the lone possible link to Anastasia!

Several days later—on June 9—Romeo told his wife, "I'm going to the country on business; be back in a week or so." On June 17, a knotted bundle of bloody clothes was found on the banks of historic, rustic Brandywine Creek in the suburbs of Wilmington, Del. A card to the International Longshoremen's Union, in a pocket, bore Tony's name. Not until two weeks later, however, was Romeo discovered, just outside of the village of Guyencourt. His head and chest had been blasted by bullets. He had apparently been given a vicious beating first—the treatment the mob ordinarily accords a suspected "canary," or one with songbird proclivities. His head was bashed in, the jaw fractured. He was one mass of bruises.

Since Tony Romeo was all smashed up near the Brandywine, no other trails have opened that might lead to Albert Anastasia. Almost any nice afternoon now, you might see the boss of the killers at some sports event, or perhaps, strolling about the grounds of his $100,000 mansion on the lordly Palisades in conservative Fort Lee, N. J. It can only be hoped that somewhere, sometime, the lid can be lifted to smoke out the impresario of homicide and make him answer to society.

The bizarre events concerning what had and had not been done about Albert Anastasia from 1940 to 1942 simmered for three years and came to a boil during a seething political campaign in 1945 in which O'Dwyer was the Democratic candidate for mayor.

The grand jury began delving into the strange factors which had been whispered for more than three years. On October 29, a presentment was handed up, bitterly attacking O'Dwyer for, among other things, having failed to follow through on the water front investigation and other probes that had showed such promise in 1940.

The action, however, occurred less than a week before the election. The County Court, as a result, felt politics was involved, and ordered the presentment expunged from the record. The jury kept at it, nevertheless, even after O'Dwyer bcame mayor. And on December 20, another presentment was placed before the court, if anything more caustic than the first. The jury listed seventeen findings, centering its strongly worded charges on an admission by O'Dwyer himself that he had "the perfect murder case" against Anastasia, but had not even ordered Albert A.'s arrest!

The jury minced few words. It charged "negligence, incompetence and flagrant irresponsibility" in Anastasia's "escape." Each finding was a cutting accusation as to why this infamous hoodlum should have been treated so lightly:

> The undisputed proof is that William O'Dwyer and Edward Heffernan were in possession of competent legal evidence that Anastasia was guilty of first degree murder and other vicious crimes. This proof admittedly was sufficient to warrant Anastasia's indictment and conviction, but Anastasia was neither prosecuted, indicted nor convicted . . .
>
> The consistent and complete failure to prosecute the overlord of organized crime . . . is so revolting that we cannot permit these disclosures to be filed away in the same manner the evidence against Anastasia (was) heretofore "put in the files."

Perhaps the most startling public revelation was that, at one point early in the Murder, Inc., probe in 1940, grand jury proceedings actually had been started against Anastasia, looking toward an indictment for murder. On the verge of completion, however, they had suddenly been dropped for some unknown reason. The presentment charged:

> We find the "perfect murder case" was presented and almost completed to the Kings County grand jury in May 1940, by (assistant District Attorney) Heffernan, who then suddenly suspended and abandoned the case. He stated this case was dropped on instructions from his superiors.

Heffernan could not recall which of his "superiors" had called him off the case. Since he was an assistant D. A., the grand jury reasoned that his superiors would be limited to the Chief Assistant or O'Dwyer himself. But O'Dwyer, who had been brought in to testify several times during the jury's deliberations, emphatically denied knowing anything about it. Along about then, the jury frankly admitted that it was baffled over the authority wielded by a clerk named Moran among a trained legal staff of prosecutors.

Actually, when Heffernan abandoned the presentation, only one vital witness still remained to testify. That one was Kid Twist Reles—the lone corroborative witness against Albert. There the case stayed, pending, right up to the time the Kid plummeted to his death—and all it needed, in all that time, was Reles' brief speech to complete it and secure the indictment!

The 1945 presentment pointed out that a written memorandum was submitted to O'Dwyer, "requesting redoubled efforts against Anastasia." Instead, all efforts to involve the commander of the trigger troop were "ignored, disregarded and allowed to remain in the office files," the jury charged sharply. It was an amazing accusation, made doubly so by O'Dwyer's twin admission, as quoted by the presentment, that he knew in April 1940 he "had a perfect case" against Anastasia, and that, although he was the District Attorney, he was unaware Heffernan "presented almost a complete case" to the jury only a month later.

"In fact," the presentment went on, "he (O'Dwyer) said that had he known of its commencement . . . he would not have permitted Heffernan to go as far, because there was a witness, a young man, whose life would be in jeopardy." (Presumably the "young man" of this 1945 testimony became the "little boy" of the 1951 statement.)

The jurors finished with a thinly-veiled regret that, but for a technicality, action could be brought against the mayor-elect of the world's largest city!

"To find penal responsibility for misconduct of a public official," they pointed out, "we are advised that, under the law, there must be wilful disobedience of duty committed within . . . the statute of limitations. This provision of law is a severe limitation . . . The law should be modified so the statute of limitations starts to run only from the time the official charged with misconduct leaves office." (See Appendix 5.)

Once more, the presentment was ordered expunged, but not because of politics this time. It recited secret grand jury testimony, which a presentment should never do, the court said. This time, in fact, no allegation of political bias could be leveled, simply because the jurors had had O'Dwyer himself confirm their findings while he was in the grand jury room, according to the presentment:

Q—You have heard the evidence, Mr. O'Dwyer, which we have heard for many weeks, and which was the basis for our presentment?

A—Yes.

Q—Will you agree with us that we were right in handing up the presentment?

A—Yes, I agree that the presentment was fully justified, and I will say so at any time.

Nevertheless, he declared, he couldn't see why any blame should attach to William O'Dwyer for letting Anastasia loose. He'd been away to war from 1942 to 1945. "Unfinished matters relating to Anastasia" should have been handled by his staff, headed by acting District Attorney Hughes, while he was gone, said O'Dwyer. "I assumed they had," he maintained. He did not, however, refer to that period in which he was in command and nothing was done, from May, 1940, when Kid Twist started talking, to November, 1941, when the Kid stopped—permanently.

The entire ugly Anastasia mess eventually dropped out of the public eye and the newspaper headlines. Five years after the grand jury censured him so severely for letting the chief of the murderers get away, O'Dwyer was nominated by President Truman (in September, 1950) to be Ambassador to Mexico. Now came as astonishing a development as any in the entire case. Interested citizens *twice* brought to the attention of the Senate the presentment charging O'Dwyer's administration with negligence, incompetence and flagrant irresponsibility in permitting an "overlord of organized crime" to escape. And still the United States Senate confirmed O'Dwyer as this nation's official representative in the second largest embassy it maintains in the world!

Nor was that all. Only six months later, in March, 1951, the Kefauver Committee, made up of the same senators who voted for O'Dwyer's confirmation in spite of the Anastasia case, was shocked to learn of that very same Anastasia case at its hearings. Yet, the Committee members, as senators, had been apprised of the entire mess only six months before!

We have sought through these pages to offer no moralizing, to deliver no great social message, to wage no crusade. Our purpose was to deal only in facts, for this was simply a factual story of the national Syndicate, the unvarnished account of organized crime in America; how it was born and grew up—and how it remains.

Nevertheless, one point must not be overlooked. Organized crime deals in billions; it well can afford to wage the war-that-never-ends against the Law. For that reason, the law enforcement officer needs every weapon he can lay his hands on, all the time. And as of now, he does not have all those he might, if there were full appreciation on the federal level, of the fact that the real battle against this menace is fought locally. The local, county and state front is the first line of defense against the Syndicate. The defenses should be made strongest there. The Joint Chiefs of Staff would hardly fortify the Pentagon Building and leave our open coasts to shift for themselves. No more should stress on battling the Syndicate be placed solely on strengthening federal enforcement. Local enforcement needs help; lots of help.

Organized crime knows no county or state boundaries, and it has its roots dug into every locality. Boundaries handcuff the local crime fighter. Remember: The vast majority of lawlessness is on the local level. The murder and assault and robbery and extortion, even the gambling, are strictly city and county and state violations. The federal government has no jurisdiction over this great mass of crime through which the mob sucks the blood from our economy. The United States Senate, therefore, should seriously study—with or without television—the local crime-fighting problem, and there lend aid on combatting the underworld.

The Kefauver Committee, in its year-long travels, concluded that the federal government has a "basic responsibility" to aid local enforcement; but nowhere among its twenty-two recommendations, in its final report, did it do anything about that "responsibility." The recommendations centered almost exclusively on suggestions for strengthening federal alcohol and income tax and immigration regulations and the like, and for establishing new, costly federal bureaus. Some of these are creditable proposals, naturally. But unfortunately, therein does not lie the cure. It is recalled, for instance, that Frank Costello's command to his henchmen is to pay their income taxes in full, and then the Federals won't bother them. The Senate's regard should be turned toward building the muscles on the local levels.

One tremendous boost would be the formation and operation of a National Bureau of Indentification. I use "National" rather than Federal here, with malice aforethought, for this should be a bureau to work with local law enforcement; not independently. It should have offices in every city, which would gather information on any and all criminals and mobs, no matter the shape and size, and would correlate and distribute such information to all the branch offices. And these branches would co-operate with local law to make the most of such information. Each branch would have, from each other branch, a complete dossier on every crime and every criminal, no matter where he might operate. And each dossier would be available in its entirety to the law agent on the local level. As it now stands, the prosecutor, all too frequently, works in the dark on a case. One prosecutor does not know what the other has—or can not get the complete information the FBI might have.

If such a bureau were functioning, a shift of scenery by a gangster would not produce the bitter example Buggsy Siegel provided in his heyday. He had been a mobster, a murderer and a hood for nearly twenty years; yet, because he had escaped any serious conviction, he became a "socialite" and "sportsman" when he went to California. And when a murder case did develop against him, the only photograph to be found was that ancient likeness in the police files in Philadelphia. A National Bureau of Identification would have long since gathered information on so notorious a character, and that information would have been available to us in Brooklyn and the prosecutor in Los Angeles—and in full. That is the advantage of the national, rather than the federal, set-up.

Every enforcement agency is naturally zealous to accomplish a cleanup itself. That very zeal, however, tends against a common front to meet the common enemy. Which brings up a suggestion for the Senate, or, perhaps, the Department of Justice, to consider ways and means for closer co-operation between local enforcement and such federal agencies as the FBI and the Justice Department, when the hunt is on for a criminal wanted by both, or when one such is to be prosecuted. In one of the Murder, Inc., trials, Judge Taylor pointed out that "when rogues fall out, it is a wise man's delight." By the same token, when honest men fall out, no one is happier than the gangster. The FBI must be admired for its unrelenting pressure on the criminal. However, the bleat of police departments across the country is that the FBI too ardently guards many of the things it learns on the local level—and which could aid the local officer. The FBI, on the other hand, has indicated more than once, that it is not too impressed with local efficiency or honesty. This cleavage, the mobster always enjoys.

There should be co-operation on the hunt for a fugitive, and free exchange of all information. The entire effort of all crime-fighting machinery should be coordinated toward the quickest way of finding the "lammister" and meting out to him the stiffest possible punishment—and let the glory and the headlines fall where they may. On simple economics alone, it would be far less costly to track down a Lepke, say, if the New York police and the FBI worked in close coordination. Why should the New York police send men to Florida or Cuba following up leads, and the FBI rush its operatives to the same spots, doing the same? Cooperation would cut the costs to begin with. And more: It would leave more men available to cover a wider territory.

And once the criminal is in the dragnet, why should there then be a squabble over which prosecutor—federal or county—will put a Lepke on trial? Or, for that matter, whether his prosecution might bring some nebulous "glory" to a rival political party? The goal should be to pick the strongest case by which such a ganglord can be put away for the longest period of time—and then all hands work to put him there.

During the Murder, Inc., prosecutions and investigations, the Federal Bureau of Narcotics, which does such a remarkable job with an undermanned staff, showed how invaluable such co-operation can be. Narcotics Agents unearthed Mendy in Kansas City, after police there had picked him up and released him fifteen times by his own count. The agents unselfishly brought the bulky killer East, turned him over to us for prosecution for murder, in spite of their own perfectly sound narcotics case against him, and then supplied information damaging to his defense—even appeared on the witness stand at his trial. All of it went a long way toward sitting Mendy in the chair—and ridding society of him. It was a perfect coordinated effort. It should be general practice.

All of these suggestions, of course, are based on the honest enforcement officer, only. And there is the hardest rub. In dealing with national organized crime, it must always be remembered that, no matter how many of the ganglords and torpedoes are eliminated today, a new crop flowers tomorrow. New talent is always on the way; always available. Already the Lepkes, the Al Capones, the Buggsy Siegels are shadows. But when they fell, the holes were quickly filled and mob business went on as usual. For, though the faces change, the blueprint remains indelible. The chief problem, then, is not in how to deal with the new faces as they come along, or the variations of the rackets these faces may conjure up. The menace that must be obliterated is the blueprint. And the blueprint for national crime calls for a foundation built upon political connivance and official corruption.

Organized crime could not last forty-eight hours if every official charged with law enforcement—municipal, state or national—were incorruptible! Nor does the corruption deal in cash only. The ganglords have ingeniously crept into officialdom in many ways, and, as we have pointed out, into the highest places. Sometimes they have done it with votes; sometimes by help of one sort or another in a political campaign; sometimes merely by "contacts" or connections they have established—or seem to have attained. One mob baron, in fact, "moved in" to the extent that he had his picture taken in a "he's-my-pal" pose with a candidate for the vice-presidency of the United States. When it was published, it won for him considerable authority. It was the same authority and power that Lepke derived from a published photograph showing him walking away from a murder charge with a police escort. The Law's greatest labor lies in amputating the gang magnate from the public official on any level.

The easy thing to say is, "Vote such officials out of office" or fire them when their fingers are found in the slime. That is the flag-waving, attention-getting shout of the crime-fighting "quack." It is telling a man who has just had his arm blown off not to look for a leak in a gas pipe with a lighted candle any more. The one sure cure is to keep the crooked official from ever getting in, in the first place. Obviously, if he never holds a position in authority—elective, appointive or party-designated—he can't do any good for the gang. That applies not only to the official who is cozy with the mobster, but to the influence peddler, as well; to any type, in fact, which capitalizes, in any way, from having his nose in the public trough. It would be far more effective for crime commissions and committees to work toward this end, rather than in delving into entrenched stenches long since exposed. On this spot, too, the U. S. Senate should put its strongest spotlight.

This may sound like an Utopian ideal, impossible to achieve. That is not the intent. Nor is there a suggestion here for a Gestapo, an OGPU or a totalitarian rose by any other name. American tradition suits us fine. But such a study on both federal and state levels is a crying need. The Senate has a bulwark to prevent just such infiltration in its own body. By senatorial rules, it can and it has refused to seat the "wrong kind" of a senator—even after his constituency has elected him by overwhelming majority. Perhaps the idea could somehow be practiced in law enforcement. Perhaps in a study, sufficiently intense, the Senate might discover some form of federal legislation or action which could legally be applied to keep from public office any whose background, at least, portends the thieving politician or the law enforcement officer "on the take."

It cannot be over-emphasized or too often repeated: the basic root of organized crime is the protection organized crime enjoys. As long as politicians and officials "do business" or hobnob with mobsters, so long will the Syndicate thrive. So long will there be organized crime. So long can Murder, Inc. wax fat and flourish on rackets and extortion and general piracy—and drop "packages" in Chicago and Los Angeles and Kansas City and Miami, as well as Brownsville.

Appendices

APPENDIX 1

POLICE RECORD OF KID TWIST RELES.

Charge	Arrests	Convictions
Homicide	6	0
Assault	7	1
Assault and Robbery	2	0
Robbery or Burglary	6	0
Grand Larceny	2	0
Petit Larceny	1	1
Possession of Drugs	1	0
Possession of Guns	1	0
Parole Violation	1	1
Vagrancy	5	0
Disorderly	3	3
Malicious Mischief	1	0
Juvenile Delinquency	1	1
Suspicious Character	1	0
Fugitive	1	0
Consorting with Known Criminals	2	0
Violating Criminal Registration	1	0

APPENDIX 2

Excerpts of newspaper stories during Lepke's 48-hour reprieve:

"Details of two new developments were shrouded in official secrecy. One was that Lepke made and signed a death cell statement about a 'deal' freighted with political dynamite, which was proposed to him when he was a federal prisoner more than three years ago."

(*New York Herald Tribune*)

"The eleventh hour statement by the gang chief . . . revealed that he had named to District Attorney Frank Hogan
a prominent labor leader, powerful in national politics, as a
man who had inspired several crimes."

(New York Daily News)

"It was reported that Governor Dewey would receive this
morning (the day Lepke died) a detailed account of District
Attorney Hogan's conversation with the one-time rackets
boss in which Lepke sought to escape the chair by involving
a number of prominent persons in his long career of crime."

(New York Sun [close to the state administration])

"According to the *Mirror's* informant, Lepke declared
(Frank) Costello has concerned himself more and more with
politics. . . .

"Lepke has named 30 politicians, high police officials and
racketeers as principals in alleged offers of 'deals' to save his
life. Lepke was said to have declared many of these individuals sought to induce him to 'frame' others for political
purposes."

(New York Daily Mirror)

APPENDIX 3

In the course of research for this book, one of the authors wrote
District Attorney Hogan for a statement about his death cell interview, seven years before, with Lepke, about which the prosecutor
has never spoken. Among the questions asked Hogan were:

Did Lepke mention any "deal" offered him by O'Dwyer or
Bals or anyone else, if he talked?

Did Lepke refer to the Guido Ferrari murder; did he mention
the late Mayor LaGuardia or Sidney Hillman in any connection?

Did Lepke mention Lucky Luciano, Salvatore Marrizano, the
clothing industry racket or the purge of Mafia?

Did Lepke refer to Joey Adonis, Frank Costello, Zwillman or
Albert Anastasia; did he reveal any political alliances or associ-

ations indicating the existence of racketeer-politico relations, particularly on the national administration level?

In reply, a letter was received from the District Attorney's office, signed by Chief Assistant Prosecutor Joseph Sarafite, one of those who accompanied Hogan to see Lepke. It said:

> The District Attorney did not request the Governor to grant any reprieve of Buchalter, nor was any other official action taken by him which could be used as a justifiable basis for revealing what Buchalter said. Beyond this statement, we are unable to answer the questions.

Thus, after seven years, Hogan still is not talking. It is interesting to note, however, that while he did not reply affirmatively to the queries—neither did he deny them.

APPENDIX 4

Excerpts from the Kefauver Committee report showing how mobsters from the gangs of various cities combine their talents in single enterprises:

> "The Wofford Hotel [in Miami] is now owned by Thomas Cassara [Chicago], John Angersola [Cleveland] and Anthony Carfano [Brooklyn], a Costello associate" (p. 180). (Ed. note: Carfano, of course, is the infamous Li'l Augie Pisano, who is a lot closer to Adonis than to Costello.)
>
> "The Greenacre and Club Boheme [in Broward County, Fla.] were operated by a group including Frank Erickson, Joe Adonis and the Lansky Brothers of New York and Mert Wertheimer of Detroit" (p. 30).
>
> "The Grand and the Sands Hotel [Miami Beach] served as headquarters for the Detroit, Philadelphia and Cleveland mobs" (p. 31).
>
> "Gamblers and bookmakers from Detroit and Chicago, and Cleveland and New York owned large expanses of property in Miami Beach and nearby" (p. 36).

"Club Arrowhead [in Saratoga, N. Y.] is operated by Joe Adonis of Brooklyn, Charley Manny [New York] and J. A. Coakley, alias O. K. Coakley, and Lefty Clark, of Detroit" (p. 107).

APPENDIX 5

Additional findings contained in the 1945 grand jury presentment alleging William O'Dwyer failed to prosecute his "perfect murder case" against Albert Anastasia:

"William O'Dwyer testified that his chief concern and paramount object was a conviction for murder of Anastasia, because Anastasia was the leader and most prominent gangster in the Brooklyn underworld; that not a single murder in organized crime was committed in Brooklyn without Anastasia's permission and approval."

"We find every case against Anastasia was abandoned, neglected or pigeonholed."

"We find that William O'Dwyer as District Attorney . . . failed and neglected to complete a single prosecution against Anastasia."

"We find there admittedly was competent legal evidence sufficient to warrant indictment, conviction and punishment of Anastasia for murder in a case described by William O'Dwyer as 'a perfect murder case.' "

"We find negligence, incompetence and flagrant irresponsibility whereby Anastasia was permitted to escape prosecution, conviction and punishment for that murder and for a number of other vicious crimes."

(Among these "vicious crimes," the presentment listed such as the looting of union treasuries, rackets, financial interests in extortions and the harboring of Lepke.)

"The neglect, incompetence and failure to proceed against Anastasia was neither denied, justified nor satisfactorily explained. The general tenor of Mr. O'Dwyer's testimony was to attribute the responsibility in all these matters to his chief aides and to the New York City Police Department. We find, however, that the Police Department of the City of New York fully performed its duties."